Vietnam's Modern Day
Boat People

Vietnam's Modern Day Boat People

Bridging Borders for Freedom

SHIRA SEBBAN

McFarland & Company, Inc., Publishers
Jefferson, North Carolina

ISBN (print) 978-1-4766-8537-3
ISBN (ebook) 978-1-4766-5009-8

LIBRARY OF CONGRESS AND BRITISH LIBRARY
CATALOGUING DATA ARE AVAILABLE

Library of Congress Control Number 2023038274

Front cover: Refugee children behind bars: from left, Nguyen Dang Koi,
Ho Thanh Thao Nhi, and Tran Nguyen Hoa Nhien in immigration
detention in Kuningan, South Jakarta, Indonesia, June 2017
(courtesy Sunshine and Aaron Biskaps)

Printed in the United States of America

*McFarland & Company, Inc., Publishers
Box 611, Jefferson, North Carolina 28640
www.mcfarlandpub.com*

In memory of my dear friend
and human rights advocate,
known as Ngoc Nhi (Ann) Nguyen,
who encouraged me to write this book.

"I'm amazed how the fine, golden threads connecting us in the universe work. We all try to do our small part, hoping for the best. Usually we don't get to see the fruit of our effort, but sometimes stories like this happen."

—Nga L.H. Nguyen, change agent,
Vietnam, August 12, 2016

"Everyone has the right to seek and to enjoy in other countries asylum from persecution."

—*Universal Declaration
of Human Rights*, article 14(1)

Table of Contents

Acknowledgments

I would never have embarked on this book without the encouragement of the late human rights advocate, known as Ngoc Nhi (Ann) Nguyen, who urged me to share our story, insisting that few modern-day Vietnamese boat people have had the opportunity to be heard in English. "After all this I think you can write a book," she once told me. "It could even be made into a movie!"

Ever since our first meeting online in July 2016, when Nhi volunteered to help translate for me in my initial attempts to contact human rights lawyer Vo An Don via Facebook, our friendship continued to grow, our support for the families drawing us closer together. Once she had introduced me to her good friend and fellow advocate Grace Bui the three of us became an indefatigable team. As Nhi said, "the world will not forget about them [the families] as long as we are here." Grace and I continue to miss her very much but know she would be pleased with our efforts to complete the work we started together.

I would also like to thank Vo An Don himself for his selfless legal advocacy and fight for justice—may he and his family attain their freedom soon—and SBS Vietnamese radio producer and presenter Mai Hoa Pham, for her enthusiastic assistance, especially for so kindly offering to translate the book into Vietnamese, making it accessible to a broader audience. Former Australian Vietnamese community and VOICE Australia president Doan Trung was providing support to the families before I became involved. I have always been able to turn to him for wise advice, and I am also grateful for the invaluable documents and translations he provided. My appreciation too for the generosity and assistance of former Canadian Senator Thanh Hai Ngo, Queensland Vietnamese community president Dr. Cuong Bui, and refugee committee chair Mr. Van Pham, Sunshine and Aaron Biskaps, everyone at JRS Indonesia, Dr. Hong Long Ha and Mrs. Trang Thu Thi Ta, Christina Nguyen, former RFA journalist, Hoa Ai Tran, and human rights lawyers, Trish Cameron and Alison Battisson, without whom we would never have achieved our goals. I am so grateful to academic Dr. Antje Missbach, for helping me with details regarding Indonesia's treatment of asylum seekers and refugees, and to legal scholars Dr. Anthea Vogl and Dr. Shauna Labman for their willingness to share their knowledge of Australian and Canadian immigration law with me. In addition, numerous supporters, who wish to remain anonymous, were integral to this project, and I thank each and every one of you.

In particular, I would like to highlight the incredible work of VOICE Canada, led by Kyanh Do, and including fellow advocates Le Luong, James Nguyen, and Khanh Lan Ho. You truly are "like a compass," to quote VOICE's website, your work and continuing advocacy efforts ensuring that "boats find a harbor." A Canadian harbor, which we know will provide the freedom for our families to pursue their dreams.

Finally, thank you to my beloved husband Ilan and children, Raphael, Gabriel, and Jonathan, who shared every step of this journey with me, whether in person or in spirit. Without your love, support, and encouragement, this book would not have been written.

Introduction

"Kids 'orphaned' as Vietnam jails parents over asylum bid": The headline grabbed my attention as I scanned the newspaper over Saturday breakfast in late July 2016.

Underneath was a photo of a downcast mother, surrounded by her four children, staring straight at the camera.

"A Vietnamese failed asylum-seeker forcibly returned after Hanoi promised the Australian government it would not punish returnees will be jailed as early as

The photograph that appeared in *The Australian* newspaper, from left: daughters, Ho Thanh Nha My, Ho Thanh Nha Tran, and Ho Thanh Thao Nhi, mother, Tran Thi Thanh Loan, and son, Ho Van Loc (courtesy Tran Thi Thanh Loan).

this week and her children sent to an orphanage after she lost an appeal against a three-year sentence."[1]

I had not even realized until then that "boat people" were still attempting to flee Vietnam. Sure, I knew that by 1982, Australia had permanently resettled around 60,000 Vietnamese refugees[2] in the wake of the Vietnam War, and that more than 200,000 migrants had come from Vietnam since then. But boat people in the 21st century? The very notion seemed anachronistic.

I had begun visiting asylum seekers in Sydney's Villawood Immigration Detention Centre in early 2016. Having long wanted to "do something" in support of refugees, I had pushed the idea to the back of my mind, constantly telling myself I was "too busy." What could I as an individual accomplish anyway? That year, however, I had finally decided to take concrete action: Like most of us, my family too had been boat people once, fleeing the dangers of pogrom-ridden Eastern Europe in the late 19th and early 20th centuries, and subsequently seeking safety and a better life in Australia and Canada.

My father's father had been fortunate enough to be allowed to settle in Toronto, Ontario, after escaping the virulent anti–Semitism of Russia, arriving on Ellis Island in 1913 as a teenager, with his widowed sister and her three children. A few years earlier, his future wife and her family had docked in Halifax, Nova Scotia, after fleeing the Polish township of Lodz.

In 1925, my mother's parents had had the foresight to leave Poland for Palestine, thus avoiding the fate of much of the rest of the family, which was decimated by the Nazis some 15 years later. My maternal grandparents would eventually make their way to Melbourne, Australia, where I would grow up, deprived of great aunts and uncles, and too afraid to confront my extended family's destruction in the Holocaust until only a few years ago.

Upon joining the grassroots organization, SASS (Supporting Asylum Seekers Sydney), I became part of a group of ordinary Australians of all ages and from all walks of life, who would meet detainees in Villawood every Thursday afternoon, bringing food to share, listening to their stories, and providing assistance when possible, be it a gift of clothing or a phone card or attempting to find an immigration lawyer prepared to work pro bono.

While most of the asylum seekers I met in detention were from the Middle East or South Asia, a few were Vietnamese. Indeed, as of May 31, 2022, there were still 101 people from Vietnam, or 7.2 per cent of the 1,402 detainees, who were being held in immigration detention facilities around Australia.[3]

Among those in onshore detention, however, people seeking asylum by boat tended to have arrived before July 19, 2013—the date when then Prime Minister Kevin Rudd had made the announcement: "From now on, any asylum seeker who arrives in Australia by boat will have no chance of being settled in Australia as refugees."[4] Henceforth, they would all be transferred to offshore Australian immigration detention facilities, then on Manus Island in Papua New Guinea (PNG) or on the South Pacific island nation of Nauru.[5]

The Australian Labor government was responding to the significant increase in the number of asylum seekers in 2012–2013, more than 30,000 people having arrived by boat over the 18-month period, often having paid people smugglers large sums of money to undertake the perilous journey. Tragically, between 2008 and 2013, 1,072 people, including at least 15 children, had lost their lives at sea.

"Stop the boats" became the slogan of the newly elected Australian Liberal-National Coalition government under Prime Minister Tony Abbott, which instituted the military-led, secretive Operation Sovereign Borders (OSB) security initiative on September 18, 2013.[6] Those seeking asylum by boat became officially known as "illegal maritime arrivals" (IMAs),[7] rather than merely "irregular" or "unauthorized," their numbers dramatically reduced. Boat "turn-backs" were used, "when it is safe to do so,"[8] with some arrivals in Australian waters being sent back on their own or an alternative vessel to just outside the territorial seas of the country from which they had departed. Australian Border Force (ABF), established in July 2015 as "Australia's frontline border law enforcement agency and customs service,"[9] also resorted to boat "take-backs," where Australia works with the country of origin or nationality to return the passengers and crew, either by plane or via an at-sea transfer from one sovereign authority to another. Between 2013–2021, Australia "reportedly removed over 800 migrants on 38 vessels."[10]

Indeed, this is precisely what had happened to the mother and children in that newspaper article. Tran Thi Thanh Loan and her family had been among 46 Vietnamese asylum seekers, who had attempted to reach Australia on a family-owned fishing boat in March 2015. Intercepted at sea by the Australian navy, they had summarily been found not to engage Australia's protection obligations and forcibly returned by boat "take-back" to Vietnam, where Mrs. Loan's[11] husband Ho Trung Loi was sentenced to two years' jail for helping to organize the "illegal departure."

In late July 2016, Mrs. Loan had just lost her appeal for leniency based on being the sole carer of their children, then aged 4 to 16. No one in the extended family could afford to look after them, and so they had been told to leave school and go to an orphanage.

"They have been crying a lot and clinging to me," she told *The Australian*. "My youngest child keeps saying 'Mummy, don't go.' My older children are worried. They feel the pressure and are scared of having neither parent around. They have asked if they can be sent to prison with me."

I could not get her words out of my mind. Hadn't this family suffered enough? I did not want to see them further torn apart. Moreover, as an Australian, I felt ashamed as well as morally responsible for their plight to some extent, as our government had sent them back in the first place, without having given them a fair hearing, thereby shirking its shared international responsibility for protecting refugees.

By that Saturday night, I had determined a course of action: The article quoted Mrs. Loan's pro bono lawyer, Vo An Don. I decided to try and contact him in Vietnam to ask how much it would cost each month for the extended family to care for the children until their father's release from jail in mid–2017. Together with my ever-supportive husband Ilan, we agreed that once we knew the amount required, we would cover the first month. "You can't do it all on your own," Ilan warned. "You'll need to raise money for them." Little did I know then where my reaction to a newspaper article would lead.

As I would quickly discover, this family's desperate situation was far from unique. Indeed, from March 2015 to July 2016 alone, the Australian navy had intercepted 113 Vietnamese asylum seekers in three separate incidents. Assessed at sea and found not to warrant protection, they had all been forcibly returned to Vietnam, where those regarded as "organizers" were incarcerated.[12]

This is the story of some of these modern-day Vietnamese boat people, and how a disparate group of volunteer advocates from Australia, Vietnam, Thailand, Indonesia, the United States, and Canada banded together to help them on their eventual journey to freedom, or as they say in Vietnamese, "*Hành Trình Tìm Tự Do.*"

Now that they are safe, I am finally able to reveal the full story behind their journey. Real names are used throughout, except when concerning their extended family members still residing in Vietnam, who understandably remain at risk and so whose identifying details have been removed. The Vietnamese vocational training institution in Chapter 6 has also insisted on anonymity for fear of being perceived in Vietnam as associated with "anti-government propaganda"—even though this is certainly not the case—and I have provided pseudonyms when necessary to maintain the privacy of all involved. Writing this book required extensive research, including an array of English-language, Vietnamese, and Indonesian sources that I often informally translated for myself via computer, as indicated by the note "(translated from Vietnamese / Indonesian)."

This is a tale that has not received much attention in western and English-language media, thereby making it even more important to share, especially as we celebrate the families' hard-won resettlement in Canada. Few books have been published in recent years that show the impact of Australia's tough border control policies on the actual lives of refugees, in comparison with Canada's relatively more humanitarian approach. Covering issues where Australian official secrecy still abounds, *Bridging Borders For Freedom* strives to fill that gap, giving voice to the experiences of Mrs. Loan, Mr. Loi and their children, among others, as shared with their advocates, in what is an inspirational story of resilience, determination, and hope. A story which highlights the extraordinary courage of "ordinary" people in their battle for liberty, showing what can be achieved when borders prove no boundary.

1

Don't Let Them
Go to an Orphanage

Contacting human rights lawyer Vo An Don, a public figure in Vietnam, proved more complicated than I originally expected. Known as "the people's lawyer" for providing free legal counsel in more than 200 cases to the poor, ethnic minorities, minors, pregnant women, and those with a disability, he was also renowned for his advocacy in sensitive political trials, defending victims of police brutality or dissidents charged with disrupting public order, attempting to overthrow the government, or conducting propaganda against the State.

My initial attempts to message him privately in English via his Facebook page went unanswered for several days. I tried ringing his office at the Center for Government Legal Aid in Tuy Hoa, capital of Phu Yen province (the most eastern rural district on the south-central Vietnamese coast), but the doorman, who answered the phone, could only manage to say "Facebook" repeatedly in response to my request to speak with the man I would come to know as Mr. Vo.

Finally, I put a public message in English on his Facebook page, asking how much it would cost for Mrs. Loan's extended family to care for her four children until their father would be released from jail the following year. Almost immediately, I was contacted privately by the late Vietnamese Australian human rights advocate, Ngoc Nhi (Ann) Nguyen (as she was known), a close associate of Mr. Vo and a former refugee herself, who offered to translate for me. We quickly became good friends and colleagues, with me constantly relying on Nhi for her wise counsel. Mr. Vo also found a translator, explaining that he had gone to speak with Mrs. Loan, but she had said she was too embarrassed to accept any help.

After he had managed to convince her otherwise, she calculated that her children's living and education expenses would amount to 7 million Vietnamese Dong (VND) each month. While that sounded like a huge sum to me, it was roughly equivalent to USD300 a month, or about USD3,600 for the year. So together with my husband Ilan, we decided to send Mrs. Loan the money for the first month. We did not know when she would be sent to jail and so we had to act quickly. She did not even have a bank account and had to arrange to open one—a process that Mr. Vo initially thought would take a week but, to our surprise, was completed within the day, with him sending me a photo of the account details.

By August 4, 2016—a week after my initial decision to get involved—Mr. Vo had posted a message of gratitude in Vietnamese to his thousands of Facebook followers. Under a large photo of me, was an explanation of the family's dire situation, with the opening statement: "Shira Sebban, a woman living in Australia, voluntarily took care of four children whose father and mother were sentenced to prison." He went on to announce that I had promised to send the money each month, concluding: "Shira Sebban is the benefactor of Mrs. Loan's family, saving four children from a dark future." We certainly had much to live up to.

Meanwhile, following our oldest son Raphael's advice, I had started an online crowd fund on the platform, GoFundMe. We called the campaign, "Don't Let Them Go to an Orphanage," setting a deadline of one month to raise an initial amount of USD7,000—enough to look after the children for two years. Nhi translated the campaign into Vietnamese, tagging many of her friends and alerting local Vietnamese communities in Australia. Within a week, we had already raised more than half the sum, with the campaign becoming among the most popular on GoFundMe. An opinion piece I wrote for *The Guardian*, titled "We're a Disparate Group of Australians Doing the Work Our Government Won't," resulted in a total of USD1,400 being donated in 12 hours.[1]

Nga L.H. Nguyen, one of the authors of the original article I had seen in *The Australian*, reported on Facebook that upon learning of the crowd fund, she had immediately called Mrs. Loan: "We both spent a few minutes crying all the happy tears on the phone." Under the headline, "The Most Magical Thing Happened," she wrote of herself and fellow journalist Amanda Hodge:

> Our hearts broke over this story of a torn family and children soon to be sent to an orphanage, all because their parents tried to give them a better future. At the time, despite telling the mother we hoped the article would bring attention to her case and those going through the same thing she is, I honestly did not believe any practical help was probable.... It's still so hard to believe something we wrote could actually make a huge difference like that to Loan and her family.
>
> Throughout this process I'm humbled by Loan's determination to save her children, Don's enduring fight for those oppressed by the system, and Shira's kindness, as well as Amanda's insistence and push for us to do justice to this story. Cases like this make it clear social justice efforts do make enormous differences in people's lives, and that love and kindness are truly what connects humanity together. Think about this next time you need your faith in fellow humans restored.

The campaign also received attention from Vietnamese media and bloggers in Washington, D.C., Vietnam, London, and Sydney, such as SBTN (Saigon Broadcasting Television Network), VOA (Voice of America), RFA (Radio Free Asia), VNWHR (Vietnamese Women for Human Rights), BBC, and Australia's multicultural media service, SBS (Special Broadcasting Service), the interviews often being posted on YouTube because the Vietnamese government scrambled the airwaves, so that was the main way some of these stations could get their message heard in Vietnam.[2]

Amongst the strangest reports I came across online was a description in Vietnamese of me as "one of the original Hebrews," with an accompanying link to a video of a group of American ultra–Orthodox Jews, clad in army uniform, singing *The Star-Spangled Banner*—an attempt to explain my Jewish faith to what must have been a most bemused audience![3]

I was attracting many new Facebook friend invitations, few of whom I knew personally. Heeding Nhi's cautionary advice that "unfortunately some of them may not be trustworthy and there may even be someone undercover from Vietnam's police force," I decided to post publicly about the campaign, thereby still reaching those interested in our progress, who could sign up as followers.

At the same time, we were preparing behind the scenes for Mrs. Loan's impending arrest, her 36-month sentence having been officially enforced by the People's Court of La Gi Township, Binh Thuan Province, on August 5, 2016.

PEOPLE'S COURT OF LA GI TOWN	SOCIALIST REPUBLIC OF VIETNAM
BINH THUAN PROVINCE	Independence—Freedom—Happiness
NO. 81/2016/QD-CA	*La Gi, August 05th, 2016*

JUDGMENT ENFORCEMENT DECISION
(For persons sentenced to imprisonment on bail)

CHIEF JUSTICE OF PEOPLE'S COURT OF LA GI TOWN

Pursuant to Articles 255, 256, 257 and 260 of Criminal Procedure Code;
Pursuant to Articles 02, 15, 20, 21 and 22 of Law on execution of Criminal Judgment 2010.

DECIDES:

1. To execute the 36 (thirty-six) month imprisonment sentence due to "Organizing for other people to flee abroad illegally."

At the Appellate criminal judgment No. 68/2016/HSPT dated July 21, 2016, of the People's Court of Binh Thuan province.
For the person serving the imprisonment sentence: Tran Thi Thanh Loan, born in 1974; Permanent residence address: quarter 2, Phuoc Hoi ward, La Gi town, Binh Tuan province. Who is a child of Mr. Tran Quy, born in 1945 and Ms. Tran Thi Phuc (died). The defendant is on bail.

2. Within 7 days from the date of receiving this Decision, the person serving the imprisonment sentence must be present at the head office of Criminal Judgement enforcement agency—Public security of La Gi town to serve the penalty. Otherwise, she will be coercively delivered to detention center to serve the sentence.

3. Public security of La Gi town is entitled to execute this Decision and notify in writing People's Court of La Gi town of the results.

Recipients:	CHIEF JUSTICE
• People's Procuracy of La Gi town;	*(Signed and sealed)*
• Criminal judgment enforcement agency—Public security of La Gi town;	
• Criminal judgment enforcement agency—Public security of Binh Thuan province;	**LE MINH CHINH**
• Justice Department of Binh Thuan province;	
• Person serving the imprisonment sentence;	
• Save Judgment enforcement dossiers.	

Certified translation of court enforcement of Mrs. Loan's jail sentence (courtesy Tran Thi Thanh Loan).

Although she preferred to cope by not thinking about it, she nevertheless introduced Nhi to her sister-in-law, whom she had authorized to access the bank account, along with her father and eldest daughter, Ho Thanh Nha My (then aged 16), thereby ensuring her family would continue to receive the monthly payments.

Mrs. Loan had been given seven days to report to her local police station in La Gi, a fishing township on the southcentral coast, from where she would be taken to prison to begin her sentence. If she did not comply, the police would arrest her at home.

Alerted by Nhi, Amnesty International subsequently released a public statement headlined: "Viet Nam: Imprisonment of asylum seeker forcibly returned by Australia would be unlawful and could be disastrous for her four young children."[4] Calling her imminent imprisonment "a callous and perverse punishment for the exercise of her right to seek asylum," the human rights organization charged that she and her husband, Ho Trung Loi, along with two other failed asylum seekers, "were convicted for exercising an internationally protected human right" and called for their immediate release. "The Universal Declaration of Human Rights ... provides for the right to seek asylum outside one's country.... Vietnam is obliged to respect and protect this right, as it is a norm of customary international law binding on all nations." Furthermore, Amnesty maintained, Vietnam, as a state party to the *Convention on the Rights of the Child*,[5] is "obliged to make the best interest of children a primary consideration in all actions concerning children, including those taken by administrative authorities and courts of law."

On August 15, 2016, Mrs. Loan was granted a temporary reprieve, the La Gi People's Court acknowledging she was the sole carer of her four children and a first-time offender. Her sentence was postponed for one year, the date falling after her husband's release. Consequently, one parent would always be able to remain with the children.

PEOPLE'S COURT OF LA GI TOWN	SOCIALIST REPUBLIC OF VIETNAM
BINH THUAN PROVINCE	**Independence—Freedom—Happiness**
NO. 08/2016/QD-CA	*La Gi, August 15th, 2016*

DECISION
TO SUSPEND THE SERVING OF IMPRISONMENT SENTENCE
CHIEF JUSTICE OF PEOPLE'S COURT OF LA GI TOWN
FINDS THAT:

After making the Decision on Judgment Enforcement No. 81/2016/QD-CQ dated August 05, 2016, for the defendant Tran Thi Thanh Loan, who must serve the 36 (thirty-six) month imprisonment penalty and being currently released on bail.

On August 08, 2016, Tran Thi Thanh Loan submitted an Application to suspend her serving of imprisonment sentence with the reason: she is the only laborer in the family with the income to raise four little children.

After studying the dossiers proposing the postponement of serving imprisonment sentence;

CONSIDERS THAT:

The proposal of postponement of serving imprisonment sentence with the reason that Tran Thi Thanh Loan is the only laborer in the family with the income to bring up four little children; first offence and after being sentenced she does not have any serious violations of the law.

According to the guidelines at point b, sub-section 7.1, section 7 of Resolution No. 01/2007/NQ-HDTP dated 02/10/2007 of the Council of Judges of the Supreme People's Court, Tran Thi Thanh Loan has met all conditions for her serving of imprisonment sentence to be suspended;

Pursuant to Articles 261 and 263 of Criminal Procedure Code;
Pursuant to Articles 02, 20, 23 and 24 of Law on execution of Criminal Judgment 2010.

DECIDES:

1. For person serving the imprisonment sentence: Tran Thi Thanh Loan, born in 1974, registered temporary address: Quarter 2, Phuoc Hoi ward, La Gi town, Binh Thuan province, who is a child of Mr. Tran Quy, born in 1945, and Mrs. Tran Thi Phuc (died), the serving of 36 (thirty-six) month imprisonment sentence due to "Organizing for other people to flee abroad" to be postponed.

At the Appellate criminal judgment No. 68/2016/HSPT dated July 21, 2016, of the People's Court of Binh Thuan province.

2. Time limit for Tran Thi Thanh Loan for the serving of imprisonment sentence to be postponed is 12 (twelve) months from 15/08/2016 to 15/08/2017.

3. To send the person serving the imprisonment sentence to People's Committee of Phuoc Hoi ward, La Gi town, Binh Thuan province, during the time of postponement.

Recipients:	CHIEF JUSTICE
• Person serving the imprisonment sentence;	
• People's Procuracy of La Gi town;	*(Signed and sealed)*
• Criminal judgment enforcement agency—Public security of La Gi town;	LE MINH CHINH
• Criminal judgment enforcement agency—Public security of Binh Thuan province;	
• Justice Department of Binh Thuan province;	
• People's Committee of Phuoc Hoi ward;	
• Save Judgment enforcement dossiers.	

Certified translation of court postponement of Mrs. Loan's sentence (courtesy Tran Thi Thanh Loan).

I was thus able to transfer the money to her for the second month, Mrs. Loan using some of it to buy textbooks, uniforms, and stationery for the start of the school year. While education in Vietnam is meant to be free, at least in primary school,[6] children from poor families often miss out, their parents unable to afford the associated costs.

With her husband—a fisherman and the family's main breadwinner—in jail, Mrs. Loan was only earning between USD5–10 a day by selling fruit, which she would buy from an orchard in the early morning. She and her youngest daughter, Ho Thanh Thao Nhi, then aged 4, would sit outside her father's home, where the family was living, until lunchtime. In the afternoon, she would walk more than half a mile down the road to another market, where she would have to pay rent, to sell the rest of the fruit at a cheaper price because it was not as fresh. If she did not sell all the fruit, that is what the children would eat for dinner.

Our campaign ended up exceeding our expectations. It attracted over 1,000 shares on social media, with more than 100 people from various cultural backgrounds and walks of life donating a total of USD7,600, the additional funds to be used to help Mr. Loi get back on his feet after his release from jail. "Your help and kindness have made me feel much more confident and less stressed now," Mrs.

Mrs. Loan's children, from left: Ho Van Loc, 13, Ho Thanh Nha Tran, 9, Ho Thanh Thao Nhi, 4, Ho Thanh Nha My, 16, with their school supplies (courtesy Tran Thi Thanh Loan).

Mrs. Loan and her youngest daughter Nhi, selling fruit in the market (courtesy Tran Thi Thanh Loan).

Loan wrote on Facebook. "Thank you from the bottom of my heart for helping my family."

"She has strong faith," Nhi told me. "She was feeling desperate and prayed to God to help her. In Vietnam caring people are rare because life is so hard that most only care for themselves. So, to her you are God's angel sent to help her and her family." Some of the donors were former Vietnamese boat people themselves, notably Sydney mother and optical assistant, Christina Nguyen, who would so generously support all our campaigns.

While many preferred to stay anonymous, others were quite outspoken in their messages of support: "This family's only 'crime' is to try to look for a better life, a birthright of any human being, yet they were let down by the Australian government, then punished by the Vietnamese government," Nhi wrote on the donations page. Several were quick to agree: "It is Australia's eternal shame that this is what happens when we turn away genuine asylum seekers. This is a great cause"; "Hopefully the refugee policy will change, and we can become a country that cares about human rights again"; and "this just shows the power of social media in helping bring about a new life for this family."

Just why had Mrs. Loan, Mr. Loi, and their four children fled Vietnam to seek asylum in Australia in the first place? Mrs. Loan has given three reasons: The State had seized their land; they had lost their livelihood (and as we shall see, risked their lives) due to Chinese incursions into fishing grounds; and as Catholics, they suffered institutionalized discrimination.

"In 2013, my mother-in-law gave us land to build a house at Street 7, La Gi township, Binh Thuan province," she told me through professional translator, Trung Sylvain Le Minh, who serves as an interpreter for VietBP2013, a benevolent Australian support e-group for those who help Vietnamese asylum seekers, of which I am a member. "My mother-in-law got the Certificate of Land Use Rights (LURC) in 1986 under her name, and then in 2013, she transferred the title to the name of my husband, Ho Trung Loi, who was entitled to control and use this land. In December 2013, while our house was under construction, the local police of La Gi, along with the coercion team, came to demolish the building; they took the bricks and stones away, and told me that the government had reserved this land for public zoning."

While all land in Vietnam was formally nationalized in 1980, and Vietnamese land law decrees that "the land belongs to the entire people with the state acting as the owner's representative and uniformly managing land,"[7] land use rights are allocated to individuals, family households, or organizations. Thus, Mrs. Loan's mother-in-law had the official right to use her parcel of land (16 feet wide by 98 feet long) for residential purposes, a right which she subsequently gifted to her son by transferring the title on the LURC, also known as the "red book," to his name.

At the same time, the Vietnamese government has the authority to "requisition" land for security purposes or public or private economic interests.[8] In the family's case, as with many others, they were told that the land in Mr. Loi's name had been designated for public socio-economic development, thereby enabling the police, together with a team of enforcers or informal police auxiliaries, to dismantle the foundations of their home while it was being built and seize their land.

"When I tried to stop them, they arrested me and took me to the People's Committee office," Mrs. Loan said.[9] "They tried to force me to sign a document agreeing to the confiscation, but I refused. They then kept me there until the evening. When I returned, I found nothing left on the land."

The police in Vietnam never act alone, Nhi explained:

> They are always accompanied by plain clothes officers and personnel, who can be under-
> cover police, security guards, volunteers, or actual thugs hired by the police.
> The police try to avoid doing the dirty work themselves because they don't want to be
> filmed abusing, beating, or robbing people. Such evidence presented to the United Nations
> or other human rights groups will be bad for the Vietnamese government. So, the uni-
> formed police usually just stand around supervising, while the other 'teams' perform the
> bad deeds. That is why it is so hard to gather evidence against the police or government,
> and people who try to take photos and film the incidents are often attacked, and their
> cameras destroyed or stolen.[10]

Mrs. Loan is not aware of what has happened to her land since then. All she knows is that the family's LURC was confiscated, and the land taken by the Vietnamese government: "I don't know whether afterwards they sold it to a private developer. The authorities always keep their intention a secret and the population doesn't know anything related to government planning until the work gets started." Her family was never compensated for their loss.

Meanwhile, in April 2014, Mr. Loi had gone on a fishing expedition to the Spratly and Paracel Islands, two fiercely disputed archipelagos in the South China Sea. Located in strategic shipping lanes and offering rich commercial fishing grounds, as well as potentially significant crude oil and natural gas reserves, the groups of islands and surrounding territorial waters are contested by various nations, notably the People's Republic of China, Vietnam, the Philippines, Taiwan, Brunei, and Malaysia.

"My husband's boat was attacked by Chinese naval forces, who stole his fish and the boat engine," Mrs. Loan explained. Mr. Loi elaborated: "They beat us, the crew and me. I was scared for my life because if I were killed, no one would even know. Previously Vietnamese fishermen had been killed by Chinese ships."

Indeed, over the years there have been numerous reports of altercations between Chinese and Vietnamese vessels, with the Chinese military and coast guard often targeting Vietnamese who have traditionally fished in the region for generations, Vietnamese officials maintaining they lacked sufficient ships and other resources to protect them fully.[11]

When Mr. Loi's boat managed to drift back to shore, he reported the incident to the local authorities in La Gi, but maintains they ignored his complaint. "We saw we had no freedom of speech and that the authorities had pushed us to the end of our ability to cope. That's why we had to leave."

Their desperation was compounded by the anti–Catholic discrimination they profess to have experienced. "Although the government did not prohibit us from adopting the Catholic religion," Mrs. Loan expanded, "it didn't like us doing so. It intimidated us as well as the priests, when they came to visit my family each month. I was followed when I attended mass in church. In prison, when my husband prayed, the guards would drag him out to beat him."

While according to the Constitution of the Socialist Republic of Vietnam, "The State respects and protects freedom of belief and of religion," at the same time, "No one has the right to infringe on" or "take advantage of" this freedom "to violate the laws."[12] Over the years, various legal and administrative regulations have continued to give the government significant, arbitrary control over religious practices so as to protect such vaguely-worded concerns as "peace and national independence and unification," "public order," "the life, health, dignity, honor or property of other people," and "the exercise of civic rights and performance of civic obligations." As legal scholar Professor John Gillespie has argued, rather than restricting "private religious worship," this "established the ground rules for state management" of religious organizations, thereby preventing "religion from becoming a rallying point for anti-government forces."[13]

Catholics, who form the largest of the officially recognized Christian minorities, constituting about six per cent of the total population, have generally experienced a mixed reception, with some reporting a marked improvement in relations, while others, like Mrs. Loan and her family, maintaining they are constantly viewed with suspicion and harassed. According to the Australian Government Department of Foreign Affairs (DFAT), among others, this difference in treatment is dependent on location and can be blamed on provincial, as opposed to national authorities.

Not everyone, however, agrees with Australia's official view: "If DFAT understood the communist party's tactics and strategy, it would understand that the party controls almost all the religious hierarchy, except in rural parts of some provinces, so it has to use force to control religious communities there," former ACT (Australian Capital Territory) Vietnamese community president (1990–1994) and Australian Vietnamese community vice-president, Nguyen Quang Duy, told me. "In short, there is no freedom, no human rights at all in Vietnam. The people can do only what the communist party sees as not a threat to its political power, so what is allowed can change from individual to individual, day to day, era by era."[14]

On March 8, 2015, after three weeks of preparations, Mrs. Loan, her husband, and their four children were among 46 asylum seekers, including 22 children ranging in age from 1–17 years old,[15] to flee Vietnam on their family-owned fishing boat, BTH 99310TS, Mr. Loi serving as skipper.

"The boat was owned by my husband and me," she later told me, explaining they had taken a bank loan to buy it. "I received from [a fellow failed asylum seeker] a sum of 520 million VND [about USD22,400]. I did not take anyone else's money. We repaired the boat, and the cost of raw materials and food for the trip was 278 million VND [around USD12,000]; we paid back the 200 million VND [roughly USD8,600] we owed the bank; and a little money was left for me to buy personal belongings for my family."

Intercepted on March 20, 2015, by Border Protection Command (BPC),[16] Australia's principal civil maritime security authority, which according to a subsequent Vietnamese legal report,[17] confiscated their boat, they were taken into custody and detained at sea until April 18, 2015—almost a month—undergoing what is known as "enhanced screening" by two Australian immigration officers. Only a few months earlier, the majority of the High Court of Australia had determined the similar detention of 157 Sri Lankan Tamil asylum seekers on board ship for more than a month in mid–2014 to be lawful under section 72(4) of the *Maritime Powers Act 2013* (Cth.).[18]

Introduced on October 27, 2012, originally in relation to a marked increase in Sri Lankan "illegal maritime arrivals" (IMAs) and extended to Vietnamese arrivals in late 2013, the controversial expedited interview process involved in "enhanced screening" is applied to "unlawful non-citizens"[19] at the discrimination of the executive. It aims to determine whether they are raising claims that "could reasonably engage" Australia's non-refoulement obligations under international law. These obligations prohibit a person's removal to a country where they have a "well-founded fear" that their "life or freedom would be threatened," the "real risk" of persecution involving "significant harm."[20] If an individual raises claims that "could potentially engage" these obligations, they are "screened in" to Australia's protection assessment process. If not, they are "screened out" and "removed to their home country as soon as reasonably practicable."[21]

After interviews, subsequently revealed in a Senate Estimates hearing to have lasted between 40 minutes and two hours, "depending on the complexity,"[22] none of the 46 Vietnamese asylum seekers were found to have "raised issues that could reasonably engage Australia's protection obligations."

In response to a question raised by Australian Greens Senator and then Spokesperson on Immigration and Citizenship, Sarah Hanson-Young, taken on notice at that hearing, assurance was provided that "Non-refoulment [sic] assessments were carried out by Commonwealth officers who are trained experts from the Department of Immigration and Border Protection" (DIBP).[23]

Various human rights organizations, as well as Australia's then Labor opposition and other minority parties, expressed concern regarding the secretive procedure: "I think that probably these people had no access to counsel or [were not] able to prepare their case. And certainly they had no access to appeal," Human Rights Watch (HRW) deputy director, Asia Division, Phil Robertson told ABC (Australian Broadcasting Commission). "So it's a shoddy process determined to send people back, and that's what's happening to this group of Vietnamese."[24]

UNICEF agreed:

> Any process that bypasses rigorous refugee assessment standards in favor of a swift resolution, risks denying asylum seekers—including women, children, and unaccompanied minors—access to a fair and comprehensive hearing of their protection claim.
>
> Without a proper assessment, the Australian government cannot determine whether it is safe to return asylum seekers to their country of origin. People seeking asylum must be given the opportunity to voice their protection claims, be granted access to legal assistance, and have an independent review of the decision.[25]

Indeed, already in 2013, DIBP had confirmed that those subject to this process are not advised of their legal rights.[26]

The Law Council of Australia reiterated its longstanding asylum seeker policy:

> All rescues, interdictions, interceptions, "push-backs," "tow backs," and transfers of persons at sea by Australian government personnel of vessels carrying suspected irregular arrivals must comply with the international law of the sea, international refugee law, and international human rights law.
>
> This includes the obligation to "respect the obligation of non-refoulement under international refugee law and human rights law, namely, not to return a person at risk to a country of risk...."[27]

By the time their interviews took place, several weeks had passed, during which the group had been moved between vessels at sea. This was disclosed in an unofficial interview conducted with one of the failed asylum seekers back in Vietnam in late April 2015, at the request of former federal president and general secretary of the Vietnamese community in Australia (1999–2004), Doan Trung. "First we were interviewed to ask for names and family relationships," the returnee said.[28] "About four days later, they took us up to what seemed to be a navy ship. After about a week, we were transferred to a ship, probably customs, where we stayed for around a week. There, immigration officials came to interview us."[29]

Mrs. Loan reported that the Australian authorities treated the group "very well," a claim with which then Commander of Operation Sovereign Borders (OSB), Major General Andrew Bottrell, would have most certainly concurred. As he told the Senate estimates hearing of May 25, 2015: "They had access to appropriate medical care, food, accommodation and ablutions of quite a high standard."[30]

On April 18, 2015, the asylum seekers were forcibly returned on a third vessel, the Australian navy ship HMAS Choules, dispatched from Darwin two weeks earlier, after the Australian government maintained it had received written "assurance" from its Vietnamese counterpart that "there would be no retribution for their illegal departure from Vietnam."[31]

While Australian authorities insist they were fairly assessed with the help of interpreters, Mrs. Loan told me that after the formal interviews, they were detained in darkness, not knowing whether it was night or day. When they begged not to be repatriated for fear of imprisonment, the crew only spoke to them in English, which they signaled they did not understand. She alleged they only realized they were being returned when they reached south-eastern Vung Tau port after a 12-day voyage—a costly exercise given the HMAS Choules' ostensible running costs of over USD145,000 per day.[32]

"When we were sent back to Vietnam, a female official—which [sic] I believe is from the Immigration Department—told us we would be safe from retribution ... and the authorities will help us to reintegrate back to Vietnam and then help us to find jobs," Mrs. Loan subsequently told Australia's ABC via a translator. She said a Vietnamese official repeated the same assurances through a loudspeaker. "I and other people were disappointed that the promise was not carried out and now our back is against the wall. I feel like I have been cheated."[33]

Major General Bottrell admitted that Vietnam's assurance had been taken "on trust," Australia not tracking "people once they have been returned."[34] Nevertheless, a spokesman for DIBP insisted that Vietnamese authorities had invited the United Nations' refugee agency to interview the group "to satisfy themselves that they have not been subject to ill treatment."[35]

Mrs. Loan, however, told me that the police immediately took the women and children back to La Gi to testify: "They locked me up for a few days but because my children were still small, they returned me." She was confined to her home, only allowed to leave with official permission. Meanwhile the men were detained for ten days in Phan Thiet, capital of Binh Thuan province. "I did not expect that my husband and I would both be arrested. When my husband was released, the locals called for 'family rights.' But when he came back, he was handcuffed and detained again. The police said I wouldn't see him for three months, and then they extended it for another nine months until the court case."[36]

SUPREME PEOPLE'S PROCURACY

PEOPLE'S PROCURACY OF
BINH THUAN PROVINCE

NO. 09/QD/KSDT/VKS-P1A

SOCIALIST REPUBLIC OF VIETNAM

Independence—Freedom—Happiness

------------*------------

Binh Thuan, June 29th, 2015

DECISION

TO APPROVE THE ARREST WARRANT FOR DETENTION
CHIEF PROCURATOR OF BINH THUAN PEOPLE'S PROCURACY

- Pursuant to Articles 36, 80, 88 and 112 of Criminal Procedure Code.
- Considering that the Arrest warrant for detention No. 01/PA92 dated June 29, 2015, of the Security Investigation Agency—Binh Thuan Public Security

For the Defendant: ***Ho Trung Loi***
Initiated due to "**Organizing for other people to flee abroad**" stipulated in Article 275 of Criminal Code is according to provisions at Point b, Clause 1, Article 88 of Criminal Procedure Code.

DECIDES

1. To approve the Arrest warrant for detention No. 01/PA92 dated June 29, 2015, of Binh Thuan Police Investigation Agency

For the Defendant: ***Ho Trung Loi***
Within 3 months and 00 day, from the date of arrest.
Due to "**Organizing for other people to flee abroad**" stipulated in Article 275 of Criminal Code.

2. To require the Security Investigation Agency—Binh Thuan Public Security to execute this Decision according to the provisions of Criminal Procedure Code.

Recipients:

- Security Investigation Agency—Binh Thuan Public Security;
- Detention Center—Binh Thuan Public security (when arresting the defendant);
- Defendant (when being arrested);
- Case files;
- Procuracy Investigation files.

PP. CHIEF PROCURATOR

DEPUTY CHIEF PROCURATOR
(Signed and sealed)

Duong Xuan Son

Certified translation of Mr. Loi's arrest warrant (courtesy Tran Thi Thanh Loan).

Indeed, Judge Pham Thai Binh, who presided over the criminal trial in La Gi People's Court on April 22, 2016, ostensibly dismissed assertions that any official reassurance had been given.[37] Mrs. Loan and Mr. Loi were among the four accused handed jail sentences, after being convicted under article 275(1) of the Vietnamese Penal Code 1999, for "Organizing and/or coercing other persons to flee abroad or to stay abroad illegally," resulting in between "two years and seven years of imprisonment."[38]

According to SBS, "the trial took place amidst allegations that the local communist party authorities had intervened to make sure the asylum seekers were heavily punished." It quoted media interviews given by lawyer Mr. Vo after the trial, in which he was reported to have said: "The La Gi township administration (local communist party) has instructed to punish heavily.... The fact that the township administration instructed the judicial authorities on the trial is completely against Vietnamese law."[39]

To quote the well-known statement made by the late Ngo Ba Thanh (as she was known), prominent lawyer and member of the Vietnamese National Assembly: "Vietnam has a jungle of laws, but when it comes to trial, we use the law of the jungle."[40]

After the court case, Mr. Loi was moved to a harsher prison in Phan Rang city, deep in the Vietnamese rainforest where, Mrs. Loan alleged, he was forced to do hard labor and was not given enough to eat. She did not see him for a further ten months.[41] The prison sentences were upheld during the appeal of July 21, 2016, whereupon she burst into tears: "The court said I was the organizer, that I asked my family and friends, and then I was the buyer of the supplies ... with these crimes, they gave me 36 months in prison."[42] She was also fined the extraordinary sum of 274 million VND (close to USD12,000), telling me: "I did not pay that amount because I could not afford it. When my husband finished his sentence, he could only pay some of the interest on the fine."[43]

While Australia's official understanding is that returnees to Vietnam will not usually "face charges as a result of making an application for protection," a spokesperson for the Department of Immigration said, "any potential criminal investigations or proceedings for people-smuggling-related offences were a matter for the Vietnamese government."[44]

Although then Minister for Immigration and Border Protection Peter Dutton referred to these 46 Vietnamese nationals as partaking in a "people smuggling venture," HRW has pointed out: "These individuals were not punished for unlawfully bringing people into another country with the purpose of financial or material benefit—the definition of people smuggling under international law.[45] They were punished for leaving their own country and helping their families, relatives and friends who willingly went with them."[46]

As Mr. Vo has explained: "The Vietnamese government believed that their crimes were punishable by law, which collectively included buying food and supplies, steering, and commandeering the ship, and propositioning people to escape with them. Generally, when refugees are returned to Vietnam, they receive minor punishments like monetary fines rather than jail time. I don't really understand why in these ... instances they were sent to jail."[47] Indeed, Mrs. Loan told VOA: "I very much hope that the international community will speak out for Vietnam to abolish these laws in order to have ... human rights for the Vietnamese people, to make life better."[48]

Meanwhile, I continued to send her money each month by international bank transfer, reassured by her regular updates via Nhi. By that stage, however, our responsibilities had increased, our focus no longer concentrated solely on her family—thanks to another request from Mr. Vo.

2

Help Care for the Children

In early September 2016, Mr. Vo asked me to help several other families, including that of failed asylum seeker, Tran Thi Lua, who had been among four more defendants punished with jail terms for helping to organize another "illegal" departure to Australia in July 2015.

The mother-of-three had just lost her appeal against a 30-month sentence on September 1, 2016. While waiting to be sent to prison, she was living with her brother and sister-in-law, together with her children, then aged 14, 11, and 4. Like Mrs. Loan, she too was a sole carer, her husband, Nguyen Long, also a fisherman, having been arrested in July 2016 for fishing in Indonesian waters near the Natuna Islands and confined to the detention center in the capital Ranai for five months, his boat and equipment confiscated. Mrs. Lua had sold a small parcel of land (13 feet wide by 49 feet long) in La Gi township in 2013 to help buy the boat for him in the first place, and so the family had been left with nothing. Without assistance, their children would not be able to continue their education.

"In 2008, I bought a piece of land and had it transferred to my name," Mrs. Lua subsequently explained to me: "In 2010, when I applied for a permit to build on the land, the government told me the land belonged to them. Even the blades of grass on the land belonged to the government. We tried hard to get the paperwork from 2011 to 2013 but failed, being constantly harassed by the authorities. So, in 2013, we sold the land to the wife of a local government chief official. I don't know whether she was allowed to build on it. In 2017, when we fled Vietnam for the second time, there was still no building on it."

Consequently, I set up another crowd fund on GoFundMe: "Help Care for the Children" would prove to be a much tougher campaign, taking a full year to raise the final amount of almost USD10,400. Once again, our aim was to improve life to some extent for such families in Vietnam. Although we still attracted some media attention and generous donations—including an anonymous one of over USD1,700—it was more difficult to raise money for a similar cause the second time around. Moreover, I let the campaign run on too long—setting a shorter time frame often better positions an online crowd fund for success.

A more serious error, however, involved sending the families what in hindsight proved to be too large a sum of money, drawing the attention, and ire, of the Vietnamese police. While in the case of Mrs. Loan, I had been careful to send small amounts each month, I did not think I had the capacity to do so for each of the families we were trying to support. Not heeding Nhi's warnings, I decided to send the full amount we had raised—USD1,000 each. Adverse consequences followed almost immediately:

Mrs. Lua and her children, from left, Nguyen Thi Uyen, Nguyen Hai Dang, and Nguyen Dang Koi, outside the court when she lost her appeal, September 1, 2016 (courtesy Tran Thi Lua).

"The police keep coming to my house to ask me about the money," Mrs. Lua complained to me through Nhi. "They ask where it comes from, what it's for, who sent it. I told them that it's from foreigners who feel sorry for my situation and decided to help me so my children can go to school."

Mrs. Lua had been going to the beach each day to dig for clams to sell at market. On occasion, she would also find some casual house cleaning work. But after I sent her the money, the police stopped her from digging for clams. "I asked them why people from overseas would help me, while the Vietnamese government does nothing to help and even causes more problems," she said. "It makes me very upset that foreigners care so much, yet the government sees them as enemies."[1]

Mrs. Lua then grew too scared to talk to me, the police having threatened that if she continued to speak to people overseas, who would say "bad things" about the government online, she would be taken to jail immediately. As Nhi explained: "In Vietnam receiving money from overseas is not encouraged and sometimes can even be seen as an offense, especially if the receiver has been deemed as a troublemaker or criminal by the government. Also, there is a possibility that sending too much money all at once can spark the greed of neighbors or even distant family members, who may pressure the family for a loan or a share. Where people are very poor, it is hard to stay virtuous."

Rather than be intimidated, however, the police intervention only made us more determined to help. We increased our fundraising target, changing our strategy to ensure I only sent a small amount each month so as not to get them into any more trouble. Mrs. Lua expressed her gratitude through the media: "I would like to thank the benefactors for their generosity," she told Washington, D.C.–based journalist, Hoa Ai Tran, then of RFA. "You have helped me pay for school and buy clothes and books for my children."[2] At the same time, she was only too aware how her impending jail term would impact on her children's future, depriving them of education and work opportunities. As she elaborated to Nhi: "In Vietnam if one person commits what is considered to be a crime, the whole family pays."

Nevertheless, on September 16, 2016, shortly after we began raising funds for the second campaign, her sentence, like Mrs. Loan's, was deferred upon request for 12 months, based on her being the sole breadwinner for three young children and only a first-time offender.

Given such harsh punishment at the hands of the authorities, Mrs. Lua had not taken the decision lightly to flee Vietnam in the first place. An English translation of the findings from investigations, conducted by the La Gi District Police from August 12 to December 14, 2015, reveals the meticulous planning that had gone into such a daring venture.[3]

Regarded as the "mastermind" behind the "illegal" escape, she was accused of initiating a meeting with a fellow organizer and mother around May 2015. Deciding to ask more people to participate, they agreed to pool the money contributed to purchase the boat and supplies required for the journey. Both women then approached various relatives to determine their interest. In total, 46 asylum seekers resolved to partake in the ill-fated voyage, most of whom contributed what they could afford. Mrs. Lua admitted to using her savings to pay 70 million VND (around USD3,000) of the total raised, which was around 440 million VND (roughly USD19,000).

As HRW deputy director, Asia Division, Phil Robertson, subsequently told the BBC, "Clearly, from the information we received, these boat journeys were organized in a traditional community style. Everyone contributed money and departed together. Australia claimed there was an issue of people smuggling and that this action represented a criminal offense. But this is totally untrue."[4]

Other family members, who left with Mrs. Lua, in addition to her three children, included her husband's younger sister and brother, Nguyen Thi Kim Nhung and Nguyen Tai, both of whom would later flee with her a second time in early 2017. In 2015, however, her husband, Nguyen Long, did not escape with his family, being on a fishing expedition at the time and thus completely unaware of their plans.

Mrs. Lua and the other organizer relied on the latter's husband to inspect the prospective boat, which they bought for 300 million VND (around USD13,000). Various family members helped to make the vessel seaworthy, while food and supplies were purchased and transported secretly to be stored on board. The police investigation notes that "all the money for the escape" was spent before the group left the country. As Doan Trung has emphasized, "No-one made a monetary profit from the trip. And all aboard sought asylum."[5]

According to the district police, they discovered the intended escape on June 18, 2015, and summoned the three to the station. Mrs. Lua, however, has assured me that she was not sent for, nor did she know that the others had been called. The couple "changed their mind and no longer held the idea of leaving the country," the police reported. "At the same time, those people who contributed financially to the escape plan became doubtful ... and thought it was a scam and they became ... abusive and threatening towards [the other woman] and Lua. Because of this ... Lua and [the couple] decided to escape illegally on July 1, 2015," first arranging for the boat to be anchored secretly in Phan Thiet.

Almost three weeks later, their boat, BTH 96282TS, reached waters about 93 miles off the coast of Dampier in Western Australia, where it was sighted at first light on July 20, 2015, by crewmembers on a tanker belonging to oil and gas contractor, Modec. The media announced that the northwest-based police search and rescue boat, Delphinus, was deployed to help locate the asylum seekers, followed by a commonwealth naval vessel.[6] After being intercepted, Australian authorities are believed to have escorted the fishing boat further out to sea the next day.

Mrs. Lua maintains the group was subsequently transferred to the Australian ship for three days, before being moved to a larger vessel on July 24, 2015, where in a similar procedure to their predecessors a few months earlier, they underwent "enhanced screening" by two officials at sea.

"At 10 P.M. on July 25, a female representative of the Department of Immigration read a document, telling us through a Vietnamese interpreter that the Australian government would return us to Vietnam," Mrs. Lua told me:

> I stood up and said, "If you send us back to Vietnam, we will be imprisoned and then how will our children live?" But the immigration representative said, "No, the Vietnamese government has made a deal with the Australian government and promised us that they won't arrest or imprison you. They will help you find jobs and help your children go to school. So, don't worry. The Vietnamese government has already promised they will never put you in prison." I asked several times what would happen to us, but I did not get any further answer from Australian immigration.

As she told broadcast journalist Kathy Trieu in a similar statement: "At that point, we decided to stop trying and if this other country didn't want to accept us, then that would be it."[7]

Having determined once again that this group of Vietnamese asylum seekers was not owed protection obligations, the Australian authorities secretly flew them back to Vietnam overnight on July 25, 2015, possibly by chartered plane.[8] Then Immigration Minister Peter Dutton refused to comment on "operational matters," while Prime Minister Tony Abbott said Australia would "act in accordance with Australia's national interests and not ... run a shipping news service for people smugglers."[9]

Mrs. Lua, however, provided me with a few more details: "At 12 midnight they moved us to the Australian coast [presumably Darwin], and at 1 A.M. they took us by bus to the aircraft, which took off at 3 A.M. There were representatives from Australian immigration and the Embassy on board as well as some army officers."

After landing at Tan Son Nhat airport in Ho Chi Minh City at 8 a.m. on July 26, 2015, the passengers said they were again assured by both Vietnamese and Australian official representatives, in scenes reminiscent of the earlier group's experience in April 2015, that they would not be punished. "One policewoman told us that on behalf of the government of Vietnam, they had pardoned us," Mrs. Lua told RFA's Vietnamese service. "They said they would let us come back to live with our community and nobody would be jailed, but they detained us, and now they prosecute us."[10]

She accused the Vietnamese immigration officials, who greeted them at the airport, of putting on a show for their Australian counterparts, for whose benefit the assurance was translated into English. "It was staged to create the impression to the Australians that we'd be well treated," she told Australia's ABC via a translator. "However, we were immediately taken to a detention centre—Vietnam didn't keep its promise.... I was held for three months and I was beaten."[11] As she explained in more detail to Kathy Trieu: "The immigration in Saigon [Ho Chi Minh City], the police of Binh Thuan province and the police of La Gi commune were all waiting for us.... They did not drive us home. They told us they would drive us home, but they didn't."[12]

Mrs. Lua told me that although she "had asked, as the representative of our group, for a letter of commitment that we would not be punished for escaping," instead, they were immediately taken by bus to La Gi police station, where the adults were arrested. Transferred that night to the Phan Thiet detention center, she and some of the others were imprisoned separately for 26 days before anyone took their statement. Only children aged 16 and under were allowed to return home.

"They said that after I tell the truth, they would let me go," she recalled to Kathy Trieu:

> They lied to me like that every day. Then on August 18, they lied to me by saying, "pack your clothes, you're going home to your children." I thought I was going home, but when they drove me home, they read the arrest order....
>
> A man there told me even if you don't sign, we will still take you away. We don't care about what we promise. We had promised that with the Australian government so they would send you back. If we didn't promise them, then they wouldn't send you back. I then asked him, "so that means the Vietnamese government lied to the Australian government?" He yelled at me; told me to shut up and even wanted to slap me. He then ordered the policemen to drag and push me into the prison van. They took me [back] to Phan Thiet.... I was there for one month and five days. During that time, he continued to lie to me and try to make me sign all kinds of papers, saying that if I sign, I could go home. I told him that he could take me wherever he wants but I won't sign anything or listen to him because he had already lied to me so many times.

She later elaborated to me: "During that time they physically beat me.... A police inspector took my testimony, and the police director of Binh Thuan province also came to threaten me, saying he would ask the court for a ten-year sentence." She never admitted to any crime.

On October 3, 2015, she was transferred to jail in La Gi, where her experience continued to be traumatic. She described this mistreatment to ABC journalist Liam Cochrane, who, alerted by Doan Trung, interviewed her in February 2017, the story briefly becoming headline news in Australia: "I was beaten and mistreated—slapped in the face, sworn at and called names—by female security guards, who when angry would place dirty linen and clothes in the prisoners' well and force us to drink, wash and cook with the dirty water."[13]

Mrs. Lua told me, "During one of the beating episodes, I bled so much that I needed to go to the hospital and was released on parole to receive medical treatment."[14] Due to this "health issue" as it was called in the prosecutor's report,[15] she was sent home on bail on November 6, 2015, where she was forced to listen to public announcements against her and her children. These were broadcast by the authorities every morning and afternoon, both in her local area and near the children's school, where they had returned about a month after arriving back in Vietnam.

"The authorities have loudspeakers at many, if not most, public spaces," Doan Trung explained:

These are used to propagate state information ... [They proclaimed that] Lua had tried to flee Vietnam, and in doing so, was, in their words, a traitor.... The announcements declaring their guilt were made well before the court hearing, which later announced that Lua and all the others were guilty as charged. The announcements stopped when the loudspeakers' airtime was required for the National Assembly elections in May 2016.

[Her two older children] Uyen and Dang were extremely upset. They cried and told their mother Lua that they felt very ashamed, they did not want to go back to school. Lua noticed that during this time, their sleep pattern was also changed, burdened with crying and their sleep was restless. Lua insisted to the two children that they must continue their schooling. The children went along with their mother's instruction and kept on attending school.[16]

As with their predecessors from the first boat of March–April 2015, all four accused, including Mrs. Lua, were again subsequently charged and convicted under article 275 of the Vietnamese Penal Code 1999 for "Organizing and/or coercing other persons to flee abroad or to stay abroad illegally," Clause 1 specifying their sentence to be "between two years and seven years of imprisonment." The same court in La Gi heard their case, the trial taking place on May 26, 2016.

Just before the court case, then Australia HRW director Elaine Pearson spoke out, telling *The Guardian* that imprisoning people for trying to leave their own country was "cruel as well as unlawful." "The Vietnamese government is prosecuting the four defendants for leaving Vietnam without the government's permission, violating their fundamental right under international law to leave their own country," she charged. "Vietnam has blatantly broken its promise to the Australian government not to prosecute boat returnees. Australia should tell the Vietnamese government to drop all charges immediately and release them."[17]

Mrs. Loan was in court to support those charged. Mrs. Lua traces their friendship back to that day: "We share the same last names so we're practically sisters."[18] Interestingly, the police investigation noted: "They have committed an offence to escape Vietnam to go to Australia to have a better life. Their motivation to escape did not mean they were protesting against the Vietnamese communist government." This interpretation of the reason for their departure was repeated at both their trial on May 26, 2016, and their appeal on September 1, 2016: "Due to difficult family circumstances, Tran Thi Lua came up with the idea to cross the sea to Australia to find a better life."[19]

Mrs. Lua, however, insists that her family's economic situation was never the issue. "It's not that we couldn't find work," she told Kathy Trieu:

We can definitely work. We still have jobs. My family has a business, has boats to go out to the sea. But when the Chinese ships attacked and seized our boats, we informed the Vietnamese authorities in our town, and asked them what they were going to do. They just nodded along and told us to continue to go out to sea. When the Chinese continued to ram into our boats, killed our fishermen, all they said was "can only look; cannot say anything." That's how life is in Vietnam. You can't say anything. There are no human rights.[20]

She was referring to an ill-fated fishing expedition her husband, Nguyen Long, had made in 2011 to the Spratly and Paracel Islands—several years before Mr. Loi—when his boat had also been attacked by Chinese ships. He had called the Vietnamese navy for help but maintains they had not responded. Like Mr. Loi, when he had returned to shore, he had reported the incident to the local Vietnamese authorities in La Gi, but they had equally ignored his complaint and, he alleges, had continued to harass the family.

"So, under that much oppression, how can we live freely in Vietnam?" Mrs. Lua asked. "We didn't have freedom, no freedom of speech, nothing at all. We didn't even have a voice to speak up. When we've spoken up, they've arrested and beaten us, leaving us without any options. When they're done, they threaten us. They say from this day forward, are you going to keep talking? So, we're left feeling like we don't have any voice at all."[21]

Together with Mrs. Loan, she certainly tried to raise her voice, Doan Trung and HRW's Elaine Pearson helping to arrange for the two women, among others, to meet privately with Australian Senator Sarah Hanson-Young in a hotel in Ho Chi Minh City on August 3, 2016. The Senator, who was replaced as Greens immigration spokesperson about a month later, had been taking a keen interest in what had happened to the families, advocating publicly on their behalf on several occasions.[22]

"Might this case be made to the Minister," Trung had lobbied via email on July 21, "that these people, who face imprisonment now and discrimination later by the state, now have a well-founded fear of persecution, and Australia should take them in now as part of its offshore refugee program?"

Mrs. Loan subsequently recalled: "We presented the issue of the Australian authorities returning us, the commitment to keep the Vietnamese government from arresting us, creating jobs, sending our children to school, but the Vietnamese government did not keep its promise. I also told the Senator that the Vietnamese police persecuted my husband and that he had difficulties with the government. The Senator said she would present this to the Australian government."

Meanwhile, Australian authorities had continued to return Vietnamese nationals intercepted in the Timor Sea, a third boat with 21 failed asylum seekers on board being secretly processed on the water and the passengers flown back from Darwin on June 16, 2016. Mr. Dutton said he could confirm the take-back because they had been safely sent back: "They claimed that they were wanting protection, it was found that they were not owed protection and they were returned to Vietnam." Prime Minister Malcolm Turnbull used the opportunity to send a strong message to people-smugglers: "It is important that their messaging, which is obviously designed to get people on boats, is countered by the facts of our steely resolve to stop them from putting peoples' lives at risk and challenging the sovereignty of our borders."[23]

The only reason why I have more information about what happened in what was the Coalition government's 28th boat take-back operation is because one of those on board, Huynh Thi My Van, has supplied me with two Australian official documents detaining her then 14-year-old daughter, Lam Huynh Nguyen, and 11-year-old son, Son Huynh Nguyen, as "unlawful non-citizens."

Issued on June 16, 2016, by the Department of Immigration and Border Protection (DIBP) at Larrakeyah Navy Base in Darwin—the main base for the Australian Defense Force in the Northern Territory—the document states that under section 189(1) of the Migration Act,

> If an officer knows or reaosnably [sic] suspects that a person in the migration zone (other than an excised offshore place) is an unlawyful [sic] non-citizen, the officer must detain the person.[24]

P004

Australian Government

Department of Immigration and Border Protection

SECTION 189(1) DETENTION OF UNLAWFUL NON CITIZENS

SECTION 189 OFFICER'S NAME:

DETAINEE NAME: Lam Huynh NGUYEN (   ).

DATE: 16/06/2016   PLACE: LARRAKEYAH NAVY BASE, DARWIN, NT.

MY NAME IS I   , I AM AN OFFICER FOR THE PURPOSES OF
SECTION 189 OF THE MIGRATION ACT 1958 ('THE ACT').

UNDER SECTION 189(1) OF THE ACT, IF AN OFFICER KNOWS OR REAOSNABLY
SUSPECTS THAT A PERSON IN THE MIGRATION ZONE (OTHER THAN AN
EXCISED OFFSHORE PLACE) IS AN UNLAWYFUL NON-CITIZEN, THE OFFICER
MUST DETAIN THE PERSON.

DARWIN, NT IS IN THE MIGRATION ZONE AND IS NOT AN EXCISED OFFSHORE
PLACE. AN UNLAWFUL NON-CITIZEN IS A NON-CITIZEN WHO DOES NOT HOLD
A VISA THAT IS IN EFFECT.

ON YOUR ARRIVAL AT DARWIN ON 16TH JUNE 2016, BASED ON THE AVAILABLE
INFORMATION, I REASONABLY SUSPECTED YOU TO BE AN UNLAWFUL NON-
CITIZEN AND I THEREFORE DETAINED YOU UNDER SECTION 189(1).

YOU ARE NOW IN IMMIGRATION DETENTION UNDER SECTION 189 OF THE ACT

Signature:........................   (Section 189 Officer)

Signature:........................   (Detainee or parent/relative)

Unreleased Australian official immigration document detaining Mrs. Van's then 14-year-old daughter, Lam Huynh Nguyen, as an "unlawful non-citizen" (courtesy Huynh Thi My Van).

Darwin, NT is in the migration zone and is not an excised offshore place. An unlawful non-citizen is a non-citizen who does not hold a visa that is in effect.

On your arrival at Darwin on 16th June 2016, based on the available information, I reasonably suspected you to be an unlawful citizen and I therefore detained you under section 189(1).

You are now in immigration detention under section 189 of the Act.

They were not in immigration detention for long, Australian authorities flying them back to Vietnam that same day.

According to *The Guardian*, "the immigration and border protection department has not commented on whether assurances were sought or received that people returned to Vietnam from the latest boat would not face persecution or prosecution."[25] By that stage, however, given the experience of the two previous groups of asylum seekers, surely Australia knew that at the very least, those regarded as having helped to organize the "illegal" departure could be sent to prison in Vietnam.

In February 2017, Darwin-based barrister, Lyma Nguyen, asked VietBP 2013 e-group members familiar with cases where failed asylum seekers had been prosecuted and faced heavy terms of imprisonment, to provide affidavit evidence, including observations of their treatment in Vietnam. She, along with other human rights lawyers and migration agents, hoped to use such evidence in judicial reviews to investigate whether their punishment amounted to "significant harm" and if so, whether complementary protection should thus be afforded to them.[26] Having recently joined the Vietnamese asylum seeker support e-group, I was among those who provided such affidavits, unfortunately with little ultimate effect.

"The affidavit was not allowed to be used on review," Lyma subsequently told me:

> It was ruled out on the basis that "the affidavit is hearsay" and "the information within the affidavit was not central to the decision to be made" and "the Tribunal below was not required to make enquiries about those matters"....
>
> The other issue is that the parents of the children you assisted, who were prosecuted in Vietnam, were prosecuted for their conduct of taking other people to Australia ("people smuggling")—and this distinction was readily made by the court, which put the asylum seekers whose review it was hearing, into another category ("victims of people smuggling").

Indeed, in June 2017, the Department of Foreign Affairs (DFAT) officially acknowledged its assessment that "long-term detention, investigation and arrest is conducted only in relation to those suspected of involvement in organizing people-smuggling operations. DFAT understands this to be the case in relation to several individuals who were on board vessels returned to Vietnam in 2016."[27]

Nevertheless, Mrs. Van, wife of fisherman Nguyen Tuan Kiet, who were both among the four defendants from the third boat—returned on June 16, 2016, charged six days later on June 21, and ultimately punished—insisted that once again, the Australian and Vietnamese authorities had made such an assurance that they would not be punished and had broken their promise: "They [officials] told us that the government of Vietnam promised the government of Australia that we would be freed when we returned to Vietnam," she told RFA. "One female representative of the Vietnamese government told us that we left Vietnam for the reason of making a living so we should not be jailed."[28]

As previously, it was Mr. Vo who drew our attention to this family's plight in mid–December 2016, Mrs. Van having traveled over 300 miles to consult him pro bono before the trial. On December 13, Mr. Kiet was sentenced to 30 months with hard labor in Phuoc Co prison, over 30 miles away from the family home in the township of Ngai Giao, capital of the rural district of Chau Duc in Ba Ria-Vung Tau province on the south-eastern coast.[29] Tried like the previous eight defendants for "organizing illegal emigration of another person," this time the Ba Ria-Vung Tau provincial People's Court decided to rely on article 349 of the new Vietnamese Penal Code 2015, which had become applicable on July 1, 2016.[30]

"I read the prosecutor's report, and I saw they are going to use the new Penal Code which has tougher jail punishments than the old one," Mr. Vo told RFA. Under the new code, Mr. Kiet was facing a sentence of seven to 15 years, while Mrs. Van could have been imprisoned for one to five years. "They think that those who illegally leave Vietnam badly affect the prestige of the country, the order of society, so they decided to prosecute them ... to warn others not to leave the country."[31]

Indeed, his view was corroborated by the People's Court of Binh Thuan province in Mrs. Lua's appeal of September 1, 2016: "The acts of the defendants are dangerous to society, not only seriously infringing on the order and management of the administrative state on entry and exit, but also causing insecurity in the locality, adversely affecting prestige and honor of nations in the region and around the world."[32]

When I later asked Mr. Vo why he had been prepared to represent such defendants for free, he replied: "They had no houses, no jobs and were imprisoned by the Vietnamese government, pushing their whole family onto the same path.... These people crossed the sea to Australia with the desire to have a better life than in Vietnam. They did not do anything wrong that the Vietnamese government should imprison them."[33]

In the end, Mr. Kiet's term was not so long as originally feared, while his wife was given an 18-month suspended sentence, with a probationary period of 36 months, preventing her from traveling outside her local area. As Nhi explained: "Her sentence is more like a good behavior bond. So long as she does not do anything to upset the government, she will not have to go to jail. But if she leaves her local precinct in search of work, she will be imprisoned immediately."

Mrs. Van was trying to support her two children and keep them in school by doing sewing work but was only earning around USD2 a day. Living in a rental property, the family was facing the risk of becoming homeless. She did not have enough money to buy lunch, and so they only ate one or two meals a day. Meat was almost non-existent. She also needed to send food to her husband each month, as he did not get enough to eat and was in poor health, having lost considerable weight since being detained immediately

Mrs. Van with her two children, Son Huynh Nguyen (left) and Lam Huynh Nguyen (right), during her husband's imprisonment in 2016 (courtesy Huynh Thi My Van).

upon their return. Without transport, it was expensive for his family to travel the long distance to visit him each month.

At that stage, we had not reached our fundraising target for Mrs. Lua and the others and did not feel comfortable taking money away to give to a new family. At the same time, we did not want to leave them with nothing: We saw they were counting on us and did not want to let them down. So, I decided to add them to the "Help Care for the Children" campaign.

Through Nhi, Mr. Vo elaborated:

> The family is poorly educated. Both husband and wife only went to school to Grade 2 and barely read and write, so they don't know much at all. Getting on Facebook and setting up a bank account are major things for them to learn to do. They need someone to take them through step by step.
>
> On top of that they are scared of the police. It took Mrs. Lua and Mrs. Loan to travel south to meet them at the court to convince them that accepting help from overseas is ok, as the police told them that overseas people only want to exploit them and get them into trouble!

Meanwhile, the day before the trial, on December 12, 2016, Mr. Dutton and Vietnam's Minister of Public Security Colonel General To Lam had signed a new Memorandum of Understanding (MOU) in Canberra to return "Vietnamese nationals with no legal right to enter or remain in Australia, including those intercepted at sea." Maintaining the arrangement was "consistent with both countries' domestic and international legal obligations" and calling it "a significant milestone in Australia's bilateral relationship with Vietnam and an important part of our broader efforts to counter irregular migration in the region," Mr. Dutton said: "The Coalition Government is committed to protecting our borders, stamping out people smuggling and preventing people risking their lives at sea.... Australia's borders are stronger than ever and our tough border protection policies are here to stay."[34]

Human rights organizations were quick to express concern, UNICEF warning "families may be at risk of return to situations where they could experience persecution and serious human rights violations." It urged "the Australian government to continue their exploring options for a common regional protection framework to coordinate predictable responses and pathways for asylum seeker and refugee children."[35]

We, however, had other worries. After speaking with Mrs. Van, Nhi told me: "I am going to try really hard to get some money for the family. I will beg my close friends for them." While there was no guarantee that we would raise any more funds, which would now need to be divided between three families, we agreed that the risk was well worth taking. All we could do was try.

I wrote an article, which Nhi translated, and Doan Trung endeavored to have placed in the local Vietnamese media. We also decided to embark on a letter-writing campaign, alerting prominent Vietnamese Australians, including executives and restaurateurs, to the plight of these failed asylum seeker families and our efforts to assist them. Stressing that our focus was non-political, I requested a meeting with each of these well-connected potential benefactors, explaining that I was not seeking donations, but rather, wanted "to discuss what could be done to help these desperate people on a larger and more secure basis than I am able to do on my own." The article was never published, and I only ever received one reply to our letter campaign—a polite, albeit firm, refusal.

Although we never learned the reason why our campaign was otherwise completely ignored, Nhi maintained that many Vietnamese living overseas continue to return to, and do business with, their former motherland and so feel more comfortable donating elsewhere. Indeed, in 2016, former Vietnamese refugees residing in Australia pledged more than half a million dollars in support of Syrian refugees.[36]

By January 2017, we were down to under USD140. As I wrote in an urgent update to our donors, "Unless more money comes in, we will no longer be able to support these seven Vietnamese children, all of whose parents are either in or awaiting jail for attempting to reach Australia by boat in 2015–16." The appeal fell largely on deaf ears, only managing to raise an extra USD500. Ever-resourceful, Nhi urged me to write to international Vietnamese advocacy organizations, BPSOS and Viet Tan.

While I never heard back from Viet Tan, Nhi conceding "it is difficult because they mostly want to support activists in Vietnam,"[37] BPSOS executive director Dr. Nguyen Dinh Thang showed a keen interest in our work. Renowned for rescuing over 25,000 Vietnamese boat people in the 1980s, BPSOS (which stands for "Boat People SOS") now assists, among others, "victims of human rights violations in Vietnam, protecting Vietnamese asylum seekers in neighboring countries and rescuing victims of human trafficking around the globe."[38]

Writing to me almost immediately from Washington, D.C., Dr. Nguyen thanked me for "bringing to our attention the plight of these Vietnamese returnees. I would like to commend you for your good work and successful fundraising efforts to help the family of Mrs. Tran Thi Thanh Loan. I would like to learn more about other families and their current conditions."

As we subsequently discovered, Mrs. Van, Mr. Kiet and their children were among 21 asylum seekers who had fled Vietnam by fishing boat on May 18, 2016. But preparations for the trip had started long before when according to Mrs. Van, her husband was approached by the other two defendants, who offered to pay him 20 million VND (around USD860) a month to sail the boat to Australia. While passengers had to pay 50 million VND (about USD2,100) each for food and fuel, the total raised being 450 million VND (roughly USD19,300), Mrs. Van and Mr. Kiet did not have to contribute financially. "They told us our family could go without paying," she told RFA. "We did not have any job back then, so we were so happy to have the offer."[39]

She explained to me that her husband acquired the boat from a friend at the request of one of the other defendants, who "was responsible for chartering the boat, but he did not pay the owner after returning home. We tried to leave Vietnam because there were no economic improvement policies and no human rights. We were prepared to sacrifice our lives to find a better life in a new country."

Even when both parents had been employed, they had always struggled to make ends meet. The Formosa disaster had also impacted on Mr. Kiet's ability to make a living as a fisherman, Mrs. Van charged, with him battling to make USD40–50 a week; some days he came back empty-handed. Indeed, this water pollution crisis of April 2016—thought to be Vietnam's worst environmental disaster—resulted in an estimated 115 tons of dead fish and other marine life being washed up along 125 miles of coastline in four central provinces from Ha Tinh to Thua Thien-Hue. On June 30, 2016, Formosa Ha Tinh Steel Corp, a subsidiary of the Taiwanese conglomerate, Formosa Plastics Group, finally claimed responsibility and agreed to pay USD500 million in compensation for the marine life disaster, which was blamed on toxic industrial waste discharged illegally through sewage pipes. By then, however, fishermen had lost millions of dollars, the Vietnamese government having banned the sale and distribution of seafood from affected areas. According to official statistics, the livelihoods of more than 200,000 people were harmed, including over 40,000 fishermen. "The companies disposed of chemical waste, which contaminated the water, and the Vietnamese government did not intervene and did not compensate us," Mrs. Van maintained.

Their voyage to Australia lasted about 25 days. "We were hungry and ill. The boat was damaged, and we drifted for a few days, waiting for fishermen from neighboring countries to help. Fortunately, we did not meet any Chinese vessels, only Indonesian and Thai fishing crews, who gave us food. At one stage, we had to stop the boat and swim, which was dangerous."

They were arrested by Australian authorities on June 10, 2016. "We were far from the mainland. The Australian government detained us for six days on their ship. They interviewed each of us and said we were lucky because one of the boats we passed had many pirates on board. They also told us there were snakes and crocodiles in the water."

After landing at Tan Son Nhat airport on June 16, 2016, the Australian government gave each failed asylum seeker 4 million VND (around USD172) to "help us restart our life," Mrs. Van said. "The Vietnamese government promised to release us in front of the Australian officials. But after they left, the Vietnamese government did not keep its promise. They took us to the Ba Ria-Vung Tau police station to be interrogated. My husband was not locked up with us because he was the captain and was immediately taken to jail where he was detained until the trial."

She told me her family was fined twice, being forced to pay 6 million VND each (just under USD260), along with the other failed asylum seekers, but also given an extra USD6,000 fine. "That was all the savings for which my family had worked so hard for so many years. The Vietnamese government said it was not our money and confiscated it for no reason. I don't understand why."[40]

As she complained to RFA: "I don't think that I committed any crime. I did not tell anybody to go with us. I did not organize the trip. I did not buy any supplies for the trip. I did not know anything. I just packed up and left when they told us they were ready to leave. I was a victim."[41] Finally released from jail in October 2018, Mr. Kiet, who had lost 22 pounds while incarcerated, had become an old man, according to his wife. "He has no job because no one dares to accept him due to his sentence," she bewailed.

I met the family for the first time on November 9, 2018, in Ho Chi Minh City, where they traveled to see me, bringing with them a Vietnamese American friend and his wife, who had offered to translate for us. Throughout their ordeal, Mrs. Van had insisted her children maintain focus on their education. Her efforts were beginning to pay off, at least for her now 16-year-old daughter Lam, who was already fairly fluent in English and proving to be a serious student, with dreams of attending university to become a nurse.

Although in the end, we had only been able to offer sporadic support, they were so grateful. Still under police observation, Mr. Kiet hoped to be able to return to fishing, if possible, in the future, and subsequently managed to secure work as a truck driver. Nevertheless, their concern remained palpable: "I want the government to

From left: Mr. Kiet, son, Son Huynh Nguyen, Mrs. Van, the author, and the couple's daughter, Lam Huynh Nguyen, Ho Chi Minh City, November 2018.

respect, listen to and handle our difficulties," Mrs. Van said. "But that can't happen in my country."

Indeed, such official harassment had played a large part in the secret decision taken by Mrs. Lua, Mrs. Loan, and another mother, Nguyen Thi Phuc, to flee with their families in a second attempt to reach Australia. A decision they did not share with us until after their departure on the night of January 30, 2017, but one which would change the course of their—and to a lesser extent, our—lives.

3

Escape for the Second Time

By February 1, 2017, we had not heard from Mrs. Loan or Mrs. Lua for several days. This was unusual as Nhi was in contact with them quite often. "Mrs. Loan has not been online," she told me. "She should get in touch tonight after she gets back from selling fruit." Little did we know that they had already fled for the second time two nights earlier.

Nor was Mr. Vo any the wiser when Nhi asked him about their whereabouts. After their appeals had been concluded, only Mrs. Loan had continued to visit him from time to time. Preoccupied with his newborn baby, he told Nhi he would try to find out what had happened and let us know.

As the days passed with no news, our anxiety increased: "I don't know if something has happened to them," Nhi confided to me. "None of them have been online. I have called Mrs. Lua and Mrs. Loan but there is no answer. I hope they have not been arrested and put in prison. Mr. Vo said he can find out, but that will take some time because the Vietnamese police work in strange ways."

Imagine our shock to read his public announcement in Vietnamese on Facebook on February 3, 2017, that he had "just learned" that three families were "on their way escaping from Vietnam to Australia by sea. Their boat has just crossed over Indonesian territory, and they are heading towards Australian waters." He warned that if they were forcibly returned by Australia again, Mrs. Loan and Mrs. Lua would face up to seven years and six years in jail respectively, as they would have to serve the remainder of their existing sentences combined with new prison terms. Both mothers had told him they would "commit suicide by jumping into the sea as they would never accept returning to Vietnam a second time." He concluded his post with the statement: "May the three families be safe and soon reach the shores of freedom!"[1]

At that stage, apart from the three mothers and their children, we were not even sure who else was on board the boat. Nevertheless, I immediately began contacting human rights organizations, such as the Refugee Council of Australia (RCOA) and Human Rights Watch (HRW), well known Australian advocates, like Refugee Action Coalition spokesperson Ian Rintoul, and legal advisers from the Human Rights Law Centre (HRLC).[2] I was in a desperate race against time to help them, in the unlikely event that they would reach Australian waters—an attempt I knew was practically doomed from the start.

As subsequently explained on a website Nhi and I established later that year, *www.vietbp.org*, as a resource for families of Vietnamese failed asylum seekers in similar straits:

To claim asylum in Australia, a person needs to be physically present on Australian territory. A person or someone on their behalf (who may be in Vietnam or elsewhere) needs to provide the asylum seeker's name and location or exact coordinates in Australian waters. A person seeking asylum should also make a request for legal help to explain the reason they left Vietnam. The person specifically needs to inform Australian authorities whether they fear for their safety if returned to Vietnam and provide details about why they hold that fear. Please note that whatever the outcome of a case, a person will not be able to apply for a visa to remain in Australia, except at the discretion of the Minister of Immigration.[3]

Having observed the considerable confusion arising among volunteer advocates each time an asylum seeker boat was rumored to be approaching Australia, I had drafted this paragraph in consultation with legal experts, not having been able to find concise advice elsewhere. But how were we going to find out the names of everyone on board as well as their location or exact coordinates in Australian waters, especially when Vietnamese sailors traditionally rely on celestial navigation? And how were they going to know to make a request for legal help on the open sea?

"There is nothing I know of specifically directed to asylum seekers still at sea or who are in Australian waters," Australian legal expert Dr. Anthea Vogl subsequently confirmed: "This is because so much of the advocacy material and services are aimed at those who have already sought asylum rather than informing people of how to do this. The limited contact and difficulty of contact prior to the making of a claim (especially for those who arrive by boat) explains the absence of resources."[4]

Pressure had been mounting on both Mrs. Loan and Mrs. Lua in the weeks leading up to their escape. We were certainly aware that both women were highly worried about their imminent and lengthy prison sentences. They had also disclosed to us, as well as to Doan Trung, that the police had threatened to beat them in jail for having spoken out to foreigners in the past. As Mrs. Loan subsequently informed SBS, "the local chief of police, Major Bui Thanh Truc, told me not to speak to any foreign media. He told me I will get what my husband got once I am in that prison."[5]

On January 21, 2017, Nhi had divulged to me that the police "seem to want to take them to jail soon. Mrs. Loan's husband is due for release, and Mrs. Lua's husband has been sent back from Indonesia. It is also possible that they want bribe money." Moreover, Mrs. Loan had reported to us that several of her friends, who had fled with her in 2015, had been summoned to the police station to answer questions about her, while Mrs. Lua had been told several times that she should elect to start her prison term early.

Nhi told the two women "to keep their ears open but maintain a low profile and let me know as soon as something happens. At the moment, the local police are just threatening them, but there is no official order from the court yet." While Mrs. Loan's husband Ho Trung Loi's sentence would not be completed until mid-year, Nhi thought at the time that he might be among those prisoners commonly pardoned by the Vietnamese government for the Lunar New Year, warning that "then the police may decide to take Mrs. Loan to jail earlier." Even after Mrs. Loan had fled with her children for the second time, we were unsure as to whether Mr. Loi had been pardoned and escaped with them, only learning subsequently from one of Mrs. Loan's sisters that he was still in jail.

What was clear, however, was how badly he was being treated in prison. "Every time I went to visit him, I would see ambulances taking prisoners out from the jail,"

Mrs. Loan later told SBS. "They've been withholding his medication from him. Swelling from high blood pressure has made it impossible for him to move around."[6]

Meanwhile, Mrs. Lua's husband, Nguyen Long, had arrived home on December 25, 2016, only to be met with more harassment: "The local police kept summoning him many times and caused him a lot of trouble," she subsequently contended to me. "So, we had to leave the country."

If Mrs. Loan or Mrs. Lua had shared their escape plans with us in advance, we would have strongly tried to dissuade them. Indeed, we had begged them never to reattempt such a dangerous journey. But they had not told anyone of their secret preparations, which had actually commenced more than a month earlier, when on January 18, 2017, Mrs. Lua and fellow mother Nguyen Thi Phuc had gone to An Loc, a small town in southern Vietnam, to look for a boat to buy, as well as purchasing food for the voyage. "We paid 245 million VND [around USD10,500] for the boat and supplies from our

Mr. Loi in prison uniform during a visit with his wife, Mrs. Loan, before she fled Vietnam (courtesy Tran Thi Thanh Loan).

savings and from money we borrowed from our siblings," Mrs. Lua later explained to me. "My husband served as skipper of the boat because he had the most experience."

It turned out that Mr. Vo had last heard from Mrs. Loan on January 28, 2017, when she had called him from a number in Vietnam to wish him all the best for *Tết* or Lunar New Year, the most important celebration in Vietnamese culture, which lasts several days and marks the arrival of spring.[7] As Mrs. Lua eventually told me, the 18-strong group, consisting of six adults and 12 children, had decided to flee during the Lunar New Year holiday period because "we knew the police did not work then." Just a few days earlier, on January 22, 2017, the three mothers had visited Mr. Vo at his home in Tuy Hoa, Phu Yen province, before going on a pilgrimage to Mang Lang Church, one of the oldest Catholic churches in Vietnam. They remain adamant that he knew nothing of their plans before their departure.

Mr. Vo posted two photos of the mothers on their pilgrimage on his Facebook page on February 9, 2017, after the families contacted him using an Indonesian sim card to ask for help. Under a headline in Vietnamese, which translates as "The Great Escape," he explained that Mrs. Lua had called him from an encrypted number and had only been able to answer a few questions before they had lost contact. "I hope the lawyers and human rights organizations in Australia get to them early to persuade Prime Minister Malcolm Turnbull to accept these families as refugees," he added. "If the Australian government returns them to Vietnam for a second time, Australia's image as a kind country will be lost in the eyes of the people."

His post the following day, February 10, 2017, was far more dramatic, announcing the group had been "apprehended by Indonesian police on Java Island at 6 P.M." and "taken to the [local] refugee camp." Doan Trung was able to speak briefly with one of the officers: "Their boat got engine trouble and went into Indonesia for repairs. This afternoon I spoke with Loan. I said New Zealand might be less cruel [than Australia]. She said her boat might not make it."

As we were soon to discover, after about 12 days at sea, their 26-foot wooden boat, BD30957TS, had lost direction, drifting into Indonesian waters where it had hit reefs in high seas, badly damaging the engine, losing the anchor, and starting to sink. After nearly ten hours, the three families had been fortunate to be rescued off the Java coast by local fishermen, who had towed them to shore at Cibanua Village in Java's westernmost province of Banten, where Indonesian police and residents had assisted them. They had lost their possessions during the ordeal.[8]

Believing that speaking to the media would help promote their efforts to find asylum in a third country, Mrs. Lua told RFA: "I asked them [the Indonesian authorities] not to return us to Vietnam. I showed them proof of our imprisonment and they told us that they would not return us.... But they said they have to wait for their boss's decision." She announced that according to Mr. Vo, "Vietnam has issued a national arrest warrant for us."[9]

Indeed, Judge Le Minh Chinh of La Gi People's Court had not wasted any time, at least in relation to Mrs. Loan. Dated February 9, 2017, and titled "Annulment of the Postponement of Imprisonment Sentence," the decision stated:

PEOPLE'S COURT	**SOCIALIST REPUBLIC OF VIETNAM**
LA GI TOWNSHIP	**Independence—Liberty—Happiness**
BINH THUAN PROVINCE	**La Gi—February 09, 2017**
Number: 02/2017/QD-CA	

DECISION
Annulment of the Postponement of Imprisonment Sentence
The Judge of the People's Court of La Gi Township
Considers that:

According to the imprisonment sentencing number 81/2016/QD-CA dated on the 5th of August 2016, issued by the People's Court of La Gi township, Binh Thuan province: Tran, Thi Thanh Loan was to be imprisoned for 36 (thirty-six) months. This person has been out on bail.

On the 15th of August 2016, the People's Court of La Gi township, Binh Thuan province, allowed the postponement of imprisonment sentencing number 81/2016/QD-CA; permitting Tran, Thi Thanh Loan to postpone the sentence. The delay period is from 15th of August 2016 to 15th of August 2017.

On the 7th of February 2017, the police of La Gi township—the executor of this sentencing order—received notice number 10/THAHS regarding the fact that Tran, Thi Thanh Loan has vanished from her residence.

Considers that:

During the time the sentence was postponed, Tran Thi Thanh Loan left her residence without the permission of the People's Committee of Phuoc Hoi Ward.

Based on Section 02, 20, 23 and 24 regarding the Application of Criminal Law in 2010.

Decides that:

1. The decision to postpone the sentence (number 08/2016/QD-CA, granted on the 15th of August 2016) is withdrawn.

2. Tran Thi Thanh Loan must turn herself in—within 7 days of receipt of this decision—to the police of La Gi township, in order to comply with the decision on the imprisonment sentence number 81/2016/QD-CA issued on the 5th of August 2016 by the People's Court of La Gi township, Binh Thuan province.

CC to

- The Accused
- VKSND La Gi township
- THAHS Agency—CAT Binh
- Thuan
- Department of Justice—Binh
- Thuan province
- UBND Phuoc Hoi Ward
- THA to file

JUDGE

(signature & stamp)

LE MINH CHINH

Certified translation of the annulment of the postponement of Mrs. Loan's jail sentence (courtesy Tran Thi Thanh Loan and VOICE Canada).

In other words, should Mrs. Loan be deported, she would go straight to prison.

Back in Vietnam, one of Mrs. Loan's sisters complained to Nhi: "The police have been swamping the area searching for them and have been harassing our family for news. They want to know the details of how they escaped and are working with coast guards to see when they actually left the country." Mrs. Lua added: "The Vietnamese police are really angry. They don't know there are 18 of us; they think there are only 16. They have been charging into houses randomly to search for people."

Indeed, according to SBS, "Vietnamese state media said authorities there would be launching a new criminal investigation into the group for leaving the country without official permission. The People's Committee of Binh Thuan Province instructed border guards and local police to 'strictly punish' those who organize people to illegally go abroad by sea, an online statement read."[10]

Mr. Vo too was under suspicion: "The Vietnamese government suspected that I was the one behind the instructions for these families to cross the sea to Australia for the second time," he subsequently told me. "They wanted to prosecute me for the crime of organizing others to flee the country, but they had no evidence to do so." Indeed, he had been battling the authorities for years, reporting regular harassment, as well as several death threats from police and "hired thugs," largely due to his work as a defense lawyer against police brutality.[11]

By then we knew the identity of each member of the group:

1. Tran Thi Lua
2. Nguyen Long (husband) and their three children:
3. Nguyen Thi Uyen (12)
4. Nguyen Hai Dang (10)
5. Nguyen Dang Koi (5)
6. Tran Thi Le (16) (dependent sister of Tran Thi Lua)
7. Tran Thi Thanh Ngoc (16) (dependent niece of Tran Thi Lua)
8. Nguyen Thi Kim Nhung (younger adult sister of Nguyen Long)
9. Nguyen Tai (younger adult brother of Nguyen Long)
10. Tran Thi Thanh Loan and her four children:
11. Ho Thanh Nha My (16)
12. Ho Van Loc (13)
13. Ho Thanh Nha Tran (9)
14. Ho Thanh Thao Nhi (5)
15. Nguyen Thi Phuc and her three children:
16. Tran Ngoc Tuan (16)
17. Tran Thi Kieu Trinh (almost 15)
18. Tran Nguyen Hoa Nhien (almost 4)

Nhi, having been given a phone number for Mrs. Lua by Mr. Vo, managed to speak with the head of the immigration office in Serang, the capital of Banten. He explained in English that while they were safe and would be treated well, if we wanted to help them further, we would have to go through the "right channel," such as the Australian Embassy, as he was not authorized to do anything else. As we later discovered through the local Indonesian media, he had already contacted the Vietnamese authorities, who were quick to demand the families' return.[12]

By the next day, February 11, 2017, Nhi and I had found ourselves drawn deeper into the saga, being asked to pay about USD400 per night for accommodation and meals for the 18 asylum seekers and two immigration officers assigned to guard them in a Serang hostel.[13] This was after Mrs. Lua had sent a message to Nhi, begging for help. Nhi spoke to a deputy director for immigration, who explained that they had entered Indonesia "illegally;" had no papers; and most likely would be sent back to Vietnam as Indonesia did not have any funding set aside to house, feed, and help "illegal immigrants."[14]

It was a Saturday, and all offices were closed; there was no one around to help. Imploring the immigration official not to extradite them straight away and explaining the urgency of their situation, Nhi asked for the families to be given a chance to obtain legal advice and consult with human rights representatives. He responded that there was nowhere for them to stay; all their belongings had been left behind; and they could not be kept at the immigration office. The police could not take them to jail because they had not yet been charged. He said he would ask his superior for instruction, but that it was most likely they would be deported immediately.

Nevertheless, upon learning we were prepared to support them temporarily, he agreed to move them to the hostel, after Nhi supplied a copy of her passport to prove her identity. This was how we ended up paying the exorbitant fees that I subsequently transferred for the next five days from the crowd funds. Although at first, we thought

Nhi with the author in February 2017.

it best to work quietly and efficiently behind the scenes, the families quickly revealed to Vietnamese broadcasters that their living costs in Indonesia were being covered by the donations we had raised.[15] Their desire for publicity backfired, however, when the local Indonesian media appeared to become involved, two people with cameras escorted by a policeman coming to the hostel and wanting to take their photos. Frightened, Mrs. Loan told Nhi that she shut the door on them, forcing them to leave.

Our immediate concern was to buy time to give the families an opportunity to obtain legal representation and protection in Indonesia before the Vietnamese authorities could succeed in having them returned. We were also keen to secure financial aid for them so that we could preserve any remaining funds for their children's future, as per our original commitment to our donors. We thus endeavored to contact the Indonesian Legal Aid Foundation (YLBHI) and the Asian Forum for Human Rights and Development (FORUM-ASIA),[16] both of which have offices in Jakarta, to see whether they could offer immediate assistance. Nhi also sent reports to, and attempted to speak with, representatives from the United Nations High Commissioner for Refugees (UNHCR) and Amnesty International, while I alerted humanitarian organizations, such as BPSOS, HRW, and Jesuit Refugee Services (JRS), to their predicament.

A JRS Indonesia representative[17] immediately informed both UNHCR and SUAKA—Indonesian Civil Society Association for Refugee Rights Protection—in the hope that a representative would visit the families in person. Established at the end of 2011, SUAKA, which is the Indonesian word for asylum, defines its mission as working pro bono "for the protection and advancement of the human rights of refugees and asylum seekers in Indonesia," including by providing legal aid, advice, and information.[18] It therefore seemed apt for me to write to them too, providing more details of the group's case, whereupon then SUAKA Legal and Development Coordinator Trish Cameron instructed Nhi to get one of the children who could speak a little English to state, "We want to apply for asylum status." Trish also notified UNHCR and International Organization for Migration (IOM)[19] to ask for their help.

Indeed, we were repeatedly advised by various human rights advocates to ask one of the children to call UNHCR to request asylum. As Nhi pointed out, however: "The 'some English' that the children speak is more like 'hello, goodbye, help me.' When you call UNHCR, you have to understand the voice instructions to navigate to get to the correct department. The children cannot do this."

Meanwhile, the Vietnamese authorities were continuing to pressure for their extradition. On February 13, 2017, Nhi received a phone call from an Indonesian immigration officer in Serang, informing her that the Vietnamese Embassy in Jakarta had contacted them asking for reports on the families as they wanted them sent back to Vietnam.[20] The officer had gone to see the group in the hostel, bringing Mrs. Lua's husband, Nguyen Long, and Mrs. Phuc's then 16-year-old son, Tran Ngoc Tuan, who could speak a little English, back to the local immigration office with him.

Once again Nhi begged for them not to be deported so soon: We were still desperately hoping we could get legal protection for them in time. For although Indonesia is not a signatory to the 1951 Refugee Convention or the 1967 Protocol Relating to the Status of Refugees,[21] it has a long tradition of hosting asylum seekers and refugees. Indeed, the right to seek political asylum, and implicitly, not to be refouled, is notably guaranteed in Indonesia's Constitution and its 1999 Foreign Relations and Human Rights Laws.[22]

Furthermore, as then SUAKA Advocacy Coordinator Muhammad Hafiz pointed out, the Presidential Regulation (*Peraturan Presiden or Perpres* in Indonesian) No. 125 of 2016 on the Handling of Foreign Refugees "confirms the definition of refugees contained in the 1951 Refugee Convention and does not continue to label asylum seekers as illegal immigrants" (art. 1[1]).[23]

According to this *Perpres*, "the handling of refugees is carried out pursuant to cooperation between the central government with the United Nations through the United Nations High Commissioner for Refugees in Indonesia and/or international organizations" (art. 2[1]). More specifically, if "a foreigner declares himself/herself to be a refugee," based on data collected by Immigration Detention Center officials by examining travel documents, immigration status, and identity, the officials "shall coordinate" with the UN through the UNHCR in Indonesia (arts. 13[2], [3], and 20).

In other words, so long as the families claimed asylum in Indonesia, the local authorities would work together with the UNHCR, which would consider their refugee status applications. They could only be deported once "finally rejected" by the UN through the UNHCR (art. 29).[24] Meanwhile, funding would be provided "for the handling of refugees" (art. 40),[25] and the Indonesian government would collaborate with the UN through the UNHCR "to provide data and information on refugees" (art. 42).

While UNHCR has actually conducted refugee status determination (RSD) in Indonesia and organized the resettlement of those accepted by third countries since 1979,[26] this *Perpres* formalized for the first time the respective responsibilities of Indonesian governmental and non-governmental bodies with regard to refugees and asylum seekers. Considerable authority was officially vested in local administration, although in reality, RSD remains in the hands of UNHCR.

Tuan later told Nhi that Indonesian immigration had enquired through a Vietnamese translator why they had left Vietnam for Australia and about the details of their alleged mistreatment in Vietnam. Nhi was subsequently asked similar questions. "They said that as long as our accommodation is paid for, we can stay," Tuan reported. "But if no one takes care of our expenses, we will be deported immediately."

We were concerned that so long as we continued to cover costs, no one else would offer to help. Furthermore, we knew we could not afford to continue paying for much longer. After all our efforts, we did not want the families to be extradited simply because we had run out of money. We were on the verge of telling the families the truth: We could only pay for their expenses for a few more days. Unless they could get the paperwork done to apply for asylum before our funds ran out, there would be nothing more we could do.

Once again, I wrote to BPSOS to request financial aid. While executive director Dr. Nguyen immediately arranged for the organization's emergency assistance team to process an application for the families to cover their costs in Indonesia and promised to "try to get some relocation funding for them," ideally to the U.S., this did not eventuate. As he explained: "It appears that it will cost about USD8,500 per month for these 18 Vietnamese boat people. And no one knows how long this situation will last. At this time, we don't have that kind of a budget."

Further efforts by BPSOS to apply for assistance grants from international organizations, by demonstrating that the adults in the group had been harmed because they defended human rights or due to their religious faith, also failed. "Note that even if the grant application is successful, we can't expect more than a few thousand US dollars," Dr. Nguyen warned, although as we were quick to point out, that amount would have been extremely helpful.

While BPSOS made us feel less alone, we were still no closer to alleviating the group's dire situation. Then, on February 14, 2017, Nhi had good news: "Mrs. Loan just let me know that two Catholic sisters came to visit them at the hostel late last night and prayed with them. The sisters only speak English and Indonesian, so they are returning with the Father this afternoon, and I will assist with the translation. Perhaps the Catholic Church can help with accommodation and food too. The nuns can support them in contacting UNHCR or even take them to the office in person."

It soon became clear, however, that the Church could only donate some food and toiletries, the nuns also being allowed to accompany the families to mass each Sunday. Meanwhile, we were still waiting to see whether Indonesian immigration would grant UNHCR permission to visit and register the families as asylum seekers.

But how to ensure UNHCR was fully aware of their circumstances? The call had to come from the families; we could not do it on their behalf. With Nhi's assistance, they sent an email to UNHCR in both Vietnamese and English, asking for an interpreter. Our hopes were raised when a nun reported to JRS that UNHCR had apparently agreed to visit the families that evening, along with an interpreter, only to be dashed the next day: "No one from UNHCR came," Nhi told me. "I rang the office myself. They said they are already aware of this group, but they just have to wait their turn. UNHCR can't tell me when that will be. If the people could speak English and could get to their office in Jakarta, it would speed up the process, but no one can enquire on their behalf. So, it is a waiting game with UNHCR. I am afraid it can take days or weeks or even months."

February 15, 2017, was an anxious day: The families had now been staying in the hostel for four nights. We knew we had to reach a decision as to whether to make any further payments. This concern was compounded by our continued worry that Indonesian immigration would soon deport them. "Apparently, last night at midnight, an immigration official came to see Mrs. Loan, asking to speak to me," Nhi reported.

> When she said it would be 3 A.M. in Australia and I would be asleep, he insisted that they try to call me. When I did not answer, he asked for my phone number. I expect him to call me some time this morning.
>
> Although we are paying for all the families' expenses, the Indonesian authorities are paying the wages of the two officers guarding them. I understand their budget funding is very small and they don't have much to spend on "illegal immigrants." On top of that, the group's phone has run out of credit. They cannot buy extra credit as they have no money, so they can't call anyone.

While Nhi thought the officer was going to ask how much longer the families would be staying at the hostel, the phone call never eventuated, it being a public holiday in Indonesia due to gubernatorial elections.

We felt frustrated, compounded by the lack of hands-on support. Some of the information we were receiving, no matter how well intentioned, was simply wrong. As Nhi complained: "We're running around, wasting so much time, while paying high living costs for them with Indonesian immigration on our backs."

Moreover, it was clear the group's fate now depended largely on UNHCR. Doan Trung strongly advised us to stop paying the hostel immediately, saying that while there was "no guarantee," he had "never heard of anyone being sent back like that" and believing the group would be taken to a detention center. He also rang Mrs. Loan to explain this to her. The JRS representative agreed. Astonished at how much we were spending on accommodation and food, he offered some reassurance: "Indonesia does not refoule people ... so I would be surprised if they force them to go back." Indeed, UNHCR assures asylum seekers in writing that it "intervenes with the Indonesian authorities to protect you from deportation to your home country for illegal stay in Indonesia."[27]

JRS also suggested that the International Organization for Migration (IOM) might become involved: "IOM usually will provide shelters once immigration refers them especially if there are children.... Your [Australian] government spends a lot on IOM services here, which usually are quite good...." Established in 1951 worldwide and active in Indonesia since 1979, IOM describes itself as "the leading inter-governmental organization dedicated to promoting humane and orderly migration for the benefit of all." Its role includes providing "humanitarian assistance to migrants in need, including refugees and internally displaced people." IOM Indonesia is one of the largest IOM missions worldwide, supported by donors including Australia.[28] Indeed, in March 2016, a spokesperson for then Immigration Minister Peter Dutton could boast: "Australia is ... by far the largest source of funds for the International Organization for Migration's activities in Indonesia."[29] This translated to about USD40 million annually, IOM's total operational expenditure in Indonesia then being around USD45 million.[30]

We had, however, already received the hostel invoice for the fifth night. When we did not pay it immediately, the hostel—unbeknown to us—decided not to provide dinner for the families. Horrified to discover the children were going hungry, our first thought was to try and contact the nuns, which was unsuccessful. Fortunately, however, Nhi was constantly in touch with Bangkok-based, Vietnamese American friend, and fellow volunteer refugee advocate, Grace Bui—also a former refugee herself—who decided to try to speak with one of the immigration guards. "At that time the officer who was guarding them came back for the night, and I told him what happened," Grace subsequently reported in a public statement on Facebook on February 27, 2017. "He bought dinner for them. He's a very nice man."

In the end, the families would stay at the hostel for one more night courtesy of the crowd funds. "Mrs. Lua's husband knelt on the floor begging the Indonesian authorities," Nhi told me. "I had to promise that the outstanding hostel bill would be paid before they agreed not to take them to the detention center."

INVOICE				
Dear Miss Ann Nhi				
Below are the detail invoice for guest (Immigration Serang)				
	Check in 2/15/17		Check out 2/16/17	
	No of Room/people	Price	No of day/times	Total
Room	6	375,000	1	2,250,000
Extra bed/people	8	150,000	1	1,200,000
Lunch	20	27,500	1	550,000
Dinner	20	27,500	1	550,000
	Sub Total			4,550,000
	Tax 10%			455,000
	Service 7.5%			341,250
	Due on Tuesday, Feb 15, 2017			5,346,250
	All Payment in IDR (Indonesia Rupiah)			
	Please make Payment by Western Union			
Thank You				

Hostel invoice for February 15, 2017.

Henceforth, they would be dependent on UNHCR, the Indonesian Directorate General of Immigration (DGI), which is under the Ministry of Justice and Human Rights, and IOM. The question remained whether we had indeed given them enough time to secure their applications for refugee status, or whether the Vietnamese authorities would succeed in having them forcibly returned by Indonesia.

On February 16, 2017, Josef Benedict, then Amnesty International director of campaigns, Southeast Asia and the Pacific, and SUAKA coordinator Febi Yonesta sent a letter to the Chief of UNHCR Representation for Indonesia, Thomas Vargas, expressing concern for the 18 Vietnamese asylum seekers. They subsequently sent a similar letter to the Indonesian government:

We are particularly concerned that, should they be forcibly returned to Viet Nam, the six adults will likely be arrested and may be the victims of torture and/or other degrading, inhuman or cruel treatment or punishment....

We urge the UN Refugee Agency, in accordance with its mandate under Articles 13 and 20 of the Presidential Decree on Refugee Number 125 of 2016, to immediately register the 18 individuals and to initiate the Refugee Status Determination procedures in due course.

Referring to Nhi's and my support of the group as "the intervention of an Australian non-governmental organization that works on refugee issues," the letter described the families as being "under effective house arrest, as they are under the watch of two immigration officers." It concluded:

Punishing an individual for exercising his or her right to seek asylum is arbitrary and unlawful. The convictions of Mrs. Loan and Mrs. Lua contravene international law and should never have been entered.... The arrests of the adults would leave the children without their parents and legal guardians in violation of the best interest of children, a primary consideration in all actions concerning children, including those taken by administrative authorities and courts of law, as per the Convention on the Rights of the Child, to which Viet Nam is a state party.[31]

As it turned out, the letter was written on the very day UNHCR conducted an initial informal interview with the families in the hostel, assisted by a Vietnamese translator. Now that we had stopped footing their bills, we anticipated they would be imminently moved to detention, where they would have to wait before being interviewed formally by UNHCR. In the meantime, however, an Australian-based relative agreed to cover their accommodation expenses temporarily, thereby further delaying their transfer to detention. Instead, they were moved to a cheaper motel, where we hoped they would be able to stay until their final interviews.

Relieved to know they were safe and would be looked after, Nhi still thought the families should be supported through the initial stages of their Refugee Status Determination (RSD), to be conducted by UNHCR. She thus asked Grace to fly to Serang so that they would have someone on hand to assist with translation. The relative offered to pay for Grace's flights, also sending her some extra money to give to the group. I too provided some cash from the crowd fund for Mrs. Loan, who was the most vulnerable, hoping to enable her to buy a mobile phone, some credit, and clothes for her four children.

"I told her you are sending money," Nhi said: "She cried and asked me to thank you from the bottom of her heart.... I don't know how long the relatives can help, but I guess not for much longer. If, and when the money runs out, they can still be handed over to the Vietnamese Embassy in Jakarta, which will ship them back to Vietnam as there are warrants out for their arrest. They are not normal asylum seekers. They are considered fugitives as they have criminal records and outstanding sentences."

Indeed, back in Vietnam, Mrs. Loan's husband, Ho Trung Loi, was under considerable pressure in jail, while extended family members were being threatened, forced to tell the 18 asylum seekers to return. As we soon discovered, Mrs. Loan's relatives had rung during her initial UNHCR interview in the hostel, making her cry so much that she fainted. The Vietnamese authorities warned "he [Mr. Loi] will never be released unless we return," she said. "At first, they told him we drowned at sea because the boat sank. He nearly went crazy with grief. Then they put him in solitary confinement, refusing to let my sister visit or send him food or medicine. She had to bribe them to see him and only managed to say we are safe before the police took him away. They told the family he will be punished for 'my mistake' and so we believe he may be beaten." She accused the Vietnamese police of "terrorizing" her extended family, preventing them from operating their fruit stall: "I'm worried the police will destroy their only source of income as pay-back and to ensure they have no money to help me and provide for my husband."[32]

As SBS reported, relations in Vietnam had been "under constant surveillance by local security forces," one complaining that "security agents have come round to our homes to ask about our relatives every day.... There are uniformed and plain clothes police watching our neighborhood and watching the street stalls where we work. They keep asking us if we know where they are."[33]

Nhi was also talking to family members in Vietnam every day to relay messages. "They know nothing, and they are worried. No one dares to visit them or to help them with anything; they are struggling. They believe their phones are tapped and are too frightened to ring their relatives in Indonesia even though they are desperate for information." Indonesian immigration officers were also vetting family calls.

Certain that they could never return to Vietnam, we were determined to do whatever we could to help them obtain refugee status in Indonesia, also continuing to promote the crowd fund in an effort to secure the children's future. Moreover, we thought it imperative to publicize the mistreatment of Mr. Loi at the hands of the Vietnamese authorities. "I am glad that despite all the headaches, things are turning out," Nhi told me. "We just need to keep persevering."

Their story was certainly attracting media attention, Mrs. Lua and Mrs. Loan fielding enquiries from their motel room. Mrs. Loan's health, however, was suffering. After complaining of headaches and dizziness for days, she collapsed and was taken to a doctor, who diagnosed an anxiety attack. "Her children were so scared," Nhi told me. "Afraid she was going to die they cried all night. I think she feels guilty that because of her actions, her husband is getting punished. I talked to her at length, telling her to pray and not to think so much, and that she has the best chance of getting asylum status. But I think it has only dawned on her now how hard the road in front of her is going to be, looking after four children in a foreign country."

By February 22, 2017, the relative was also running out of money, having paid over USD2,700 for their accommodation and meals. While we were hoping the families would be interviewed imminently by UNHCR, they met with IOM, before being moved to a still cheaper boarding house adjoining an Islamic center and mosque in Serang.

Meanwhile, Grace had arrived, taking a three-hour bus ride that morning from Jakarta's Soekarno-Hatta International airport to see the families. "The Indonesian immigration office, IOM, and the UN knew I was coming, and especially the immigration office was happy that I was going to come and help them," she wrote a few days later in a public statement on Facebook, headlined "18 Vietnamese Asylum Seekers in Indonesia." "They [the families] were very excited to see me. We met with IOM and registered them."[34]

The situation changed, however, after the arrival of several Indonesian immigration officers later in the afternoon. "They started to interrogate me and told me what I was doing is illegal. These families are illegal, and they are under immigration control, so anything I do with them, I need the approval of immigration. They asked me to leave right away."

When Grace protested that her trip was common knowledge and questioned why it was only now being deemed illegal, she did not receive an answer. Urged to persuade the group to return to Vietnam, she refused, whereupon one of the officers told her to gather the families together.

> He told them they should return to Vietnam because they would have a better life there than in Indonesia. They were crying and begging him not to kick them out. They shared with him what would happen if they returned to Vietnam. He told them he didn't believe their story that Vietnam would put them in jail because Vietnam is a good country....
>
> He asked them what they would do if no country accepted them for immigration. They said they wanted to stay in Indonesia. They said anywhere but Vietnam because they would be persecuted if they are returned to Vietnam. I think he was playing a mental game with them, and I think it's the cruelest game. Seeing the families kneeling down on the ground and begging him not to kick them out, and the officer was just smiling and laughing....
>
> I do believe the Vietnamese government is behind all of this. The Vietnamese Embassy is trying to put pressure on the Indonesian immigration office ... in the end, he told me to tell them if the Vietnamese Embassy demanded them back, then Indonesian immigration would send them back. He said Indonesia wants to keep a friendly relationship with Vietnam.[35]

Behind the scenes, Nhi attributed the apparent change in attitude of Indonesian immigration to Grace having been described in the original version of an Australian ABC story[36]—due to a miscommunication on my part—as "an experienced immigration worker ... traveling from Thailand this week to assist with the case." "They did not want Grace to be there," she confided to me:

> They did not allow her to help. They even threatened to deport Grace.... She is there on a visitor visa. They said if you are an experienced immigration worker from Thailand and you want to come here to work on the case, you need to apply for a work visa and approval from Indonesia....
>
> I had to call immigration to explain that it was a misunderstanding, that I am the one responsible for asking Grace to help and that she ... only comes as a friend [of mine] to see what she can do. She is not "working on the case."

The offending description was subsequently removed, and a clarification issued, but not before Vietnamese media had distorted the truth still further, VOA announcing that "a convoy of UN officers" would be coming from Thailand to Indonesia to interview the families.[37] "It has become fake news," Nhi despaired. "It's gone viral on Facebook. Vietnamese people are thinking, 'wow, it's so easy to get asylum, just get to Thailand and Indonesia and you can get a UN interview within a few days!'"

No one was allowed to see them anymore, although Nhi continued to speak to them every day by phone, the families telling her that Indonesian immigration was constantly trying to persuade them to return to Vietnam. IOM also returned the funds we had given them. "They said the families are not allowed to have money while they are in their custody," Nhi explained. "They can only receive food and clothing by post, so Grace has gone to buy supplies as they have nothing. Now that no one is paying for them anymore, they are no longer free like before but are being treated as 'illegals.'"

As academic Dr. Antje Missbach has explained, until 2018, IOM was usually notified "not least because they need to reimburse costs accumulated ... such as for temporary accommodation in hotels, schools, and mosques; food; and additional security staff and night guards. The IOM usually bears all expenses until those arrested have been transferred to an immigration detention center, a process that may take several weeks because of overcrowding."[38] Needless to say, we were not expecting to be reimbursed.

Nhi and Grace turned to Amnesty International, with whom they were volunteering as advocates and translators, in the hope that the organization would become more involved. We agreed that if, and when the group was granted asylum status, it would be easier to promote the crowd fund campaign because then "we would be able to talk freely without worrying about how it would affect their case."

SUAKA Legal Aid Coordinator Trish Cameron also provided reassurance, telling us: "UNHCR is advocating for this group every day. I am in contact with UNHCR about this every day." Indeed, on February 26, 2017, Nhi reported that "someone from UNHCR came to their boarding house with an interpreter from Jakarta, but Indonesian immigration did not allow them to enter. They said there had to be permission from head office before anyone is allowed to see them."

While we knew UNHCR representatives were continuing to negotiate on their behalf with senior-level government officials in Jakarta, the outcome was still far from certain. "UNHCR might grant them their asylum, or they might not, but we will not give up," Grace said. "Right now, what we can all do is pray for them. Their chances are very slim, but I do believe in miracles."

The following day, we thought the 18 asylum seekers had finally been registered with UNHCR. "Now they can formally apply for refugee status," Nhi rejoiced, "and Indonesia can't send them back to Vietnam until UNHCR says they don't qualify. So at least they will be safe for several months. IOM will continue to pay for their accommodation and basic needs. I am not sure if Indonesian immigration is going to move them to another place or not; I think they will." As it turned out, however, we were celebrating too soon: their registration would not be finalized for almost another month.

On March 1, 2017, an Amnesty International researcher visited the families to deliver all Grace's purchases, including rechargeable phone cards, as well as the money I had sent to Mrs. Loan. "Amnesty had to obtain permission first," Nhi explained:

> Everything we send has to be checked and recorded by the immigration officers. The nuns have been visiting every second week so far and will bring food when they can but visiting them is hard now because you have to apply and get approval. Mrs. Loan can't go out shopping, but at least she has some money now and can ask the guards to do so on her behalf. She wants to buy extra food for the children like fruit and noodles. They are supplied daily with a large pot of rice and curries, but they are not getting fruit or vegetables.

Amnesty International warned us that even once they had been registered, the determination of their refugee status could take a year or longer, UNHCR lacking capacity and resources.[39]

That day, two Indonesian policemen came to visit the families, accompanied by a Vietnamese translator. After much anxiety and confusion, we managed to work out that they had been seeking information about the group. "They asked questions about whether anyone in Australia or Thailand had helped us plan the trip," Mrs. Loan subsequently told Nhi.

While the families waited for the UNHCR interviews that would decide their fate, we remained concerned about the complete disruption to their children's education since fleeing Vietnam. Although we knew they needed to be recognized as refugees before we could even contemplate potential schooling, I began to contact various refugee educational facilities, while Nhi spoke to Vietnamese translators working in Indonesia so that we could better understand the difficulties they would confront.

We did not always agree on how they should behave, particularly regarding the media. Believing that publicity could aid their quest for recognition as refugees as well as draw attention to Mr. Loi's mistreatment in jail in Vietnam, Doan Trung and I were now keen for them to speak to the press. Nhi and Grace, however, were more cautious, remaining adamantly opposed until their registration had been completed or at least until we had received some kind of guarantee from UNHCR or SUAKA.

"I had to buy them a new sim card and throw away their old number because so many reporters and people have contacted them and I feel that it is not safe for them at this moment," Grace said. "They are being monitored by the immigration officers very carefully. I learned when I was there that the Indonesian government is very sensitive about refugees in their country. If there is too much publicity about this case, it could make things uncomfortable for the government, both internally and in relations with other countries. We should only approve activities that directly benefit them."

Nhi agreed:

The three youngest children, from left: Nguyen Dang Koi, Ho Thanh Thao Nhi, and Tran Nguyen Hoa Nhien; behind is Ho Thanh Nha Tran (courtesy Grace Bui).

They are actually not allowed to have a phone. They had two of their phones confiscated and hid the two phones they have left in the toilet. Every time they use the phone they have to hide in the closet. So, the authorities obviously don't want them to have contact with outside people. Having the media write about them is like saying to the Indonesian officers that they still have a phone and that is how they contact people outside Indonesia. That may prompt them to do another search to take the remaining phones away and then we won't be able to contact them at all.

The police in Vietnam are still telling the families they will be returned. They have received many threats about being sent back. I don't know if these threats are real or not, but the UN still has not interviewed them. Our emails to UNHCR and SUAKA receive no reply. What can we do?

So, if anyone wants to advise them to speak out to the media, that person will have to bear responsibility in case it somehow jeopardizes their safety. I am not willing to take that responsibility, and neither is Grace. Are you?

The problem is they are not normal refugees. Strictly, they are fugitives. If the Indonesian government wants to return them to Vietnam, they have all the reasons to do so. The only reason they were not returned immediately was because we paid big money.... But I am worried too much media will enrage the Vietnamese government and they will put pressure on Indonesia to return them.

Nor did the immigration guards always behave appropriately either, taking several of the older children out late at night and offering them alcohol in exchange for agreeing to deliver packages of supplies from their relatives in Vietnam.

Finally, on March 20, 2017, we received the long-awaited news that UNHCR was registering the group. "They just finished with Mrs. Lua and her family," Nhi told me. "Tomorrow will be Mrs. Loan and Mrs. Phuc and their children. They will be issued an asylum seeker case number each. So, they are safe now. I think we can let the media know about their situation." Grace concurred: "Just want to let you know that everything is done," she wrote the following day. "The UN staff gave the families 1 million Indonesian Rupiah (IDR) [around USD70]. The UN also gave presents to the immigration officers and the lady who is staying with the families.... Indonesian immigration is always there. They were there both days while the UN was working with the families."

It took a little time for the case numbers to be issued as could be seen from the photocopied *Code of Conduct for Asylum Seekers and Refugees in Indonesia*, which UNHCR provided to Mrs. Loan, with a handwritten comment at the top of the page: "No case number—woman at risk; family with 4 children."

BBC Vietnam soon produced an article, announcing they could now "enjoy asylum status" and including an interview with Grace, who was quoted as saying "the Muslim center where they are is very spacious and clean; they are well-fed and supervised and not allowed to go out ... 'Life is quite comfortable,' commented Ms. Bui after visiting the three families in February." The piece concluded with a statement from Mrs. Phuc: "Every day we pray to get refugee status. We would rather die than return to Vietnam."[40]

The three mothers, together with Nhi and Grace, all complained about the inaccuracy of the BBC piece, which was receiving considerable attention among Vietnamese readers. "It has many thousands of views and hundreds of shares," Nhi told me. "But most of the comments were against the families, and it may encourage others to try secretly to head for Australia again.... Reading it one gets the impression that they had been treated very well by the Vietnamese government, but still tried to leave again and now live in luxury, so there is no need to help them!"

Although Mrs. Lua and Grace were under the impression that UNHCR would return the following week for another interview, printed information supplied by the organization itself was more circumspect: "You will be scheduled an interview as soon as possible after your registration but do be aware of a waiting period which is dependent on the number of asylum applications received by the office." While the length of time between registration and interview should not exceed six months, in Indonesia "the average waiting period ... ranges from 18 to 24 months depending on the priority and complexity of the case."[41]

Back in Vietnam, a meeting was held at local police headquarters to which one of Mrs. Loan's sisters and Mrs. Lua's sister- and mother-in-law were invited. "I told the UN about the sentences that are awaiting them if they are returned to Vietnam," Grace said. "Mrs. Lua and Mrs. Loan will receive 30 years; Mrs. Phuc will get 20 or 25 years, and all those aged 17 or over will go to jail." Such long jail terms were hard to reconcile with Mr. Vo's original predictions and with the punishments I had read in the Vietnamese Penal Code. Surely, they were merely threats, but we could not be sure. "That happens a lot in Vietnam," Nhi said, "verbal threats without any paperwork so that you can't formally complain."

Although we subsequently ascertained that the feared sentences had been exaggerated, the local police did pay a visit to Mrs. Loan's and Mrs. Lua's homes, which extended family members surreptitiously filmed, sending as proof. "The police left a phone number.... They said they will have warrants for their arrest," Grace said.

Photograph taken covertly by Mrs. Loan's extended family members in Vietnam of local police (both in uniform and plain clothes) visiting the home of Mrs. Loan's mother to interview one of her sisters (center) (courtesy Tran Thi Thanh Loan).

Meanwhile, she stepped up her advocacy on the families' behalf, sending documents and urging UNHCR to conduct second interviews as soon as possible: "I said the only way we could save them was for their refugee status to be approved as soon as possible."

According to UNHCR guidelines, applicants considered to be "'manifestly in need of protection intervention' are persons who may be subject to immediate refoulement or arbitrary arrest or detention in the host country, or who may have other serious legal or protection needs." Such applicants may be referred to Accelerated RSD Processing, involving "reduced waiting periods" and "shortened timelines."[42]

In the end, Mrs. Lua and Grace were right: UNHCR returned from March 29–31, 2017, with an interpreter. As stipulated, each adult was given "the opportunity to give detailed reasons about why you left your country and why you cannot or do not want to return. You need to bring with you any documents which you think are important, including identity documents, and which could help your claim."[43]

Mrs. Loan later told me: "They asked me questions about what happened to me in Vietnam and why I had to leave. I also showed them my Vietnamese documents. I didn't have a lawyer. The interview lasted two or three hours." Nhi was more descriptive: "She told me she made the interpreter cry, and the UN officer was very moved." They were not the only ones. "Yes, I don't cry, but I cried when I heard her story," Grace admitted.

JRS has provided more information about what happens at an RSD interview conducted by UNHCR: "An eligibility officer will ask open-ended questions to gain information from the asylum seeker in chronological order. The focus … is not simply to determine whether they meet the definition of a refugee in accordance with the Refugee Convention, but also to assess credibility, whether they fall within UNHCR's extended mandate definition or whether they are to be excluded from international protection."[44]

UNHCR has stressed that refugees are to be identified not "as a matter of certainty, but as a matter of likelihood." A credible applicant would present "a claim which is coherent and plausible, not contradicting generally known facts, and therefore is, on balance, capable of being believed."[45] In accordance with standard procedure in Indonesia, as in other Southeast Asian countries, the group was not given a copy of their statements.[46]

While waiting to see whether the three families would be recognized as UNHCR mandate refugees, Nhi and I turned our attention back to the crowd fund, with Grace urging her friends to donate. The group was now feeling a little more relaxed: "Mrs. Loan told me that the lady who was staying with them 24 hours a day has left," Grace reported, "and no one from immigration has stayed around, so they feel comfortable talking on the phone."

We also commenced work on developing a website in both English and Vietnamese in the hope that it would draw attention to the families' plight and encourage donors to support our campaign, as well as serving as a resource for others in similar situations. At the same time, we were keen to discourage other prospective Vietnamese boat people from attempting such a journey to Australia, warning them about its harsh border protection policies and including some of Operation Sovereign Borders (OSB) "Overseas Public Information Campaigns" in Vietnamese.[47] We had come

Logo from our website, www.vietbp.org.

Promotion for the refugee and human rights panel discussion and campaign fundraiser (courtesy Emanuel School).

up with a name, "Viet BP: Helping you Stay Safe," and logo of two hands cupping a boat in a storm. Enlisting the assistance of a web designer based in Thailand, and a translator from Melbourne, both friends of Nhi's, we were able to launch the website, www.vietbp.org, by mid–2017.

Nevertheless, it remained a constant struggle to raise money for the families, especially given the increased pressures we faced: In a few months, we had gone from endeavoring to support Mrs. Loan's family of five in July 2016 to assisting five families—three in Indonesia and two in Vietnam—comprising 29 people, including 16 children. Despite our hopes and efforts, media attention had not promoted donations, nor did our website ever really gain traction within the Vietnamese community, although occasionally the group benefited from the generosity of those who had once been in a similar situation: "We are a small furniture business here in USA and we are committed to help the boat people. Believe it or not, I used to stay in Bataan [province in the] Philippines over 20 years ago. So, when I saw them in the news, it kind of broke my heart. I hope they can come to America (only hope under President Trump's administration) because if they do, I can help them … just like when I first came to America. We thank America and we are committed to give back to help others."

In the end, our crowd fund, "Help Care for the children," dragged on for the rest of 2017, culminating in one final burst of effort, when we really pushed to meet

Mrs. Loan (fourth from left) with her children, Loc, My, Tran, and Nhi, Mrs. Lua (third from right) with her two sons, Koi and Dang, and sister-in-law, Nguyen Thi Kim Nhung (right), on April 2, 2017, just before they entered detention in Jakarta (courtesy Tran Thi Thanh Loan and Tran Thi Lua).

our ultimate target of around USD10,000 by personally contacting all those we knew who had not yet donated. Organizing a refugee and human rights panel discussion at my children's school, involving asylum seekers sharing their stories, also contributed much-needed funds.

By then all three families had long been granted refugee status, their UNHCR refugee cards dated May 5, 2017—a little over a month after their RSD interviews.[48] The group itself had only been notified on May 23, 2017, when two UNHCR representatives had visited them to share the good news. By that stage, however, the families had spent almost two months in detention, having been taken to the center located within the Directorate General of Immigration (DGI) in Kuningan, South Jakarta, on April 4, 2017.

4

Life in Detention

While Nhi and I had long expected the families to be transferred to an Immigration Detention Center (IDC),[1] they themselves were not alerted in advance. "We were taken by surprise," Mrs. Lua recalled, recounting the events of April 4, 2017. "At 4 p.m., a bus took all 18 of us to detention, along with three guards. There were two more cars with guards, I don't know how many."

The journey took about four hours. Upon arrival, the families were immediately separated. "They locked women and young children up on one side, men and teenage boys on the other. We could not go out. When it was time for lunch or dinner, they would open the door to give us food and then close it again."

The pressure to return to Vietnam continued. "Sometimes they advised us to go back; they told us Indonesia would not provide a good future for our children. But we said that if we returned, we would die, so eventually they stopped." While in detention, Mrs. Lua provided more detail of the day-to-day impact, particularly on the younger children:

> We're given ... two days when one of the nice officials may come, feel bad for our children, and let them out of the rooms to play in the larger workspace. There they can run around and play for a little bit.
>
> But on the days when the stricter official comes by, the children just stand by and observe. For us adults seeing the 30 meters [almost 98.5 feet] of open space, it doesn't look like much, but the children enjoy it. They're excited to have space to run around in. Every day they count down the days until they get to run around and play again. On the days they know the nicer man is coming by, they wake up early, brush their teeth, rinse their mouths, eat breakfast, and wait. They just stand right by the door and wait for him. When I watch them waiting, I just want to cry. It makes me want to cry just talking about it and picturing them waiting by that door and screaming with excitement when it's finally open. As soon as he opens the door, they run out to play.[2]

The older teenagers were also adversely affected: "When they drove us to the Jakarta detention center, I didn't think they would lock me up," Ho Thanh Nha My, Mrs. Loan's oldest daughter, subsequently reflected. "When we arrived, we thought it was a hotel, but when we went inside, we saw it was a place to lock up refugees. I was unsteady and my mother fainted. Living there, we were confined by four walls, unable to see the sun, so we were often sick and uncomfortable." Tran Thi Thanh Ngoc, Mrs. Lua's niece, agreed, explaining how her emotions changed from feeling "so happy and lucky" when she first saw what she thought was a "large apartment building," to fear: "I felt heartbroken for our dark life at the time ... after a while I stopped thinking about what I was scared of and I began to pray; I knew there were challenges."

Mothers and children behind bars in detention, Jakarta, June 2017 (courtesy Sunshine and Aaron Biskaps).

Although Grace, Nhi, and I would battle to have them freed, our efforts would prove largely in vain. As an IOM representative told Grace the day after they were moved to Jakarta, "We cannot get them out of detention as they are under supervision of immigration, and IOM is only facilitating their basic needs and helping the Indonesian government." SUAKA coordinator Febi Yonesta urged us to petition UNHCR, despite being unsure of our chances of success. "As far as I know, there is no bailing mechanism under the immigration system," he messaged Grace. "However, both the immigration [law] and the presidential decree also said [*sic*] the possibility for children, pregnant women, sick people, and elders to be placed outside the detention upon approval from the immigration headquarter and based on guarantee from IOM for accommodation.[3] The problem is that the current immigration general director has put a tough stance against asylum seekers by not releasing them from the detention. We have previous experience where attempt to release the asylum we're not successful [*sic*]." Nevertheless, Grace remained undaunted. UNHCR "told me to go to SUAKA and SUAKA told you to contact UN," she told me. "Well, I'm going straight to immigration.... I think we can try to use the children to get them out."

The nuns and some parishioners from the international congregation Franciscan Missionaries of Mary (FMM) continued to visit as JRS volunteers, bringing instant noodles and other basic provisions to supplement the two regulation meals provided in detention, breakfast not being included. At our request, they kindly donated an extra blanket for each of the 18 detainees, refusing our offer to cover the cost. Unable to go outside even to hang their laundry, the families were forced to sleep on low mattresses without pillows or sheets; if the blanket provided was wet, they had to go without. Unfortunately, however, Indonesian immigration prevented the nuns from bringing in the kettle needed to boil the noodles.

In late April 2017, Mrs. Loan told us that Australian Embassy officials had come

The youngest children: from left, Koi, Nhi, and Hoa Nhien in detention, June 2017 (courtesy Sunshine and Aaron Biskaps).

to her hometown of La Gi in Binh Thuan province to investigate her and Mrs. Lua's claims, Grace alleging:

> The Vietnamese government paid an extended family member to lie to the Australian Embassy that the Vietnamese authorities didn't do any harm when they returned. They were paid 500,000 VND [a little over USD20] per night ... others were also invited and offered money but didn't go.
>   Mrs. Loan got so angry because the families are worried that it might affect their chances with the UN. I told her to calm down. The people who work for the Australian Embassy in Vietnam are not stupid. It has nothing to do with Australia because they are in Indonesia, but of course Australian Embassy officials needed to do an investigation because it is their government that originally returned these people to Vietnam without a chance to see the UN.

Initially the extended family in Vietnam undertook to record a verbal statement as to what had transpired, which Grace intended to send to UNHCR. "They told me the

Conditions in the detention center located within the Directorate General of Immigration (DGI) in Kuningan, South Jakarta, 2017.

A standard meal in detention, 2017 (courtesy Sunshine and Aaron Biskamps).

Vietnamese government is staging these meetings and bribing people to come to tell lies to the Australian officials," Nhi explained:

> It did so over three days in three different towns, Binh Thuan, Tan Tien, and Tan Thang.... Questions were designed so that attendees could only answer "yes" or "no." They were not allowed to speak freely to tell the whole story....
>
> The one family member who took bribes to go to two meetings did so because they were approached by town officials, who asked whether they had obtained a permit for new improvements added to the front of their house. They understood this as a threat, meaning if they did not attend, it would be easy for the authorities simply not to return their "red book," or land use rights certificate [LURC], without which the police can confiscate their house.

Although in the end, Mrs. Loan managed to send Grace the recording, we did not hear back from UNHCR.

Ever since first meeting the families in Serang in February 2017, Grace had been planning to visit them again, seeking permission to do so from Indonesian immigration and purchasing clothing and toiletries for them. I was keen to join her, and we agreed to meet in Jakarta on June 1, 2017. "Mrs. Loan asked if you could buy a phone for her daughter so she can get on the Internet and study," Grace said. "Her cell phone screen is cracked in many places so she can't see out of it very well." Determined to help all 12 children access educational resources while in detention, we relied on the crowd funds to buy phone tablets—one for each family—books, and stationery. Grace was also hoping the children would be able to use Facebook Messenger to access weekly English as a second language classes that she was helping to organize in Bangkok for Montagnard asylum seeker youth.[4] "Since we got onto the boat, each of us only had one set of clothes," Mrs. Lua and Mrs. Loan explained. "Wherever we were taken when we first arrived here, we walked barefoot without shoes. Later an international campaign raised enough money to buy shoes and clothes so we could change."[5]

While preparing for our trip, we continued efforts to draw attention to the families' plight. At Grace's and Nhi's suggestion, I wrote to then first Canadian Senator of Vietnamese origin, Thanh Hai Ngo: "If they are fortunate enough to be recognized as refugees, it could take many more years for a third country to be found for their resettlement. I am wondering whether Canada might be able to come to their rescue given your generous immigration policy?"[6]

On May 11, 2017, I received the following reply:

> Despite their assurance that refugees would face no sanctions or retributions for leaving the country, the government of Vietnam continues to jail, beat, torture, and prosecute refugees returned to them by the Australian government. The occurrence of these violations of basic human rights and civil liberties are at the core of why many are choosing to flee and are well known by the Canadian and Australian governments....
>
> Given the strong relationship between the Canadian and Australian governments, we will discuss and bring this reoccurring issue on Vietnamese refugees to the attention of the Australian High Commission and to the appropriate authorities here in Ottawa, Canada.
>
> Thank you as well for bringing this list of potential refugees to my attention. Please note that Canada's immigration policies only recognize refugees in immigration detention centers who have been validated by the UNHCR.[7] I understand this long process often keeps immigrants and their families in difficult situations. It is therefore preferable

to consider options once official documentation from the UNHCR has been processed.

Meanwhile, on May 9, 2017, retired U.S. Ambassador Grover Joseph Rees III had visited them in detention, with Grace providing translation support via phone from Bangkok. A former Ambassador to East Timor, Professor Rees had previously served as Chief Justice of the High Court of American Samoa. An experienced attorney and legal academic, he is a strong defender of human rights, who has also worked as Senior Counselor for International Initiatives for BPSOS, executive director, Dr. Nguyen, having first introduced us to help with international advocacy if necessary.

On May 12, Grace reported that immigration officers from Serang had

Retired U.S. Ambassador Grover Joseph Rees III visiting the families in detention, May 9, 2017.

questioned the families in detention, urging them to sign a document, which not understanding, they refused to do:

> The officers still think someone in Australia helped the group to escape Vietnam.... They asked questions that they should have already known, like what port did you leave from Vietnam; who advised you to come to Australia; how much fuel did you have; did you have your passports with you and other documents like your ID card.
>
> Then they asked why they didn't hear from me after I left Indonesia. I said that after they told me I couldn't translate for the families and threatened to jail me, I visited Jakarta for two days and then left. They apologized many times for their actions and told me their boss had ordered them [to behave that way].
>
> The same officer as last time again tried to persuade the families to return to Vietnam. He said to think about the children, but the families replied that was [precisely] why they had left. He asked me what would happen to them if they returned, and I repeated what I had said in Serang ... that the government had already told them how many years they would spend in jail.... He said Indonesian immigration is not deporting them.

Continually concerned about their conditions in detention, notably the children's lack of sunlight and fresh air, Grace petitioned the immigration officers, as well as writing again to IOM and UNHCR. "I sent in the mothers' complaints and asked if they could be removed from detention," she reported. "When IOM came, they were so nervous and just said they only need doctors to come in and see them when they are sick, and their children need to go to school." Although during a subsequent visit from UNHCR, they managed to sum up the courage to request to be moved out, Grace doubted whether "the UN will even take that into consideration. I also asked about the result of the interview, but they can't say anything until the final result. Right now, we just have to be patient."

I too wrote—in hindsight, naively—to IOM's then chief of mission in Indonesia, Mark Getchell, on May 15, 2017, requesting "advice as to the possibility of them being moved to community housing so that the families can be reunited, and the children can continue their education." My email went unanswered for nearly a year: In March 2018—almost two months after they had finally been released from detention—I received a response from Mr. Getchell, explaining in detail that in such circumstances IOM was unfortunately unable to assist.[8]

I should have known IOM's "irregular migrant care management" role also included servicing the many immigration detention premises—the 13 centers (*rudenim* in Indonesian) and 20 temporary facilities—spread across 13 of the 33 provinces of the Indonesian archipelago: "IOM provides counselling, medical care, food, shelter, education and vocational support to people both within and outside of immigration detention centers."[9]

Nonetheless, overcrowding remained a recurring problem in most of the detention centers, which were originally intended for "foreigners" awaiting deportation, and not specifically refugees. Total capacity was officially 1,200 detainees in the *rudenim*, or 3,000, if the temporary facilities were included. In practice, however, some 3,865 persons of concern to UNHCR, including around 980 children—among

Children displaying books received from Viet Toon.

the most vulnerable supposedly meant to be given "preferential care"—were being detained in the detention centers alone at the end of May 2017.[10]

Ever since the families had been detained, we were determined to establish a support network for them on the ground. With the assistance of then Washington-based RFA journalist Hoa Ai Tran, who had been covering their story for some time, we strove to reach out to the small Vietnamese community in Jakarta. Unable to find a Vietnamese-English tutor, who could visit the children on a regular basis, she told us about the Van Lang Vietnamese Language & Culture Education Center, based in San Jose, California, in the hope that the children could access its curriculum online. Although this proved too difficult, Viet Toon, a Vietnamese non-commercial publishing company in Virginia, kindly donated a series of books, which Hoa Ai duly delivered, when she decided to use some of her holiday leave to join us in Jakarta at her own expense.[11]

She also found an American-Vietnamese former body builder and personal trainer, Sunshine Biskaps—an erstwhile "boat child" herself—who offered to coordinate donations of second-hand clothing through the Jakarta expatriate community and American Women's Association of which she was the president, as well as children's books and other necessities. While Sunshine did not have teaching experience, she suggested the possibility of giving the group English lessons, together with a friend.

Around mid–May, we were hearing rumors that the families might be imminently moved to a better facility in Jakarta. "They will stay in a room together, but they will not be locked up," Grace said. "IOM will not deliver food to them anymore, but the families will receive money and do their own shopping. The kids might be able to go to school." While the families insisted their transfer had been decided by the "big boss of immigration" himself as room was now needed in detention for "70 Chinese illegal immigrants," little did we know that their long-desired move to community housing (also known officially as "alternatives to detention" or ATD) was still many months away.

On May 22, a UNHCR official visited the families to monitor how they were coping in detention—one of a total of 386 such visits that the organization made to IDCs around Indonesia that year. The very next day was when two UNHCR representatives personally delivered their refugee cards, the only official notification of their new status. They were among some 1,760 refugees to be issued identity cards in 2017.[12]

"We shouted loudly and burst into tears of happiness," Mrs. Phuc later told me. "We felt like we have a new life." Doan Trung phoned to congratulate them: "Since I first knew them some 18 months ago, I've talked with Loan and Lua perhaps 20 times," he told me. "Each time their voice was worried, scared, or tired. This was the first time I heard joy in their voices and that was lovely!"

Elated, we alerted JRS and SUAKA, which had already been advised by UNHCR itself. "Well done for all your hard work supporting them also," SUAKA Legal Aid Coordinator Trish Cameron wrote. "My legal role in advocating for this group is now complete, as I am not able to assist with resettlement, however the steps you are taking are fantastic and more than most refugees have access to. I wish you every success with this.... It sounds like the families you have been helping have a lot of support from many people in Jakarta now, which is fantastic. Please keep me updated with

The original UNHCR refugee card belonging to Mrs. Lua's youngest son, Koi, then aged 5.

any news of their resettlement, the good news I hear is a ray of sunshine among all the pressures here."

Vietnamese media outlets were quick to publicize their official recognition as refugees, quoting Mrs. Loan: "UNHCR said they will soon work with IOM and Indonesian immigration to get us out of here."[13] Grace confirmed this in a phone interview from Bangkok the following day: "Yesterday morning UNHCR entered the refugee camp of the immigration department. They called me and I spoke directly with UNHCR. They said these people were granted refugee status. The refugees remain there and are waiting for UNHCR and the immigration department to arrange for them to go to a third country."[14]

More good news was to follow with Mr. Loi's release from jail in Vietnam on May 29, 2017, two months' short of completing his two-year sentence—but only after he had been forced to sign a document, retained by the police, stating he had not been mistreated. Frequent beatings and kicks to his face and head had damaged his sight in his left eye; one of his kidneys had been affected; and he had lost considerable weight, which he attributed to having been fed poisonous food, causing his blood pressure to skyrocket, and leading to a stroke.

Despite the fact that the Constitution of Vietnam (art. 20[1]), in addition to other laws, explicitly protects the individual against torture, and although party to such treaties as the *International Covenant on Civil and Political Rights* (ICCPR) and the *United Nations Convention against Torture and Other Cruel, Inhuman or Degrading Treatment or Punishment* (UNCAT), Vietnam's jails are notorious for the harsh treatment of both general inmates and political and human rights activists, known as "prisoners of conscience," regardless of denials by authorities. As a Vietnamese colleague, who wishes to remain anonymous, told me: "Vietnam is a signatory of many

GENERAL DEPARTMENT VIII
SONG CAI PRISON
No:378/GCN

SOCIALIST REPUBLIC OF VIETNAM
Independence – Freedom – Happiness

NO
24811604464
CERTIFICATE
Completed the prison sentence

SONG CAI PRISION GUARD
Pursuant to Article 40 of the 2010 Law on Criminal Enforcement;

Pursuant to the judgment No. 29/2016/HSST dated April 22, 2016 of the People's Court of La Gi town, Binh Thuan and Pursuant to the Decision on judgment execution No. 56/2016/QĐ-CA dated May 27, 2016 of the People's Court of La Gi town, Binh Thuan,

CERTIFIES

Full name: HO TRUNG LOI   Gender: Male   Year birth: ▉
Other name: Domicile: Binh Thuan
Registered permanent residence: Quarter 2, Phuoc Hoi Ward, La Gi Town, Binh Thuan
Father's name: Ho Van Trong (died)   Mother's name: ▉
Ethnic group: Kinh   Nationality: Vietnamese
Crime: Illegally organizing other people to flee abroad
Date of arrest: 30/7/2015;   Penalty: 2 years
Has been reduced: 1 time = 2 months
Until now, he has completely served his prison sentence
Residing in Quarter 2, Phuoc Hoi Ward, La Gi Town, Binh Thuan
Additional penalty: No
Ho Trung Loi must present himself to the People's Committee of Phuoc Hoi Ward, La Gi Town, Binh Thuan Province before June 6, 2017

THE CERTIFICATE HOLDER
(Signed)

Rolling hand of the certificate
holder (Right index finger)

Ninh Thuan, May 30th, 2017
PRISON GUARD
(Signed & Sealed)

Ho Trung Loi

Recipients:
- The certificate holder
- People's Court of La Gi town, Binh Thuan
- Police of La Gi town, Binh Thuan
- People's Committee of Phuoc Hoi Ward, La Gi Town, Binh Thuan
- LLTP QG-BTP Center
- Department of C53/A93-BCA
- Save HSPN

- Name list no 853
- Issued at: PC81B Binh Thuan's Police
- Date: 31/07/2015

Major Phan Hong Lam

*Note: If you have issues of community integration, direct contact or send mail to the following address: Department of Education and Community Integration. General Department VIII, Ministry of Public Security- No. 17/175, Dinh Cong, Hoang Mai, Ha Noi (Tel: 0435.401.405; Email: Congdong786@yahoo.com.vn)

CERTIFICATE OF TRANSLATION
I, Soesilo, certify that I am a sworn translator by virtue of Decree of Governor of Special District of DKI Jakarta No.527/55. I am competent to perform the translation and certify that above is a true and accurate translation from original document shown to me.

SK Gub DKI Jakarta
Address: Taman Laguna ... Jakarta ... Indonesia 17435
Tel. 021-8452 ... www.arsindyatrans.co.id

Certified translation of Mr. Loi's certificate of release from jail (courtesy Tran Thi Thanh Loan).

international conventions to protect human and religious rights. This then begs the question, why do they breach their international obligations? And more importantly, why has the international community been silent on those breaches?"

Under police supervision for the next six months, Mr. Loi was unable to travel out of his local area without permission. "The authorities came to his house and told him just to let them know when he wants to leave town," Grace told me. "They congratulated him because Mrs. Loan became a refugee."

Meanwhile, plans for our impending trip were progressing. Sunshine reported that she had gathered boxes and bags full of items for the families, and we arranged

From left, then RFA journalist Hoa Ai Tran, the author, and Grace Bui, June 2017 (courtesy Hoa Ai Tran).

to meet at the detention center on June 2, even though we were still hoping they would be released before then. Reaching Jakarta two days earlier, Grace and Hoa Ai managed to see the families once prior to my arrival on June 1. At Grace's suggestion, we had agreed to keep my visit a surprise. When she kindly picked me up at the airport, she recommended we take advantage of the fact that one of the "nice" officials happened to be on duty at the detention center and go that very evening to meet them.

Somehow, however, the group must have guessed because no sooner had we arrived outside the immigration building in south

Guard unlocking the grille door to allow visitors to join the refugee families in the cell (courtesy Sunshine and Aaron Biskaps).

The three youngest children, Nhi, Hoa Nhien, and Koi, posing with a donated tricycle in detention, June 2017 (courtesy Sunshine and Aaron Biskaps).

Jakarta when Mrs. Loan, Mrs. Lua, and Mrs. Phuc came running down the road to embrace me: the kind guard had allowed them out of detention to greet me, with RFA on hand to record our meeting.[15] Laden with supplies, we made our way to the third floor where the detention center was located, greeting the children in a reception area. In the video, you can see the mothers ushering us through a metal grille door into a corridor, followed by an Indonesian guard. There, just as they described, were two padlocked cells opposite each other: To the left, one for the men and older boys, and to the right, the other for the mothers and children. Also confronting was the cell at the end of the corridor, where I was told the "real criminals" were confined. Fortunately, Mrs. Lua's husband, Mr. Long, together with his younger brother, Nguyen Tai, Mrs. Loan's son, Ho Van Loc, and Mrs. Phuc's son, Tran Ngoc Tuan, were released from their cell and allowed to join us in the female quarters. While the accommodation was modern and clean, there were no windows or natural light. Incapable of communicating other than by gestures, I was fortunate to be able to rely on Grace and Hoa Ai. We presented our gifts, but at the families' request, took the phone tablets away to be fitted with sim cards.

The next morning, Grace and I returned as planned with Sunshine and her band of supporters, as well as a Vietnamese translator. This time, however, it was not as easy to gain entry: A "stricter" official must have taken over the shift. "I'm on the way to the detention center and my Vietnamese friend is already there," Sunshine texted.

Advocates visiting the refugee families in detention (Sunshine is at the center, with the author third from right, and Grace Bui seated far right) (courtesy Sunshine and Aaron Biskaps).

"They are not allowing her access to the families even after she mentioned your names. I have a car full of donations for them.... Please call me as soon as you get this message or provide me with a name and phone number of a local Indonesian contact."

Eventually, after clearing security, a hijab-clad female guard first insisting that Grace pull on a pair of jeans over her shorts, we were allowed upstairs. Not only did Sunshine have box loads of supplies, but also children's tables and chairs and a tricycle, although unfortunately, the English-Vietnamese dictionaries I had ordered online had not arrived in time. But first the guard had

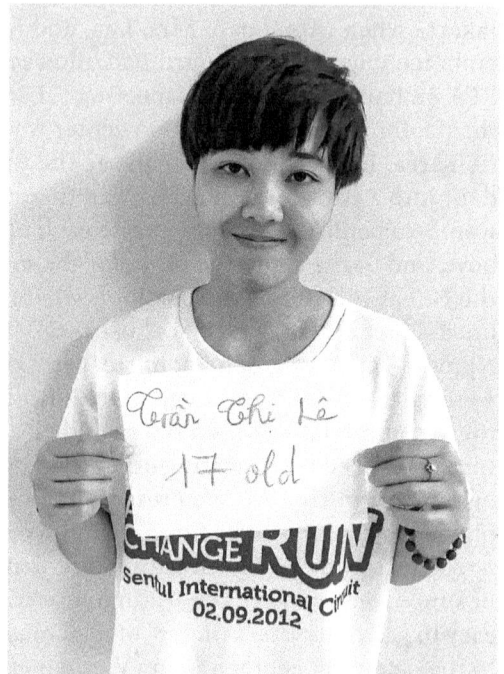

Mrs. Lua's sister, Tran Thi Le (courtesy Sunshine Biskaps).

Sunshine (right) and her husband Aaron reading to the children (courtesy Sunshine and Aaron Biskaps).

to unlock the cage-like cell doors, the families clustered behind them, waiting to greet us.

We took advantage of the opportunity to get to know each other better, despite the language barrier. Using her initiative, Sunshine took photos of each of the 18 detainees, holding a sign with their name and age, and read books to the children, together with her Australian husband, Aaron.

After Grace's return to Bangkok later that day, Sunshine and I met at a hotel with Sister Lidwina, principal of Pius Senior High School in Tegal, Central Java, who

Aaron saying goodbye to Mrs. Lua's youngest son, Koi (courtesy Sunshine and Aaron Biskaps).

From left, the author, Sunshine, and Sister Lidwina.

Eating fruit for the first time in months (courtesy Sunshine and Aaron Biskaps).

undertook what turned out to be a three-hour journey in standstill traffic on a Friday afternoon to see us. Able to speak some Vietnamese, she had been instrumental in providing initial support to the families upon their arrival in Indonesia.

While we remained eternally hopeful the families would be imminently moved to community housing, a JRS representative explained over dinner that the head of immigration would have the final say, the entire process taking as long as six months. In the meantime, if we became aware of any human rights violations in detention, we should alert JRS, which would try to help.

On June 3, Sunshine and I returned for what would be my last visit to the detention center. Bringing back the phone tablets, now complete with sim cards, Sunshine also delivered more supplies, including watermelon and papaya: It was the first time in five months that the children were able to enjoy such fruit.

She had even managed to find an experienced teacher, who initially offered to give the children lessons in rudimentary English during her holiday break. "How do I go about doing it? Can we just walk in any time? Or do we need to make an appointment?" the teacher innocently asked. "Kindly let me know how I can be of service. I would love to do my part."

Departing Jakarta later that day after an emotional farewell, my suitcase was now empty—save for a giant, multi-colored lobster woven out of flexible plastic bags that had taken the mothers a week to make. I felt confident we had done our best to establish a local network, headed by Sunshine, upon which the families could rely, whether they remained in detention for a while longer or were fortunate enough to be released to a community shelter. Sunshine agreed: "I'd like to see them often to build a nice rapport."

I landed in Sydney to a message from Senator Ngo's then Director of Parliamentary Affairs, asking whether I could send "full documentation and an update for each of these refugee claimants? This would help us bring their cases forward." I immediately contacted Grace, requesting she ask the adults to take a photo of each of their 18 refugee cards and send to me to forward to the Senator, along with an explanation we were compiling of each family's situation.

Meanwhile, she had heard that UNHCR had been working with Indonesian immigration and IOM to secure community housing, where the group would finally be moved the following week. No sooner had this plan ostensibly been established than it was thrown into doubt. On June 6, detention center guards told the families "They were to be sent somewhere," writing down the instructions, which Mrs. Phuc's daughter, Tran Thi Kieu Trinh, translated into Vietnamese: The first group of nine would fly out on June 13, followed by the second group three days later. This sounded

Gift for the author from the mothers in detention.

ominous: Would our support network be rendered useless before it even had a chance to be put into operation?

Sunshine, who happened to be visiting that day, attempted to ask a guard, but was told only that they would be taken to the airport:

> I'm a bit disappointed they don't seem to be remaining in my area as I was hoping to help teach them with the team of tutors I've put together. I've bought two kettles, plastic chopsticks, soup spoons, and small non-ceramic bowls. I've also collected more clothes specifically for the younger children, shoes too, new stationery, books, and toys as well. The families have requested luggage for their belongings. I pulled out a couple of zip-up bags from my closet, which will suffice. I will look for more. I only want to bring in essentials and what they will want to take with them on their flights. Whatever they cannot use, I'll donate to local charities here.

A flurry of phone calls and emails followed to UNHCR, JRS, and SUAKA as we tried to clarify their destination and lobbied for them to stay in Jakarta. While I was concerned they could be deported, this was thought unlikely as Indonesia had not tended to treat refugees that way in the past. More probable, or so we hoped, was that they would be moved to an IOM shelter elsewhere.

As we soon discovered, however, they had been scheduled to be sent to Semarang IDC on the north coast of Central Java, which was designated for families. From what we could understand, quick intervention by UNHCR now meant they would instead be housed in community accommodation near Jakarta. "Fantastic!" Sunshine said. "I plan to visit along with their new teacher. She has experience and is extremely passionate, so she will be a huge asset to the children. We'll bring the books and materials now that we know they are staying in Jakarta."

Joy turned to consternation yet again the next morning, when Mrs. Loan repeated to Grace that the guards were insisting immigration would send them elsewhere on Java Island. Sunshine still hoped they would stay near Jakarta. "Every day I'm doing something for the families. Today I went to the shops and bought a few more items.... So now I am left not knowing if I should bring in more or not. My whole office is lined with what I've gathered for them."

In the interim, a UNHCR official told Grace: "Grateful if you can advise them that they do not have the luxury of choosing their movement. Immigration has the sole authority of transfer, while both IOM and UNHCR are only in an advisory role."

On June 8, as Mrs. Loan had asked, Sunshine gave her the equivalent of around USD350, which I had transferred from the crowd fund. While she had called for the remaining money to be given to her husband, we agreed to send him enough to cover the urgent medical attention he now required, wanting to conserve what we could for the children's future. "The families are again requesting a sewing machine and table," Sunshine wrote to Grace:

> I'm confused as I didn't think they were staying. I attempted to tell them in my broken Vietnamese that they would not be allowed to take a table with them. I'll look for a small sewing machine. I hope it will be able to get into the cell and onto their flights. They are also asking for hair-cutting scissors and an electronic trimmer set. The boys' hair is getting too long. But I'm a little hesitant as I was told no sharp metal objects allowed into their cell.... The security guard told me I could not buy them stainless steel cutlery, so I doubt I can bring hair-cutting shears.... I'm not really sure they'd be able to have sewing needles either. How strict are they? ...

Grace advised her to check with the guards first. "If you bought them and they hurt themselves, they might hold you responsible. They can request a haircut from IOM." The group expressed their gratitude by giving Sunshine multi-colored, plastic woven name-bracelets for each member of our families.

By June 10, I had already received a response from Senator Ngo's office: "Thank you for all these additional documents. We have brought them to the highest authorities within Canada's immigration department for their immediate consideration. We will update you as soon as we receive updates from them."

That evening, a senior Indonesian immigration official came to talk to the families in detention, asking whether they wanted to move out of Jakarta. Certain they would refuse and would explain their reliance on the newly established support network, we were disappointed to discover they had agreed. "They said yes because a translator told them they had no choice," Grace subsequently told me. "Mrs. Loan wanted to tell the officer she wished to stay. But some of the others told immigration they would be happy to move." Realizing the implications, they begged Grace to resolve their predicament: "They had a chance last night and they blew it."

On June 12, IOM brought in the paperwork, translated into Vietnamese, asking the group to sign. Titled "Declaration of Voluntary Movement," the document stated:

I understand that on DGI [Directorate General of Immigration] request IOM will move me (and my family) from Directorate General of Immigration detention room to Semarang Immigration Detention Center.

I appreciate that IOM will continue with the migrant care support for me and my family until durable solution is established.

I also confirm that I understand the text mentioned above and declare that I am signing on my free will.

"It's voluntary," Grace explained. "Immigration didn't force them to move. Tuan, Mrs. Phuc's 17-year-old son, signed the form. There is nothing we can do now." The question remains, however, as to whether the families were really free to choose for themselves or whether the authorities were simply following procedure: What would have happened had they refused to sign?[16] "I am sure that even if the families had firmly refused to go, they would have been forced to," Nhi later reflected. "Also, in their situation and frame of mind, they are very scared and worried most of the time. They would not have the confidence to fight."

JRS urged us to stay positive: "Best to ensure there will be support for them wherever they go," a representative told me. "Semarang IDC is quite open and there will be more families with children. From what I heard, it's still no community accommodation, but JRS will try and find some volunteers. Let's make sure there is access to education."

By then, the *Sydney Morning Herald* (SMH) had finally agreed to publish my article announcing their recognition as refugees.[17] I also gave a public talk—the first of what would prove to be many—to a small audience at the University of New South Wales. The following day, Hoa Ai's Vietnamese exclusive about visiting them in detention appeared, quoting Mrs. Loan: "On behalf of all 18 people, may I express our deep emotions and gratitude to the government of Indonesia, the United Nations, and IOM, Mrs. Shira, Mrs. Grace Bui, Mrs. Ngoc Nhi for their companionship and attention to us. We are calling upon their assistance in helping us achieve a new life in a third country."[18] "We have come a long way with them," Grace reflected. "A lot of headache, heartache, joy, sorrow, tears, and laughter. I would never forget this experience."

After all the adults had signed the "Declaration of Voluntary Movement," we expected them to be transferred to Semarang IDC as early as July 1. Nevertheless, their actual move did not occur until several weeks later. In the interim, the guards grew stricter, hampering Sunshine's continued largesse, despite her tip and cigarette money. Security had already been tightened, with visitors being escorted to the ninth floor to obtain permission from a supervisor before being allowed to see the families. Now extra steps were introduced: A detention center guard would interview Sunshine about how she knew them; her papers would be inspected, and some gifts rejected, such as uncut melons—purchased along with other groceries thanks to a donation from a local Vietnamese restaurateur—because knives were not allowed in the cells.

"They were also denied a few coloring books and some plush toys for whatever reason," Sunshine wrote to us on June 14:

> I wasn't able to bring in a Lego box for the kids either. They were happy to get the play dough though!
>
> The men and older boys were kept locked up and not allowed to mingle together. It was sad to witness the father, Long Nguyen, unable to interact with his kids. The older boys appeared distant, understandably. I squeezed two fresh whole chickens through the cell bars and saved the rest for the moms, girls, and young boys. The guards were very strict, requesting me to leave when they said, which was right in the middle of lunch, only 30 minutes after they let me in.

Sunshine (center) enjoys lunch with female members of the refugee group in detention (courtesy Sunshine and Aaron Biskaps).

> I was told they have a maximum weight limit of 20 kilos [44 pounds] per person when they fly. They made it clear they do not want me bringing in any more material donations, as the guards want to limit what comes into their cells. They were mostly concerned with the tables and chairs I brought in for the children ...

Although the teacher had decided not to continue her efforts, one of Sunshine's friends managed to send in some children's books, while the "nice" guard even donated two suitcases.

June 14 was also when Mr. Van Pham—a former boat person himself—wrote separately to both Grace and me on behalf of the Queensland Chapter of the Vietnamese Community in Australia (VCA-QLD), generously offering to privately sponsor all the families. He had considerable experience in social development, having long contributed to the northwest Melbourne Vietnamese community before moving to Brisbane: "Now we would like to sponsor them to settle in Brisbane, Australia. But we don't know which country they are looking for and how to make a sponsor application with the Australian government's requirements? If it's possible and with your help ..., we're going to mobilize our community in Queensland to support them to settle here."

JRS had first raised the possibility of the families being sponsored for resettlement during my visit to Jakarta, explaining UNHCR would lobby third countries that had signed the Refugee Convention, according to acceptance quotas, but the process could take a long time. The group could also apply for private sponsorship if they had immediate family overseas, but this could be very expensive. A representative suggested approaching an immigration lawyer prepared to work pro bono, but I knew from my other refugee advocacy work in Sydney how hard they were to find.

Whereas Australia officially allows refugees outside the country, who satisfy certain health, character, and other requirements, to apply for a visa themselves with support (known as "self-referred refugee applications"), the chance of being accepted, even after waiting for years, is minimal. Priority is officially given to those referred by, or registered with UNHCR, or who have "close family members in Australia," or "proposers residing in a regional area."[19] Canada, in contrast, does not generally accept direct applications from refugees at all. Referrals for resettlement can usually only be made by UNHCR and similar organizations, private sponsors, or as the result of an agreement or arrangement with a foreign state or institution.[20]

In fact, I had written to Refugee Council of Australia (RCOA) chief executive officer, Paul Power, who assured me in an email dated June 23, 2017, which he reiterated on April 26, 2020, that RCOA

> drew the matter to the attention of the Assistant High Commissioner for UNHCR, Volker Türk, and other senior officials in Geneva at the opening plenary of UNHCR's annual consultations with NGOs [non-government organizations] in June 2017, referring to your article in the *Sydney Morning Herald* and suggesting that this appeared to be a clear breach of Australia's non-refoulement obligation under the Refugee Convention. We also emphasized the importance of finding resettlement for the women and children. Mr. Türk acknowledged that the matter had been brought to his attention, saying that he would look into it and, if necessary, raise it with the Australian government.[21]

Later that month, Mr. Power visited Ottawa and met with an advisor of Senator Ngo to discuss the case.

Meanwhile, UNHCR had already warned the families themselves about the difficulties of resettlement when they had first registered as asylum seekers back in March 2017: "Resettlement is NOT a right and hence is not automatically processed after refugee status is granted." Furthermore, according to the Code of Conduct drawn up by UNHCR: "The chances for successful resettlement are globally very limited. **Therefore, as a recognized refugee, you should understand that <u>not all recognized refugees will and can be</u> resettled in a third country.**... The resettlement process can be a very lengthy one and the waiting period and final decision do not rest with UNHCR but with the resettlement country."[22]

Another UNHCR brochure available on-line was even more hard-hitting: "Resettlement countries offer only a limited number of resettlement places every year, benefitting less than 1% of the refugee population worldwide. As Indonesia hosts a relatively small number of refugees compared to other countries of asylum, the number of resettlement places provided for refugees in Indonesia is far fewer than anyone would hope. There are simply far more refugees in Indonesia than there are places for resettlement. You should therefore understand and accept that you may never be able to benefit from resettlement from Indonesia...." Indeed, in 2017, the total population of concern in Indonesia, as recorded by UNHCR, stood at around 13,800, including 4,000 asylum seekers and 9,800 refugees, only about 760 of whom departed for resettlement.[23]

The two other "comprehensive" or "durable solutions" promoted by UNHCR and facilitated by IOM were even more impossible: The families could neither return safely and voluntarily to Vietnam nor integrate permanently with formal rights in Indonesia, which was their "country of refuge" or "first asylum."[24]

Hence the attraction of private sponsorship. While we thought they had more chance to be accepted for protection by Canada, despite having no immediate family members living there, I agreed to explore Mr. Van Pham's magnanimous suggestion on behalf of the Queensland Vietnamese community. On June 15, 2017, the mothers did a live broadcast with American Vietnamese interviewer Thanh Tam Nguyen, streamed on Facebook and YouTube:

From left, Tran, Koi, Sunshine holding Hoa Nhien, and Nhi (courtesy Sunshine and Aaron Biskaps).

"We need to get a third country to notice them," Grace told me. "Some of the audience said they will write to Canada to support our request for the families' resettlement."

By June 17, Sunshine was finding it difficult to "share quality time" with the group even during the amenable officer's shift. "I guess it all depends not only on the guards on duty, but also on the front door security and the immigration officials on the ninth floor. Unfortunately, with their strict regulations, I'm not sure if they want future visitors. I'm happy to have brought them a little happiness and comfort during their stay. I'll continue to do my best to help them with basic needs while they are in Jakarta."

She was much missed, Mrs. Loan's oldest daughter My revealing to me later how she had "kept fighting every day for Sunshine to visit us." Sunshine's last attempt on July 7 proved unsuccessful, the guards not allowing her to enter. "I was able to drop off the equivalent of around USD350 for Mrs. Loan [donated from the crowd fund], and a few boxes of food, clothes, and shoes. I doubt I'll be back much as the guards have made it nearly impossible to visit with them ... such a shame and very frustrating!" Concerned the group was now languishing in limbo, I begged her to try again some weeks later. "I'd like to go to read to them or have a meal together," she replied on July 23, "but sadly, these no longer seem to be options.... I wish them well!"

By then Grace had informed us their date of departure would be July 28. At the same time, the Queensland Vietnamese community was persisting with its sponsorship idea, president Dr. Bui Trong Cuong[25] writing to me: "I'm arranging to see [Home Affairs] Minister Dutton in the next few weeks. Please give me: The cases' ID, the names of all members, their dates of birth, the dates when they were sent back to Vietnam, the punishment in Vietnam, harassments, difficulties that happened to the children, when did they escape again, the day when they were granted refugee status, and as many details as you can. All the failed asylum seekers were told they won't be punished. In the meantime, if possible, please contact their relatives in Australia. Please keep in touch."

Although Dr. Bui initially thought his community might be able to join with Australian relatives to co-sponsor the families, that plan never eventuated. Only too aware of Australia's strict border protection policies, notably in relation to those who had attempted to arrive by boat, we strongly counseled against approaching the Australian government at this stage. Nevertheless, I was excited about potential, albeit more modest, possibilities under the Community Support Program (CSP), the latest version of which had only been introduced that month. What if the Queensland Vietnamese community could find a local business prepared to privately sponsor one of the families, supporting both their visa application and settlement for 12 months?

Welcomed as "following in the footsteps of Canada," Australia's new private sponsorship program was part of an increased quota in the number of refugee and humanitarian entrants, under which up to 1,000 could now be proposed for resettlement by individuals, families, businesses, and community groups.[26] Although precise details had not as yet been revealed, candidates for the "Global Special Humanitarian visa subclass 202" would have to satisfy a host of humanitarian and "human capital" requirements, including being outside both Australia and their home country, where they faced "substantial discrimination amounting to gross violation of human rights"; meeting "minimum health standards"; being aged between 18 and 50; being "of good character"; having employable skills; and formally agreeing to "respect the Australian way of life and obey Australian laws."[27]

At first, Nguyen Thi Phuc and her three children appeared to tick most, if not all, the boxes. A small fish business owner in La Gi township, Binh Tuan province, she and her husband, Tran Van Yen, a fisherman, and their young family, were among the group of 46 Vietnamese failed asylum seekers, who had attempted to reach Australia in March 2015. Like Mrs. Loan and Mr. Loi, they had initially fled Vietnam due to Chinese incursions into fishing grounds and in quest of religious freedom, having suffered institutionalized discrimination as Catholics under the communist regime. "We lost our livelihood but were still penalized by having to pay higher taxes," Mrs. Phuc later told me. "My husband and I had also been beaten by an attacker, who accused us of stealing a pair of flip flops." Unlike Mrs. Loan and Mr. Loi, however, Vietnamese authorities did not regard them as organizers of the trip. Indeed, they had only paid Mrs. Loan the equivalent of USD500 so she could buy milk, fruit, and other supplies to sustain their family on the journey.

"Upon our return, I was imprisoned and tortured for seven days before being released with a 27-month parole sentence," Mrs. Phuc complained:

> The government did not allow me to continue my business and so I became jobless. I was summoned frequently to report at the local police station with many difficulties caused.... They hired thugs to follow me 24 hours a day just because I illegally crossed the border. I did not commit a crime....
>
> My children were subjected to the ridicule of the teachers and the school. The teacher asked how illegal maritime escapees could afford to learn and said any attempt to learn would be in vain. Then the teacher took my child to the foot of the flagpole to show an example of an illegal maritime escapee. My child was an above average student but was given a bad mark for conduct and had to repeat Year 9....
>
> At the court hearing the magistrate said that I escaped overseas with the intention of working as a prostitute and sold my younger siblings to a whorehouse. I stood up to try to protest but she pounded the table and did not allow me to speak. I had no right to respond; the thugs following me flustered me, making me forget everything I had just done.

PEOPLE'S COMMITTEE OF	SOCIALIST REPUBLIC OF VIETNAM
PHUOC HOI WARD	Independence—Freedom—Happiness
-----------------------	----------*----------

Phuoc Hoi, October 06, 2015

INVITATIONS

In order to improve the role and responsibility of the public in building a movement for the entire people to protect national security and defense, prevent and fight against crimes and social evils, People's Committee of Phuoc Hoi ward sincerely invites:

Ms. Nguyen Thi Phuc
At 1.30 P.M. on October 09th, 2015 (Friday afternoon)
To be present at the Meeting-hall of Phuoc Hoi People's Committee (Opposite Tran Vu Gasoline station)
To attend the **Propaganda and Dissemination of legislation on crime and social evil prevention and fighting**.
Please attend fully, on time and at the right place for the meeting to achieve good results.

CHAIRMAN
(Signed and sealed)
Ha Thanh Binh

Certified translation of summons for Mrs. Phuc (courtesy Nguyen Thi Phuc).

Meanwhile, her husband was given a 24-month suspended sentence and attempted to resume fishing in an effort to support his family. Also constantly expected to attend the police station, he maintained this was a deliberate attempt "to prevent us from going to work. They often mocked us, followed us, went to our home to disturb us."

Their punishment in Vietnam was far more severe than that described by Australia's Department of Foreign Affairs (DFAT), which continues to assert that while "all individuals involved in people smuggling operations, whether as organizers or travelers," are detained for questioning, "would-be migrants who have employed the services of people smugglers at worst only face an administrative fine, including in cases of multiple illegal departures."[28]

By the time his wife and children had fled again in January 2017, Mr. Yen was already in Indonesia, having been arrested together with Mr. Long, among others, on July 24, 2016, accused of fishing illegally in Indonesian waters. "I was not familiar with the area and had not realized that I had done so," he later explained. Originally jailed for a year, he was transferred on January 16, 2017, from detention in Ranai, Natuna Islands, to the Tanjung Pinang IDC on Bintan Island, in Riau province, Sumatra,[29] and was set to be deported to Vietnam on June 16, 2017.

He subsequently described life as a detainee in Tanjung Pinang, which had been refurbished and enlarged to a maximum capacity of 600 with IOM assistance in 2008. The three-story *rudenim* building had around 12 blocks of dormitories, each designed to accommodate about 30 inmates, as well as six isolation rooms[30]:

> In prison, we got three meals a day: one bowl of rice in the morning, two bowls at lunch, two at dinner. But we didn't get any other food. If we were given a small piece of chicken, the people who distributed the meal would retain it for themselves. We bought shrimp instant noodle soup and asked for hot water to cook it, then mixed it with the rice to complete the meal.... We took water from the well. During the time I was in custody, I was allowed to go out only once a month, as well as on gym days and public holidays, but I had to remain within the prison area.

Although Mr. Yen would manage to remain in Indonesia and apply for asylum seeker status, it was unclear as to whether he would ever be reunited with his family, and so the Queensland Vietnamese community decided to confine its sponsorship efforts to his wife and children.

After the group of 18 refugees was flown to Semarang IDC on July 28, 2017, we did not hear any news for two days. "Mrs. Loan told me their phones were confiscated when they arrived," Nhi subsequently explained. "They only have one phone left, but it has run out of credit." Not, however, before they had managed to send three photos: One of the group at Terminal Three of Jakarta's Soekarno-Hatta International Airport prior to their departure, and two of the conditions at Semarang, which were clearly much harsher than what they had experienced in detention in south Jakarta.

"Mrs. Loan said they have no freedom," Nhi confirmed. "They get locked in together all day; at night they can't even go downstairs to the communal bathroom. Food-wise, they have to give money to the guards, who will go out to buy it for them. They cook for themselves, but the guards always take a portion."[31] Constantly under camera surveillance, their cell was also considerably smaller and not as clean as in Jakarta.

Concerned, I contacted retired Ambassador Rees, JRS, and other refugee advocates to see whether anything could be done to improve their situation. "They have

The group poses at Jakarta's international airport before flying to Semarang.

Conditions in Semarang IDC.

been told they will stay there for at least a year and possibly for two or three years until they find resettlement in a third country," I wrote to JRS. We were also worried they would exhaust their finances. While I had understood IOM would pay for their meals and shelter, the families were clearly relying, at least initially, on the crowd fund. "That was why I did not think it a good idea to spend money on phone tablets," Nhi pointed out. "While in a refugee camp, they need the money for survival more than education."

Fortunately, support was soon at hand: "I got a message from Mrs. Loan saying they nearly ran out of money, but IOM is now supplying food," Nhi reported on August 3.[32] "A UN team visited today, bringing milk and fresh fruit. She also managed to get some credit for her phone." In due course, IOM would arrange occasional beach excursions too.

At JRS' advice, I wrote to a local Catholic priest, asking if he would visit the families. "They dearly want to be able to attend mass, but are not allowed out, even on Sunday," Nhi complained. "Mrs. Loan said they sought the guards' permission and will keep begging." The Father requested leave from the head of the detention center to visit the families together with two nuns in the hope of ascertaining whether such restrictions were only temporary.[33] "The main problem will be the language barrier," a JRS representative explained, asking whether I could arrange for a translator to help via phone from Jakarta. I suggested Nhi or Grace, but neither was given official permission. "They're not allowed to use the phone or go online," Nhi relayed on August 5. "They have to do so secretly. So, they cannot access the phone tablets you gave them or attend any online classes."

Moreover, the adults had more serious concerns, needing to keep a close eye on their children, who were particularly vulnerable due to the proximity in which they were now forced to live with other asylum seekers. While Semarang IDC's official capacity was 60 "illegal immigrants," there were already 84 residing there on June 30, 2017, a month before the families arrived.[34] At one stage, we feared that one of the older girls had been molested. Subsequently examined by a doctor, she was given antibiotics against infection, but when her mother asked the guards to show her CCTV footage of the alleged assault, they refused. As usual Grace reported the incident to UNHCR and IOM.

Continuously striving to provide emotional support to the families took its toll, particularly on Nhi and Grace. "They constantly call me. They are not well educated and so need help with everything," Nhi disclosed. "Initially I thought I would help with some translation, but for a year now, it has taken so much of my time and money. It is interfering with my study and main line of work. Because you don't speak Vietnamese you don't realize how much work and pressure Grace and I have been under in the last year to help the families and to help you with this. I think the workload and stress contributed to me getting so sick."

At least when members of the group fell ill, local Indonesian doctors had usually allowed Grace to provide translation, although it took IOM considerable time to arrange medical appointments. By September 2017, however, we had been instructed that "outsiders" were no longer allowed to interpret for detainees in Semarang, Mrs. Phuc's request for Nhi's assistance during her consultation for depression denied. "The doctor told her depression in the refugee camp is widespread and reassured her just to try to live the best way she can." "I was scared and sad to be imprisoned," My later told me. "We were cramped, eating, and drinking inadequately, and when we went to bed, we couldn't sleep. There were so many mosquitos. I wanted to be free. I had no education and no contact outside the prison area. Every day I prayed to God for us to quickly leave."

Eventually some of the restrictions were lifted, phone tablets permitted once more; the families able to go on a four-hour outing each week to attend Sunday mass; the children free to use the playground, with the boys joining woodworking classes. Mrs. Phuc and her children were moved to separate quarters downstairs, meaning they could only communicate with the rest of the group by phone. "Here I could run and jump," Mrs. Lua's niece, Tran Thi Thanh Ngoc, added. "Sometimes teachers came to teach us English and *Bahasa Indonesia*."[35]

In mid–August, Mrs. Loan had reported that according to the head of the detention center, they were to be moved to Jakarta, but unsurprisingly, the transfer did not eventuate, even though they still lived in constant hope. "They go to some English lessons but mainly learn Indonesian," Nhi informed me on October 17. "They were told they will not be moved out of there until they are fluent enough in Indonesian to live independently. They get enough basic food, but if they want extra, like fruit, they have to give money to the guards, who will buy it for them."

On a brief trip to Melbourne, I finally met Doan Trung in person, who revealed he had also been liaising with Queensland Vietnamese community president Dr. Bui about sponsorship possibilities.

The next day, October 22, I received the most wonderful message from Mr. Van Pham in his capacity as new VCA-QLD refugee committee chair:

Author with Doan Trung.

The Queensland Chapter of the Vietnamese Community in Australia has decided to sponsor Mrs. Nguyen Thi Phuc and her three children as the result of meeting in the last two weeks. Before we can process the sponsorship procedure, we would like to seek the following:

1. To receive certified hard copies of all the Nguyen family's information including refugee status and photos;
2. To seek a letter confirming the Nguyen family's wish to come to Australia for settlement;
3. To form a sponsor group to handle the case;
4. To organize a financial campaign to receive donations and support from the Vietnamese community to sponsor her family.

While VCA-QLD would be responsible for the last two steps, which Mr. Van Pham initially estimated would be achieved in one-to-three months, he needed our assistance to obtain the necessary documents. "If you can get a confirmation letter from Mrs. Phuc in both Vietnamese and Indonesian, and have it certified, that would be better for us when filling out the visa application and discussing it with our Vietnamese community." Mrs. Phuc duly sent the letter, albeit in Vietnamese only, on October 23.

Three days later, Senator Ngo's Director of Parliamentary Affairs wrote: "I have little updates to bring to your attention other than how the Vietnamese Canadian community is in the process of fundraising the required significant funds to privately sponsor this large group of refugees, and submitting an application with the government of Canada. We will make sure to keep you appraised as this endeavor progresses."

On November 17, we obtained more good news from the Senator's office, introducing us to Kyanh Do and James Nguyen from VOICE Canada, "a community sponsorship group who can be of assistance moving forward." A member of the Senator's staff was also assigned as the "main contact for this case." Henceforth, we would work together with VOICE Canada on what Senator Ngo's office called "the ideal refugee resettlement path."

Formally registered in the U.S. in 2007, VOICE, which stands for Vietnamese Overseas Initiative for Conscience Empowerment, is a not-for-profit, with the vision of "a strong, independent, and vibrant civil society in Vietnam."[36] Its independent Canadian affiliate was set up in 2014, president Kyanh Do, a chartered accountant and former boat person himself, working with a team of Vietnamese volunteer advocates to sponsor refugees the way they themselves were helped in the past.

I immediately wrote to Kyanh asking whether he would speak directly with the families in Indonesia. On November 24, we had the first of many conference calls with Dr. Bui and Doan Trung, in his capacity as VOICE Australia president. It was important to find a way to work together towards the best outcome, and we agreed that should the Queenslanders fail, the Canadians would take over. "While Queensland wants to help sponsor Mrs. Phuc's family, there is no guarantee they will succeed," I explained to Nhi and Grace. "Nevertheless, they are going to try. Meanwhile, Kyanh Do told us the Canadian Vietnamese community is prepared to privately sponsor all 18 of our family members to come to Canada! To do so they will need to raise a lot of money. We are going to try to work together to help the Canadians do so."

Unlike the Australians, they certainly had considerable experience, VOICE Canada having sponsored more than 100 Vietnamese refugees from Thailand over 2014–2017, as well as several refugee families from Syria, with a sponsor approval rate of close to 100 per cent, under Canada's flexible Private Sponsorship of Refugees program (PSR). Established in 1978, in response to the Indochinese refugee crisis, PSR has been estimated to have involved approximately two million Canadians in the resettlement of more than 300,000 refugees in 40 years, reunifying many families along the way. Providing a "complementary pathway" in addition to the country's regular government-assisted humanitarian intake,[37] it is the oldest and most successful private refugee sponsorship program in the world.[38]

Approved by Immigration, Refugees and Citizenship Canada (IRCC)[39] to be what is known as a Sponsorship Agreement Holder (SAH), VOICE is one of many incorporated organizations in Canada—usually religious, ethnic, community, or humanitarian—to have signed an ongoing legal agreement with the Canadian government to "help support refugees from abroad when they resettle in Canada." It does this either by sponsoring refugees itself or by working with others in the community to do so. Refugees can either be "named," or "sponsor-referred," like the group in Indonesia, or more rarely, nominated by an overseas visa office, often after reviewing files provided by UNHCR. Indeed, Canadian privately sponsored refugees are "the only category of resettled refugees in the world where sponsors, communities and former refugees themselves can name specific persons for sponsorship."[40] In an effort to ensure "timely protection" of refugees, the government limits the number of new applications that SAHs outside Quebec can submit: In 2019, the cap was set at 10,500 people, with an increase to 12,500 in 2021, in addition to any places unused in 2020 due to the COVID-19 pandemic.[41]

Originally planning to sponsor three or so Syrian families, VOICE had launched a national fundraising campaign, Vietnamese Canadians for Lifeline Syria (VIETCAN4LLS) in 2015, setting a target of

Vietnamese Canadians for Lifeline Syria (VIETCAN4LLS) is a national campaign, spearheaded by VOICE Canada, to mobilize organizations and individuals across Canada to aid with the Syrian refugee crisis. We, Vietnamese Canadians, can empathize with the plight of the Syrian refugees, as we too had to flee our country 40 years ago after the Communist took over Vietnam in 1975. Many of us were very fortunate to be able to come to a great country such as Canada, whose government and people opened their arms and hearts when we were all so desperate. It is time for us Vietnamese Canadians to give back by mobilizing our community to help the Syrian refugees.

MISSION

· Raise at least $100,000 to sponsor 3 Syrian refugee families.
· Create awareness and engage our community to get involved and give back.
· Create a network for Vietnamese organizations and individuals who would like to help the Syrian refugees.
· Provide support for the Vietnamese organizations and individuals through the sponsorship process.
· Act as the liaison between Lifeline Syria and other Vietnamese organizations and individuals.
· Be fiscally responsible and transparent with all funds raised and disbursed.
· Unite Vietnamese groups across Canada to work together towards one initiative.
· Showcase to the world that Vietnamese Canadians care and are ready to pay it forward like how the world had helped us in the late 70's.

DONATE TODAY

There are three easy options to donate:

Option 1 - Donate to VOICE Canada
Write cheque payable to VOICE Canada
289 Old 16th Avenue, Richmond Hill, Ontario, L4B 3N1
Memo: Syrian Refugee

Option 2 - Donate to Phap Van Buddhisst Cultural Centre (tax receipt will be issued)
Write cheque payable to Phap Van Buddhist Cultural Centre
420 Traders Blvd E. Mississauga, ON L4Z 1W7
Memo: Syrian Refugee

Option 3
Please donate online by visiting our website or visit http://bit.ly/VietCan4LLSyriaDonateNow

www.VietCan4LifelineSyria.com

For additional inquiries, please contact: Ky Anh Do (416-417-8098), Lê Quốc Tuấn (416-475-8836), Le Luong (647-818-8088), James Nguyễn (416-738-5561), Nguyễn Quang (647-588-3205), Trúc Tâng (416-854-7711)

VOICE Canada's 2015 national fundraising campaign, Vietnamese Canadians for Lifeline Syria (VIETCAN4LLS) (courtesy VOICE Canada).

CAD100,000: "We are boat refugees ourselves," advocate James Nguyen explained. "So, this is our way ... to give back...."[42] The response was overwhelming, enabling six families to be sponsored.

With regard to the Vietnamese refugees in Indonesia, Kyanh explained, VOICE now planned to get 20 adult Canadian citizens or permanent residents from the Toronto, and more specifically, Mississauga Vietnamese community, divided into what is known as "Groups of Five" (G5), to sponsor the 18 in four family groups.[43] Meanwhile, VOICE Australia and VCA-QLD would decide whether they were in a position to contribute financial support.

We had big dreams. While Mrs. Loan's and Mrs. Lua's families would hopefully one day be able to re-establish their lives in Mississauga, Mrs. Phuc and her children were seemingly blessed with two options: Would they prefer to go to Ontario with the others or join extended family in Brisbane? As I wrote to Mrs. Loan: "Everyone will hopefully now have a sponsor—whether in Canada or Australia—people care about you and want to help you." And to Mrs. Lua: "You have a goal and something to look forward to—freedom in Canada—hopefully within one year. So please tell everyone including the children, and you all should focus on trying to learn some English as well as Indonesian."

The reality was much harsher. Still languishing in detention, Mrs. Lua insisted she had heard the group would be moved to Jakarta before Christmas. It was unclear whether they would end up in detention again or finally in long-awaited community housing. In late December, Mrs. Loan informed us their transfer had been postponed for another few weeks. Mrs. Phuc's son Tuan confirmed the delay during a video call with Dr. Bui when we met for the first time in Brisbane.

Kyanh had also finally managed to speak with the families: "I told them we now have enough sponsors and are working on collecting some money. I will absolutely try to get things done as fast as we can.... I am very happy to ... let them know our intention and our determination to resettle them in Canada."

While in Brisbane, I met with Nhi as well to discuss how to tackle the Canadian immigration forms Kyanh had sent for us to help the families complete.[44] Our immediate problem was getting them translated into Vietnamese. "I had a look at the only form for Canada I can download so far," I told her:

> Here is the information I don't know:
> I need each of their full names written in Vietnamese.
> For each adult, I need to write in English the family name and first name of their father and mother, as well as their mother's maiden name, each of their parent's date, town, and country of birth, and date of death.
> I also need to know for each applicant whether they have been convicted or charged with any crime in any country?
> Have they applied for refugee protection in any country before or with UNHCR?
> Have they been refused refugee status before in any country?
> Have they been refused admission to any country?
> Have they been jailed before?
> Have they any serious disease? If yes, we need to give details.
> I need education details for everyone, especially specific years for high school or trade school, the name of the high school, city, type of certificate, field of study.
> For adults, I need details of what they have been doing for the past ten years, starting with the most recent: dates, activity, city, status, name of employer, school.
> Are they a member of any organization, including political, social, youth, or student?

Have they had any government positions?

Have they done military service? Dates, branch of service, rank, dates of active combat, reason for end of service.

I need all the addresses where they have lived for the past ten years; it cannot be a post office box.

They also need to sign each document.

Nhi's reaction to this overwhelming request was succinct: "This is a LOT of information and a LOT of work, and it will also take them a LOT of time to get done. I will have to translate the questions for them; they will have to write down all the answers; then I will call you, verbally translate what they have written, and you will have to note down the information to rewrite in proper English."

In the end, we decided on another approach. Noting this was only one of many forms to complete for each adult and preferring Nhi to focus on her health concerns, we agreed to ask another translator. "But if you cannot find anyone else, I will do it," she promised. "You know I never say no to helping people if they need me." On the recommendation of VOICE Canada advocate Khanh Lan Ho, I approached Sydney-based professional translator, Trung Sylvain Le Minh, who kindly agreed to become involved. Henceforth, I would go through each form, sending him lists of questions by email to translate into Vietnamese. Each adult would then send their written responses back to Trung to translate into English for me to fill in their forms. A long and arduous process that would take at least 100 hours over the next eight months to complete with the precision required.

Mrs. Lua (left), her husband, Mr. Long (right), and their three children, and Mrs. Loan (second from left) and her four children preparing to board the plane at Ahmad Yani International Airport, Semarang, on their way to Jakarta, February 8, 2018.

"Khanh Lan, James, and I will work on the sponsors' portion of the application," Kyanh wrote to me on December 18, "and it would be great if you could help Loan, Lua, Long, and Phuc to complete their portion. Let's commit to submit the application as soon as possible." As it turned out, Khanh Lan would be one of the G5 sponsors, while James did government advocacy work with businesswoman and advocate Le Luong, charged with the actual sponsorship paperwork and reviewing the applications before submission. Not only was VOICE Canada ensuring all private sponsorship requirements were undertaken, but their administrator also arranged certified translations of important documents, with Le supporting me every step of the way, ensuring we worked closely together.

On January 26, 2018—which happens to be Australia Day—Mrs. Loan sent a message: "Today all family Vietnam carry to the hotel. Live at the hotel wait go to Jakarta [*sic*]." From this we deduced the group was finally out of detention. Transferred to a hotel in Semarang, they would wait until February 7, 2018, when they would sign another IOM declaration, enabling them to be flown to Jakarta the following day. They would then be transported to community housing in Tangerang, a city on the western border of the capital, marking the beginning of a new chapter in their quest for liberty.

5

Communal Living

Fathers Reunited

"Each family has their own room. We have freedom and are no longer in jail." With these words Mrs. Loan encapsulated what the transfer from detention to open community housing meant to the group, who were among over 1,600 refugees released by the Indonesian government in 2018. By December, only one per cent, or around 120 of all UNHCR-registered refugees in Indonesia would remain in detention.[1] Indeed, since mid–2014, Indonesia had been one of 12 focus countries in UNHCR's "Beyond Detention" campaign, which aimed to end the detention of asylum seekers and refugees, striving to ensure that "Alternatives to Detention" (ATDs) would be available and implemented and that all children would be released by 2019.[2]

The families after their arrival at Jakarta's Soekarno-Hatta International Airport on February 8, 2018.

The families' relocation in early 2018 coincided with press coverage of the growing phenomenon in Indonesia of independent asylum seekers or refugees, who could no longer afford to live unaided, camping in front of overcrowded detention centers, especially in Jakarta, in a desperate bid to gain access. Prepared to "sacrifice their freedom for food," they believed, as the families' experience actually showed, that "the only way to be considered for a place to live with international ... assistance [was] to be processed at a detention center."[3]

From March 15, 2018, however, this would no longer be possible, no new cases being referred to IOM due to a "reduction or tightening of assistance from the Australian government," which IOM interpreted as a "termination" of Australian funding for newly arrived or "independent" refugees and asylum seekers. As a JRS staff member explained, "Now we have the situation that [Indonesian] immigration doesn't want to take anyone into the detention centers because that would mean immigration would have to pay for food, healthcare and so on, which means that detention is phasing out, it's ending, which is a good thing."[4]

Thankfully, having been granted refugee status long before the cut-off date, the families were now moving in the opposite direction. After almost ten long months in two detention centers, they had finally been allocated nine rooms on the fourth floor of an IOM low-cost refugee-housing complex in Tangerang, an urban center on the

Tai, Mr. Long, Mrs. Lua and her three children, Mrs. Loan and her four children outside their new accommodation in Tangerang, February 8, 2018.

western outskirts of Jakarta—one of around 42 community housing facilities funded by Australia via IOM across about six of the 34 Indonesian provinces.[5]

Henceforth, they would sleep two to a room in relatively comfortable accommodation, in line with normal Indonesian housing conditions, which Mrs. Loan would later describe as being "like a vacation home. All rooms are the same; each has two wardrobes, two beds, a refrigerator, a bathroom, an air conditioner, a TV, and a table." Their compound was also conveniently located near public transport, local markets, and medical services.

Despite our initial euphoria, however, their freedom was still severely curtailed. While they were now able to come and go largely as they pleased and could shop and cook for themselves, they were still not allowed to work or, at least initially, study formally, the children notably unable to attend local schools. Indeed, only around ten per cent of the 4,000 or so refugee children frequented public school in Indonesia—even though in theory there was no general prohibition against doing so since mid–2018, when some local governments, including in Tangerang, began to make agreements with IOM to allow limited numbers into their public education system, the Indonesian government formalizing their access to national schools a year later.[6]

"Usually, the language barrier is the biggest obstacle to enrolling refugees into public schools," CWS (Church World Service) Indonesia Country Representative Michael Koeniger explained in response to my original inquiry in April 2017. "The children need to be able to speak enough Indonesian to follow the class." To be registered for school, potential students also usually needed proper documentation.[7] Although CWS was the body through which UNHCR implemented both formal and non-formal educational and vocational training programs in Indonesia,[8] it was unable to assist the families directly: "CWS only operates in Jakarta and unfortunately we don't assist any Vietnamese refugees, so we have no contacts that would speak Vietnamese or could give advice (usually other refugees are a great source for advice for refugees and asylum seekers)," Mr. Koeniger told me. "Sorry I can't be more helpful."

Still, we were not prepared to give up. "Our immediate focus is to find a school, which will accept the 12 children," I announced on our website when the group was first released. "Resettlement in a third country—the ultimate solution to their plight—could still be a long time away, although we are working on that too."

Once the families were settled in Tangerang, Mr. Koeniger suggested we contact a nearby refugee center as well as CRS (Catholic Relief Services) and Islamic philanthropy institute Dompet Dhuafa, both of which provide education services for refugees, among other responsibilities.[9] Unfortunately, none of these avenues ultimately proved successful, nor were my attempts to approach the few existing refugee schools, most of which cater to the large Iranian and Afghan Hazara communities.[10]

While CWS shared our request with both UNHCR and IOM, this too did not bear fruit. "IOM has their own education program and policy, and since the families live in their accommodation, their enrolment to public schools is being assisted by IOM," then CWS urban refugee program manager Andi Juanda clarified:

> Further, the last update we received from IOM is that the new enrolment to public school will start in July 2018. And the enrolment is subject to the space availability in the public schools and the result of school's selection interview ... and the children do not have

sufficient *Bahasa Indonesia* skills to be enrolled to public school. As such, in the meantime, the children could join home-schooling classes that will start again in early March (*Bahasa* is one of the subjects), and the adults could join *Bahasa* class so they could teach the children as well. This information has been shared with the families since their arrival.

Indeed, IOM teachers were soon coming to their compound, offering separate 90-minute classes in English to children aged 6–10 and 11–15 twice a week, as well as Indonesian language lessons more sporadically. "As for me, because I am 18, IOM does not allow me to attend," My subsequently told me. "Hope you and the [overseas] community help us to get to go to school like many other children.... We long to leave here soon so we can go to school and fulfil our dream." Mrs. Phuc's son Tuan agreed: "My life is much better, but here more sadness because I have no education to improve my knowledge."

Initially, IOM also provided Mathematics and Social Studies lessons for the children, who could, in addition, access an English language center, Yayasan LIA,[11] some distance away once or twice a week. "Mrs. Loan asked if you still have some of her money left," Grace wrote, "so she could cover the transportation cost for her children." We decided to use the rest of the crowd fund for that purpose—sending Mrs. Loan the money via Grace since refugees are not allowed to open a bank account in Indonesia—but by mid–2018, those lessons and trips to the center, among other IOM services, had stopped. "I don't know why," Mrs. Loan said. "Now IOM does not allow it ... some people said IOM spent a lot of money for it so they should stop."

Whereas IOM maintained the Australian government's cap on its funding from mid–March 2018 would not affect the refugees it currently supported, this was clearly not the case, also spelling the end of most adult and vocational training services.[12] Nevertheless, over the following years, IOM would still offer an occasional course, such as in mid–November 2019, when refugees in Tangerang were encouraged to enroll in a morning session devoted to frozen food, being asked to choose between cake decorating, coffee brewing, or soap making in the afternoon. Almost half the group decided to participate, the majority opting for soap making. "I choose

My (right) volunteering as a pre-school aide with student Yalda at JoyCare.

frozen food and cake decorating," Mrs. Lua told me excitedly. "I, my sister, and my niece will go to the class. Le and Tai will learn about coffee maker [*sic*]."

The families had quickly proved resourceful in helping themselves. In May 2018, My and two of the other older girls, Mrs. Phuc's daughter, Tran Thi Kieu Trinh, and Mrs. Lua's niece, Tran Thi Thanh Ngoc (known as Vy), secured volunteer work, training to be pre-school aides at JoyCare, a local playgroup and daycare center, which offered a refugee assistance program.

"With limited access to the public services available (such as education, healthcare, etc), refugees struggle daily to find hope," the organization's website stated. "JoyCare wants to reach out to this community and welcome them to our family! We have had the privilege of opening up a class (2–5 y/o) and subsidizing their tuition fees."[13] In late 2018, JoyCare founder and then program director Sandy Ooi reported that sponsors had been found to cover tuition fees for eight of the 14 refugee children enrolled and that "three refugee teenage volunteers [are] being trained in vocation."

Sandy and her American co-worker Nanci Long also helped the girls access online classes in English, Mathematics, and Chemistry or Biology, with plans to add Computer Science in the near future. "Our Providence Anglican Church started the Learning Lab," Sandy explained, "an online, self-driven, home-schooling program." Focusing on educating refugee youth in Indonesia, the curriculum prepares "them to test for a high school equivalency diploma that will enable them to pursue higher education."[14]

From left: Trinh, Ngoc (Vy), and My in the Learning Lab.

Trinh described a typical week: "From Monday until Friday I teach at JoyCare from 8 A.M.–12 P.M. After school I take a nap. In the afternoon I learn English by myself with my mom and my sister. Every Tuesday I'm learning online, and on Saturday and Sunday I'm learning, helping my mom, and going to church." By July 2019, Mrs. Lua's daughter, Nguyen Thi Uyen, had joined the group, volunteering each weekday morning and now studying together three afternoons a week. Meanwhile, Sandy had moved Vy to another of her daycare centers "so she can get some experience working with non-refugee children…. Sometimes the girls are too relaxed

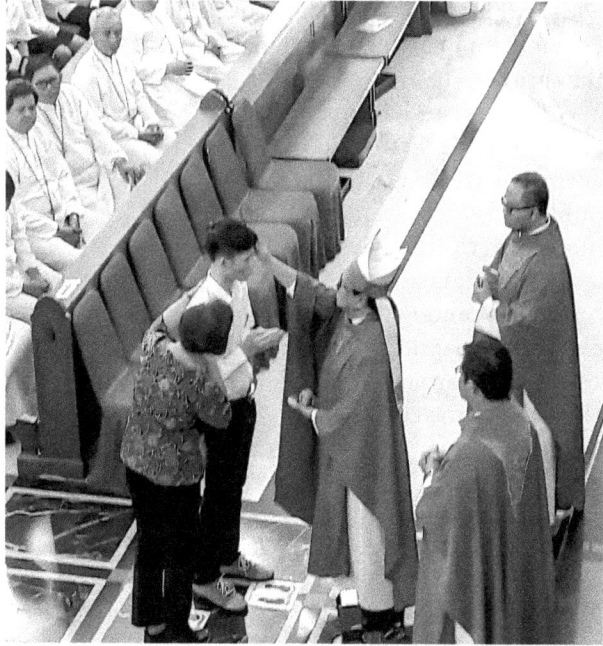

Mrs. Loan's son, Ho Van Loc, being confirmed (courtesy Tran Thi Thanh Loan).

Mrs. Loan's and Mrs. Lua's families at their children's confirmation, November 10, 2019 (courtesy Tran Thi Thanh Loan and Tran Thi Lua).

with the kids because they are so familiar, and they are living within the same 'standard.' I want them to understand that in the real world, the expectations are higher than what they are used to."

In contrast, Tuan initially remained determined to be accepted into the Indonesian public-school system, going by motorbike to attend lessons with an Indonesian language tutor at a refugee center in the hope of eventually passing the test and selection interview. "I failed," he told me in June 2019:

> Other subjects got great score, but they told me my *Bahasa* score was low, just 40, so I cannot access the class, and they tell me if I want to join, I need to pay 2 million IDR [around USD140] each year. So now I am waiting for IOM—If they accept the payment, I could join. I waited for six months and studied hard, but it is zero.... I want to ... improve my knowledge. That's my free right; we should try. Waiting here, I do not know when we will go, so [in] front of my eyes, which things good I must catch [*sic*].

Mrs. Loan in the church grounds (courtesy Tran Thi Thanh Loan).

Continuing to learn Indonesian with the local Catholic community, he also strove to better his English by borrowing university textbooks from friends and volunteered with Christian charities as well as the local Catholic Church, which the families attended without fail each Sunday—their only formal outing for the week.

Although I was willing to sponsor his studies, if necessary, in the end, he managed to clarify that it was his language difficulties that were preventing him from being enrolled. By July 2019, Sandy and Nanci had come to the rescue once again, setting up an additional Learning Lab online class, attended three mornings a week by a group of refugee teenage boys from such diverse countries as Sri Lanka, Iraq, and Afghanistan, and including Tuan and Mrs. Loan's son, Ho Van Loc. "We coach and direct them," Sandy elaborated, "but it is about 95 per cent self-directed. I tell them if they break rules, they get replaced in the program. Ain't nobody got time for that!" Tuan wrote to say how much he was enjoying the classes: "I study every day. I know many friends. They so great and they from many different countries [*sic*] ... from them I learned many things...."

In early October 2019, his tenacity finally paid off with the award of a refugee

Dear: Shira Sebban

"Hello miss shira". How are you, this
is the Fist time I write letter, Thank you
for help My Family.

- My name is Loc, I'm 17 year old,
and I am is son of Loan and Loi.

Today I Writing this letter Cause
Share with you about My
life in Indonesia.

Ever since I move Tangrang to jankata
My life very boring, 1 week I have 3days
come to class and many day else I'm just
sleep and study in My room, day by day
I Just Think "how can I improve My english"
for better and My sister, she have a friend
name sandy, miss. Sandy Talk with my
sister about learn english on computer, That's
So Great" and my sister request me join to
Sandy class and I accept her request and
Join sandy class,

First page of a letter written by Loc to the author in July 2019, shortly after he joined the Learning Lab.

residential scholarship to undertake a four-year hospitality management program at UPH College. A private Christian senior high school in Tangerang, the college, which has more than 1,000 students from 34 Indonesian provinces, is under the auspices of Pelita Harapan University, billed as the first in Indonesia to introduce programs completely taught in English. Henceforth, Tuan would live in the dormitory on campus, having embarked on a comprehensive course for which students normally need to satisfy numerous pre-enrolment requirements, including supplying identity documents and legalized copies of academic results, as well as paying a "development fee" of 47,000,000 IDR (around USD3,300) plus tuition fees of 19,750,000 IDR (just under USD1,400) per semester.[15] He had learned about the opportunity from the associated Harvest Mission Community Church (HMCC),[16] where he had become an enthusiastic member, responding to a subsequent IOM appeal to "qualified and interested" refugees.

"It is not easy to approach anything without conditions," Tuan told me, explaining that he had waited a long time after attending an interview and sitting the admission test to learn he had been accepted, undertaking to approach his studies seriously and follow school rules. He subsequently managed to help his sister Trinh with her enrolment. They had never been part of such a large institution: "I joined at mid-term; that's why I just run and ask. In school we have swimming pool, basketball stadium, soccer field, futsal, badminton, and some things else but cannot observe whole [sic]...."

Noting that other students had a computer, he asked me to help him acquire a laptop with a price tag of 8,900,000 IDR (over USD600). Keen to encourage his studies and initially thinking I could share the cost with several past donors, I contacted the school to better understand its policy. An added complication was how to send him the money: "I tried many way but no body ready [sic] give me bank account," he lamented. I was urged, however, to communicate directly with Tuan and visit UPH's website to learn more about the Hospitality Management Program. "Better yet, visit the university if you happen to be in the country."

In the end, we were unable to supply the computer: There were simply too many competing demands on our limited funds, Tuan's request coinciding with Mrs. Lua's urgent need to have her court documents translated in the hope of assisting her family's resettlement.[17] "No matter just help Mrs. Lua," he graciously acquiesced. "Thank you, Mrs. Shira, please help her." For although he had managed to secure his dream of attaining a formal education, he never lost sight of the group's ultimate goal, accepting that he might not be able to complete the course should they be resettled in a third country.

Meanwhile, the adults strove to learn largely independently—IOM providing those aged 16 and over with two-hour English classes twice a week—not easy for parents who had either never been to school or had mostly left in Grade 3. They also took responsibility for supplementing the younger children's education. "In the morning, when I finish cooking, I study English," Mrs. Lua told me. "I study alone. When I don't know [how to] read, I asked my daughter. My children [by] themselves study an English program on the Internet in the morning, and in the afternoon, they study math on YouTube. My sister-in-law

Tuan in his trainee chef uniform (courtesy Tran Ngoc Tuan).

teaches my youngest son. She found programs and downloaded them on the phone tablet you gave me." "I don't go to school; I study at home," Mrs. Lua's younger sister, Tran Thi Le, added. "I wake up, pray, and teach myself English; the rest of my time is spent socializing. The Indonesian community is very friendly. Life in Indonesia is good but not stable. I'm really scared. I hope the [overseas] community will help me settle in a third country so I can return to school soon."

Finally, in late September 2019, the youngest child in the group, six-year-old Hoa Nhien, was accepted by a local Christian primary institution, which would become known as KANIA School. Her mother Mrs. Phuc explained that she had learned about the school from some women, who belonged to the Protestant church, and had gone to enquire whether her daughter could be enrolled. "I knew the cost was very high. I said I would do anything for my child to go to school.... She has to speak *Bahasa*, but they also teach English."

While the school normally charged a one-off payment of 1,000,000 IDR (around USD68) for registration fees, uniform, activities, field trips, and books, as well as 100,000 IDR for tuition per month (around USD6.80), the family was only asked to pay half: "They know that we are refugees and no work [*sic*] ... Every 16 days I give money. I will pay the tuition for my child."

Mrs. Decy, responsible for the school's curriculum as well as teacher training, was pleased with the little girl's development. "It is a delight to have Nhien in our school.... The family has been cooperative as well to help Nhien to progress in her study." Partnership between staff and parents is the basis of educating children "in the same vision," she explained: "Our school is helping the students to learn the Word of God through school subjects (Bible based). When the students understand what God's will in their life is, then they can know the purpose of why they need to study. They don't just go to school because everyone at their age goes to school. Coming to school isn't a burden but a delight."

While I was keen for the other young children to have the same opportunity, the school, as we quickly discovered, only had one more place available that year. Nor could it offer as generous a discount as it had to Hoa Nhien, although Mrs. Decy stressed that as a non-profit, it subsidized all students whose families could not afford to pay the regular fees. Such monthly payments were out of the question for Mrs. Loan, so I offered to help her youngest daughter Nhi, by then aged 8. Total cost for the rest of the academic year would be 1,900.000 IDR (around USD130) as she had missed the first three months. After being tested in Indonesian and Mathematics, she was immediately accepted and began school the next day. I would continue supporting her education until the family finally left Indonesia, eventually splitting the costs with SBS Vietnamese radio producer and presenter Mai Pham when they later doubled under the online learning constraints imposed during the COVID-19 pandemic.

Each adult received a monthly

Nhi proudly poses in her new school uniform, October 2019 (courtesy Tran Thi Thanh Loan).

allowance from IOM of 1,250,500 IDR, or around USD88 (about USD3 a day), children allocated 500,000 IDR each (USD35), from which they were expected to pay all expenses. This amount, provided to the roughly 7,700 refugees and asylum seekers under IOM care, was considerably higher than what UNHCR could afford to pay, its efforts confined to cases of exceptional need.[18]

"Every month, on the day I receive the IOM subsidy, I go shopping for food for one month," Mrs. Loan told me. "Every morning I prepare meals for the whole day. IOM doesn't allow us to work so I just stay home learning English via YouTube and taking care of my family.... In the afternoon I go out for a walk and interact and socialize with Indonesians. From time to time, I call my friends in Vietnam." Mrs. Phuc described her newfound contentment: "My life is happy. I feel better here than in Vietnam. I exercise in the morning, then cook, and teach my young children Vietnamese cooking after the day is over."

Meals were prepared in their communal open-air kitchen on the top floor, the families often choosing to eat sitting on the floor in the hallway to avoid the heat. IOM also subsidized basic medical care, enabling them to attend *Puskesmas*, the network of public community health clinics, for a minimal fee. Not being eligible for national health insurance, however, refugees and asylum seekers could not afford more complicated and expensive treatments unless IOM agreed to pay upfront.[19]

Indeed, notwithstanding their efforts, there was no prospect of the families being integrated permanently with formal rights in Indonesia, which was their "country of refuge" or "first asylum," now known increasingly as a "transit state."[20] Despite there being no coherent refugee policy with consistent regulations, they undoubtedly remained barred from officially participating in the economy and legally earning money. Unable to obtain local identity documents, they could neither formally access the labor and housing markets, nor benefit from social services, thereby fostering further dependency on basic aid provided by IOM and other nongovernment organizations. As UNCHR has made clear: "In Indonesia, only voluntary repatriation and resettlement are currently available to refugees."[21]

And chances for resettlement, notably by UNHCR, were minimal. Determined to prioritize "appropriate temporary

Mrs. Phuc cooking (courtesy Nguyen Thi Phuc).

Sharing a meal. On left: Mr. Long, son Dang, Mrs. Lua, son Koi. On right: Mr. Loi, Mrs. Loan, daughter Tran.

stay measures as well as livelihood opportunities," the organization ran a poster campaign, funded by European Union Humanitarian Aid, in late 2017, encouraging those registered with it to "prepare for your future":

- With such **limited places for resettlement** from Indonesia, focus energies on **activities that will enrich your life**.
- Use your special **talents and skills** by volunteering to **support other refugees** and **your host community**.
- Engage in **sports** and other positive **recreational activities**.
- Learn **Bahasa Indonesia** to engage with the Indonesian people who have welcomed you into their community.
- Participate in local **Indonesian cultural events**.
- Take advantage of **educational opportunities** for yourself and your children.
- Enroll in **vocational training** programs and online **university** courses.
- Expand your skills and experience through **internships and apprenticeships**.
- Always **respect the laws and customs of Indonesia**, and remember that you are a **guest in this country**.[22]

The families were doing their best, but still, the fact that they were in a "protracted refugee situation," considered outsiders or long-term guests of a "reluctant host," forced to live in "tolerated transit" for an indefinite period without "adequate and dignified means of subsistence"—a situation which has been described as "benevolent neglect"—only made us more determined to help them secure "effective protection" elsewhere.[23]

In the meantime, the Queensland Vietnamese community (VCA-QLD) had launched its financial campaign to privately sponsor Mrs. Phuc and her children with a fundraising dinner and entertainment, held in a Vietnamese restaurant in Brisbane on March 3, 2018. At Dr. Bui's invitation, I gave a speech, which in retrospect was far too long, the translator diligently repeating each sentence in Vietnamese to the understandably restless audience. A video prepared by Mrs. Phuc and her children was also shown, and during the evening, she spoke directly with the sell-out, 300-strong audience by phone from Tangerang. Around USD12,000 was raised that night, Dr. Bui presented with numerous donations of AUD100 bills, largely saved from hard-earned wages. Another function, held at the Linh Son Buddhist Temple in Darra, Queensland, on May 12, 2018, raised a further USD10,000 or so—"successful beyond expectations," to quote Mr. Van Pham.

The question of what to

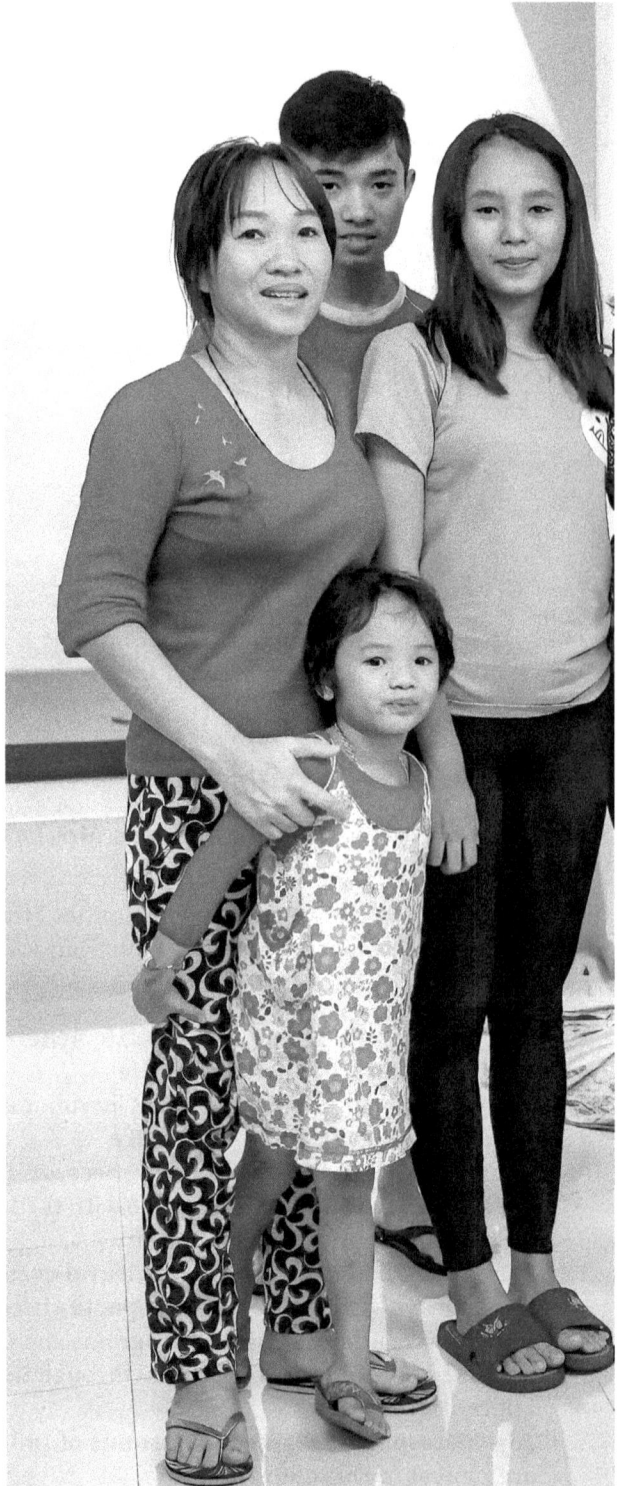

From left: Mrs. Phuc with Nhien, Tuan, and Trinh (courtesy Nguyen Thi Phuc).

Mr. Van Pham and fellow VCA-QLD Refugee Committee member My-Linh Do addressing the crowd at the fundraising function in Brisbane on March 3, 2018 (courtesy Dr. Cuong Trong Bui).

do with such a substantial sum was becoming more pressing, although at that stage, we were still under the illusion that we could proceed with an application under Australia's new Community Support Program (CSP), redirecting the money, should we fail, via VOICE to its Canadian counterpart, Private Sponsorship of Refugees program (PSR).

While Sunshine continued to collect clothing, books, and school supplies for the families, duly arranging a delivery to Tangerang, the group had been summoned to the UNHCR office in Jakarta to collect their new refugee cards on March 9, 2018. Underpinned by a biometric data collection system, UNHCR hoped the new technology would "enjoy greater recognition from government officials and provide enhanced protection" for registered asylum seekers and refugees.[24]

By then, I was urging VCA-QLD to go through the requirements for Australia's Global Special Humanitarian Visa subclass 202, for which we still hoped Mrs. Phuc and her children would be eligible. We were becoming particularly concerned about the fast-apparent myriad of fees—according to the official website, "there is no visa application charge for this visa unless you are proposed under the Community Support Program"[25]—as well as the character requirements.

Temple Abbess, The Venerable Thich Nu Tri Luu, presenting Dr. Bui with the check on May 12, 2018 (courtesy Dr. Cuong Trong Bui).

"You may have to provide a police certificate from each country you have lived in for 12 months or more during the past ten years after you turned 16 years of age," I told Dr. Bui and Doan Trung.[26] "I do not know how Mrs. Phuc could arrange this with Vietnam—it would be impossible, I would suggest." Nevertheless, I agreed to assist by having a closer look at the application forms required by Australian immigration, while VCA-QLD sought legal advice. Their solicitor, Hien Thi Nguyen, did not mince her words: "A migration agent and lawyer who takes on an obvious losing case, giving a client false hope, can face disciplinary action, regardless as to whether it was on a pro-bono basis.[27] ... Another solution, which is more appropriate with better chance of success, will be for the Vietnamese leaders here to work with UNHCR and to seek help from Vietnamese leaders in USA, UK, Canada, Germany, or France to see whether they can help sponsor the family to any one of these countries where refugee law is more flexible."

Although we were only too aware the families stood little chance of being formally referred for resettlement through UNHCR, Dr. Bui agreed: "We have to be

UNHCR No.:

Removed for Security

Name / Nama:

Tran Nguyen Hoa Nhien

Date of Birth / Tanggal Lahir: Sex / Jenis Kelamin:
Perempuan - F

Country of Origin / Negara Asal:
Viet Nam

Issued Date /   Expired Date /
Tanggal Pengeluaran: Tanggal Habis Berlaku:
08/03/2018   08/03/2021

UNHCR
The UN Refugee Agency

2017BAP008545

The new UNHCR refugee card issued to then almost five-year-old Tran Nguyen Hoa Nhien.

realistic and think more about the waiting time and the education of the children. The best solution we have now is to wait until the end of March. By then we will discuss again. We have received strong support from the community. I still have some hope."

At the same time, we had seemingly hit a hurdle in the Canadian immigration application process, which required those refugees privately sponsored by "Groups of Five" Canadian citizens or permanent residents (G5) to provide valid proof of refugee status recognition by UNHCR or a foreign state.[28] And no, the families' refugee cards—the only official evidence they had—were not acceptable.

Known as a "mandate letter" or "refugee status recognition certificate," this status-certifying document was not routinely provided by UNHCR in Indonesia.[29] Fortunately, however, my Sydney-based colleague Alison Battisson, founder and director of charitable law firm Human Rights for All,[30] came to our rescue and the mandate letters were quickly produced, the families returning to UNHCR's Jakarta headquarters to collect them in person on March 22, 2018. "We have a reception site for refugees on the side of the building for crowd control purposes," a UNHCR official explained to Alison, requesting the families give advance notice of when they intended to arrive. "Sometimes we got hundreds of refugees coming and building management got nervous [*sic*]."

Mrs. Phuc was given two copies of her family's letter, one certified just in case we decided to proceed with her Australian application. In preparation, I had also sent her son Tuan a link to the Vietnamese version of the booklet, *Life in Australia: Australian Values and Principles*—required reading for adult potential visa applicants, who are also expected to sign what is known as the "Australian Values Statement."[31]

(((o))) UNHCR
United Nations High Commissioner for Refugees
Haut Commissariat des Nations Unies pour les réfugiés

UNHCR
Representation for Indonesia

Menara Ravindo, 14ᵗʰ Floor   Tel. +62 21 2964 3602
Jl. Kebon Sirih, Kav – 75   Fax +62 21 2964 3601
Jakarta Pusat 10340   Email: insja@unhcr.org
Indonesia

19 March 2018

Notre/Our code   18/INSJA/HCR/30468

Re: **Status Confirmation – Tran Thi Lua and Family**

To whom it may concern,

Upon their request, I would like to confirm the status of the following individuals:

Case Number	Name	Sex	Place of Birth	Date of Birth	Country of Origin
	Tran Thi Lua	Female	Ha Tinh, Vietnam		Vietnam
	Nguyen Long	Male	Phan Thiet, Binh Thuan, Vietnam		Vietnam
	Nguyen Thi Uyen	Female	Phan Thiet, Binh Thuan, Vietnam		Vietnam
▮▮▮▮▮	Nguyen Hai Dang	Male	Phan Thiet, Binh Thuan, Vietnam		Vietnam
	Nguyen Dang Koi	Male	Phan Thiet, Binh Thuan, Vietnam		Vietnam
	Tran Thi Le	Female	Phan Thiet, Binh Thuan, Vietnam		Vietnam
	Tran Thi Thanh Ngoc	Female	Phan Thiet, Binh Thuan, Vietnam		Vietnam
▮▮▮▮▮	Nguyen Thi Kim Nhung	Female	Phan Thiet, Binh Thuan, Vietnam		Vietnam
▮▮▮▮▮	Nguyen Tai	Male	Phan Thiet, Binh Thuan, Vietnam		Vietnam

(((o))) UNHCR

UNHCR hereby confirms that the individuals registered with UNHCR on March 2017 and were recognized as refugees on 28 April 2017.

I understand from the individuals that you have requested our confirmation of their status in relation to private sponsorship submitted by a family member residing in Canada.

I hope this clarifies your concerns, and should you require further information please contact our Office.

Thank you for your kind attention and for your continued cooperation with our Office.

Sincerely,

Jeffrey Savage
Senior Protection Officer

Mrs. Lua's family's mandate letter (courtesy Tran Thi Lua).

The official added some unsolicited advice: "Private sponsorship is quite financially demanding. The family will have to spend their own money to travel to Jakarta for interview with the destination country, and often immigration insisted for the refugees to pay the escorts. Have the family discuss about the financial implication that cannot be covered by either UNHCR nor IOM [*sic*]?"

Simultaneously juggling the various requirements of Canadian and Australian immigration, I immediately forwarded the mandate letters to Kyanh Do at VOICE Canada before writing to VCA-QLD's solicitor, Hien Nguyen, to express my growing concerns, noting: "The Canadian questions are much friendlier and easier than the Australian ones."

The Vietnamese authorities may not have regarded Mrs. Phuc and her children as organizers of their original attempted escape to Australia in March 2015, but as far as the Australian government was concerned, they had tried on two separate occasions to reach Australia "illegally by boat," and we knew this would be held against them. Moreover, the Australian immigration forms insist on asking whether other family members are already in Australia, and if so, what their status is. "If Mrs. Phuc happens to have a sibling already in Australia who is not a citizen, she needs to declare this openly," I wrote to Hien. "Canada does not have a similar provision."[32]

We had other concerns pertaining to Mrs. Phuc's demonstrated ability to speak and write "adequate English"—she could always learn, we reasoned; the requirement for applicants to satisfy "the regional and global settlement priorities" of the Australian government[33] and the priority given to those prepared to "live and work in regional or rural Australia"; as well as the lengthy visa processing times, the authorities warning: "The decision process could take many months, or even years. The number of applications we receive for resettlement each year is far greater than available visas."[34]

Our main worry, however, centered on the high financial cost involved: "If we go ahead and apply and Mrs. Phuc gets rejected, will the more than AUD27,000 [USD18,600] in visa application fees be returned to the Queensland Vietnamese community so you can donate it (as per our understanding) to help VOICE Canada sponsor her and her children privately to settle in Canada instead?"

At first, the situation seemed unclear. After all, the CSP private sponsorship scheme was brand new and not all details had been revealed yet. Nevertheless, we knew that refunds were generally only paid in limited circumstances.[35] Hien was more direct: "As to the application visa fee, it will not be refunded. I have tried to recover for clients in these circumstances and have not been successful. Given the above scenarios, it may be more worthwhile to go through Canada. I have spoken to a very experienced barrister on her matter—and the future looks no good." Trung concurred: "I'd lean towards abandoning Australia and asking VOICE Canada to take her on. The main consideration to abandon Australia, though, is not money but likelihood of rejection."

On March 27, 2018, the Australian government published the list of Approved Proposing Organisations (APOs), or community groups formally appointed to connect private sponsors with potential CSP applicants and manage their visa process.[36] APOs were also meant eventually to help new arrivals settle into Australia and achieve financial independence within the first year. They could charge varying, non-refundable fees for their services—in addition to the already steep visa application fees—the total cost mounting to AUD100,000 (just over USD69,000) for a family of five.[37] By now, it was clear that should Mrs. Phuc's visa application fail, VCA-QLD would be left greatly out of pocket.

"So, it is important to decide if you wish to proceed with Mrs. Phuc, or whether you want to support her through Canada instead, or sponsor another refugee family with a better chance?" I wrote to Dr. Bui. "Otherwise, you may miss out on a refugee place…. It would be a good idea for the Queensland Vietnamese community to decide which APO you wish to work with and perhaps to ask them for some advice."

Hien urged Dr. Bui to leave the ultimate decision to Mrs. Phuc: "Given the success rate to Australia is very small,[38] … whilst to Canada it may be higher, talk to Mrs. Phuc Nguyen and determine where does she and her family want to go? … Also, perhaps Mrs. Phuc should apply to BOTH countries—and then go to whichever country accepts her and her family. In the event of Australia, I am happy to check the forms once completed." Trung disagreed: "To me, Canada is the way to go, but this decision is for Dr. Bui et al to make."

Indeed, another consideration was that while Australia only allocated up to 1,000 places for CSP applicants within its refugee and humanitarian quota, the fees charged subsidizing government expenditure, private sponsorship places in Canada were increasing each year and were additional to other programs. In 2017, the Canadian government announced a "multi-year Immigration Levels Plan," intending to welcome 57,000 people through its Private Sponsorship of Refugees program (PSR) over the next three years. Furthermore, "most of the growth in resettlement spaces" was in this category. By early 2022, in the wake of the COVID-19 pandemic, projected numbers would jump to a target of just over 85,000 privately sponsored refugees between 2022 and 2024.[39]

The situation came to a head in mid–April when following discussions with both its legal advisor and Mrs. Phuc, the Queensland Vietnamese community decided not to continue with its pursuit of an Australian visa. "If Australia is so difficult, please send my family to Canada," Mrs. Phuc told me. "Wherever if that better for my family. Any way you got we'll follow."

It was the right decision: As we should have realized earlier, Mrs. Phuc and her children actually had zero chance of being accepted by Australia because they had registered with UNHCR in Indonesia after July 1, 2014.[40]

Even an apparently routine requirement such as providing a photo of each family member for the Canadian visa applications proved difficult due to the language barrier. The detailed photo specifications listed in English on the website were obviously incomprehensible to them, despite the helpful images included,[41] and although we supplied a written Vietnamese translation, the group had trouble communicating the instructions to the Indonesian commercial photographer. In the end, after numerous phone calls, texts, and unacceptable photos, I contacted Sunshine, who arranged for them to consult a translator fluent in both Indonesian and Vietnamese.

No sooner was one drama averted, however, than another would arise. On April 19, 2018, a standard request from IOM that each adult sign a document, also known as a "declaration of compliance," agreeing to remain in their assigned Indonesian accommodation to continue to receive IOM support services,[42] resulted in mass panic and a call to Kyanh Do at VOICE Canada for reassurance, before they finally all signed. "The problem is when they are scared, they will just do whatever and not fully understand the consequences," Nhi commented.

We were hoping to submit all the applications to Immigration, Refugees and Citizenship Canada (IRCC) by the end of May 2018, but that was before Mrs. Loan's husband, Ho Trung Loi, unexpectedly arrived in Jakarta. "Today I am happy to inform you that my husband came to Indonesia to visit us," she blithely announced to me on Facebook Messenger on May 23. "I feel very happy."

We were delighted too—until upon further questioning, she revealed that he planned to stay with the family for about three weeks before returning to Vietnam "because he is not [recognized as] a refugee and if he stays here for a long time, he will find it hard to go abroad."

The last we had heard of Mr. Loi, he had returned to work as a fisherman, albeit under police surveillance and confined to his local surrounds of La Gi township, Binh Thuan province. For the past several months, however, he had apparently been free to travel further afield. I had not realized he even had a passport—the rest of the family had arrived in Indonesia without papers—but Mrs. Loan now explained he had obtained one in 2014, before the family's first attempt to flee to Australia, and she eventually sent me a copy.

It turned out, as Nhi discovered, and I reported to Kyanh: "He just tried his luck and somehow his name was not blacklisted so he bought the ticket and boarded the plane." Asked how he could afford the flight, he explained he had borrowed the sum from his brother. Or at least that was what we believed at the time, the true story only revealed years later by Mrs. Loan's nephew, Bao Anh Tran, who as a flight attendant with Vietnam Airlines, had proved integral to Mr. Loi's departure.

"One day, I received a flight schedule including a flight to Jakarta," Bao recounted to me in August 2022 from the United Kingdom where he was now safely resettled.

That night, I texted my aunt via Facebook, offering to bring her food. After thinking for a while, she told me that all she wanted was for me to help bring my uncle to Indonesia to be reunited with his family. I was worried because while as an ordinary citizen, it was easy to go abroad, my uncle was a newly released inmate still on probation.

I advised my aunt not to proceed, but she did not agree and insisted on borrowing money to buy plane tickets. We decided my uncle would fly with me. He was suffering from temporary amnesia due to being beaten on the head by the police and tortured too much. We planned to leave our homes at 2 A.M. so that we wouldn't be followed by the police, and no one would notice; then get in the car to the airport to catch the flight at 8.20 A.M.; and we discussed how to deal with airport police and customs if detected. After weighing my luggage and getting my ticket, I told my uncle to start queuing up at customs for the exit stamp, and I went through the security gate for the crew.

This was the most important moment. We were all worried, including our loved ones at home, watching our progress, and praying for a good trip. If we got through customs with our passport stamped, we would be successful. Otherwise, my uncle would be arrested again and could be taken to court and continue to be tortured in prison. We said goodbye to each other and arranged to meet at the door of the plane.

After I completed my exit procedures, I stopped and looked at my uncle, who was waiting for customs to stamp his passport for exit. He appeared to be having some problems as the customs official was asking many questions. I decided to take a risk, going up to my uncle and talking to the officer to get him through. I clipped USD200 into my uncle's

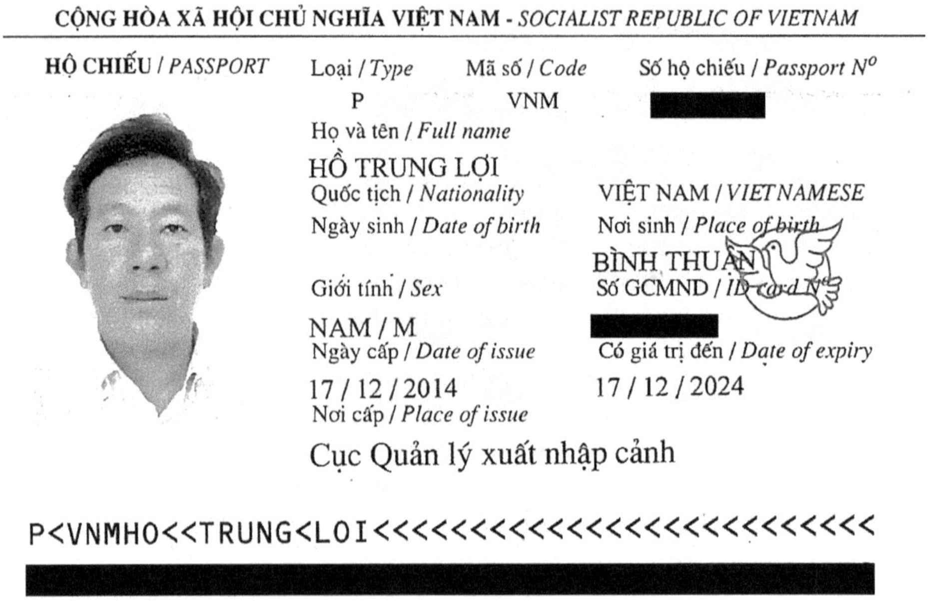

CỘNG HÒA XÃ HỘI CHỦ NGHĨA VIỆT NAM - *SOCIALIST REPUBLIC OF VIETNAM*

HỘ CHIẾU / *PASSPORT*   Loại / *Type*   Mã số / *Code*   Số hộ chiếu / *Passport Nº*

P   VNM

Họ và tên / *Full name*

HỒ TRUNG LỢI
Quốc tịch / *Nationality*   VIỆT NAM / *VIETNAMESE*

Ngày sinh / *Date of birth*   Nơi sinh / *Place of birth*

BÌNH THUẬN

Giới tính / *Sex*   Số GCMND / *ID card Nº*

NAM / M
Ngày cấp / *Date of issue*   Có giá trị đến / *Date of expiry*

17 / 12 / 2014   17 / 12 / 2024
Nơi cấp / *Place of issue*

Cục Quản lý xuất nhập cảnh

P<VNMHO<<TRUNG<LOI<<<<<<<<<<<<<<<<<<<<<<<<<<

Above and below: **Mr. Loi's passport including his departure stamp from Vietnamese immigration (courtesy Ho Trung Loi).**

passport as a bribe, and the officer turned a blind eye and stamped his passport immediately. We then got on the plane and flew to Jakarta. When we arrived, we were so happy and broke down when we saw each other. We thought we were dreaming, as we never believed we would be able to leave Vietnam.[43]

While the family would never have been reunited without Bao's help, it was Mrs. Loan's sheer courage and persistence that had convinced her nephew to act in the first place—and there were consequences, as Bao would discover after returning to Vietnam: "I went back to my hometown, where I learned the terrible news that the Vietnamese government had

VIỆT NAM - IMMIGRATION
THỊ THỰC — *VISAS*
2 3 MAY 2018

9

IMMIGRATION INDONESIA
VISA EXEMPTION
SOEKARNO - HATTA

2 3 MAY 2018

PERMITTED TO ENTER AND STAY
FOR 30 DAYS FROM DATE SHOWN ABOVE
"WORK PROHIBITED"
"NOT EXTENDABLE"
ART. 43 ACT. 6/2011

sent many police to our family home to scare and interrogate us, demanding that we hand over Mr. Ho Trung Loi, but everyone said they didn't know where he was. Then, because I had participated in political activities against the state, I quit my job at Vietnam Airlines. I crossed the border to Cambodia to fly to the UK, where I was granted refugee status."

Back in May 2018, we could not understand why Mr. Loi would go back to Vietnam given what he had gone through and how he had been treated. As I told Kyanh, "We would love him to apply for refugee status with UNHCR in Jakarta and stay with his family and then resettle with them in Canada. But we don't know if this is possible and don't want to make his life worse."

VOICE Canada advocate Le Luong agreed: "I wouldn't recommend him going back to Vietnam or else he might not get back out. He might be arrested when he returns since his family is in Indonesia." Moreover, she added, if Mr. Loi could go back to Vietnam without incident, "Canada will question why he is able to return, and the rest of the family cannot. This may jeopardize everyone's application, not only his family."

As I pointed out to Le, however, both Mrs. Loan and Mrs. Lua were "the ones really at risk who can't go back. There was a wanted ad on Vietnamese television for them just last week.... Mr. Loi is not in this situation—he served his entire sentence and has not tried to escape by boat again." Indeed, Grace Bui had shared the authorities' continued interest in the two mothers on Facebook on May 18, 2018: "For the past two days the Vietnamese government posted a wanted poster on TV for Mrs. Tran Thi Lua and Mrs. Tran Loan."

I decided to consult Australian human rights lawyer Alison Battisson who agreed to discuss with UNHCR's Jakarta office. Asked by Mrs. Loan for our views, we urged her husband to apply to stay in Indonesia as a refugee. "But we don't want to make him do the wrong thing," I cautioned. "That's why we're seeking advice first. IOM is not taking any new refugee cases since mid–March 2018, and we don't want him to end up separated from his family or in detention." Alison was less dramatic: "Does the family have sufficient resources to support Loi in Indonesia without IOM support? If so, that appears best." Nhi confirmed: "They can support him with their existing allowances. He does not eat much, Mrs. Loan said!"

Grace emphasized, however, that official procedure must be followed: Mr. Loi could not simply apply for asylum, without anyone helping to guide and translate for him. Otherwise, he would never get an interview. Nhi agreed: "I don't want him to rush and mess up his chance.... I worry if he just walks in and applies and gets a 'no' right from the start because he speaks to the wrong person, that will be a disaster."

To make matters worse, as we soon discovered, the couple had panicked. A lawyer in Vietnam, who was a friend of Vo An Don, had advised that should Mr. Loi fail to apply for refugee status, he could "just go home peacefully and he should be ok," Nhi explained. "When they were told it could affect everyone, Mrs. Loan was so scared she rented a hotel [room] to stay with Mr. Loi, and even planned to run away with him, which is illegal and would get all of them into big trouble with IOM."

In the end, Grace agreed, at Nhi's request, to fly to Jakarta once more to provide support. "I have been working with the UN and they are going to accept Mr. Loi," she told me on May 31, 2018, "but it would be a while for them to squeeze him in and his visa is running out on June 22. I am planning to go there and register him directly with the UN."

His initial UNHCR registration interview was held on June 11. "Grace came in with Mr. Loi, but a few minutes later, Grace came out," Mrs. Loan later described. "Someone worked with UNHCR to translate for him by phone." Grace also subsequently helped to arrange his photo as per Canadian specifications. "Today my

UNHCR No.:   *Removed for Security*

Name / Nama:
Ho Trung Loi

Date of Birth / Tanggal Lahir: Sex / Jenis Kelamin:
                                   Lelaki - M

Country of Origin / Negara Asal:
Viet Nam

Issued Date /   Expired Date /
Tanggal Pengeluaran: Tanggal Habis Berlaku:
27/06/2018   08/03/2021

Removed for Security

2017BAP012881

UNHCR
The UN Refugee Agency

The bearer of this card is registered and under UNHCR's protection mandate. If you have found this card, please return to:

Pemegang kartu ini adalah seseorang yang terdaftar dan dibawah mandat perlindungan UNHCR. Jika anda menemukan kartu ini, mohon kembalikan kepada:

UNHCR Indonesia
Menara Ravindo Lt. 14
Jl. Kebon Sirih Kav. 75
Jakarta Pusat 10347
Indonesia

Tel: (62-21) 2964 3602
Fax: (62-21) 2964 3601
Email: insja@unhcr.org

Kartu ini Hak Milik UNHCR

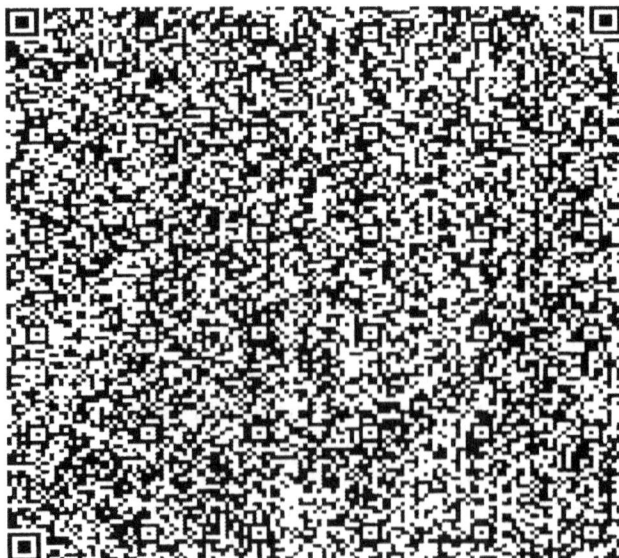

Front and back of Mr. Loi's UNHCR refugee card (courtesy Ho Trung Loi).

husband went to UN," Mrs. Loan reported, "and very happy when my husband UN granted the paper [*sic*]." She forwarded an official UNHCR "Under Consideration Letter,"[44] which stated that he had applied for refugee status in Indonesia and was "considered a person of concern to UNHCR," who "should, in particular, be protected from forcible return to a country where he ... could face threats to his ... life or freedom."

A second interview was scheduled for June 20, after Grace had left Jakarta. "We need to wait until the UN decides if he is going to pass the interview," she told me the following day. "It might take a month or more for them to do so." To our surprise, he was issued a UNHCR refugee identity card a mere week later.

The card was accompanied by an official notification—in English, Farsi, Arabic, and Somali—explaining that he had been recognized as a refugee by UNHCR and that while the new ID card did not specify the grantee's status, it incorporated "a range of security features, including a link to a mobile phone application that will allow Indonesian authorities to confirm your registration with UNHCR when necessary."

Once again, UNHCR took the opportunity to emphasize the minimal chances of resettlement available to refugees in Indonesia: "You will be contacted in the event you are identified for resettlement, but with the very limited resettlement opportunities available for refugees in Indonesia this is unfortunately not likely. Only the most vulnerable refugees in Indonesia can be prioritized for resettlement. Resettlement is not an automatic right available to all refugees."

Indeed, by 2018, the number of resettlements from Indonesia was down to about 400 people a year—less than three per cent of the total refugee and asylum seeker population of around 14,000.[45] Worldwide, the statistics were even starker, UNHCR maintaining: "An unprecedented 70.8 million people ... have been forced from home. Among them are nearly 25.9 million refugees, over half of whom are under the age of 18." Only 92,400 of the 1.4 million estimated to need resettlement—0.066 per cent—were actually resettled, including 55,680 with UNHCR's assistance. Canada admitted over 28,000, including close to 19,000 who were privately sponsored—more than any of the other 24 countries involved, although as Canadian legal scholar Dr. Shauna Labman

Mr. Loi reunited with his family once again, September 2018 (courtesy Tran Thi Thanh Loan).

has commented, "Unfortunately, this accomplishment speaks more to the diminishment of resettlement places elsewhere than to increases in Canada."[46]

While in Indonesia, Grace had also intended to try to assist Mrs. Phuc's husband, Tran Van Yen, who was still languishing in Tanjung Pinang detention center on Bintan Island. This was after Mrs. Phuc had finally clarified—after considerable confusion—that she wanted to include him in her Canadian visa application. She had originally asked Grace to approach UNHCR on his behalf in June 2017, when having practically completed his one-year sentence for fishing illegally in Indonesian waters, he had been on the verge of being deported to Vietnam. In response, UNHCR had requested further information about his situation, Mr. Yen later revealing that a staff member had come to see him the following month in what he called "the transit waiting center" in Tanjung Pinang to which he said he had been transferred from prison. IOM had also visited him, according to Grace, and had agreed to begin paying his expenses.

"At the waiting center they detained me alone in a room; there was a bathroom and toilet," Mr. Yen told me. "People got better food; they drank spring water.... When the time came for meals, they handed food through an aperture in the iron fence. When the time came for cleaning the room, then I was allowed to go outside.... Every two weeks or once a month, when they needed someone to do cleaning work, weeding, or garbage pickup, they got me out to do these jobs. After I completed the job, they put me back in my room."

He maintained he had been transferred again four months later, in mid–October 2017, this time to what he referred to as the "refugee detention center" in Tanjung Pinang:

> I was shut up in a small area, together with six Thai people, who were not refugees and were waiting to be returned. The door was locked 24 hours a day. I was very sad because I did not know who to talk to. I stood near the doorway and looked over to the other side and saw a crowd of people whom I knew were refugees.
>
> For a while, they were transferred to a new center, but somehow, I was left behind. At that time, rice was not distributed every day as before. Money was given out so each person could go out to buy food.

Indeed, a new IOM shelter or ATD ("Alternative to Detention") for 500 refugees had been opened on Bintan. Residents were allowed to move freely during the day but were required to sleep there at night. They were also given a small allowance for food and incidentals.[47]

Mr. Yen's initial registration interview with UNHCR took place in April 2018, after permission had been obtained from Indonesian immigration. "When the UN first interviewed me, they gave me a document," he told me. "I asked the translator, who said it was a temporary protection to prevent me from being sent back to Vietnam."

An Amerasian adopted at birth, Mr. Yen did not know his Vietnamese mother or American father, Grace explained. He had agreed to try to locate his relatives on his father's side, originally with the assistance of the non-profit organization, Amerasians Without Borders (AWB), the founder of which, Jimmy A. Miller, was her friend.[48] "If we find anyone related to him, the State Department will process his paperwork. I will try to talk to the UN.... The problem is Yen is on another island.... I am trying to get some donations from my friends so I can fly there to help him."

As it turned out, Indonesian immigration did not allow Grace to see Mr. Yen, although UNHCR still agreed to interview him for the second time on June 20, 2018. "I'm happy," Grace told me. "I'd rather have the interview." Before leaving Jakarta, she also went to the U.S. Embassy to see what could be done for him. While she was prepared to appeal should he fail, UNHCR Indonesia recognized him as a refugee, along with Mr. Loi, on June 27, 2018, although Mr. Yen would not be released from detention and reunited with his family until early September. "Good news," his son Tuan told me on July 10. "I talked with the UN about my dad. He will come here in a few weeks. Thankful for your help and Ms. Grace [who] helped my family.... Just wait ... everything will be ok."

Although we had not known until then when the two remaining fathers would be recognized as refugees and reunited with their families, we had still thought it important to include them in the Canadian visa application process. For, in some cases, Canada allows "non-accompanying" family members to "follow later under the provisions of the One Year Window (OYW) of Opportunity," on condition that they have been declared on the original application.[49] Now that they had been reunited, however, we needed to redo their forms to take note of their changed circumstances, resulting in further delay.

Once again, we relied on Alison Battisson to secure the updated mandate letters from UNHCR's Jakarta office, incorporating both fathers on the respective lists of their family members, as required by IRCC. Arranging an official photo of Mr. Yen was more difficult as he was still in detention. "Madam I not sure when my father will release [*sic*]," Tuan wrote on July 25. "We try to tell detention immigration to go

TRAN VAN YEN

TUESDAY 31 JULY 2018
TRI, JL.LAYAR RAYA NO.77
KELAPA DUA TANGERANG
INDONESIA
ARVAL STUDIO FOTO

Front and back of Mr. Yen's photograph for Canadian immigration (courtesy Tran Ngoc Tuan).

outside just take a picture but the[y] not allow.... They said must have the permission from UN or IOM." A week later, however, with the assistance of Mrs. Lua, Tuan somehow managed to send the required photo to VOICE Canada. We still do not know how they did it.

Once he had sent through his father's signatures—again while Mr. Yen was still in detention—we were finally able to submit the family's completed visa application—the last one of the now 20-strong group—to IRCC. VOICE Canada had been able to find still more private sponsors, who were generously prepared to provide formal support via temporary "Groups of Five" (G5).[50] Acting as volunteer "guarantors," they collaboratively undertake to develop detailed settlement plans, including estimated living costs for one year, from receiving the new arrivals to arranging lodging, care, and assistance within their local community so as to help them "adjust to life in Canada"—all at about a third of the then estimated cost of the Australian private sponsorship program, refugee applications to Canada not involving visa or processing fees.[51]

As it transpired, Mr. Yen was not that far behind the other adults, who had only signed their visa application forms a little earlier in response to a call from Kyanh, after we realized that no matter how many emails I sent, clearly marking where they should sign, they simply did not understand. A further delay arose when their local photocopying shop was closed for holidays, and another when Mr. Loi's original photo never reached VOICE Canada and had to be redone.

"Unfortunately, we have to submit a complete application package," Kyanh explained. "The application will be returned if we miss any piece of information." Indeed, some members of the group had never used email before, their forms being returned simply for including the same address as their more technically minded relatives, Canadian immigration requiring an individual one for each applicant.

Another hurdle involved formally requesting to link Mrs. Lua's application to those of her younger sister, Tran Thi Le, and niece, Tran Thi Thanh Ngoc, both of whom were then minors, classified as "de facto dependents,"[52] who relied on her as their primary caregiver. Finally, on August 31, 2018, Kyanh was able to report: "Le Luong has completed the last three applications. They were mailed to Immigration Canada today. We have now officially submitted all applications. Let's hope Immigration Canada will move quickly.... We are looking forward to welcoming everyone to Canada."

By then, we had realized, however, that while the group was waiting to be resettled, Mr. Loi would not be allowed to live with his family—a direct consequence of the Australian government ending IOM automatic funding for new arrivals in Indonesia after March 15, 2018. "He will have to stay in a hotel until he is resettled to a third country," Grace told me. Mrs. Loan confirmed this added complication and expense. "Now my family is having trouble," she wrote, explaining that IOM representatives had come to speak with the group in mid–July. For the over 5,000 new refugees like Mr. Loi—755 alone had arrived in the first seven months of 2018—"IOM cannot subsidize anything for food, medical examination, money, or housing.... He is not allowed to attend English classes for refugees; when he is sick, he cannot go to IOM's hospital; he must be treated in a private hospital; he stays together every day with his family; at night he has to return to the hotel to sleep."[53]

Indeed, the rules for living in their housing complex, printed in numerous languages, and pinned next to the main door and on every floor, clearly stipulated: "Guests from outside dormitory must handover their identity to security guard. The guest cannot stay overnight and must leave the dormitory at the latest by 10 P.M."[54] "I am not monitored by the police or IOM, but the building manager follows me by camera," Mrs. Loan explained. "If I'm absent for many days without reason, they will notify IOM. But with my husband monitored by IOM, … before they told manager to go to my room at 11 P.M. to check my husband was not staying." At first, she rented a room for him in an empty house nearby, paying 900,000 IDR (USD65) each month—a large proportion of an adult's monthly IOM allowance—before finding a cheaper option, costing 700,000 IDR (USD50), about 20 minutes away.

In contrast, once Mr. Yen was reunited with his family on September 9, 2018, he was allowed to live with them, IOM allocating an extra room on another floor of the same refugee-housing complex in Tangerang. "My life is now comfortable," he told me. "I get more freedom." Noting that the monthly benefits the family received did not cover all their expenses, especially those of their three children who "are growing up every day with more needs," he added that his "wife's siblings provide some

Mr. Yen and family on the day they were reunited, September 9, 2018 (courtesy Nguyen Thi Phuc).

additional support to fill in the gap. Here they don't allow us to work. If someone tries to work underhand, and gets discovered by the police, the police would report them to IOM, which would cut their benefits off." They would also run the risk of being returned to detention.[55]

By September 14, IRCC had notified all the families, as well as those offering to privately sponsor them, that the Resettlement Operations Centre in Ottawa (ROC-O) had received their applications. A long road lay ahead—according to official statistics, as of that month, there were "applications for more than 44,200 refugees waiting to be processed"[56]—but at least no further forms had so far been returned. Hopefully we would pass the "completeness check"—the first stage of the assessment—and a file could then be created for each case, an application number assigned for future correspondence with IRCC.

As soon as Mrs. Phuc had told VCA-QLD Refugee Committee chair Mr. Van Pham that her husband had been officially recognized as a refugee and reunited with his family, he reached out to Kyanh, requesting that Mr. Yen be included in their Canadian visa application. "Phuc, Yen, and their children are already named," Kyanh reassured him. "The whole family will be interviewed together and hopefully will

1065 Canadian Place Suite 307, Mississauga, ON L4W 0C2, Tel. 416-417-8098, Fax 905-212-7087

August 28, 2018

To: Dr. Bui Trong Cuong

Dear Dr. Bui Trong Cuong,

On behalf of VOICE Canada, I would like to thank the Australian community for their generous contribution of $27,983.00 CAD received on August 20th, 2018.

Please rest assured that 100% of the Australian community's contribution will be used to sponsor the family of Mrs. Nguyen Thi Phuc.

It is our hope that we will have more chances to work together to help even more refugees.

Sincerely,

Tuan Le, VP
VOICE Canada

Thank you letter from VOICE Canada to the Queensland Vietnamese community (courtesy VOICE Canada and Dr. Cuong Trong Bui).

travel to Canada together." The Queensland Vietnamese community had already transferred the money it had raised for Mrs. Phuc's family to VOICE Canada in mid–August 2018, VCA-QLD president, Dr. Bui, officially updating members and donors the following month.

Six months later, on April 9, 2019, Mrs. Lua forwarded to us the notification she had received from ROC-O that the sponsorship application for her family had been approved: They had passed what is known as "Phase 1." "In case you haven't heard, the file of Mrs. Lua's family has been transferred to the office in Singapore for the next step," Grace wrote. "Good news." I took the approval of this particular G5 application largely for granted: "This is very exciting, although not at all surprising," I wrote to Kyanh, who together with his family, had so generously put themselves forward among the sponsors. "I knew you would be approved given your meticulous work and wonderful sponsorship history."

Meanwhile, that same day back in Vietnam, the fate of Vo An Don was seemingly sealed: "I have lost my license to practice law forever, with no apparent recourse available," he announced in Vietnamese on Facebook after the People's High Court in Da Nang, central Vietnam, upheld a decision to disbar him. Already on November 26, 2017, he had been struck off his local legal association's lists—just days before the appeal of prominent human rights activist and blogger, "Mother Mushroom" (Nguyen Ngoc Nhu Quynh)—thereby prevented from being part of the legal team representing her. Accused of "abusing freedom of speech" by liaising with foreign media, "allegedly defaming" and "making false denouncements against the prestige of the communist party, the state and Vietnamese lawyers," whom he had criticized for corruption,[57] he had been ultimately stripped of his practicing license by the national Vietnam Bar Federation (VBF) on May 21, 2018—despite more than a hundred of Vietnam's roughly 14,000 attorneys writing to request the Standing Committee reconsider its disciplinary action. In September

Mr. Vo (right) carrying one of his children, with Mrs. Lua (left) and Mrs. Loan (center), when they met to prepare for court in April 2016 (courtesy Tran Thi Thanh Loan and Tran Thi Lua).

2018, his Facebook page had been shut down for several months before he had managed to convince management to restore it.

Known as the "farmer lawyer" because he had to resort to farming to support his young family, he had sued the Minister of Justice in December 2018, requesting that he be allowed to resume his legal practice, all to no avail. He was not alone: "Since 2017, Vietnamese authorities have intensified the suppression of human rights lawyers, who have been harassed and/or had their practice license revoked."[58]

Never one afraid to speak his mind, Mr. Vo told me he had no regrets, and was continuing to provide legal assistance to those in need: "The imprisonment of those who tried to reach Australia by boat, and those who crossed the sea for the second time, is one of the reasons why the Vietnamese government permanently deprived me of my legal practice. Although I was stripped of my license, I never regretted what I did for people in dire straits. What I have done is to contribute to the fight for justice against an oppressive government."[59]

We too had been prepared to fight for justice in Vietnam, albeit in a far more modest way, helping a failed asylum seeker family learn how to stand on their own two feet.

6

Standing on Their
Own Two Feet

In late March 2017, I had begun receiving calls from a Vietnamese number at odd hours, often in the middle of the night. Over the next four months, they had continued, although I never managed to answer in time. "Can you believe it, Nhi?" I eventually asked in early August. "Do you remember I kept telling you I was getting many phone calls from Vietnam, and I didn't know from whom? I gave you the name 'Due.' Well guess who that is? We know his mother. All these months he's been trying to reach me.... Now I've finally realized who he is, and I apologized to him."

Nhi, however, remained unconvinced. "That's weird. I talked to her a few times, and she did not say anything about her son trying to reach you.... I asked around if anyone knew who it could be, and no one knew.... He made no attempt to contact me or Grace." I refused to share her doubts, insisting I had "solved" the mystery by searching for his name in my computer files, where I had found it in an old report translated by Doan Trung about some of the most struggling families Mr. Vo had asked us to assist, if possible. "Are you sure it is him and not someone pretending to be him?" Nhi, ever cautious, persisted. "I thought Mrs. Cam would have told me if her son was trying to reach you and could not. Anyone can register a sim card under that name.... Let me add him as a friend on Facebook and I will let you know when he accepts, and I can talk to him."

As it turned out, we were both wrong: A member of their family had certainly been calling me, but it was actually the younger son Tu, then aged only 13. Such tenaciousness in someone so young was impressive: He was determined to seek help to alleviate his family's plight. "His mother does not know he gets online," Nhi confirmed. "She said to thank you; the money you sent helps a great deal. The family is really struggling. She has to work 12–14 hours a day, mostly washing dishes. She gets up at 6 A.M. and does not get home until nearly midnight. Their [younger] son is on the street selling lottery tickets and only finished Grade 3. They hardly have time to sleep!"

With her husband suffering from a disability and no longer able to work, Mrs. Cam was willing to do odd jobs for anyone who would employ her, and was also working as a cleaner, digging for clams, and helping people around their yards. Meanwhile, her younger son Tu would get up early every morning to go to a distribution center to buy lottery tickets and then walk the streets trying to sell them. "There is even the risk of getting robbed of the tickets," Nhi added. "The most they can earn a day is USD2, but sometimes no one hires her, and they make nothing."

Mrs. Cam's long and irregular working hours, compounded by caring for her frail, elderly father, who was frequently hospitalized, made it difficult for us to contact her. As a result, so as not to trouble Nhi or Grace too much, I even resorted to asking other Vietnamese friends to let the family know whenever I managed to send some money sporadically from the crowd fund, "Help Care for the Children," which she would also use to buy medication for her husband.

At 15, the eldest son Due was now the main breadwinner. Having lost his job at a café, he had found work in another eatery. His wage—under USD3 a day—was the only stable income on which the family could depend. He had also become the man of the house and the only one who could do heavy work, including physically carrying his grandfather.

For some time, we had wanted to find a more sustainable way to help the family long-term. Gradually we were coming to the realization that encouraging and supporting Due to seek appropriate vocational training could eventually lead his family to stand on their own two feet, which would ultimately become the name of our third crowd fund campaign in August 2018. As we wrote to potential donors: "We all know the saying, 'Give a person a fish, and you feed them for a day. Teach a person to fish, and you feed them for a lifetime.' Won't you help make this a reality for Due and his family?"

Some 12 months earlier, however, it was hard to see how we would ever reach that point. An online search had revealed a possibly suitable institution that was in the process of recruiting around 40 candidates, as it did on a regular basis.[1] "While applicants are normally aged 16–22, I think Due should give it a go and at the very least enquire," I told Nhi. "The college is holding open days next week—one in the south and the other in the north. I know he doesn't live there and would have to travel, but we can help him. Then if they say he's too young, he can plan for next year if this is something that interests him."

Nhi's initial phone call to the family was met with a swift, albeit respectful, knockback. "He will have to leave home to study, and although the course is free, he won't get a salary. He needs to be at home to look after the family and they need his income to survive." But I refused to give up: The situation was becoming untenable with younger brother Tu having begun to message me each month, borrowing a friend's phone and using Google Translate to beg for money which, if no donations had been forthcoming, I would try to provide from my own pocket. At the same time, his determination remained inspiring: We could not contemplate abandoning his family.

By October 2017, I had thought of a possible solution: Why not try to raise enough funds to cover Due's café wages? Nhi remained unconvinced: "I think it would be wonderful if he can break off to go to the center for his future, but first we need to get his and the family's agreement." Predictably, this proved a formidable challenge. "$5 a day is $35 a week," I persisted. "Even if we say $50 a week, that would still be $200 per month or $2,400 for the year. We could raise that money for them. We could raise double that too and help them pay for some assistance in the home for the heavy lifting and aiding the grandfather so that the young man can get a future for himself and be able to help his family much more in the long run."

With her husband still requiring medical treatment, Mrs. Cam understandably remained reluctant to let her older son leave home. "They rely heavily on him for everything," Nhi explained, "from how to talk to doctors to reading the medical instructions for his father.... She is more keen to get a small sum to start some form of family business rather than let her son go, but was afraid to say so outright.... Their mentality is different. She herself is not well educated, so she does not see things the way we do.... Hopefully she will see the logic in your plan to help them, that it will be better in the end."

Indeed, crowd funding to send an adolescent on a two-year intensive, accredited vocational training program seemed a more certain proposition than backing an unknown business. "I cannot just raise money for anything," I told Nhi. "Mrs. Cam would need to have a well thought out and detailed plan as we have to remain accountable to donors."

After several fruitless attempts, Nhi could no longer continue. "I am sorry, but you will have to find someone else to help with Mrs. Cam's family. I am not doing very well. I am too tired and talking to her is stressful because it is difficult to get her to understand your point of view." Doan Trung kindly took up the gauntlet, but we continued to have trouble contacting the family. Having decided not to send any more money until we had ascertained their decision, I was fast running out of time to run a crowd fund campaign before the next enrolment deadline.

By mid–2018, however, Tu, who seemed to have become the family spokesman, was asking whether we had applied to the institution on his older brother's behalf, and Nhi agreed to try speaking to his mother again. She had little choice, the family having grown accustomed to relying on her interpreting skills: "Mrs. Cam just sent me a message saying that anything you need from her please communicate through me because she does not understand and has to ask or pay people to translate for her.... She told me she has sent in the application and will let us know if it is approved. She also said her younger son would like to learn carpentry rather than going back to school. He has talents with his hands but not for academic study. What do you think?"

Loathe for him to end his education at such a young age, we convinced her to consider other options as well, but the news was not good. "She has asked around and said there is no night school or tutoring available for Grade 4. Such services do not exist in Vietnam as no one cares about it. The only option is for Tu to attend public school, but even then, there is no guarantee he will be accepted into the class."

Meanwhile, with Mrs. Cam's cooperation in itemizing her family's predicted expenses, we set up the campaign. SBS Vietnamese program producer and presenter Mai Hoa Pham provided an added boost by interviewing Due and me for the weekly radio broadcast, *Seeds of Love*, which aired on August 9, 2018, in the early part of the campaign, and other Vietnamese media followed suit. "My family owes a lot of debt, and I don't know when it will go away," Due told journalists. "My dream is to have a career to help them."

Initially struggling to attract Vietnamese donors, I wrote an open letter to a local communal newspaper, which unfortunately was not published. Nhi also promoted the campaign to her almost 40,000 Facebook followers, while Sydney-based supporter Christina Nguyen kindly translated a posting for Vo An Don to share with his close to 70,000 followers. "There are several people in Vietnam who want to donate too," Nhi confided, "but they are not allowed to send money out of the country, so they asked me for a local number in order to transfer money directly."

Ultimately, donations exceeded our expectations, reaching over USD8,000 in four weeks, notably thanks to the generosity of Mai Pham's friends, Dr. Hong Long Ha and Mrs. Trang Thu Thi Ta, who offered to complete the campaign, as well as the Melbourne-based Australian Vietnamese Women's Association.[2] Mrs. Cam relayed her gratitude via Nhi: "She and her family feel deeply indebted. She still can't believe there would be someone as kind, and she never dreamt that her two children would have the opportunity to learn and have a proper career. She does not know how to say thanks enough."

At the college's invitation, she accompanied Due to its Ho Chi Minh City office in early September so he could complete a questionnaire and sit basic literacy and mathematics tests. "The poor kid is really stressed because he has never traveled far before in Vietnam," Nhi told me. "He only goes to work and then back home and does not leave his village. Can you send her some money so she can take him by bus please? I just sent him a message telling him he will like Saigon and think of it as an adventure. If she has some money to take him sightseeing a bit and maybe for some nice food, he will love the trip."

Told to return on September 19 for a final test and interview, we remained optimistic that Due would pass—even though only one in seven applicants gets through—and began to prepare for what we thought would be his imminent flight to Hanoi to embark on a month's trial period, as per the rigorous trainee recruitment process. "I don't think they will reject him," Nhi said, "but the training may be a big struggle as they demand quite a high standard. Hopefully he can rise to the expectations."

As with all "suitable applicants," a representative also visited the family's home, checking his background and speaking with neighbors. Trung liaised with its recruitment officer, informing her about our fundraising campaign, while upon request, I provided further information about their personal circumstances.

Meanwhile, younger brother Tu was embarking on his carpentry career. "Grandma, my tuition fees are 20 million VND [about USD860]. This fee is just paid once. It will teach me success."[3] Recalling that sending a similar amount in the past had caused trouble, I asked Nhi to investigate further. "I am a little concerned," she reported on October 8. "Mrs. Cam said it is not for a school, but just a family friend who is a carpenter and owns a shop. He offered to teach him and feed him lunch so that he can spend the whole day at the shop learning. Since it's not a school, he can learn for as long as he needs, until he has acquired enough skills to work in the shop himself. But there won't be any certificate. What do you think? She said he is too young otherwise to attend proper training classes or school."

Striving to keep costs down, we stipulated that we could only spare around USD35 a month for two years or USD70 a month for one year. But the prospective employer was not satisfied: "She said the man agreed to accept 5 million VND [about USD215] first, then 3 million VND [around USD130] each month, and she will take photos [of the receipts] for you. In Vietnam, that is the usual cost for a private course, also the average income for a laborer. Due is being fed while at the shop too.... That is how they operate. They don't do anything by the book; they only go by verbal agreement, and they can change anytime.... The problem is many Vietnamese people think that overseas benefactors are like the golden goose, so they will try to get as much money as possible."

Pointing out that paying the higher fees—without even the prospect of a formal qualification—would limit what we could do for the family once Due left home—we persisted with our original offer, which the carpenter eventually accepted, commencing lessons even before receiving the first payment.

After considerable confusion as to when the vocational training college would announce its decision, I decided to reach out directly to its founder and chairman to explain the family's plight. Although not normally involved in the recruitment process, he responded that they already had all the information needed about Due.

On October 24, 2018, he provided me with their decision:

> I have gone through all the reports for the last two months and with a heavy heart I have some bad news. Due has failed the interview round and is not successful in our intake this time.... I have spoken to this young man directly and he is just too immature.... Having said this, we are open for him to reapply in six months' time.... A program such as ours requires commitment, perseverance, and self-discipline.... Although our hearts say YES, our experience says NO—because we don't want to set him up to fail. We hope for your understanding. I wish I could bring you better news. Of course, if you have any more candidates for the program—please do not hesitate to send them along to us.

While I continued to hope that Due would soon mature enough to be able to take advantage of their invitation to reapply, Nhi was more pessimistic, suggesting he embark on another qualification closer to home instead. "He is from a remote village; he is very shy; he is terrified of being away from his family, and both his parents are illiterate. Immaturity cannot suddenly change in six months. Deep down he does not want to do the course. Even if he manages to pass the interview, with such an attitude, how can he cope with the two years' training? I will try to speak to him to see where his heart lies."

Meanwhile I had arranged to meet the college founder in Ho Chi Minh City on November 9, 2018, while my husband was attending a conference. Why not ask Mrs. Cam and her sons to join us? "She was so excited she couldn't sleep last night," I subsequently reported to Nhi. "We hugged—it was very emotional.... Due told his mother today he just wasn't ready.... All he has to do is have another interview, but if he decides he doesn't want to go, he has to tell us his plans, so we remain fully answerable to donors. Before he met him, the chairman may have had the impression that Due felt entitled because of overseas money, but now he understands how devoted he is as a son."

Indeed, as he told me, "Due is trying to please his parents, who are pressuring him to go, but he also feels guilty as he doesn't think he should leave his mother in her time of need because of his deep love for her." The college would enable Due to have the childhood he never had, including holidays, sports, and leisure time—everything he had missed out on by working so hard for his family. Moreover, while military service is still compulsory in Vietnam, its students are among those eligible for an exemption.

As for Tu, rather than spending hard-earned funds on uncertified carpentry tuition, the chairman believed it would be far better to find a private teacher to help him catch up his primary studies while selling lottery tickets at night, also generously offering to help him enroll in high school. If his heart remained set on carpentry, there were numerous vocational training options to consider.

"Poor boys," Nhi sympathized. "I hope they give it a go. They have been away from school so long they have lost all confidence."

"I love my mother so much," Due wrote to me after our meeting. "I have seen her becoming miserable, sacrificing so much for the family. I want to help her, but I don't know how."

Over the following months, we continued to stay in contact with the family. Trung would call every so often to discuss plans, but Tu remained adamant that he wanted to continue with his "apprenticeship" for the year, while Due did not seem any closer to making a decision. "If they don't want to go ahead, then I don't think we can continue to support them and use the crowd fund in ways other than what we told donors," I wrote to Nhi in desperation. I also warned Tu: "Please think very carefully because once you use the money, it is gone, and I cannot get it again. I want the best future for you."

By mid–February 2019, however, Due had agreed to undergo another interview. Once again, I sent money to enable him and his mother to take the bus to Ho Chi Minh City, only discovering subsequently that the college had assigned a local graduate to keep in contact with him over the preceding months. The interview was eventually scheduled for April 16, Due looking far more relaxed when it was over. "They said his answers were more mature than previously," his younger brother told me. "They asked him to wait for the results."

On May 1, we finally had good news: "My brother has been successful. On May 6, he will be present in Hanoi. Can you send him money?" Tu, however, had also reminded me payment was due for his bimonthly carpentry fees, and in confusion, due to the language barrier, I had only sent enough to cover his apprenticeship. Meanwhile, the plane ticket had already been booked, but Mrs. Cam did not have the money to pay for it, and she had also announced a desire to buy her older son new clothes ahead of his departure.

There no longer being enough time to send more money, I suggested they delay the carpentry dues, but these had already been paid. I asked Nhi to try to reason with Mrs. Cam but to no avail. In the end, I decided to call on the chairman. "No need for clothing as he should come as he is," he reassured me:

> The rest we will provide over time. Please remember his fellow classmates are all or some in even worse situations than he is....
>
> I need your commitment / word that you won't send him money for the two years no matter how tough it gets here (so I can slowly move him away from this dependency he seems to have on you or any foreigner). The allowance you give him plus all paid for education/live in is sufficient. If you have already raised the money, then I suggest you sponsor him through our program.... Congratulations—you will see a very different empowered young man at the other end.

Having reached an understanding that the crowd fund was needed to support the family during Due's absence, we agreed the college would find him a sponsor as we continued to work together in a communal effort.

Due duly flew to Hanoi just in time to start the course, while I subsequently reimbursed the school for the plane fare as promised. Posing for a photo at the airport without the trace of a smile, he clearly carried the weight of responsibilities far beyond his years. Not to mention family expectations, as encapsulated by younger brother Tu: "My mother has to take care of everything, and she doesn't complain. My relatives only hope that my brother will succeed so that he can take the burden from her later."

"I do not know what to say," Due wrote on the eve of his departure. "I promise I will study English and train well for my career so that I can speak English with Grandma often. I thank you and the other benefactors for helping my family. I will try my best."

Only a week into the course, he had begun to try writing in English. "It is very good and fun," he said, expressing the hope that we would be able to share another meal in the future. To his Facebook friends he explained that he was "learning to listen," while from the photos that the family continued to share with me, it was clear that Due was soon feeling more at home in his new surroundings. "Yes, my brother is very good, he is undertaking new challenges," Tu confirmed. The chairman wrote too: "He is settled and happy. Thought you should know."

On June 19, 2019, we learned that Nhi had passed away from cancer. A private person, she had only shared with me a few weeks earlier just how ill she was, and my husband and I had flown to Brisbane to say goodbye. A strong human rights advocate to the end, Nhi had never wavered in her support of the refugees we were endeavoring to help. We felt her absence keenly. As Mrs. Loan said, "we see her like our family."

Concerned about what would happen to younger brother Tu once he had completed his year with the local carpenter, I had refused to extend his uncertified apprenticeship, determined to follow the chairman's advice: "My recommendation is for you to have a condition and expiry date for your support, or he will continue to use your kindness and not become proactive. I have access to many vocational training institutes in different trades in Vietnam. Let me know if you need help?"

For months I urged Tu, now 15, to make an appointment to discuss his prospects. We were also keen to help Mrs. Cam realize her dream of starting a small grocery business, the chairman kindly offering to review her plans before I would release the money in stages to help contribute to her success. My hope was that once no more funding was forthcoming for Tu's training, they would take more urgent action. As the college founder has explained, "they often only think of the present, of how to survive day-to-day. They don't look at their long-term future."

Weeks would go by, however, without a word, apart from a request that I advance the next payment as the grandfather had fallen seriously ill. Concerned, I asked whether the college could send the local graduate back to visit the family and encourage Due to motivate his younger brother. "They say he needs a bit more time to think about what he wants to do," the chairman explained. Meanwhile, he and I continued to stay in contact by email, meeting sporadically in Sydney whenever possible.

While Tu no longer contacted me—ostensibly because his mother's phone was broken and remained unrepaired—Due would dutifully respond to my questions. In mid–October 2019, he sadly announced that his grandfather had died. My first impulse was to offer to send him home, but he explained the burial had already taken place. Remembering the founder's advice, I restricted myself to conveying condolences to the family.

Then in early November, he revealed his younger brother was working as a waiter for about 3 million VND (around USD130) a month and assured me that he seemed happy. Perturbed, I wrote to the chairman:

> I am assuming that given I refused to pay any further for his carpentry "apprenticeship," the family must have told him he had to get a job to contribute to income? I am quite sad because my understanding is he loved carpentry, and as you will recall, I so wanted him to

come to discuss his future with you. I also had hoped to help their mother set up a grocery business (as per her expressed interest) ... Obviously if he is happy, then perhaps once Due graduates, we should look at seeing if the younger brother can come to the college. Any advice would be appreciated. Is someone able to discuss with Due? I am having great difficulty communicating.

A week later I received the following response:

I think you would be proud of the reply Due has given me to relay back to you. He said perhaps letting his brother work in a cafe is not a bad idea.... He tried many times and feels that his brother just doesn't and won't understand. He asked you to let his brother be for a while longer—when he is more mature and less stubborn, you and his family will be able to help him properly. Due has grown up and that's a very mature thing to say—don't you think? He wanted to text you many times to explain but felt his English was not adequate yet. He said when he finishes college, he will be able to communicate properly with you.

By December 2019, I was receiving requests from Due and his brother to fly him home for Lunar New Year celebrations the following month. Although I had originally budgeted for several flights so he could see his family, I could not forget the commitment I had subsequently made not to send any more money "no matter how tough it gets." "The chairman said the college provides everything you need, and I should let you take the bus like everyone else," I wrote to Due. "If I spend the money on the plane fare for you, there will be less for your family, and I'm still hoping your brother and mother will want to do something to help their future too." Upon further discussion, however, it became clear that this was a singular occasion: There would be no other extended holidays during the course, Due being expected to work during the second year. "Thanks for [taking] care of me so much," he said upon receiving the ticket. "I will never forget you; you help me a lot. I love you so much!" Mai Pham commented on his growing confidence when she conducted follow-up interviews for her weekly broadcast, *Seeds of Love*, which aired on SBS on March 12, 2020: "Due said he has found his future," she told me, "He now has a new life."

The onset and spread of the COVID-19 virus, however, would brutally disrupt even the best-laid plans. While Due remained safely ensconced in quarantine with those he now called his "college family" in Hanoi, by early April, his family were struggling to make ends meet, both Tu and his mother having lost their jobs. I now faced a dilemma: Should I send what was intended to be bi-monthly financial support early, thereby providing immediate relief, albeit at the risk of depleting our hard-earned resources before Due was in a position to take responsibility for their care? It was clear we needed to modify our strategy, but how? I urged the brothers to discuss and suggested they contact the college founder before relying on me to bail them out.

It turned out that three weeks earlier, Mrs. Cam had told Due she was interested in establishing her own business and had urged him to contact the chairman on her behalf. "I was planning to fly to Ho Chi Minh City to visit her and go through her business plan," he told me when I too rang for advice, "but she never called." Due subsequently revealed that he had asked his mother to delay until the disease outbreak had subsided, and so I agreed to continue shouldering financial responsibility for the family via the crowd fund whenever required.

Their meeting finally took place in Ho Chi Minh City at the beginning of May, by which time I was drawing down on the crowd fund monthly—at this rate, reserves would be depleted fast. It had taken the pandemic to make Mrs. Cam realize she had to take action to help herself. "I gave her an update on Due and shared our expectations, stressing I am not your inspector," the chairman told me. "But while you want the best for her and would trust her completely if you were spending your own money, the crowd fund must be transparent."

To our pleasant surprise, she had already begun setting up a rudimentary grocery store in front of her home and was planning to work from morning to night. To turn even a small profit of around VND200,000–300,000 (USD9–13) a day, or roughly USD275–400 a month, it was agreed that she would need to think bigger, making coffee and eventually serving breakfast for locals, paying a cousin to assist her so as not to overwork herself. The business would have to be registered and taxes paid, the college founder even offering to fly down with Due—"for moral support and buy-in because he loves his mother and so should be involved"—to use funds I had set aside to buy the necessary provisions, chairs and tables, a street vendor stall.

Tu, however, had still not given his future serious thought—other than expressing a wish to move to Ho Chi Minh City, where he cockily assumed he would find a job in a coffee shop. Asked whether he had a trade in mind, he nominated signwriting, even though he had not researched the cost of training or what was involved. Why not carpentry at least? Any enjoyment had been tempered by injuries to his hands. The chairman did not mince his words: "No one will hire a 16-year-old in the city. You will be exploited, and we won't assist you to endanger yourself."

In the interim, it was decided he could assist his mother in what we anticipated would eventually develop into a Vietnamese-style convenience store. She too now hoped he would ultimately opt to apply for admission to the same vocational college as his older brother—as indeed we were encouraging another teenager still on our radar, Son Huynh Nguyen, to do later that year.[4] "It is so important we provide these youth with opportunity, so they do not find themselves in risky situations," the institution's head of marketing and partnership engagement agreed.

Mrs. Cam painstakingly prepared her long list of provisions, which the chairman and Due planned to buy for her in early June, when they intended to fly from Hanoi to Ho Chi Minh City, renting a car to drive to the village. Asked to research the price of each item, she was careful to keep to our budget of USD1,700, which I transferred from the crowd fund, along with the cost of Due's airfare, the chairman paying for his own ticket and car hire as his "contribution to the family."

"Their lives have been blessed," was Mai Pham's reaction when I excitedly told her the good news. "It's so touching and thrilling to see. It is a fortune for many people in Vietnam. And it is a result of love, caring, and compassion. My goodness, I can't find words to express my gratitude to see what you all have done for them."

"Her smile makes it all worth it," the chairman said of Mrs. Cam. "She feels empowered." The business gradually became more established, Tu loyally supporting his mother, grateful for the regular work. So long as the crowd fund remained operational, however, they continued to call on me every two months for additional cash injections, which I calculated would last until February 2021, after which all the money would be gone. I hoped they would be able to manage on their own by then, as Due would still not have graduated. He was certainly going from strength to strength, the chairman praising him for his independence—"uses his head and is compassionate." The next message was more revealing: "He is doing really well. He has a girlfriend now also!"

Mrs. Cam's initial provisions list included everything from cigarettes, beer, and soft drinks to a fridge, scales, and storage chest, as well as sacks of rice, cooking and dairy products, coffee, and green tea (author's collection).

By the end of October 2020, the college had also agreed to accept our other candidate, Son, after a similar rigorous process, initiated and led by his older sister Lam. "Our family is very grateful for what you have done for us over the years," she generously wrote. "You are our benefactor." But all we had really done was inform them about the opportunity. "After meeting you and listening to advice, he did research," she added. "Leaving school has nothing to do with his passion and dreams."

During her brother's brief visit home for *Tết* (Lunar New Year) in February 2021, Lam proudly shared that she had been accepted into a four-year nursing diploma program at a private local university and would commence her studies, pandemic-permitting, the following month. Initially admitted into a more expensive course elsewhere, she had at first thought to defer for a year, receiving free training as a manicurist from a friend in an effort to support herself. Her devoted mother, Mrs. Van, also took in extra sewing to try to cover the fees, but ever-resourceful, Lam soon found a cheaper option, enabling her to bring her enrollment forward. "I will do some part-time job to help my mom," she told me, "nails, or anything else like cashier or waitress."

By March 2021, Lam had commenced her nursing studies, only for them to be interrupted by another COVID lockdown due to the Delta variant that would drag on for six months. Nevertheless, she was able to continue her course online and remained upbeat: "My mother recently started raising two pigs to earn extra income. Everything is okay." While it had taken her brother time to adapt to his college surroundings, he too would soon flourish, Lam revealing that he loved the chairman and had come to consider him a second father. "So sweet," the chairman replied, "I am working to build his confidence." His efforts were certainly paying off, with Son soon winning second prize in a college competition.

The following month, I received a message from Due: "I and my class passed the final assessment, and I am really thankful to my supporters. I hope to see you soon." While I had originally hoped to travel to Hanoi for his graduation, this no longer seemed possible due to the pandemic. One positive though was that the college had arranged three months of work experience for its new graduates to tide them over before the Vietnamese job market would hopefully reopen. While COVID would further interfere with these plans, there being no flights to Hanoi for months, Due managed to continue training as well as enjoying some rest and recreation at the beach resort where he had originally been flown to work. With graduation postponed until June 2022, he decided to accept a job there once the situation had stabilized.

Son at Tan Son Nhat airport in Ho Chi Minh City, November 1, 2020 (courtesy Lam Huynh Nguyen).

"He is an exceptional boy, and you should be very proud," the chairman wrote. "He has grown into the mature, kindhearted, and professional man that I knew he would be. When his class passed their assessment and a few days later had to say goodbye, they hugged and cried the whole night. This is an indication of how much they have grown and how close knit a family they have become. So Due has friends and family who will walk with him. Thank you for changing his and his family's life. I heard the store is doing well and they will soon serve breakfast."

By the end of 2021, he and his former classmates were back in Hanoi, preparing for an English language test, a high score on which would give them

Son in Hanoi (courtesy Lam Huynh Nguyen).

the opportunity to compete for one-year apprenticeship positions in Australia. "He has gone leaps and bounds this one," the chairman wrote. Son, on the other hand, had left the program and was working and living in Hanoi with a friend, the college having helped them find a job so they could assist their families. "We will keep you posted on his progress ... and will continue to provide support and mentoring." The pandemic, however, would compel him to return home, with the aim of seeking employment in Ho Chi Minh City when possible. His sister, now a second-year nursing student, had finally managed to move to the university campus, visiting her parents every Saturday. She would eventually win a four-year 40 percent scholarship to study nursing in the U.S.

In May 2022, I unexpectedly received a text message from Due: "My graduation will be on June 21. So that will be grateful if you can spend your time to come over [sic]." Finally, my long-term dream to celebrate his achievements in person looked like becoming reality. Upon learning, however, that his mother was too scared to leave the store unattended to attend the graduation herself, I arranged for Tu to fly to Hanoi—his first visit to the capital—thereby ensuring that at least one family member would be present, although Due did send his parents a recording. Reunited at the ceremony, we toured the college facilities the following morning, before I flew to Ho Chi Minh City, having decided to take the opportunity to visit Mrs. Cam's business, which I soon discovered had been established in the front room of her rudimentary home on the outskirts of a fishing township.

As we sat together at a brightly colored plastic children's table and chair set, she told me through a translator, "When I am here, I don't remember the hard times, and I'm at peace." She revealed that Tu had returned to carpentry, enabling him to help her pay the rent, electricity, and water bills, as well as supporting her in the shop by buying basic household goods to sell, and assisting his father, who had managed to return to work on good days, fishing from the beach. Tu was even paying off a bright red motorcycle, which took pride of place in the sparse shop beneath the alter to the ancestors and paintings of Jesus and Mary.

Time will tell if these young adults realize their true potential, but as the college founder has taught us, when you give someone love and empowerment, the future is limitless.

7

Towards Resettlement
in Canada

Meanwhile, back in 2019, the families in Indonesia were still waiting to see if they would be accepted for resettlement in Canada. No one else's private sponsors had been approved—apart from the seven members of Mrs. Lua's family (including her "de facto dependents," sister Tran Thi Le and niece Tran Thi Thanh Ngoc)—and even they had not heard anything since the processing of their application by the Immigration, Refugees and Citizenship Canada (IRCC) office, based at the Canadian High Commission in Singapore, had commenced on April 15, 2019. Just when would their refugee interviews be scheduled?

Months went by without word; we remained on tenterhooks. On May 30, I finally expressed our concern to Kyanh Do and Le Luong, sharing Mrs. Loan's growing apprehension: "My family is waiting for the papers to arrive, so I am very worried...." Whereas VOICE Canada remained hopeful that we would soon hear, I was keen for us to contact the Resettlement Operations Centre in Ottawa (ROC-O) for a case status update. After all, it had been more than nine months since we had received the Acknowledgment of Receipt (AOR) of their applications.

By early July, Kyanh was equally uneasy: "Many Groups of Five [G5] got rejected for very minor and general reasons," he wrote. "We just have to wait and see for a bit more." He had attached a report on the results of an online news poll, headlined "the majority of Canadians against accepting more refugees."[1]

Canada's rapid acceptance of refugees had certainly peaked between late 2015 and early 2016, with the resettlement of more than 25,000 Syrian refugees under new Prime Minister Pierre Trudeau in about four months.[2] Moreover, with the tightening of official U.S. attitudes against refugees under President Donald Trump, Canada had begun rejecting more claims from the increasing numbers irregularly crossing its border on foot between official ports of entry.

Indeed, in the lead-up to the October 2019 federal election, the Liberal government had introduced amendments to the *Immigration and Refugee Protection Act* (IRPA), notably deeming ineligible those overland asylum claimants who had previously filed for protection in a designated "safe third country" (STC). Obviously, Canada's continued support of immigration was at least partly "contingent on the perception that the state remains in control of the border."[3]

Despite IRCC assurances that this influx of "irregular border crossers" since 2017 "are not queue jumpers and are not taking the place of refugees who are coming to Canada from abroad for resettlement," and the increase in budgetary support to respond to such pressures, Kyanh maintained that "IRCC still has to divert staff and resources to determine the eligibility of those crossing the border."[4]

Nevertheless, on the whole, Canada has retained its self-image and international reputation as a welcoming country, willing to share the "international burden," with more than half of the 62,000 Syrian refugees resettled between 2015 and 2020 being privately sponsored.[5] Moreover, since 2017, the Global Refugee Sponsorship Initiative (GRSI), led notably by the Canadian government and UNHCR, amongst others, continued to draw inspiration from Canada's private sponsorship model to promote community-based refugee resettlement in other countries.[6] In 2019, Canada would accept around 30,000 out of 107,800 refugees from 26 countries—"the highest number of refugees worldwide, for the second year in a row."[7] VOICE Canada too was continuing its private sponsorship work, with one Syrian family still to arrive, as well as championing the cases of 50 more Vietnamese refugees from Thailand.[8]

Still, to ease Mrs. Loan's anxiety, I suggested she send a case status inquiry directly to ROC-O. She received a reply almost immediately, telling us what we already knew: Her sponsorship application had been received and was being processed. I quickly discouraged Mrs. Lua's sister- and brother-in-law, Nguyen Thi Kim Nhung and Nguyen Tai, from following suit. Their family's distress was palpable, the two siblings having had to lodge separate applications, neither of whose sponsors had yet been approved.

On July 10, 2019, our fears were confirmed; both had been refused, ROC-O criticizing their sponsors' settlement plans for lack of information. "Overall, I am not satisfied the responses … demonstrate adequate planning on the part of the sponsoring group," the officer wrote—even though, as Kyanh emphasized, "their applications were prepared very similarly to those of Lua, Le, and Ngoc. IRCC has been rejecting many applications lately."[9]

Mrs. Lua's family was despondent: They were inseparable, having lived together and supported each other in Vietnam, during their original thwarted escape, and now in Indonesia. Asked about personal qualities that would assist them in successfully settling in Canada, both siblings had highlighted their devotion and responsibility in helping to care for their relatives. Would Canadian immigration now tear them apart?

There was still a chance they could be accepted: "If the situation has changed substantively or new information has emerged to overcome the current deficiencies," ROC-O concluded, "you may submit a new and complete application." I tried to reassure Mrs. Lua, telling her that if her immediate family was allowed to emigrate first, they could prepare the way for her sister- and brother-in-law, making their life easier in the long run. "This is clearly a setback for us," Kyanh conceded. "But please do not despair. We are committed to redo the applications for Tai and Nhung. We will find new sponsors and resubmit the applications with more details and better description of our settlement plan. Please be patient."

According to IRCC's "projection for processing times," immigration applications from Indonesia received on or after July 31, 2018, were now taking 31 months on average from "the day we receive your complete application" until "we make a decision," with an added proviso: "After your visa is approved, you may need more time to get departure documents."[10] This meant that even Mrs. Lua's family could not expect to arrive in Canada until around mid–2021—despite the fact that the Canadian government continually promised to process such permanent resident applications more efficiently.[11] In hindsight, how naïve I was to think they would arrive so soon.

No matter, we were committed for the long haul and had more immediate, if seemingly mundane concerns, Mrs. Loan announcing that one of her family's sponsors had moved house. I messaged Kyanh, who rang her immediately: "We just have to update the information," he reassured her. "We will take this opportunity to better describe our settlement plan to hopefully enhance your chance of being approved." Mrs. Loan's family's case was more complicated, as he subsequently explained, their original sponsorship having been revoked or in official language, "withdrawn," due to a change in personal circumstances. As per monitoring requirements, VOICE Canada immediately transferred their application to new sponsors with the time and ability to make the required financial commitment.[12] "Wow, thank God," Mrs. Loan replied when told her application had been resubmitted. "This news is so good…. I'm so happy."

In contrast, Nhung and Tai had to start all over again. While I helped them redo their forms, VOICE Canada focused on collecting sponsor information, striving to complete the process as rapidly as possible to avoid still further delay. In the end, both were exceptionally sponsored under SAH (Sponsorship Agreement Holder), their applications eventually resubmitted in mid–November 2019 after the requisite police checks were finally completed. "VOICE has only six-to-ten spots annually," Kyanh explained, "and we normally reserve SAH spots for those who do not have UNHCR refugee status."

As required, each SAH and G5 had to guarantee to provide them with the "care, lodging, settlement assistance, and support" they would need for up to one year from the date of their arrival in Canada, or until "the refugee becomes self-sufficient, whichever comes first."[13] According to official financial guidelines, the estimated total annual settlement cost in 2019 ranged from USD12,700 minimum for one adult to USD27,300 for a family of six, an extra USD2,100 being required for each additional member.[14]

This would include, as VOICE Canada members detailed in their settlement plans, "residing at the home of one of the sponsors where there are spare bedrooms and access to wireless Internet, cable and phone until we can find a suitable apartment." Their plans also incorporated a range of responsibilities, from providing start-up assistance, like household essentials, food staples, and education supplies, to monthly financial payments, expected to be at least equal to social security,[15] to cover the refugees' daily living expenses. In addition, they offered help with such diverse tasks as translation and completing paperwork, enrolling in English classes and schools, finding a job or training, counseling, and communal and cultural orientation, often by linking refugees to various settlement services (Service Provider Organizations [SPOs]).[16]

Indeed, costs are contained through government involvement: "An unspoken but major reason that private refugee resettlement happens in Canada is because various levels of government are willing to pay for education, health, and social services on par with those of citizens."[17] This does not prevent some from criticizing the way the scheme has developed, arguing that it devolves "the cost and labor of resettlement to private residents."[18]

G5s would also explain "Canadian culture and values," offer "ongoing friendship," and put refugees "in touch with religious organizations based on their faith as they can provide additional moral and emotional support if necessary." In short, as explained by the government-funded Refugee Sponsorship Training Program (RSTP), which guides VOICE Canada, among other SAHs: "Sponsoring groups should support their efforts in gaining self-sufficiency and independence and in undertaking activities that will best support their longer-term integration."[19]

The new, meticulously detailed sponsorship undertaking and settlement plan for Mrs. Loan's family generously covered all bases, including renting a three-bedroom apartment, with furniture provided by in-kind donations; "already secured employment"; language-training and public schools within walking distance; and "initial free medical, eye, and dental checkups … done by a group of volunteer medical practitioners." In the unlikelihood that suitable rental accommodation could not be found, the family would be welcome to stay with one of their sponsors for up to a year.

Meanwhile, nothing had yet been done on a public communal level in Canada to prepare for the families' potential arrival, apart from an interview arranged for me with the Canadian Vietnamese newspaper, *Thoi Bao*, published in February 2019.[20] "We will have a few events to raise money for our Indonesian refugees at the end of 2019 and in early 2020," Kyanh decided. Deducting the Queensland Vietnamese community's donation, VOICE Canada still needed to raise over USD85,000, but they remained undaunted: "Financial considerations are not the major issue. What matters is whether people are willing to become private sponsors." As the year progressed, however, with little news, fundraising was further delayed: "We don't want to collect any money until we have confirmation that they have been accepted and made welcome to Canada," Kyanh told me in November 2019. "We'll probably do so a few months before they arrive."

Back in Indonesia, Mr. Yen was still trying to prove that his father was American. Another organization, Home for Amerasians,[21] had taken charge of his quest, sending him a DNA kit, which he received in early August 2019, imploring: "You help me prayers for me to find my father [*sic*]." Within days, he had collected and mailed back the sample, the non-profit group, which as of that month had already helped 250 Amerasians in Vietnam, paying for his paternity test with AncestryDNA.[22] "We will use it to find his paternal family," volunteer Kieu Gould assured me. By November, several first- and second-generation members of Mr. Yen's American extended family had been located, although he was still looking for his father. Would he come to be eligible for resettlement in the U.S., and how would that affect his Canadian application?

Realizing the families' dream under Canada's Refugee and Humanitarian Resettlement Program (RHRP) would mean they would all be granted permanent residency upon arrival, generally becoming eligible for citizenship after living in the country for three years and meeting other requirements, such as filing income tax returns and attaining language skills. Indeed, refugees, who comprise about 15 per cent of permanent residents admitted each year, are more likely to become citizens than any other immigration category in Canada—even though in practice, they might have to wait five years before the process is finalized.[23]

We fully expected them each to be accepted as eligible for resettlement as members of the "Convention Refugees Abroad" class,[24] for which they seemingly met all the criteria: They were outside both Canada and their home country of Vietnam to which they could not return due to a "well-founded fear of persecution," and they had "no reasonable prospect, within a reasonable period" of another "stable option for protection." In addition, considering "their resourcefulness," "presence of their sponsor," "potential for employment," and "ability to learn to communicate in one of the official languages," they would certainly "be able to become successfully established in Canada" within three to five years. Moreover, Convention Refugees are admitted to Canada in far higher numbers than other humanitarian applicants.[25]

With its description as an "Act respecting ... the granting of refugee protection to persons who are displaced, persecuted or in danger," the wording of the IRPA itself also gave us great hope, its listed objectives for refugees including

> 3(2)(a) to recognize that the refugee program is in the first instance about saving lives and offering protection to the displaced and persecuted;
> (b) to fulfil Canada's international legal obligations with respect to refugees and affirm Canada's commitment to international efforts to provide assistance to those in need of resettlement.

Mrs. Lua, Mr. Long, their three children, as well as Mrs. Lua's sister, Tran Thi Le, and niece, Tran Thi Thanh Ngoc, were the first members of the group to undergo "Phase 2," or the "eligibility assessment," a Canadian Visa Officer in Singapore finally reviewing their applications to determine whether they had met the Convention Refugee definition. But first each of the four adults had to undertake an interview with a Migration Officer, which took place at the Canadian Embassy in Jakarta on November 15, 2019. Preparation for the occasion would prove to be an international team effort. "My paper has just returned," Mrs. Lua told me excitedly upon receiving her "interview convocation letter" about a month earlier. "I am go to Jakarta interview. I so happy. Happy cry. [*sic*] Thank you so much."

The interview would be conducted in English or French, it being the family's "responsibility to bring an experienced interpreter.... It is preferable to hire a licensed interpreter who works for a translation agency or language school. If this is not possible, you may select an interpreter who is a member of your community...."[26] While Mrs. Lua immediately settled on Grace, she was initially unsure of her availability, and interviews could "not be rescheduled unless there are extenuating circumstances," applicants having to provide "a detailed explanation" involving "compelling reasons." Failure to attend could result in an application simply being refused. Neither relatives nor close friends being allowed to serve as interpreters for this purpose, we resorted to recommendations. None of the Jakarta-based, Vietnamese-speaking translators suggested, however, were available that day, nor indeed was a friend of Sunshine's, who had previously assisted members of the group with medical appointments. Fortunately, in the end, Grace herself was able to make it, flying in briefly from Bangkok to meet Mrs. Lua and her family at the Canadian Embassy.

The convocation letter included a long list of documents, which they needed to bring to the interview, along with five photos per applicant. Grace explained the requirements so they would understand what to prepare. I would also have to update their Canadian immigration background information forms, but first needed to write an acceptance email in English for Mrs. Lua to send, confirming they would all attend the interview on the appointed date. An added complication was that they were unable to open their Canadian papers online, resulting in Kyanh scanning the PDFs for the family to print out and sign.

Keen to have the myriad of documents related to her Vietnamese court case and appeal officially translated, Mrs. Lua obtained a quote for 5,600,000 IDR (close to USD400), which several Australian-based donors generously agreed to cover. We were determined to provide the family with the best chance to be accepted for resettlement, even though according to IRCC guidelines, "applicants rarely present documentary evidence in support of a claim of persecution."[27]

About ten days before the interview, IOM summoned the family to hospital for health checks and vaccinations, covered by Canadian immigration. Medical examinations are part of Phase 3 or the "admissibility assessment," along with security and criminality checks, although screening normally only takes place after applicants have been found to be eligible.[28] If, as seemed highly likely, more than six months were to elapse before their resettlement was finalized, the medical tests would need to be repeated.

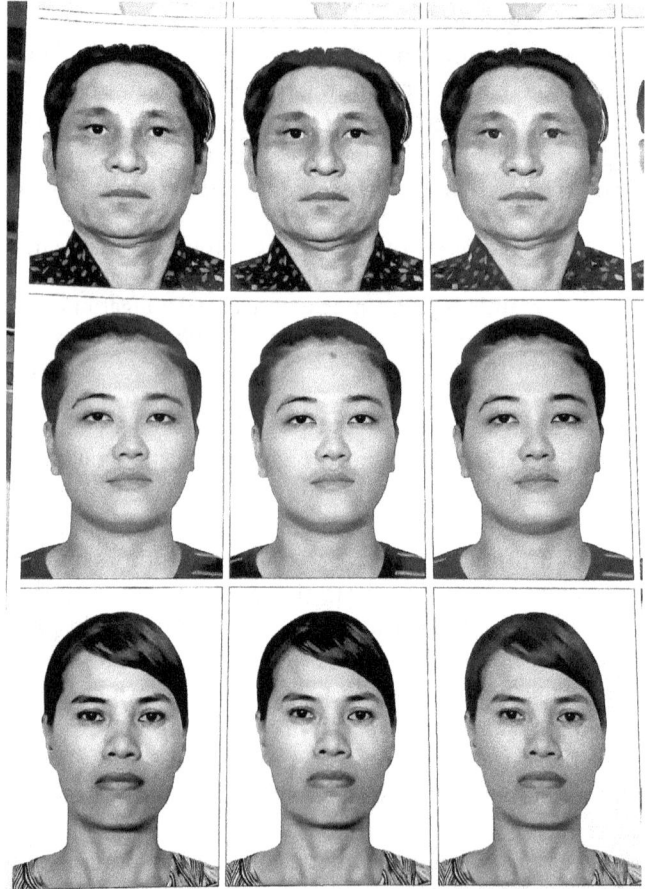

Photos of Mrs. Lua (bottom), her sister Tran Thi Le (center), and husband Mr. Long (top), in preparation for their refugee interview at the Canadian Embassy, Jakarta, November 2019 (courtesy Tran Thi Lua).

With 36 hours to go, we discovered that part of Mrs. Lua's blow-by-blow account of her trials and tribulations at the hands of the Vietnamese, Australian, and Indonesian authorities, which she had handwritten almost two years earlier, had somehow been overlooked, resulting in a last-minute translation effort by Doan Trung. Finally, the family made it to the Canadian Embassy, but not without multiple last-minute panicked calls to me when they could not find Grace directly upon arrival.

Hours ticked by, while we waited with bated breath for the result. Then a crushing text from Grace: There would be no outcome that day, the Canadian official having decided to investigate their case further. The adults had been separately interviewed in turn, but some of their answers were "vague, unclear, and inconsistent" due to nerves, Grace said. While Mrs. Lua begged me to pray for them to be accepted, I remained hopeful that the documents submitted as part of their file would help

Outside the Canadian Embassy, Jakarta, before their refugee interview, November 15, 2019, from left: Dang, Mr. Long, Mrs. Lua with Koi, her sister Tran Thi Le, niece Tran Thi Thanh Ngoc, and daughter Uyen (courtesy Tran Thi Lua).

clarify matters. "I know Lua's case is genuine," Trung wrote to me. "It'd be wrong if she meets more difficulties than others."

Indeed, fairness and impartiality are crucial to the decision-making process, IRCC guidelines emphasizing that officers must explain why they prefer one factor over another, focusing on those that are "directly applicable" or "particularly significant." Moreover, while "a refusal cannot be based on credibility alone," a "Convention Refugee applicant must establish the facts underlying their claim of persecution on a balance of probabilities but need only show that there is a reasonable chance that they would face persecution in the future." Examples of "persecution" provided to officers include "a flagrant violation of a basic right, such as denial of a fair and impartial trial, particularly when combined with unduly severe punishment."[29]

Barely a week after their interview, Vietnamese television screened another wanted notice for Mrs. Lua and Mrs. Loan: "The authorities will keep on posting it every year as long as we are still free," Mrs. Lua explained.

The rollercoaster ride of ups and downs would continue unabated, with Nhung's and Tai's SAH sponsorship applications being approved and dispatched to Singapore merely days after having been resubmitted. Meanwhile, Mrs. Loan and Mrs. Phuc and their families had been waiting for more than a year to hear whether their

G5 sponsors had been approved, the acceptance email ultimately arriving in early December 2019. "I did not have to contact anyone," Kyanh assured me. "The approval just came through. I do believe in the system. I am very happy for everyone."

This time, we decided not to wait for the scheduling of their interview date, which judging from Mrs. Lua's family's experience, could still be months away. Determined to be more organized now that we knew what to expect, I encouraged the rest of the group to obtain a quote for the certified translation of all their Vietnamese legal documents. Once again Dr. Hong Ha and Mrs. Trang Ta inspired their friends to donate more than the required 6,800,000 IDR (close to USD500). "We sincerely thank you for helping us," Mrs. Loan said. "I can't say anything more than just pray to God for many gifts for your family."

In mid–December, the Australian government, together with IOM, UN, and unnamed "partners in Vietnam," released a trailer and short video in English and Vietnamese on YouTube. Titled "A Documentary of Illegal Migration," it purported to focus on "real stories as reported to IOM and partners" involving fishermen, deemed "irregular maritime migrants." Portrayed as being motivated to try their luck in Australia in 2018 solely for economic reasons, their boat was battered by storms, their supplies contaminated in an oil spill, before being intercepted by Operation Sovereign Borders (OSB) and forcibly returned to punishment and increased debt in Vietnam.

Under the banner, "Zero Chance," then OSB Commander Major General Craig Furini intoned the oft-repeated message: "Australia does not allow anyone who tries to come to Australia illegally by boat to live or work in Australia. If you attempt such a journey, you'll be caught and quickly returned to Vietnam. You will have risked your life, wasted your money, and you'll be banned from coming to Australia for life. There are no exceptions."[30]

Interestingly, even though the controversial, retrospective lifetime ban on asylum seekers who arrive by boat had been in the offing since 2016, it had still not been finalized by the time the video was released, nor has it become law since.[31] This is in sharp contrast to "Zero Chance" campaigns, which Australian authorities have continued to run in such countries as Sri Lanka, Afghanistan, and Indonesia.

Not surprisingly, the increasing international spread of the COVID-19 virus in early 2020 would prove a major setback, profoundly obstructing the progress of our plans. Not only were there now major travel restrictions, with IOM and UNCHR temporarily suspending resettlement on March 17, 2020, and Canada notably closing its borders and canceling all imminent refugee arrivals the following day,[32] but the Singapore Visa Application Centre (VAC) was "temporarily closed until further notice." This meant that the families' refugee interviews would also be further delayed.

While the Canadian government's official processing time for privately sponsored refugees from Indonesia was still 31 months, there was now a new proviso, warning that such projections "may not accurately reflect any disruptions caused by the novel coronavirus (COVID-19)." By mid-year, Canadian authorities were no longer able to provide processing timelines for specific applications and were working on ways to virtually finalize "priority applications" of Canadians trying to return home, "vulnerable populations," and essential service providers. Meanwhile, refugee resettlement programs had been "temporarily paused," to be resumed "as conditions permit." It was clear the families were in for an even longer wait. "Sadly, I am sure there will be further delay and stricter conditions imposed on our refugees," Kyanh lamented.[33]

To make matters worse, we had serious concerns for the refugees' health, Indonesia, and notably Jakarta, being particularly severely impacted by the virus, with what would prove to be the highest infection rate and death toll in South-East Asia.[34] By mid–March 2020, Mrs. Loan had already expressed concern, restricting her children's movements, while still focusing on their education. "Some people infected with coronavirus live near my place," she told me. "We are limited [*sic*] to go out. Almost we stay home, my children [do] worksheets at home." At IOM's insistence, Mrs. Phuc's children, Tuan and Trinh, remained quarantined at home, struggling to continue their studies online with UPH College. Furnished only with mobile phones and having exhausted their data allowance, I agreed to pay for Wi-Fi temporarily. Nevertheless, as per the Indonesian government's protocol, refugees were eligible for COVID-19-related services, notably testing and treatment provided by the Health Ministry, while UNCHR, together with local governments and partners, were distributing sanitation kits, including face masks and disinfectant.[35]

Hoping that Indonesian schools would soon reopen, we remained concerned for three of the youngest children in the group, denied a formal education since fleeing Vietnam in early 2017: Mrs. Loan's daughter, Tran, who had got as far as Grade 4, and Mrs. Lua's two sons, Dang, who had only reached Grade 5, and Koi, who had been too young to attend school in Vietnam.

"We are collecting money for the refugees here during COVID-19," Grace told me from Bangkok, "but no one thinks about the ones in Indonesia. So, I said we need to help them too." The USD900 she raised would help the families buy food during the pandemic, enabling them to set aside funds to cover school fees. At the mothers' request, I turned to Mrs. Decy once more to inquire whether any more room was available at the Christian KANIA school attended by the other little girls.

Revealing that Koi had sat entrance tests several months earlier to determine his grade level, she replied that he could now enroll for the coming academic year. In fact, Mrs. Lua had already made an appointment to discuss the curriculum and fees, agreeing to pay the school each month and maintaining that IOM would contribute a subsidy. As for the older children, "we are sorry that we have no classes as yet for Grades 4 and 5," Mrs. Decy wrote. "We can recommend other private schools, but the fees will be around six times or much higher than us.... How about a tutor rather than having no one helping with their studies? I know someone who can help. Let me know if you are interested."

Upon learning that Dang and Tran were now teenagers, however, the tutor deemed them too old. Rather than simply allowing them to return to their own online English and Mathematics programs, Mrs. Decy suggested we contact Sekolah Lentera Harapan (SLH), a network of 26 schools around Indonesia with close to 10,000 students of all ages, which according to its website, is "designed to provide a high quality education for less fortunate people."[36] Indeed, UPH College was part of the SLH network, whose head office was also in Tangerang. The response from the acting administrative coordinator was initially positive. After more than three years, it seemed as if our aim of securing formal educational opportunities for all 12 children was finally about to be realized, enabling them to be counted among the roughly 580 refugees enrolled in accredited national schools in June 2020.[37] Unfortunately, however, COVID-19 would play havoc with our plans once more, the coordinator writing again that month to explain that Indonesian schools, closed since mid–March, would not be reopening as originally envisaged for the new education year, with learning to continue online.

By late July 2020, Canadian immigration was slowly resuming, with some refugees "starting to arrive as countries and organizations reduce travel restrictions. We expect more refugees to slowly start arriving over the next few months." Even more heartening was the estimated reduction in processing times for privately sponsored refugees from Indonesia first to 18 months, then by September 2020, to 15 months, down to 11 months by November 2020, and by February 2021, a mere seven months, based on "how long it took us to process most complete applications in the past 12 months."[38] Nevertheless, the contrast with the families' actual situation in Indonesia could not have been starker, with daily life at a complete standstill, even though the Singapore VAC had reopened, albeit with "limited services" subject to pandemic-preventative measures.

Indeed, the Canadian government revealed that it was now resettling about 250 refugees per week. To compensate to some extent for the dramatic shortfall in immigration in 2020, it announced a new ambitious Immigration Levels Plan for 2021–2023, with projected admissions of between 43,500–68,000 "refugees, protected persons, humanitarian and compassionate and other" in 2021 to between 49,000–70,500 in 2023, positioning "Canada to maintain its leadership in refugee resettlement." More specifically, a targeted 22,500 privately sponsored refugees—more than one third of the total—were to be resettled during each of the three years. Not everyone was impressed: "None of Canada's resettlement numbers are particularly high," academics Dr. Shauna Labman and Dr. Adèle Garnier wrote. "Compared to economic and family-class immigration to Canada, humanitarian admissions are already the smallest stream, representing less than 15 per cent."[39] Nevertheless, by 2022, numbers had increased still further, with projected admissions of between 60,000–88,000, including 31,255 privately sponsored, set to rise to 64,000–93,000 in 2023 with 30,795 privately sponsored, before falling slightly to 56,000–85,000, including 23,000 privately sponsored, the following year.[40]

The families too remained frustrated at their lack of progress: "I and everyone still not yet [sic], and refugees from IOM have flights to Canada every day," Mrs. Lua vented in August 2020. "I saw them go, I also happy for them [sic]. I ask them and they said the Embassy of Canada and England will open to interview refugees from next month." Stuck at home, she focused on perfecting her rice paper roll skills, contemplating the possibility of opening a food business in Canada one day.

At my suggestion, Mrs. Loan contacted the Singapore VAC for an update, only to be told there was nothing for her to do but wait:

> Please note that your application is currently in our interview queue. There is no timeline at this time, but we will notify you once an interview date has been set. At this time, you are not requested to provide any additional documents....
>
> You should be aware that the application for immigration to Canada as a Convention Refugee in the Privately Sponsored Refugee category is a lengthy process, and that the approval of the sponsorship does not in any way guarantee the applicant's acceptance for permanent residence in Canada. All applicants must meet the eligibility and admissibility criteria for immigration to Canada. As such, please wait to hear from us.

The families were among 45,000 PSR applicants across the world, still waiting to be processed by Canadian visa officers, the resumption of official processing remaining a "moving target." Indeed, most refugees who had managed to reach Canada were those whose cases had been finalized prior to border closures in March 2020, with only just over 9,200 being admitted by the end of that year, including around 5,300 who had been privately sponsored. In total, a mere 22,800 refugees would be resettled worldwide in 2020—the lowest number in almost two decades—about 400 of whom traveled from Indonesia, a nominal 27 being privately sponsored. The following year, Canada resettled around 20,400, including about 9,500 privately sponsored, of the 57,500 refugees resettled worldwide, 457 of the 13,175 refugees registered with UNHCR in Indonesia departing to resettlement countries by the end of 2021, including 59 who were privately sponsored.[41]

As schools gradually began to reopen in Indonesia, Mrs. Phuc's older children, Tuan and Trinh, made the difficult decision to return to their UPH dormitory, IOM subsequently requesting that Tuan sign a "living outside (self-accommodated) form," warning that their "current beds" at home with their family "will be given to other beneficiaries [who] may need [sic]." Should they wish to return to community housing in the future, IOM would "relocate" them to similar accommodation "wherever available at the time you request. (Other community housing under IOM Tangerang might be possible.)" In other words, they risked being permanently separated from their parents and younger sister. By November 2020, Tuan had confirmed that not only were new people living in their old room, but both he and his sister had fallen ill with COVID-19 and were in isolation at UPH: "Don't worry, we are young and have good immunity," he said, admitting they had not initially told their family. "I don't want they worry about us [sic]. And they will panic." While their "secret" was soon discovered, they fortunately made a quick recovery as predicted.

Meanwhile our efforts to secure some sort of formal education for Dang and Tran continued, the SLH coordinator finally putting us in contact with the UPH scholarships manager in February 2021. It had taken four years to reach this point, and we no longer had the heart to share such small steps with their mothers for fear of further disappointment. By mid–2021, we still had not had a response from either institution. In desperation, I reached out to Learning Lab founder Sandy Ooi, now based in New York City, who reassured us that once online classes resumed post-COVID-19 Delta variant outbreak, both teenagers would be welcome to join the refugee home-schooling program. In the end, only Tran was prepared to embrace the then still hypothetical opportunity, Dang preferring to study English and Mathematics with his sister's and aunt's support. They would also attend IOM-run English classes, Tran opting to study music as well. "She learns on her own about musical notes, musical instruments," big sister My confirmed. "She share with me she want to register music class when she come to Canada [sic]."

We had already had to inform Mrs. Lua that even if the families were fortunate enough to be vaccinated against COVID-19, they would have to wait their turn in the visa processing queue. "We still have not heard anything new from our Canadian immigration," Kyanh told me in February. "We spoke to the staff at the Immigration Minister's office, but all they said was 'everything is in progress.' I guess we just have to wait. I hope with the availability of the vaccine now, things will move faster."

IOM provided a glimmer of hope when it called for registration from adults, particularly female, proficient in both written and verbal English, for online courses in digital marketing or video editing. Quotas were limited and applicants had to write a "motivation letter," as well as submitting their CV. My and her brother Loc jumped at the opportunity. I was now in regular contact with My, her English having dramatically improved. She would ring me with any queries on her family's behalf, and we would also correspond regularly by Facebook Messenger. At Mrs. Loan's request, I agreed to pay for the family's internet connection for the duration of the course: "IOM hire a teacher for my children," she told me proudly. "They will study by Zoom or Google Meet. When my children finish class, they will give certificate that course [*sic*]. That's good for my children."

In late March 2021, out of the blue each family received an email from the Singapore VAC, announcing that the assessment of their Canadian permanent residence application would finally proceed. They had 30 days within which to submit a list of documents, many of which we had already included with their original applications in August 2018. One difference was that some of the forms needed updating as IRCC had since introduced newer versions. Another was that within the group, some who had been children when we first applied on their behalf, were now adults and so needed to submit their own forms. This time applicants were specifically asked: "If you or any family member have ever been refused any kind of visa ... to any country, provide a copy of ... each refusal letter for each family member, whether accompanying or not. If you do not have a copy ..., provide a written explanation of the refusal, including the country, the date ..., the purpose of the trip, an explanation of your understanding of the reasons ..., and an explanation why it is not possible to provide a copy...."

In response, we decided to submit all documentary evidence as part of their files, including the translations we had arranged of their court papers. Each family's deadline fell on a different date in the last week of April 2021. Le Luong, Kyanh, and I agreed to continue our team work to ensure all requirements would be met, including allowing sufficient time for each applicant to sign. While a general email from IRCC and ROC-O assured sponsors and refugees that "due to the pandemic, you will have 90 days to respond instead of the usual 30 days," no such extension was afforded the families.

A month later, they were among those alerted by IOM in Jakarta that their refugee interviews would take place in mid–June in a hotel via video link with the Singapore VAC. Considerable confusion ensued, as in preparation, IOM had set a 24-hour deadline for applicants to submit a myriad of forms for Canada's Government-Assisted Refugee Program (GAR). We explained to the families that fortunately, they were not in the same invidious position as some of their fellow refugees, their PSR applications having already been submitted—twice!

Nevertheless, I still had to prepare interview acceptance emails in English for each family to send and help them inquire as to whether they needed to arrange their own interpreter as had previously been expected of Mrs. Lua's family. I also had to complete Supplementary Information forms for Mrs. Phuc and family—the only ones not asked by IRCC in advance—providing, with Tuan's assistance, details of their travel history over the past ten years as well as of their active social networks. Once again, an email from IOM, this time in Tangerang, caused panic among the refugees, giving them only 24 hours to complete this form. Although I tried to reassure the other families that it had been submitted as part of their renewed applications the previous month, we ended up resending at IOM's insistence, "just to be sure."

Each family's interview was to be held at a different time on June 15, 2021, IOM having hired an interpreter for the day—apart from Nhung and Tai, who were now behind in the queue following the resubmittal of their sponsorship applications 18 months earlier. Mrs. Lua constantly fretted about their fate, only relaxing somewhat when Kyanh explained the delay was purely for administrative reasons. Nevertheless, we ensured the certified translation of all their documents so that they would be well prepared when finally summoned for interview.

When Mrs. Lua and Mr. Long finally emerged—scheduled first, their interview had started late due to technical difficulties and had taken three hours, double the allocated time—they sounded happy: "They said two or three days will have results [*sic*]," Mrs. Lua told me. Her young sister and niece had done particularly well, answering the questions directly in English without the interpreter's assistance.

Mrs. Loan's family was not so confident. "They asked about religion and my mom's land," My explained. "My mom tell them they thrown off my land and destroy my house [*sic*]. He said he was not convinced by the land. He asked for a copy. But my mom said she didn't have any copy [*sic*]."

She was referring to a receipt for the amount of 1,580,000 VND (under USD70) for a permit for which her mother had paid so as to be allowed to commence building the home that the Vietnamese police and an enforcement team had subsequently destroyed when they seized the land on the government's behalf.[42] Upon request, Mrs. Loan had given the receipt to the authorities on the understanding that it would be returned in due course, which of course it never was. In any case, if it had been handed back, she would have burned it along with all other "incriminating" documents before having fled, for fear of endangering her extended family still residing in Vietnam.

Asked why the family had not moved to Ho Chi Minh City to escape the anti–Catholic discrimination they had experienced, Mrs. Loan, a good fisherman's wife, answered simply: "There is no sea there." Strikingly, her husband was not asked any questions about his time in Vietnam's jail system, while My, in attempting to explain how she was treated at school after the family's forced return in 2015, broke down crying and could not continue.

As for Mrs. Phuc, the official ran out of time to interview her, Mr. Yen, and their two oldest children, Tuan and Trinh. We waited in hope for their appointment to be rescheduled but heard nothing until late July 2021, when the family received another email from IRCC, giving them 30 days to submit another document each for the young adults to the Singapore office—even though we had already done so three months earlier. Keen to humor the Canadian authorities, we immediately did so again.

Meanwhile, Mrs. Lua's sister, Tran Thi Le, had suddenly received an automated message from the Canadian High Commission in Singapore on behalf of IRCC, telling her that while her permanent residency application was being processed, she now qualified for free "pre-arrival services to help you prepare for your new life in Canada." "I don't understand that I only got this information," she asked me. "Why everybody doesn't receive it [*sic*]?" I encouraged her to make the most of her new-found "status," helping her to acquire an e-copy of the Participant Workbook from Canadian Orientation Abroad (COA), which she duly went through with My. Funded by IRCC and implemented by IOM, the practical program aims to improve integration outcomes for refugees resettling in Canada by preparing them in advance for what to expect.[43] "Trinh and I love the workbook, it's really helpful," Tuan commented upon receiving the e-copy from My at my request. I hoped that the young adult members of the group, now equipped with better English skills, would share their newly acquired knowledge with their parents, My assuring me she would prepare a summary in Vietnamese. "But I need time to do because I have many thing to do for a day [sic]."

Both Mrs. Loan's and Mrs. Phuc's families subsequently received invitations to attend the Canadian Embassy in Jakarta for collection of their biometrics (finger-prints and photos)—part of "Phase 2" or the "eligibility assessment."[44] Although their excitement was growing, Mrs. Loan crying tears of joy, we urged them to stay calm: All their applications were still marked as "in process," meaning that a decision had not as yet been made. "I told them biometrics doesn't mean they passed the inter-view," Grace said.

It turned out that Nhung and Tai were not that far behind, both finally receiv-ing—much to Mrs. Lua's relief—an email from the Singapore VAC about the immi-nent processing of their Canadian permanent residence applications. Having the procedure down to a fine art by now, Kyanh, Le, and I were able to submit their files within days: July 7, 2021, marked the culmination of all our efforts; henceforth all we could do was wait. "From what Lua and Loan told me about their interviews, it sounds like they went well," Kyanh told me. "I'm an optimistic kind of guy, and I think they will all be accepted."

By then restrictions on travel to Canada had begun to ease, those applicants with a valid Confirmation of Permanent Residence (COPR) document,[45] including pri-vately sponsored refugees, having been allowed to enter the country since June 21—although as an IRCC sponsor letter warned, overseas processing was still limited: "We ask for your patience and understanding while we work to increase final deci-sions and arrivals." The Canadian government had also announced it would spend close to USD2.4 million over the next two years on improving pre- and post-arrival support services for privately sponsored refugees, soon adding special immigration and humanitarian programs for 40,000 Afghan refugees in the wake of the Taliban takeover of Afghanistan on August 15, 2021.[46]

Checking how long it would now take for a privately sponsored refugee applying from Indonesia to be processed was met with the stark message: "No processing time available." Nevertheless, in October 2021, the G5 sponsors for Mrs. Phuc's family—the only family still awaiting interview[47]—suddenly received an email from IRCC requesting their 14-day quarantine plan as "our records show that you sponsored a refugee(s) who may now be able to travel to Canada." Failure to provide the plan would delay their arrival. "Looks like good news," Kyanh commented. "Le and I will work on COVID isolation plan immediately." Detailed support measures included purchasing food and other life necessities to be home delivered; a volunteer doctor who would call every day to check on their health; as well as the owner of the home where they would be staying, who would ensure they were well cared for. Meanwhile, Mrs. Phuc had some news of her own: At age 43, she was now six months pregnant with her fourth child. "Do you know the date we will go?" son Tuan asked when I told him about the quarantine plan. As usual having no idea, I urged him to continue focusing on his studies.

Eventually receiving COVID vaccines at a private hospital,[48] all three families had also been undergoing immigration medical examinations (IME), everyone meeting the Canadian pre-departure health requirements, apart from Mrs. Loan's son Loc, who was diagnosed with a pneumothorax or collapsed lung, much to his family's surprise as he did not have any symptoms. Tall and very thin, the physician urged him to gain weight, and he was given a course of physical therapy, covered by IOM. With the family's permission, I shared his medical results with a rehabilitation medical specialist and refugee advocate colleague in Sydney, who explained the confusion: There were three reports, each with a different outcome. According to one, Loc's lungs were clear, another stated he had tuberculosis, while a third referred to the pneumothorax. Our underlying concern was whether he had active tuberculosis, which without treatment, could make him inadmissible to Canada for "endangering public health."[49] Further tests were scheduled, as well as appointments with a nutritionist and pulmonologist. If he was found to be contagious, he would need a six-month course of antibiotics before his family would be allowed to depart for Canada.

It would be several months before the anxious family was informed, much to everyone's relief, that he had been given a clean bill of health.

Discovering that he was watching YouTube videos to learn how to design game apps, Mai Pham, Sandy, and I supported his purchase of a suitable laptop computer, with his sister My's assistance, so he could learn hands-on. "Thank you for helping me achieve my dream," he told us in a video message in English.

Ensuring the Learning Lab was functional after such a long hiatus took several months, Sandy needing to organize considerable repairs from afar. Upon learning the former local director would not be returning, she decided to hand management responsibilities to a committee comprised of the oldest students, including My. "I am so proud of these young adults," Sandy told me. "Very responsible.... They are learning to use excel sheets, canva graphic design, and more." My explained further: "We will handle about the bus, make a rule in Learning Lab, preserve computer and creative account for new members [sic]." She had also been revising the high school curriculum on her own during lockdown. "When I go to Canada, I would like to go to school for get diploma [sic]," she told me. "Then I register to college."

With over 30 refugee teenagers enrolled, the fastest Wi-Fi connection installed, class schedules set, and *angkot* drivers employed to transport students from home to the premises,[50] itself provided for free by a generous donor, My and her team were on a final walkthrough when they discovered the roof had shattered. Hopes for repairs to be completed by January 2022 appeared dashed when Sandy learned that building management had been charging the Learning Lab a monthly "environmental" or maintenance fee throughout the pandemic, even though the center had been shut. "So that's another 26,000,000 IDR or USD1,800," she posted on Facebook. "I know the money will come. I'm just so upset at all the stumbling blocks the students need to face just to get into the facilities—to study! So much time wasted! Most refugees in Indonesia do not have access to public education.[51] Forget Covid, they haven't had formal schooling since they sought refuge in Indonesia! My heart breaks every time one of the students asks me when Learning Lab will reopen. I'm sorry guys.... I hope soon." Less than four days later, the financial shortfall had been covered by further donations, and the renovation permit was well underway, thus finally enabling the roof repairs to begin. "I wanted to post a victory, and not just my complaints," Sandy wrote. "My heart is at peace now."

With minimal control over their own lives and forced to await an outcome for so many years, tensions would often arise, particularly between the older family members, who were confined in such proximity. The situation came to a head in early November 2021, when Grace contacted me from the U.S. on behalf of Mrs. Loan, who had requested she translate for me in a meeting with the entire group. This was the first time I would meet the two fathers, Mr. Loi and Mr. Yen, in person, albeit online. It quickly became apparent, however, that the main purpose of the discussion was for me to confirm that everyone was of good character, providing reassurance that no one was speaking ill of the others behind their back.

Soon afterwards, relief was finally at hand, with Tuan announcing the good news to me the following week. His family had received a text message from IOM Tangerang Operations Team, announcing they would pick them up from their dormitory on the afternoon of December 1, 2021, and take them to the airport ahead of their flight to Canada that evening. "Mrs. Shira on December there is so cold [*sic*]," Tuan wrote. "Could you help us to prepare sweaters?" Reassuring him their sponsors would meet their needs on arrival, I excitedly rang Kyanh, not realizing it was the middle of the night in Mississauga. He did not seem to mind, commencing plans immediately to find an appropriate apartment for the family as per their settlement plan.

Continuing our conversation the next day, he revealed that he had only just discovered from Mrs. Lua that all the adults had been doubly vaccinated against COVID-19 and so possibly did not need a quarantine plan after all. "We do the plan as requested," he explained. "The IRCC representative at the airport will tell us what the restrictions are." As it turned out, given none of the children had been vaccinated in Indonesia, their parents were expected to quarantine with them for two weeks upon entry.

While the effects of the pandemic meant that VOICE Canada had not been able to fundraise fully in preparation for the families' arrival, it was fortunate that the Queensland Vietnamese community had already provided more than enough to support Mrs. Phuc and her growing family. Kyanh charged me with the responsibility of explaining that all would be well so long as the adults were willing to work, VOICE being prepared to introduce them to the job market. I assured him this would not be a problem: Having been prevented from working in Indonesia for so many years, they had shown great initiative in seeking out opportunities for advancement whenever possible, particularly for their children. In a conference call with Dr. Bui and Doan Trung, we agreed to consider private fundraising within our personal circles should it prove necessary.

An IRCC Notice of Arrival email forwarded from their sponsors confirmed that the impending birth of the new baby was behind the decision to allow Mrs. Phuc and family to fly at this time: "She needs to travel before 32 weeks of gestational age." Arrangements would also be made for her to consult a family physician within a week post-arrival followed by an obstetrician within the month. "It's such a Christmas gift for Phuc's family that opens up a big hope for others," Mai Pham commented.

Mrs. Lua's family, including her sister Le and niece Ngoc, were not far behind, with IRCC requesting their quarantine plan in late November 2021. Meanwhile, Kyanh and his team had found a brand-new condominium for Mrs. Phuc's family, with Le Luong putting out a call for donations on Facebook: "Urgent! Furniture and household items needed for refugees arriving next week: Sofa, microwave, dishes, utensils, blankets and bed linen, pots and pans, anything. Please pm [personal message] me if you have anything you can donate." The response was overwhelmingly generous: "I've been picking up clothes and household supplies all afternoon," Le told me on the weekend before their arrival. "Out of seven places, I only picked up from three and my car was full. I'll have to make sure some is shared with the other families but the eight-year-old is getting a lot of new or very gently used stuff…. When I came to Canada, I was still wearing hand me downs until my teenage years."

Around six dedicated VOICE Canada volunteers had helped prepare for the family's arrival, supported by another eight who assisted in collecting clothing, household goods, and furniture, and in setting up the apartment. "It takes a village," Le told me. "In this case, we have a very strong network of volunteers, donors, and advocates." Meanwhile back in Indonesia, although Tuan nonchalantly assured me at first that "we just wait by God plan [*sic*]," he eventually confessed, "We['re] so nervous, scar[ed], and excited…. I have no clue about Canada. I just worry for my mom and the baby. I am so nervous [about] what will happen and what to do?" Asked whether they wanted to see photos of their new beautifully arranged home, they preferred to wait until they could enjoy the surprise in person.

Mrs. Phuc contacted me eagerly from Jakarta's Soekarno-Hatta International airport just before departure. Not having passports, the family members had each been issued with a "Single Journey Travel Document for Resettlement to Canada." Their Canadian government transportation loan was to be repaid in full within three to eight years, as is common practice, monthly repayments commencing within one year of their arrival.[52]

A day and a half later, including a stopover of just under ten hours in Istanbul, they landed at Toronto Pearson International Airport, Tuan immediately alerting me that they were in the Air Canada terminal. Thinking they were about to appear, I urgently contacted Kyanh and Le, only for them to respond later from their car, where they were required to wait due to COVID restrictions until IRCC had processed all the family's paperwork and an IOM representative had helped collect their luggage and accompanied them outside. Only then could their advocates and sponsors finally welcome them to Canada, giving out warm clothing and taking celebratory photos, SBTN (Saigon Broadcasting Television Network) conducting a brief curbside interview.[53] While we knew they had been granted permanent Canadian residency immediately on arrival upon being authorized by Port-of-entry officials with the Canada Border Services Agency (CBSA),[54] a subsequent check of their Confirmation of Permanent Residence (COPR) document confirmed our highest expectations: Canada had indeed recognized them as Convention Refugees, conferring protection.[55]

Once they had found their bearings, it did not take them long to find work, with the support of their sponsors: Mr. Yen making sushi rolls, Tuan working in construction—"I love this job"—while Trinh was employed in a candy factory until the restaurant where she had been going to work would resume full operations post–COVID. Understanding she would need to self-fund her future studies, she also approached

From left, Vietnamese Veterans Association of Ontario former president Thien Tran, Kim Tran and husband Kyanh Do, sponsor Can Nguyen, Mrs. Phuc, Mr. Yen, Trinh, Hoa Nhien, Tuan (holding the Republic of Vietnam heritage and freedom flag), sponsor Lien Nguyen, and Le Luong (courtesy of VOICE Canada and journalist and photographer Vu Xuan Sa on behalf of *Thoi Bao*).

the local grocery store, offering to work nights and weekends. While they would change jobs several times over the next months, adapting their plans to suit their changing circumstances, they would always remain employed.

No sooner had Mrs. Phuc and family arrived in Mississauga than Mrs. Lua received an email from IOM confirming her family's flight on January 19, 2022. "We're so excited right now," she texted me. "We are thankful because if not have you, we don't have the happiness today [*sic*]. You have a good heart. And we never forget you. You are always in our hearts.... And I hope Loan's family and my brother and sister [-in-laws'] documents will come soon."

Indeed, Grace and I were also waiting for Canadian immigration to announce the date so that we could make plans to accompany Mrs. Loan who, while delighted at that prospect, understandably remained on tenterhooks despite all efforts to reassure her: "For the past four weeks my sponsor has not received a letter from the immigration department," she told me. "I don't know what's wrong with our family's document. I also ask IOM medical. They said they already sent our document to immigration last month.... As you know, I look forward my sponsor call me every day [*sic*]." I repeated my reassurance that her family's application had probably been delayed due to her son's ostensible medical misdiagnosis in addition to their change of sponsor in 2019. "Oh wow, how lovely it is for you and Grace to think about accompanying Loan, let alone actually doing it," Trung commented, "This is beyond amazing!"

While Mrs. Lua and family packed their bags, Kyanh had managed to find them a place to live. "It was -20°C [-4°F] outside but Lua Tran's new home is filling up with so much love and warmth," Le shared on Facebook on January 16, 2022. "We are excited for their arrival later this week and can't wait for them to start their new life in Canada. If you have any extra mattresses, blankets, gently used winter clothing, or furniture, please pm me. Anything helps!"

It had been a busy weekend for VOICE Canada, with Le and Kyanh also facilitating an international zoom meeting involving four different time zones so that Grace, who was visiting her family in Seattle, and the three Australians, Dr. Bui in Brisbane, Trung in Melbourne, and myself in Sydney could get a progress report from Mrs. Phuc, Mr. Yen, and Tuan as to how the family was settling into their new home. With much of the meeting conducted by necessity in Vietnamese, I was content to observe the proceedings, until Le shared that Mr. Yen's gratitude for our support had brought tears to her eyes. Dr. Bui was keen to send several thousand more dollars raised by the Queensland Vietnamese community in support of VOICE's efforts for the families, while Kyanh joked that he knew Mrs. Lua's sponsors well and would be prepared to ask for more assistance if necessary. Given he and his family were their sponsors, he would not have far to go.

Mrs. Lua, her husband Mr. Long, three children, sister Le and niece Ngoc duly arrived on January 21, 2022. After clearing immigration and taking the now customary photos outside the airport, Kyanh only momentarily contemplating cancelling due to the extreme cold—"frostbite happens after a few minutes"—they made their way to their spacious apartment accompanied by their VOICE Canada sponsors and volunteers. Kyanh introduced me to the support team via video link, while Le Luong provided a tour of their new home, enabling me to greet the new arrivals, shouting to be heard above the cacophony of excited chatter. Mrs. Lua's message of gratitude was succinct: "Because of everyone helping me I have a good life today."

From left: Mrs. Lua's sister Le, niece Ngoc, daughter Uyen, son Koi, Mrs. Lua, son Dang, and husband, Mr. Long (courtesy of VOICE Canada and journalist and photographer Vu Xuan Sa on behalf of *Thoi Bao*). "What a gutsy woman Lua is!" Trung mused. "Seeing her smiling brings a smile to my face. For so long I heard only their voices during dark times."

Three days later, Mr. Long was already working, labelling boxes, while his wife, her sister and niece were preparing for a job interview with a tool and die manufacturer. They were immediately hired, starting work the following week in a factory assembly line, interspersed with interviews with Vietnamese media outlets.[56] "These are jobs referred to us by other refugees whom VOICE Canada sponsored," Kyanh explained. "They are working at this company and helped get Lua, Le, and Ngoc in." Husband and wife were soon working together: "I'm sorry I was busy to say hello to you [sic]," Mrs. Lua told me. "From Monday to Thursday I work at factory and from Friday to Sunday I work at bread store."

Less than a month later, her children had started school, the first time in over five years since son Dang had had the opportunity of formal education. Mrs. Loan's daughter Tran was not far behind, the Learning Lab finally reopening in Jakarta in early March 2022. "She likes it very much," older sister My reported. "But she prefers it when the class can be directly guided by a teacher.... She doesn't like me to teach because I'm very strict in studies. But some questions she didn't understand. She will ask me."

Only brother Loc languished at home, waiting for his second COVID-19 vaccine before he was eventually able to rejoin the class in late April. Meanwhile, Mrs. Phuc had given birth to her daughter, Quinna Nguyen Tran, on February 13—the first Canadian citizen in the family. "I don't want her name same as others [sic]," she wrote, explaining the family's choice of a western (Irish) name.

Several more months would pass rather uneventfully, with Mrs. Loan only becoming more depressed, before Kyanh finally shared an IRCC email received by her sponsors on May 9, 2022, requesting their quarantine plan. By this stage, the official processing time for privately sponsored refugees from Indonesia as per the IRCC website was ten months for the sponsorship application and 25 months for the refugee application, based on how long it had taken to process most

Tran on her first day at the Learning Lab, March 8, 2022 (photograph by Ho Thanh Nha My, courtesy Tran Thi Thanh Loan).

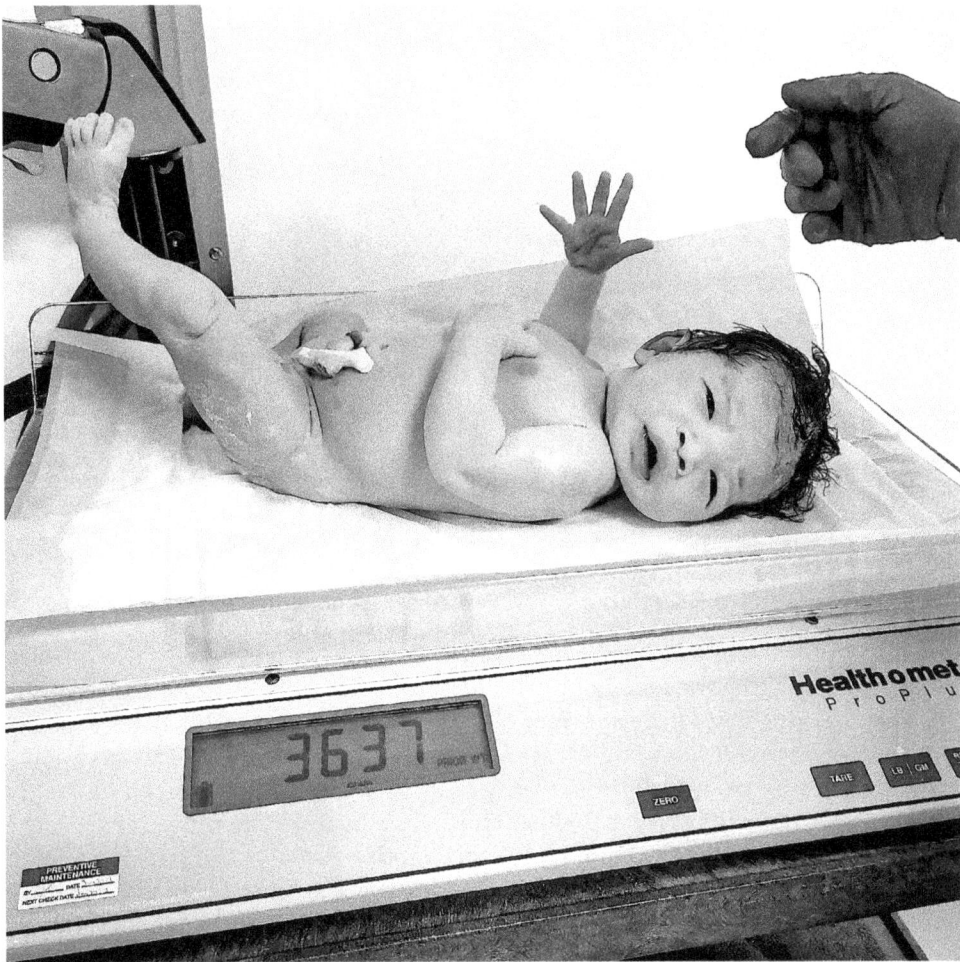

New-born Canadian citizen, Quinna Nguyen Tran (courtesy Nguyen Thi Phuc).

complete applications over the past six months[57]—a fairly accurate estimate, as it had turned out, for Mrs. Loan and family. While My had already planned on approaching her little sister Nhi's school to discuss enrolling for the new Indonesian academic year, this no longer seemed necessary.

Assuming a similar departure schedule as for the other two families, we estimated that IOM would announce their scheduled flight to Canada in about seven weeks' time. As Grace was already intending to undertake advocacy work in Mississauga then, I would be accompanying the family as promised, but on my own. It also seemed likely that I would be traveling to join them in Jakarta straight after my trip to Vietnam for Due's graduation.[58]

As it turned out, I had just over a week between trips. On June 23, 2022, accompanied by a driver and translator, I traveled to the families' hometown of La Gi in Binh Thuan province—just under 100 miles from Ho Chi Minh City—to meet their relatives. Slowly making our way between homes, parents, siblings, in-laws, nephews, and nieces all expressed gratitude for the opportunity their refugee family members had been given for a new life in Canada. It was well into the afternoon when we

From left, Lam, the author, Mrs. Van, Mr. Vo, and Son, June 24, 2022.

were finally able to enjoy the lunch arranged by Mrs. Loan's siblings at a nearby beach resort, before making the four-hour drive back to the city.

The following day, I had the honor of finally meeting Vo An Don in person, after he accepted the invitation to breakfast at my hotel, which involved taking a 12-hour bus trip each way from his home in Phu Yen province. We were joined by his former clients, Huynh Thi My Van and her children, Son and Lam, the latter serving as translator.[59] Showing us the callouses on his hands caused by the farming work he had been forced to undertake to support his young family since being disbarred four years earlier,[60] Mr. Vo clarified that he had been invited to join me in La Gi, but had considered it unsafe to do so, warning that I too was now probably under surveillance. He also apologized for not having met me during my previous visit to Vietnam in 2018, explaining that he had not been allowed to leave his local area at that time. Even now, his family remained isolated, the authorities spreading negative rumors about them, which encouraged the local community to shun them. His ability to fulfil his lifelong aim of assisting the less fortunate in Vietnam having been completely circumscribed by the loss of his legal license, Mr. Vo revealed that he had applied for asylum in the U.S. and had already undergone three interviews, expecting imminently to learn the outcome.

I was also struck by the way in which Mrs. Van and her daughter Lam could still recall the small kindnesses shown to them by Australian officers in 2016 in stark contrast with their Vietnamese counterparts. Indeed, Mrs. Van went so far as to say that if she ever had the chance to return to Australia, she would like to visit Darwin— the very city where she was taken to be forcibly removed—because she remembered being given medication for a headache there. "Australian officials were really kind, especially to women and children," Lam confirmed.

On July 4, 2022, I flew to Jakarta from Sydney to join Mrs. Loan and family ahead of their departure the following evening. Two of her sisters, whom I had just met in Vietnam, had come to visit along with a nephew, enjoying their first reunion in many years, with the knowledge that it could be many more before they saw each other again. After waiting hours for me to obtain a visa on arrival, eight of us—including My, Nhung, and Tai—crammed into a taxi, driven by a Hazara Afghan refugee and family friend, to take me to my hotel in the vicinity of the refugee housing complex in Tangerang, where they had lived since February 2018. By now it was late, and all restaurants were closed. Undaunted, My and Nhung accompanied me to the corner store, speaking in fluent Indonesian with the shopkeeper—a legacy of their years there. My also relievedly shared that her entire family had passed the "fitness-to-fly" COVID-19 check.[61]

The next day, I was finally able to see their IOM accommodation for myself. We walked up the four flights of stairs to their rooms on the top floor, an African resident obligingly carrying my suitcase: "We won't see you again," he told Mrs. Loan's youngest daughter Nhi, now 11, who was showing me around together with My. Each level resembled the others, a long, white-tiled corridor leading to the modest rooms, rows of shoes neatly arrayed outside the locked doors. The focal point of each floor was an external, communal kitchen, with a separate hotplate or stove top for each individual or family.

The author with Mrs. Loan, July 5, 2022.

Mrs. Loan's family was the only one departing that day, and everyone wanted to participate in their joy. Dressed traditionally or in western clothing, fellow residents from an array of countries, some of whom I discovered had been there for as long as eight years, came to say goodbye, wish them well, give them a hug, and pose for a photo. The fortunate ones excitedly shared the news that they too were being accepted by Australia, Canada, New Zealand, UK, or U.S., but did not know exactly when they would leave. Others were still waiting in hope, their resettlement process delayed for years due to the COVID-19 pandemic, Taliban takeover of Afghanistan in August 2021, Russian invasion of Ukraine in February 2022, or another crisis. Waiting for the IOM bus to arrive to take us to the airport, Mrs. Loan and I sat together on a mattress on the floor of her small, airconditioned room, hibernating from the stifling heat, surrounded by her family.

They had 12 pieces of luggage between them as well as a myriad of cabin bags, including seven sturdily wrapped boxes of frozen seafood, which their neighbors helped load on to the bus. When upon arrival at the airport, the airline insisted that they only bring two or three, My, as family representative, stood her ground: "I was so nervous, but I told them I had done my research, and we were eventually allowed to being all seven," she said.

We had agreed to leave the announcement of their departure to Mr. Vo, who duly posted on social media to his numerous followers. The actual journey went smoothly, with an IOM representative meeting the refugee families, of whom there

From left: Mrs. Loan, Loc, Tran, Mr. Loi, Nhi, and My (courtesy of VOICE Canada and journalist and photographer Vu Xuan Sa on behalf of *Thoi Bao*).

were several, at each airport to give them their papers—an IRCC-issued Single Journey Travel Document for Resettlement to Canada and boarding pass—shepherd them through customs, and ensure they were looked after, especially during the close to ten-hour layover in Istanbul. IOM had also prepared them in advance as to what to expect after arriving in Canada, My revealing that her family had spent two hours on a "Canadian Orientation Abroad" session[62] the previous week with the Thailand office: "We had so many questions for them to answer, which is why it took so long."

A kind IOM official at Toronto Pearson International Airport allowed me to join the family in immigration after going through customs myself. Following a lengthy wait in a reception area, they were ushered into a glass booth for their first screening interview with an officer from the Canada Border Services Agency (CBSA), who checked their documents were in order and asked a series of routine questions: "What is your permanent address in Canada? Has anyone in your family been convicted of a serious crime in your home country? How much money do you have with you? Is everyone on the same visa application? Is this your first time in Canada?"

My answered each question calmly and succinctly: "Yes, both my parents were found guilty in Vietnam and sentenced to jail." Listening at the doorway, my heart skipped a beat: Surely that prison term was integral to their refugee status? The official, however, moved straight on to the next question on his script. After another long delay during which their paperwork was finalized, they were called in to sign their Confirmation of Permanent Residence. Finally, the moment for which we had

From left: Trinh, Hoa Nhien, Sandy with baby Quinna, and Tuan.

all been longing: They had been authorized to enter Canada as permanent residents—among the projected 31,255 privately sponsored to be admitted in 2022—and were no longer refugees.[63]

Having collected their luggage, we were excitedly met by VOICE Canada advocates and sponsors, notably Kyanh Do and Le Luong—our first face-to-face meeting—as well as Grace, Mrs. Lua, and her sister Le. Posing for celebratory photos, Mrs. Loan did a curbside interview, before everyone made their way to the family's spacious new home in Mississauga.

The next days involved a whirlwind of celebrations: Learning Lab founder Sandy Ooi had flown in from New York City as a surprise for the children, and we made sure to share dinner with Mrs. Loan's family on their first evening, and to visit Mrs. Phuc's family, meeting baby Quinna. My gift to each home was an English-Vietnamese dictionary that I had been keeping for them since 2017, when the online order had failed to arrive ahead of our first meeting in Indonesian detention. Grace and I also did a detailed interview with Canadian Vietnamese newspaper, *Thoi Bao*, published the following week.[64]

Best of all, Mr. Vo had texted to say that he and his family had been accepted as refugees by the U.S. The week culminated in a dinner at Kyanh and wife Kim Tran's home, attended by many VOICE Canada supporters to welcome the newcomers. It was inspiring to meet such generous sponsors who had once been refugees themselves, friends of Kyanh's since their college days, upon whom he knew he could depend. It was also impressive to see Kyanh and Kim's home basement, which had

From left: Dang, Mrs. Lua, Nhi (front), Ngoc (back), Mrs. Loan, Tran, Koi (front), My, Uyen, Mr. Loi, Le, and Loc at Kyanh Do and Kim Tran's home (courtesy of VOICE Canada and journalist and photographer Vu Xuan Sa on behalf of *Thoi Bao*).

Saying goodbye to the families, as Mrs. Lua (left) and Mrs. Loan (right) accompany the author to the detention exit in Jakarta, June 3, 2017 (courtesy Sunshine and Aaron Biskaps).

been converted into a massive storage area, from which new arrivals were able to collect whatever they needed, from kettles to furniture and mattresses. Even those who had only been in Canada for a few weeks themselves were prepared to volunteer in whatever capacity they could to assist others who arrived after them. Most heartening was to observe Mrs. Phuc's and Mrs. Lua's families quietly donating part of their wages to charity. "So empowering and important for their self-respect," Kyanh commented, revealing that by mid–2022, VOICE Canada had sponsored more than 135 Vietnamese refugees, with 25 more waiting to be resettled

From left, Mrs. Lua, Mrs. Loan, the author, and Grace at Toronto Pearson International Airport, July 13, 2022.

from Thailand.[65] My favorite photo was taken at Kyanh and Kim's home that night: It shows the promise of the next generation, preparing to soar.

I spent my last day in Toronto with Mrs. Loan, Mrs. Lua, My, and Grace, the two mothers insisting on accompanying me to the airport. Now working two jobs from morning to midnight, Mrs. Lua had taken time off to join us. Reflecting on our journey as I waited for the plane to take off, I posted on social media: "Just over five years ago we bid an emotional farewell to each other in detention in Jakarta. We had no idea then that we would be saying goodbye in Toronto, free and equal. I am so excited about your future as you embark on your new life in Canada."

Postscript

It has been six years since I sat down to breakfast with the newspaper on that Saturday morning in late July 2016 and first read of the plight of Mrs. Loan and her children. Their long battle for resettlement has certainly not been for the faint-hearted, whether refugee or advocate. Nevertheless, together we have learned to persist, gaining strength from each other, and developing ties so close we now consider ourselves family.

Celebrating *Tết* (Lunar New Year) on what would turn out to be for the last time in Indonesia in February 2022, Mrs. Loan messaged in English:

> Today I write [from] my heart to express what you have given to my family during the long time my family has had a lot of difficulties, you have given all your heart. The love you have for my family is so great mentally and physically for a long time, you are not tired of the difficulties, you do your best.... When I'm very tired but having you by my side makes me mentally strong, you are my guardian angel, ... my children always remember you, they always try to study well and be obedient so as not to disappoint you. The family does not know what to say other than to pray for your family's health every day to continue to help other families with similar circumstances.

I responded by expressing our love and admiration for her family's resilience and determination to help themselves: "You rarely ask for anything and you all try so hard in difficult circumstances. These qualities make us want to assist you even more."

It may take a village to raise a child, but in our experience, it takes a global network to assist a refugee. In mid–2022, with the number of forcibly displaced people having surpassed 100 million, including 26.6 million refugees, UNHCR estimated more than 2 million would need to be resettled the following year, an increase of 36 per cent.[1] Confronted by such numbers, it is easy to be daunted—what are three families, or 21 lives, in this human ocean of suffering and need? Yet, I remain convinced that it is within the power of each of us to make a difference, especially if we join forces and work together. Nor does assisting third world refugees involve much financial outlay. As renowned Australian philosopher Peter Singer argues, "if we can provide immense benefit to someone at minimal cost to ourselves, we should do so."[2] Moreover, as advocates, we are free to contribute as our abilities, means, and constraints allow. It is the refugee who must courageously take center stage in their own life drama if they are to succeed.

These three families were the first to flee Vietnam successfully in recent times, Vo Anh Don confirmed during our last meeting in June 2022, revealing their escape to be the main reason why he and his family were banished from both the law and their community. "If someone goes overseas and obtains citizenship elsewhere and then returns to Vietnam, they are admired," he explained. "But if someone flees the country and is rejected and forcibly returned to Vietnam, they are treated harshly and can be sentenced to up to 15 years' jail. They are criticized for avoiding paying tax and shirking their financial responsibilities to the country. The government also encourages their local community to shun them, and this black mark remains next to their name forever."

Not only does this reality impact the failed asylum seeker, but their extended family too. As I discovered during my last visit, relatives had been forced to change jobs or settle for a more modest career, staying under the radar and ensuring they did nothing to upset the authorities.

This on the ground experience flies in the face of the official view of Australia's Department of Foreign Affairs (DFAT), which continues to assert that "being a failed asylum seeker is not generally stigmatized." But then, such an assertion is not surprising, given Australian authorities have now completely and blatantly obliterated any memory of what these families endured in Vietnam: "Authorities occasionally question returnees from Australia upon their arrival in Vietnam. The interview process generally takes between one to two hours and focuses on obtaining information about the facilitation of any illegal movement on their part. DFAT is not aware of any cases in which returnees from Australia have been held overnight for this purpose."[3]

Reading through the close to 2,000 congratulatory messages from fellow Vietnamese citizens sent within the week after Mrs. Loan and her family reached Canada, I was struck by the general tone of admiration: "They are determined; knowing that the risk is very high, they still decided to go and achieved what they wanted."

On August 7, 2022, Mrs. Loan sent me a warning: "My sister is being investigated about you and Mr. Vo An Don. My sister told the police she didn't know you … [except] from Facebook. I think you should be wary when going back to Vietnam. Because you are in the sights of Vietnamese communists." Concerned, I reached out to Mr. Vo, who explained that the Vietnamese security police had "invited" Mrs. Loan's family to clarify our relationship after seeing his post on Facebook about our departure to Canada: "The purpose of the police 'offer' was to intimidate me and Mrs. Loan's family because they were very disgusted that Mrs. Loan and many others crossed the sea for the second time. The communist state, they are only good at oppressing people in the country. For foreign nationals like [you], they are very respectful and never dare to touch them."

Asked whether I should at least take down the photos on social media from my recent trip to Vietnam, he provided reassurance: "The fact that [you] visited some families in Vietnam with people crossing the sea [sic], the Vietnamese government respects these families very much … [and] does not dare to do anything to them." Mrs. Loan concurred: "My sister … only offered to work with the police for about half an hour and then they let her go."

As it turned out, however, Mr. Vo and his family would not be so fortunate. Scheduled to depart on September 27, 2022, IOM officials accompanied them to Tan Son Nhat airport in Ho Chi Minh City, where he duly announced their departure on social media, only to be stopped by Vietnamese police and ordered to return to their hometown of Tuy Hoa in the middle of a storm. The airport police were acting on a request from the police of Phu Yen province, where the family lived, to "postpone" their exit for "national security reasons" under article 36 of the Law on Exit and Entry

Welcoming Nhung and Tai to Canada on September 28, 2022, from left, Le Luong, *Thoi Bao* journalist Vu Xuan Sa, Vietnamese Veterans Association of Ontario former president Thien Tran, Kim Tran and husband Kyanh Do, Mr. Loi, Nhung, Mrs. Lua, Mrs. Loan, Tai, Mrs. Lua's son Koi, and sister Le (courtesy of VOICE Canada and journalist and photographer Vu Xuan Sa on behalf of *Thoi Bao*).

Nguyen Thi Kim Nhung (left) and Nguyen Tai, Mississauga, September 30, 2022 (courtesy Kyanh Do).

of Vietnamese Citizens No. 49/2019/QH14 (November 22, 2019). The action was almost immediately condemned by HRW deputy director, Asia Division, Phil Robertson: "The reality is Hanoi doesn't want Vo An Don traveling overseas where he could speak freely about the litany of harassment, discrimination and abuse he's suffered because of his choices to represent politically sensitive clients in Vietnam's kangaroo courts.... Now the authorities are blocking him and his family from seeking opportunities outside of Vietnam. This travel ban ... shows how the Vietnam government is prepared to use every dirty, abusive trick to silence the very few lawyers left in the country who dare stand up for the principle that everyone deserves legal representation."[4]

Almost a year later, as we were preparing this book for publication, Grace suddenly contacted me: "I heard the second person leaving Vietnam after [President] Biden's visit is Vo An Don. Have you heard anything or just a rumor?" I immediately reached out to Mr. Vo and was overjoyed to receive his response: "The Vietnamese government lifted the exit ban on me when President Biden visited Vietnam. Currently, my family is waiting for the U.S. Consulate to notify us when to settle in the United States."

It turned out that the official agreement had been negotiated ahead of the U.S. President's visit of September 10, 2023, Mr. Vo being informed two days earlier via a phone call from Phu Yen provincial police. He was one of four activists to be allowed to leave, the Biden administration believing he had been "wrongly detained by the country's Communist government."[5]

Mr. Vo subsequently told RFA that while his children's education had not been hindered over the past year, Vietnamese plainclothes security officers had often kept watch over his family and encouraged the neighbors to do the same, making them feel insecure. Since the verbal announcement by the police, monitoring had stopped, the officers texting him to "let them know when you leave."[6] That date finally arrived on October 25, 2023, when the family flew to the U.S., landing the next day.

This wonderful news, however, lay well ahead back on September 27, 2022, which not only was the original departure date for Mr. Vo's family but also coincidentally for the last two members of the group in Jakarta, Nguyen Thi Kim Nhung and Nguyen Tai. Bittersweet for us as advocates then was their flight to Canada. Nonetheless, this meant we had finally fulfilled our commitment both to the families and to the memory of our dear friend and indefatigable human rights advocate, Ngoc Nhi (Ann) Nguyen (as she was known). Initially motivated by my shame and sense of moral responsibility at their treatment at the hands of the Australian government, their story has become, and continues to be, so much more.

So, let's leave the final word to Nhung, Tai, Mr. Vo's young family, and all the others who arrived before you. Your journey to freedom may at last be over. But what you choose to do with that freedom is only just beginning. Over to you to write the rest of your story.

Appendix 1

Doan Trung, "Statement About Two Groups of 46 Vietnamese Asylum Seekers—The 'Plane Group' and the 'Choules Group,'" Unpublished, January 7, 2016 ᐧ

Trung Doan 01/07/2016

Notes about terms:

- The "Plane group" was flown back in July 2015 by Australia on a (possibly chartered) plane
- The "Choules group" was brought back in April 2015 on HMAS Choules

First, in A below, I state information about the Plane group and the Choules group given to me by various sources, mainly the boatpeople themselves. Then in B, I provide a table containing my translation of itemized contributions and costs of the Plane group's boat trip.[1] According to this information, no-one made a monetary profit from the trip. And all aboard sought asylum.

A. Statement Summarizing What the Plane Group and the Choules Group Told Me

- A Vietnamese official welcomed the Plane group back; he said aloud that Vietnam would not punish or detain them and would help them to settle back in if needed. These statements were interpreted into English for Australian officials present.
- Five boatpeople have been in indefinite detention, under repeated questioning; all have been told by police that they will be jailed for several years; at least one has been charged, and at least one (who is not detained) has been made unemployable because their papers are marked as an illegal departee.
- Of the Plane group, one has now been given the Charge Sheet.
- Note that the alleged crime is not people-smuggling in the sense that most Australians understand it. The authorities have not alleged that anyone profited financially from the trip. The alleged crime is leaving Vietnam without authorization by the authorities (from whom they flee).

161

- Of the Plane group, two have been in indefinite detention since their return, a third person was also in indefinite detention but due to ill health is now under house arrest, not allowed to leave home.
- Of the Choules group, two have been in indefinite detention since their return.
- During these months of indefinite detention, the Vietnamese police questioned them several times about their departure, activities, and finances of the trips.
- Apart from formal investigations, in at least one case, in December [2015] a Vietnamese person posing as an "international official" met some boatpeople. Some boatpeople were misled into thinking that that person was sent by the Australian government to help them. But that person asked, in a friendly manner, questions of a similar nature to the above.

The sources of the information I summarized above are

- the Plane group: Four boatpeople, plus one of their relatives, told me directly;
- the Choules group: One person in Australia who is a relative of one boatperson told me, and one boatperson told a person in Vietnam who investigated under my guidance.

Statement by Doan Trung, Based on Transcript of Telephone Conversation with Tran Thi Lua, Unpublished, September 28, 2016

STATEMENT BY MR TRUNG DOAN

Former Federal President of Vietnamese Community in Australia

1. I write to state facts as I learned from Vietnamese asylum seekers whose boats were stopped and who were returned by Australia back to Vietnam in 2015, in relation to the treatment that they and their schoolchildren got from the Vietnamese authorities.

2. I am willing to testify as a witness. And I am willing to provide a sworn affidavit.

3. A brief outline of my background: I was a twice-elected Federal President of the Vietnamese community's peak representative organization, the Vietnamese Community in Australia, my two terms started from the beginning of 2000 and ended at the end of 2003. My understanding of Vietnamese asylum seekers is deep and spans decades, starting with being their interpreter in the late 70s, helping form community representative organizations, and continuing as an advocate for their humane treatment from the late 90s till now.

4. On September 20, I telephoned Mrs. Lua Tran ("Lua"), a Vietnamese asylum seeker and, with her permission and prior knowledge, I recorded the call then provided the audio file to a lawyer who is helping Vietnamese asylum seekers. The transcripts of that conversation form the supporting materials for this Statement.

5. Lua and 45 other people, each person a relative or friend of at least some of the others, pooled their moneys to obtain a boat and sailed to Australia in early July 2015 to seek asylum. The boat was intercepted by Australia, and in late July 2015 they were brought back to Vietnam.

6. Upon accepting them back, a Vietnamese government official, in front of Australian government officials, gave a verbal assurance to the returned asylum seekers, to the effect that no-one would be punished for leaving Vietnam on that trip. The assurance was translated into English for the benefit of Australian government officials. The asylum seekers, and the Australian official officials, were assured by this assurance. Later, at a May 2015 Senate hearing recorded in the Hansard, an Australian government official, Operation Sovereign Borders commander Major-General Andrew Bottrell, confirmed that the Australian

government had been provided written assurance by the Vietnamese authorities that boat people would face *"no retribution for their illegal departure from Vietnam."*[1] In the Attachment, I copy the relevant texts from the Hansard.

7. The above confirmation was in relation to another boat, which also happened to contain 46 Vietnamese asylum seekers. The 46 people were returned to Vietnam in April 2015. I have spoken to people from both boats, and both groups confirmed that they were given such verbal assurance in front of Australian officials. Therefore, I believe that Vietnam gave written assurance in relation to both groups.

8. As soon as Australian officials left the scene, the returnees were taken back to their home province, where each person underwent a brief questioning session. A short time later, Lua and two men were detained for being the people who started the idea of the escape and who went to see their relatives and friends asking if they wanted to join in. Loan Tran ("Loan") (a fellow female boatperson, and the wife of one of the two men) was similarly accused but was not held in detention.

9. Due to being physically beaten on their legs, both men have become paralyzed in their legs. Lua was also physically beaten such that she vomited blood. For this, she was taken to hospital, then released on remand.

10. Lua has three children: Nguyen Thi Uyen ("Uyen") a 12-year-old girl, and boys Nguyen Hai Dang ("Dang") 10 years and Nguyen An Koi 3 years.

11. About a month after the above three children were returned to Vietnam, the two older children were able to return to school.

12. I noted that in Vietnam, the authorities have loudspeakers at many if not most public spaces. These are used to propagate state information.

13. The authorities ran public announcements publicly giving the names of Lua and of her children, stating that Lua had tried to flee Vietnam, and in doing so was, in their word, a traitor. These public announcements were made once each morning and once each afternoon, on public loudspeakers in Lua's local area and also those next to the schools attended by Lua's children. The announcements declaring their guilt were made well before the court hearing which later announced that Lua and all the others were guilty as charged. The announcements stopped when the loudspeakers' airtime was required for the National Assembly elections in May 2016.

14. Uyen and Dang were extremely upset. They cried and told their mother Lua that they felt very ashamed, they did not want to go back to school. Lua noticed that during this time, their sleep pattern was also changed, burdened with crying and their sleep was restless. Lua insisted to the two children that they must continue their schooling. The children went along with their mother's instruction and kept on attending school.

15. The public announcements also called out Loan's name and the names of her children. Loan told me a few months ago that one of her children actually stopped going to school for at least several days. Eventually, as insisted upon by Loan, her children continued with their schooling to this day. During my September 20 conversation with Lua, Lua said the same to me.

Statement made at Springvale South, Victoria, this Twenty Eighth day of September 2016

   Mr. Trung Doan

Please see ATTACHMENT →

Attachment to Trung Doan's Statement
Extracts from Senate Hansard of May 25, 2015
Page 120 of Hansard, from the 8th line

Senator HANSON-YOUNG: What has been done to ensure their safety once they have been returned to Vietnam? Do we know what has happened to them?

Major Gen. Bottrell: There was an engagement with the Vietnamese and, as the minister has previously announced, there was a level of comfort provided that—

Senator HANSON-YOUNG: A level of comfort?

Major Gen. Bottrell: there would be no retribution for their illegal departure from Vietnam—in a sense, an assurance from the government of Vietnam that there would be no retribution for their illegal departure from Vietnam.

Senator HANSON-YOUNG: So Vietnam has waived its own laws for this special group of 46—is that correct?

Major Gen. Bottrell: I cannot speak on behalf of the Vietnamese or their laws; what I can say is that there was a level of assurance provided that there would not be any retribution for their illegal departure from Vietnam.

Senator HANSON-YOUNG: Is that assurance in a written form? How did that assurance come about?

Major Gen. Bottrell: It was in a written form, but, given that it was an engagement at an official level between Australia and Vietnam, I am not able to disclose the detail of that.

Letter from Amnesty International and SUAKA to Chief of UNHCR Representation for Indonesia, February 16, 2017

Ref: TIGO ASA 21/2017.001

Chief of UNHCR Representation for Indonesia Menara Ravindo, 14th Floor Jalan Kebon Sirih Kav. 75, Jakarta Pusat 10340 Indonesia

16 February 2017

Dear Thomas Vargas

Amnesty International and SUAKA (Indonesian Civil Society Network for Refugee Rights Protection) write to express our concern for 18 Vietnamese asylum seekers, six adults and 12 children, currently in Indonesia. We are particularly concerned that, should they be forcibly returned to Viet Nam, the six adults will likely be arrested and may be the victims of torture and/or other degrading, inhuman or cruel treatment or punishment. Two of the six have already been convicted for having previously left Viet Nam for Australia and have already had prison sentences imposed which they are yet to serve.

We urge the UN Refugee Agency, in accordance with its mandate under Articles 13 and 20 of the Presidential Decree on Refugee Number 125 of 2016, to immediately register the 18 individuals and to initiate the Refugee Status Determination procedures in due course.

On 31 January 2017, the 18 individuals (their names are written below post-script) left Viet Nam by boat in the hope of reaching Australia. They had passed Indonesia on 10 February when, according to information we have received from trusted partners, their engine failed and they drifted back to Java Island, where the boat hit rocks and started to sink. When ashore, they were taken to a detention camp by Indonesian police. Having arrived in Indonesia without authorization, the 18 are at risk of being returned to Viet Nam. However, following the intervention of an Australian non-governmental organization that works on refugee issues, they were permitted to leave the detention centre for a hotel ... in Serang, Banten province. They remain in the hotel, under effective house arrest, as they are under the watch of two immigration officers.

The 18 individuals wish to seek asylum in Indonesia. The details of the case are complicated as it involves individuals who were part of two separate groups who had previously left Viet Nam by boat for Australia, only to be intercepted in Australian waters and forcibly returned to Viet Nam in March and July 2015, respectively. In August 2016, Amnesty International issued a public statement detailing both cases....

Two members of the group currently in Indonesia, Mrs. Tran Thi Thanh Loan and Mrs. Tran Thi Lua, currently face prison sentences in Viet Nam arising from the two previous attempts to flee to Australia. The details of their cases are as follows:

Mrs. Tran Thi Thanh Loan

After being sent back to Viet Nam, and despite assurances made by Viet Nam to the Australian authorities that no one would be imprisoned upon arriving back in the country, Mrs. Tran Thi Thanh Loan was arrested along with her husband and two others and charged under Article 275 of the Penal Code, which describes the crime of 'Organizing and/or coercing other persons to flee abroad or to stay abroad illegally.' She was convicted in April 2016 and given a three-year sentence. Mrs. Loan's husband, Ho Trung Loi, has been in prison since July 2015, and is now serving a two-year sentence. Mrs. Loan remained free on bail pending her appeal. She and her four children are among the 18 currently in Indonesia.

Mrs. Tran Thi Lua

In a separate but almost identical case, Mrs. Tran Thi Lua was among four people convicted under Article 275 after a boat they were traveling in was intercepted by Australian authorities and they were forcibly returned to Viet Nam in July 2015. Two men in the group of four were given two-year sentences and sent immediately to jail whereas two women, one of whom is Mrs. Lua, were given three-year sentences but remained at liberty pending appeals. Mrs. Lua, her husband and their three children are among the 18....

Mrs. Loan and Mrs. Lua both had their sentences deferred for one year, which were due to end shortly, although the exact date that they were due to be brought into custody again and sent to prison is unclear. We have spoken with a partner human rights organisation that has been in direct contact with both women since 2015. The women informed them that in the weeks leading up to their departure for Australia, they both feared that when sent to jail they would be beaten badly for speaking to international media (including the Australian Broadcasting Corporation) and Vietnamese language media based outside Viet Nam about their cases. Both women told the organisation that they have received threats from officials that they should not contact media outlets and will be punished if they do. According to the organisation, one of the women is carrying an audio recording of such a threat from a high-level police official and also a dossier of all the past media articles about her case. They stated to the organisation in advance of traveling that they would rather commit suicide by jumping into the sea than be sent back to jail in Vietnam.

Mrs. Lua told the organisation that she is terrified of jail and does not think she would survive her three-year sentence, most likely because of the treatment she received during previous imprisonment. She spent 10 weeks in jail about 500 km from her home upon being returned to Viet Nam in July 2015, before she was charged. She stated to the partner organisation that this experience traumatised her.

She described being beaten and mistreated by prison guards, who slapped her face, shouted threats and profane language, and verbally insulted her. She told the organisation that on one occasion she vomited blood after being beaten by guards. Mrs. Lua told the organisation that when angry, the guards would place dirty linen and clothes in the prisoners' well and then force them to drink, wash and cook with the dirty water.

While Viet Nam ratified the Convention Against Torture and Other Cruel, Inhuman or Degrading Treatment or Punishment in 2015, torture and other ill-treatment continue to be systematic within Vietnamese places of detention. In July 2016, Amnesty International released a report titled *'Prisons Within Prisons—Torture and Ill-Treatment of Prisoners of Conscience in Viet Nam,'* which outlines a pattern of torture and cruel, degrading, inhuman treatment and punishment of prisoners of conscience in Viet Nam (see *here*),[1] including enforced disappearances, prolonged solitary confinement, physical violence by police, prison staff and other prisoners known or believed to be working at the instigation of officials, and the withholding of medical treatment to those in need, causing severe pain and suffering. As in the case of Mrs. Lua, described above, prisoners of conscience are usually held in facilities far from their homes where it is more difficult for them to receive emotional and material support from their families and friends.

Torture of other detainees and prisoners who are not considered prisoners of conscience is also widespread, as described in *'Public Insecurity: Deaths in Custody and Police Brutality in Viet Nam'*, a 2014 report by Human Rights Watch which documents the beating to death of dozens of Vietnamese detainees (see *here*).[2] While researching the "Prisons Within Prisons" report, Amnesty International received information about beatings of prisoners who are not considered prisoners of conscience. This information was not included in the report.

Punishing an individual for exercising his or her right to seek asylum is arbitrary and unlawful. The convictions of Mrs. Loan and Mrs. Lua contravene international law and should never have been entered. In the event that they are forcibly returned they will face certain jail time and, in our opinion, the likelihood of torture and/or other ill-treatment in punishment for leaving Viet Nam a second time and fleeing their prison sentences. We also believe that the other four adults face the very real prospect of arrest, torture and/or ill-treatment in the event that they are forcibly returned to Viet Nam. The arrests of the adults would leave the children without their parents and legal guardians in violation of the best interest of children, a primary consideration in all actions concerning children, including those taken by administrative authorities and courts of law, as per the Convention on the Rights of the Child, to which Viet Nam is a state party.

Yours sincerely,

Josef Benedict
Amnesty International Director of Campaigns, Southeast Asia and the Pacific

Febi Yonesta,
Coordinator of SUAKA (Indonesian Civil Society Network for Refugee Rights Protection)

Chapter Notes

Introduction

1. Amanda Hodge and Nga L.H. Nguyen, "Kids 'Orphaned' as Vietnam Jails Parents Over Asylum Bid," *Australian*, July 29, 2016, http://www.theaustralian.com.au/news/nation/kids-orphaned-as-vietnam-jails-parents-over-asylum-bid/news-story/fdb6751c38007ea02371b802315e57a9.

2. The term "refugee" is defined in the United Nations General Assembly, *Convention Relating to the Status of Refugees*, July 28, 1951, 189 UNTS 137 (Refugee Convention), art. 1A[2]) as applying to any person who "owing to well-founded fear of being persecuted for reasons of race, religion, nationality, membership of a particular social group or political opinion, is outside the country of his nationality and is unable or, owing to such fear, is unwilling to avail himself of the protection of that country."

3. Australian Government Department of Home Affairs, "Immigration Detention and Community Statistics Summary," May 31, 2022, 9, https://www.homeaffairs.gov.au/research-and-stats/files/immigration-detention-statistics-31-may-2022.pdf. Officially established on December 20, 2017, the Department of Home Affairs (DHA) built on the former Department of Immigration and Border Protection (DIBP). For more details see https://www.homeaffairs.gov.au/about-us/who-we-are/our-history. Detention of asylum seekers arriving by boat without a valid visa has been mandatory in Australia since 1992.

4. Kevin Rudd, "Transcript of Joint Press Conference—Brisbane," July 19, 2013, https://pmtranscripts.pmc.gov.au/release/transcript-22763.

5. The Manus Island Regional Processing Centre was closed at the end of October 2017, the Supreme Court of PNG having found it to be illegal on April 26, 2016, because it breached the Constitution's right to personal liberty.

6. Liberal Party of Australia and National Party of Australia, *The Coalition's Operation Sovereign Borders Policy*, July 2013, https://perma.cc/DV5E-HUN6.

7. Letter from then Minister for Immigration and Border Protection Scott Morrison to DIBP Secretary Martin Bowles, October 16, 2013, and

"Scott Morrison Defends Decision to Call Asylum Seekers 'Illegals,'" *Guardian*, October 21, 2013, https://www.theguardian.com/world/2013/oct/21/news-asylumseekers-immigration-government. For an in-depth discussion of Australia's changed official narrative surrounding asylum seekers arriving by boat see Ben Doherty, *Call Me Illegal: The Semantic Struggle Over Seeking Asylum in Australia* (Oxford: Reuters Institute for the Study of Journalism, 2015), 46–48, 61, 65–66, https://reutersinstitute.politics.ox.ac.uk/sites/default/files/2017-10/Call_me_illegal_The_semantic_struggle_over_seeking_asylum_in_Australia_0.pdf.

8. "Any determination of when it is 'safe to do so' is made by the commanding officer of an intercepting vessel" (*Turning Back Boats*, Research Brief, UNSW Kaldor Centre for International Refugee Law, last updated August 2018, 3, https://www.kaldorcentre.unsw.edu.au/sites/kaldorcentre.unsw.edu.au/files/Research%20Brief_Turning%20back%20boats_final.pdf.

9. https://www.abf.gov.au.

10. UN Human Rights Council (HRC), *Report on Means to Address the Human Rights Impact of Pushbacks of Migrants on Land and at Sea*, A/HRC/47/30, May 12, 2021, 13, https://documents-dds-ny.un.org/doc/UNDOC/GEN/G21/106/33/PDF/G2110633.pdf?OpenElement. See Commonwealth of Australia, Senate, Legal and Constitutional Affairs Legislation Committee, *Estimates*, Immigration and Border Protection Portfolio, February 23, 2015, 137, https://parlinfo.aph.gov.au/parlInfo/download/committees/estimate/726d2567-78be-48ef-a9df-f7302dbb884c/toc_pdf/Legal%20and%20Constitutional%20Affairs%20Legislation%20Committee_2015_02_23_3235_Official.pdf;fileType=application%2Fpdf#search=%22committees/estimate/726d2567-78be-48ef-a9df-f7302dbb884c/0000%22.

11. I have chosen to reflect the style of address we use in our regular interactions in which we refer to each other as Mr. or Mrs. followed by our first name as a mark of respect.

12. In August 2018, another 17 Vietnamese asylum seekers were notably apprehended when their fishing boat ran aground near the mouth of the crocodile-infested Daintree River in North

Queensland and sent back to Vietnam. See, for example, Anne Barker, "Suspected Asylum Seekers Found in Queensland Spark Warnings of Exodus from Vietnam," *ABC News*, August 30, 2018, https://www.abc.net.au/news/2018-08-29/fears-suspected-asylum-seekers-part-of-flood-from-vietnam/10179322.

Chapter 1

1. Shira Sebban, "We're a Disparate Group of Australians Doing the Work Our Government Won't," *Guardian*, August 24, 2016, https://www.theguardian.com/commentisfree/2016/aug/24/were-a-disparate-group-of-australians-doing-the-work-our-government-wont.

2. Nor were companies like YouTube immune: "The government continued to pressure firms such as Facebook and Google to eliminate 'fake accounts' and content deemed 'toxic,' including anti-state materials" (U.S. Department of State, Bureau of Democracy, Human Rights and Labor, *Vietnam 2018 Human Rights Report*, 20–21, https://www.state.gov/wp-content/uploads/2019/03/VIETNAM-2018.pdf); see also Human Rights Watch (HRW), *Vietnam: Events of 2018*, 2, http://www.vietnamhumanrights.net/english/documents/HRW_2019.pdf.

3. Apparently, this report has since been removed.

4. Amnesty International, "Public Statement," August 11, 2016, ASA 41/4653/2016, https://www.amnesty.org/download/Documents/ASA4146532016ENGLISH.pdf.

5. UN General Assembly, *The Convention on the Rights of the Child*, November 20, 1989, 1577 UNTS 3.

6. According to the Constitution of the Socialist Republic of Vietnam (November 28, 2013), art. 61, "the state shall ... guarantee compulsory primary education which is free of charge."

7. Socialist Republic of Vietnam, Land Law No. 45/2013/QH13, art. 4. See also Vietnamese Constitution, art. 53.

8. See, for example, 2013 Vietnamese Land Law, arts. 13.4, 16, and c 6 and Vietnamese Constitution, art. 54.

9. People's Committees act as executive bodies and are responsible for administrative duties, including managing land, at the local level on behalf of the state.

10. This view is corroborated by ACAT, BPSOS, CAT-VN, CSW, LIV, and VN-CAT, *Report to the United Nations Committee Against Torture for the Examination of the First State Report of the Socialist Republic of Vietnam*, 65th session, Geneva, November 12, 2018—December 7, 2018, 12, https://www.acatfrance.fr/public/joint-report-for-the-examination-of-vietnam-by-uncat_1.pdf; HRW, *No Country for Human Rights Activists: Assaults on Bloggers and Democracy Campaigners in Vietnam*, June 18, 2017, https://www.hrw.org/report/2017/06/19/no-country-human-rights-activists/assaults-bloggers-and-democracy-campaigners; Department of Foreign Affairs and Trade, *DFAT Country Information Report Vietnam*, January 11, 2022, 29, [para. 5.4], https://www.dfat.gov.au/sites/default/files/country-information-report-vietnam.pdf: "Sources have also reported that local police sometimes use contract 'thugs' and 'citizen brigades' to harass and beat political activists and religious adherents perceived as undesirable or a threat to national security."

11. See, for example, Ben Bohane, "South China Sea: Vietnam Prepares for Dangerous Days Ahead as the Country's Fisheries Clash with Chinese Authorities," *ABC News*, December 9, 2016, http://www.abc.net.au/news/2016-12-09/south-china-sea-vietnam-prepares-for-dangerous-days-ahead/8101192; Pamela Boykoff, "Vietnam Fishermen on the Front Lines of South China Sea Fray," *CNN*, July 12, 2016, https://edition.cnn.com/2016/05/22/asia/vietnam-fisherman-south-china-sea/index.html; Ben Kerkvliet, "Vietnamese Fishermen Versus China," *New Mandala*, July 6, 2016, http://www.newmandala.org/vietnamese-fishermen-versus-china/; Nguyen Xuan Quynh, Andreo Calonzo, Philip J. Heijmans, Hannah Dormido, and Adrian Leung, "China is Winning the Silent War to Dominate the South China Sea," *Bloomberg*, July 11, 2019, https://www.bloomberg.com/graphics/2019-south-china-sea-silent-war/?leadSource=uverify%20wall; Vo Hai, "Prioritize ASEAN-China Cooperation on Equal, Humane Treatment of Fishermen: Vietnam," *VNExpress*, November 3, 2020, https://e.vnexpress.net/news/news/prioritize-asean-china-cooperation-on-equal-humane-treatment-of-fishermen-vietnam-4186530.html; International Crisis Group, *Vietnam Tacks Between Cooperation and Struggle in the South China Sea*, Asia Report No 318, December 7, 2021, 23–25, https://icg-prod.s3.amazonaws.com/318-between-cooperation-and-struggle_1.pdf; "Vietnam Fisherman Recounts Attacks by China Coast Guard in South China Sea," *South China Morning Post*, October 14, 2022, https://www.scmp.com/news/asia/southeast-asia/article/3196026/vietnam-fisherman-recounts-attacks-china-coast-guard-south.

12. Vietnamese Constitution, arts. 24(2) and (3).

13. John Gillespie, "Human Rights as a Larger Loyalty: The Evolution of Religious Freedom in Vietnam," *Harvard Human Rights Journal* 27 (2014): 125-126, https://web.archive.org/web/20180409231343/http://harvardhrj.com/wp-content/uploads/2014/07/V27_Gillespie.pdf. See, for example, Socialist Republic of Vietnam, Ordinance on Beliefs and Religions No. 21/2004/PL-UBTVQH11, arts. 8(2) and 15 and Decree No. 92/2012/ND-CP Detailing and Providing Measures for the Implementation of the

Ordinance on Beliefs and Religions, art. 2. These were both used as a foundation for their replacement, the 2016 Law on Belief and Religion No. 02/2016/QH14 (see notably art. 5.4) and implementing Decree No. 162/2017/ND-CP, which came into effect on January 1, 2018, well after Mrs. Loan and family had fled Vietnam.

14. Interview with Nguyen Quang Duy, June 18, 2020, and *DFAT Country Information Report Vietnam*, January 11, 2022, 13, 14, [paras. 3.14, 3.15, 3.17, 3.21].

15. Commonwealth of Australia, Senate, Legal and Constitutional Affairs Legislation Committee, *Estimates*, Immigration and Border Protection Portfolio, May 25, 2015, Questions taken on notice (BE 15/038 and 112), https://www.aph.gov.au/Parliamentary_Business/Senate_estimates/legconctte/estimates/bud1516/DIBP/index.

16. This multi-agency taskforce within DHA, comprising both Australian Defence Force and Border Force officers, was renamed the Maritime Border Command (MBC) in July 2015. For more information see https://www.abf.gov.au/about-us/what-we-do/border-protection/maritime. These extraordinary powers to detain and transfer people at sea were granted under the *Migration and Maritime Powers Legislation Amendment (Resolving the Asylum Legacy Caseload) Act 2014* (Cth.).

17. Report of appeal, La Gi People's Court, July 21, 2016 (translated from Vietnamese), original supplied by Mrs. Loan. Unfortunately, the document is incomplete, several pages having been irreparably damaged by rain leaking through the roof of her home.

18. *CPCF v Minister for Immigration and Border Protection* [2015] HCA 1, January 28, 2015, https://jade.io/article/365019. See also Ben Doherty and Paul Farrell, "Detention of 157 Tamil Asylum Seekers on Board Ship Ruled Lawful," *Guardian*, January 28, 2015, https://www.theguardian.com/australia-news/2015/jan/28/detention-157-tamil-asylum-seekers-on-board-ship-ruled-lawful; Helen Davidson, "Australia Reportedly Uses Navy Ship to Return Asylum Seekers to Vietnam," *Guardian*, April 17, 2015, https://www.theguardian.com/australia-news/2015/apr/17/asylum-seekers-to-vietnam; United Nations High Commissioner for Refugees (UNHCR), "UNCHR Legal Position: Despite Court Ruling on Sri Lankans Detained at Sea, Australia Bound by International Obligations," Press Release, February 4, 2015, https://www.unhcr.org/54d1e4ac9.html.

19. An "unlawful non-citizen" is a non-citizen who does not hold "a visa that is in effect" (*Migration Act 1958* (Cth.), ss. 13(1), 14(1) (Migration Act)).

20. See Refugee Convention, art. 33(1); UN General Assembly, *Convention against Torture and Other Cruel, Inhuman or Degrading Treatment or Punishment*, December 10, 1984, 1465

UNTS 85 (UNCAT), art. 3; and *International Covenant on Civil and Political Rights*, December 16, 1966, 999 UNTS 171 (ICCPR), arts. 6 and 7, which are reflected in the terms of Australia's Migration Act, s. 36. See also Commonwealth of Australia, Senate, Legal and Constitutional Affairs Legislation Committee, *Estimates*, Immigration and Citizenship Portfolio, May 28, 2013, 44–70, https://parlinfo.aph.gov.au/parlInfo/download/committees/estimate/0f70343a-b92d-45d8-b692-58b9623ba9cd/toc_pdf/Legal%20and%20Constitutional%20Affairs%20Legislation%20Committee_2013_05_28_1971_Official.pdf;fileType=application%2Fpdf#search=%22committees/estimate/0f70343a-b92d-45d8-b692-58b9623ba9cd/0000%22.

21. See Australian Government Department of Immigration and Citizenship, *Enhanced Screening Policy Guidelines*, April 2013, 1–37, https://drive.google.com/file/d/0ByW2V3f-jYBRMEllNEsOX3haN28/edit.

22. Commonwealth of Australia, Senate, Legal and Constitutional Affairs Legislation Committee, *Estimates*, Immigration and Border Protection Portfolio, May 25, 2015, 118, https://parlinfo.aph.gov.au/parlInfo/download/committees/estimate/0c5973fa-5b41-457f-af39-57df2971a205/toc_pdf/Legal%20and%20Constitutional%20Affairs%20Legislation%20Committee_2015_05_25_3493_Official.pdf;fileType=application%2Fpdf#search=%22committees/estimate/0c5973fa-5b41-457f-af39-57df2971a205/0000%22.

23. Senate Estimates, May 25, 2015, Question Taken on Notice (BE 15/164). Legal academics, Alex Reilly and Rebecca La Forgia, have argued that the difficult decisions expected of Commonwealth officers during the enhanced screening process place an "unreasonable burden" upon them. See "Secret 'Enhanced Screening' of Asylum Seekers: A Democratic Analysis Centring on the Humanity of the Commonwealth Officer," *Alternative Law Journal* 38, No. 3 (2013): 143–146, https://journals.sagepub.com/doi/10.1177/1037969X1303800302. Eve Lester, on the other hand, highlights "the technique of decision-lessness that clothes with legislative authority, and absolves public officials of responsibility for, unbridled and unchecked executive action" (*Making Migration Law: The Foreigner, Sovereignty, and the Case of Australia* (Cambridge: Cambridge University Press, 2018), 59).

24. Samantha Hawley, "Asylum Seekers Returned to Vietnam by Australian Navy Had Claims Assessed at Sea, UNHCR Says," *ABC News*, April 21, 2015, https://www.abc.net.au/news/2015-04-21/vietnam-asylum-seekers-returned-australian-navy-screened-at-sea/6407848; see also Chris Uhlmann and Peta Donald, "Australian Navy Returns 46 Asylum Seekers to Vietnam After Intercepting

Group en Route to Australia," *ABC News*, April 20, 2015, https://www.abc.net.au/news/2015-04-20/government-criticised-over-boat-secrecy/6404950.

25. "UNICEF Statement on Australia and Vietnam Signing MOU to Return Vietnamese Asylum Seekers," Sydney, December 13, 2016, https://vietbp.org/2017/08/14/unicef-statement-on-australia-and-vietnam-signing-mou-to-return-vietnamese-asylum-seekers.htm.

26. Senate Estimates, May 28, 2013, 62–65 (chief lawyer, Legal and Assurance Division, Immigration and Citizenship Portfolio, Vicki Parker). As pointed out by legal expert Professor Mary Crock, "Under the *Migration Act 1958* [s. 256], immigration detainees have a right to legal advice about their detention, but only upon their request. There is no statutory obligation on immigration officials to advise people of their rights" ("'You Have to Be Stronger Than Razor Wire': Legal Issues Relating to the Detention of Refugees and Asylum Seekers," *Australian Journal of Administrative Law* 10 (2002): 57, https://www.researchgate.net/publication/228185845_You_Have_to_Be_Stronger_than_Razor_Wire_Legal_Issues_Relating_to_the_Detention_of_Refugees_and_Asylum_Seekers).

27. Law Council of Australia, *Australia-Vietnam 2016 Human Rights Dialogue: Civil Society Consultation*, DFAT, June 20, 2016, 10, paras. 27 and 28, https://www.lawcouncil.asn.au/docs/11b58e10-02bd-e611-80d2-005056be66b1/3158_-_AU-Vietnam_Dialogue_2016.pdf. See also Claire Higgins, "Protecting Refugees and Australia's Interests," in *Fresh Perspectives in Security*, Centre of Gravity Series Paper 51, ANU Strategic and Defence Studies Centre, March 2020, 32, http://sdsc.bellschool.anu.edu.au/sites/default/files/publications/attachments/2020-03/cog_51_web.pdf and Violeta Moreno-Lax, *The Interdiction of Asylum Seekers at Sea: Law and (Mal)practice in Europe and Australia*, Policy Brief 4, UNSW Kaldor Centre for International Refugee Law, May 2017, 9–10, https://www.kaldorcentre.unsw.edu.au/sites/default/files/Policy_Brief4_Interdiction_of_asylum_seekers_at_sea.pdf: "Direct returns to ... Vietnam ... under Operation Sovereign Borders ... are incompatible with the prohibition on refoulement."

28. The name of the returnee has been withheld to protect their identity.

29. "Enhanced screening" involves "asking each of the asylum seekers a set of four questions and determining their refugee status on the basis of their answers to these questions (the asylum seeker's name, country of origin, where they had come from, and why they had left) without a right to appeal a negative decision" (Andreas Schloenhardt and C. Craig, "'Turning Back the Boats': Australia's Interdiction of Irregular Migrants at Sea," *International Journal of Refugee Law* 27, No. 4 (December 2015): 538, https://doi.org/10.1093/ijrl/eev045). Following an Australian Human Rights Commission (AHRC) inquiry in 2015, DIBP added another question as to whether interviewees "have any concerns about being returned to their country of origin" (AHRC, *Report into the 'Enhanced Screening' Process*, 26–27); see also Senate Estimates, May 28, 2013, 47–48 (first assistant secretary, Refugee, Humanitarian and International Policy Division, Immigration and Citizenship Portfolio, Alison Larkins).

30. Senate Estimates, May 25, 2015, 111.

31. Major General Bottrell, Senate Estimates, May 25, 2015, 120 (see Appendix 2) and Question Taken on Notice (BE 15/164), and Davidson, "Australia Reportedly Uses Navy Ship."

32. Heath Aston, "Australian Navy to Hand 50 Asylum Seekers Back to Vietnam," *Sydney Morning Herald* (*SMH*), April 17, 2015, https://www.smh.com.au/politics/federal/australian-navy-to-hand-50-asylum-seekers-back-to-vietnam-20150417-1mnew5.html and Davidson, "Australia Reportedly Uses Navy Ship."

33. Jessica Longbottom, "Vietnam Jails Four Asylum Seekers Over Voyage to Australia Despite 'No Retribution' Promise," *ABC News*, May 26, 2016, http://www.abc.net.au/news/2016-05-26/asylum-seekers-jailed-in-vietnam-despite-no-retribution-promise/7449516.

34. Senate Estimates, May 25, 2015, 120–121.

35. Nicole Hasham, "Tony Abbott Tight-Lipped on Suspected Vietnamese Asylum Seeker Boat," *SMH*, July 21, 2015, https://www.smh.com.au/politics/federal/tony-abbott-tightlipped-on-suspected-vietnamese-asylum-seeker-boat-20150721-gih1ij.html.

36. "Người Úc Giúp Thuyền Nhân Việt Bị Hồi Hương," *VOA*, September 3, 2016, http://vietjoy.com/viewtopic.php?f=18&p=86926 and "Việt Nam Thẳng Tay Xử Tù Người Vượt Biển Sang Úc: Bản án Tàn Bạo Và Vô Nhân Đạo," *VietInfo*, August 18, 2016, http://vietinfo.eu/tin-viet-nam/viet-nam-thang-tay-xu-tu-nguoi-vuot-bien-sang-uc-ban-an-tan-bao-va-vo-nhan-dao.html (translated from Vietnamese).

37. Joel Keep and Mai Hoa Pham, "Women Flee Vietnam for Second Time Following Turn-Back from Australia," *SBS*, February 15, 2017, http://www.sbs.com.au/news/article/2017/02/14/women-flee-vietnam-second-time-following-turn-back-australia.

38. Socialist Republic of Vietnam, Penal Code No. 15/1999/QH10, art. 275(1).

39. Keep and Pham, "Women Flee Vietnam." "Communist party-controlled courts receive instructions on how to rule in criminal cases, and have issued increasingly harsh prison sentences ..." (HRW, *Vietnam: Events of 2018*, 1).

40. See, for example, "Rừng Luật Và Luật Rừng," *VietInfo*, September 9, 2014, http://vietinfo.eu/luat-vn/rung-luat-va-luat-rung.html (translated from Vietnamese).

41. *VOA*, September 3, 2016.

42. *VietInfo,* August 18, 2016.

43. This is far more than the amount stipulated in the legislation. See discussion in Chapter 2, endnote 40 below. According to the legal report of the appeal supplied by Mrs. Loan, a fellow failed asylum seeker also had to pay "440,000,000 VND [about USD19,000] for the illicit profits to supplement the state housing fund" (translated from Vietnamese).

44. Longbottom, "Vietnam Jails Four Asylum Seekers."

45. This definition is contained in the UN General Assembly, *Protocol against the Smuggling of Migrants by Land, Sea and Air, Supplementing the United Nations Convention against Transnational Organized Crime,* November 15, 2000, art. 3a: "'Smuggling of migrants' shall mean the procurement, in order to obtain, directly or indirectly, a financial or other material benefit, of the illegal entry of a person into a State Party of which the person is not a national or a permanent resident." For further discussion on Australian official attitudes to people smuggling see, for example, Antje Missbach, *The Criminalisation of People Smuggling in Indonesia and Australia: Asylum Out of Reach* (Oxford and New York: Routledge, 2022).

46. HRW, "Vietnam: Show Rights Commitment at Australia Talks," August 1, 2016, https://www.hrw.org/news/2016/08/01/vietnam-show-rights-commitment-australia-talks.

47. Kathy Trieu, "Lua and Loan, Two Asylum Seekers Rejected by Australia," *Loa Broadcasting Vietnam,* Episode 76, July 19, 2017, audio, 20:24, https://vietbp.org/2017/09/05/lua-and-loan-two-asylum-seekers-rejected-by-australia.htm.

48. *VOA,* September 3, 2016.

Chapter 2

1. Shira Sebban, "Saving the World, One Life at a Time," *New Matilda,* October 15, 2016, https://newmatilda.com/2016/10/15/saving-the-world-one-life-at-a-time/.

2. Hoa Ai Tran, "Mạng Xã Hội Và Niềm Tin Từ Thiện," *RFA,* December 6, 2016, https://www.rfa.org/vietnamese/in_depth/social-media-and-charity-fund-raising-12062016140941.html (translated from Vietnamese).

3. I am indebted to Doan Trung for this document, which he translated himself.

4. "Phúc Thẩm Vụ Vượt Biên Đến Úc," *BBC,* August 31, 2016, https://www.bbc.com/vietnamese/vietnam/2016/08/160831_australia_asylumn_seeker_vietnam (translated from Vietnamese).

5. Doan Trung, "Statement About Two Groups of 46 Vietnamese Asylum Seekers—The 'Plane Group' and the 'Choules Group,'" unpublished, January 7, 2016, based on information provided mainly by the boat people themselves. See Appendix 1 for the complete statement.

6. "Suspected Asylum Seeker Vessel Heading for Dampier off WA's North West Coast," *ABC News,* July 20, 2015, https://www.abc.net.au/news/2015-07-20/suspected-asylum-seeker-vessel-seen-heading-for-dampier-wa-coast/6633146.

7. "Lua and Loan."

8. Doan Trung also raised this possibility in his unpublished statement of January 7, 2016 (see Appendix 1).

9. Nicole Hasham, "Vietnamese Asylum Seekers Returned by Plane in the Dead of Night: Reports," *SMH,* July 27, 2015, https://www.smh.com.au/politics/federal/vietnamese-asylum-seekers-returned-by-plane-in-the-dead-of-night-reports-20150727-gil671.html. For further discussion of the usage of such military language, see Mungo MacCallum, "Asylum Seekers and the Language of War," *Drum,* January 14, 2014, https://www.abc.net.au/news/2014-01-13/maccallum-operation-sovereign-borders/5196708.

10. "Vietnamese Face Punishment for Attempt to Flee the Country," *RFA,* April 1, 2016, https://www.rfa.org/english/news/vietnam/vietnamese-face-punishment-04012016142103.html.

11. Liam Cochrane, "Vietnamese Asylum Seeker Returned by Australia Says 'A Bullet Would be Better,'" *ABC News,* February 23, 2017, https://www.abc.net.au/news/2017-02-21/vietnam-asylum-seeker-returned-by-australia-speaks-of-beatings/8288226.

12. "Lua and Loan."

13. "A Bullet Would be Better."

14. Her allegation was supported by an unpublished statement of September 28, 2016, by Doan Trung, based on the transcript of a recorded phone conversation he had with her on September 20, 2016. See Appendix 2 for the complete statement.

15. See RFA, "Vietnamese Face Punishment."

16. Doan Trung, unpublished statement of September 28, 2016. He also revealed that Mrs. Loan made similar allegations about public broadcasts shaming her and her children after their forcible return to Vietnam (see Appendix 2, paras. 11–15).

17. Ben Doherty, "Vietnamese Asylum Seekers Forcibly Returned by Australia Face Jail," *Guardian,* May 24, 2016, https://www.theguardian.com/australianews/2016/may/24/vietnamese-asylum-seekers-forcibly-returned-by-australia-face-jail; see also HRW, "Vietnam: Drop Charges Against Boat Returnees," May 24, 2016, https://www.hrw.org/news/2016/05/24/vietnam-drop-charges-against-boat-returnees. Amnesty International said much the same in its public statement of August 11, 2016.

18. Trieu, "Lua and Loan."

19. Report of appeal, People's Court of Binh Thuan province, September 1, 2016, supplied by Mrs. Lua (translated from Vietnamese). The

Court specified that the more than 11 weeks Mrs. Lua had already spent in jail would be deducted from her 30-month sentence.

20. "Lua and Loan."

21. "Lua and Loan."

22. See, for example, "Abbott Government Must Lift Veil of Secrecy on Operation Secret Boats," Media Release, April 18, 2015; "Minister Needs to Come Clean on Boat Arrival," Media Release, July 20, 2015; "Grave Concerns for the Plight of Vietnamese Asylum Seekers," Media Release, July 31, 2015. The Greens have since removed these press releases from their website.

23. Jane Norman, "Election 2016: Peter Dutton, Malcolm Turnbull Confirm Vietnam Asylum Seeker Boat Turn-Back," *ABC News*, June 22, 2016, https://www.abc.net.au/news/2016-06-22/dutton-turnbull-confirm-vietnam-asylum-seeker-boat-turn-back/7532368; see also Commonwealth of Australia, Senate, Legal and Constitutional Affairs Legislation Committee, *Estimates*, Attorney-General's Portfolio, October 17, 2016, 201–202, https://parlinfo.aph.gov.au/parlInfo/download/committees/estimate/516239db-3ab5-4777-8b43-33f6d160c55d/toc_pdf/Legal%20and%20Constitutional%20Affairs%20Legislation%20Committee_2016_10_17_4510_Official.pdf;fileType=application%2Fpdf#search=%22committees/estimate/516239db-3ab5-4777-8b43-33f6d160c55d/0000%22.

24. Under the Migration Act, ss. 189(1) and (3), whether an "unlawful non-citizen" is in the migration zone or in an "excised offshore place," they must still be detained. A legal device created by the Australian government, the "migration zone" includes Australian-controlled territories as determined by the government, within which a non-citizen must hold an Australian visa. Prior to September 2001, it consisted of the mainland and some external territories (see definition in Migration Act, s. 5(1)). From that date, legal amendments excised the territories of Ashmore and Cartier Islands, Christmas Island, and Cocos (Keeling) Islands from the migration zone, which limited "offshore entry persons" from applying for a visa on arrival (see the *Migration Amendment (Excision from Migration Zone) Act 2001* (Cth.) and the *Migration Amendment (Excision from Migration Zone) (Consequential Provisions) Act 2001* (Cth.)). On October 30, 2012, the entire Australian mainland was excised from the migration zone, the *Migration Amendment (Unauthorised Maritime Arrivals and Other Measures) Act* (Cth.) being assented to on May 20, 2013. Subsequently that year, it was decided that "unauthorised maritime arrivals" to Australia would henceforth not be able to make any valid visa application (Migration Act, s. 46A).

25. Ben Doherty, "Vietnamese Asylum Seekers Turned Back After Being Processed at Sea," *Guardian*, June 22, 2016, https://www.theguardian.com/australia-news/2016/jun/22/vietnamese-asylum-seekers-turned-back-after-being-processed-at-sea.

26. Part of Australian law since 2012 (Migration Act, ss. 36(2)(aa), 36(2A)-(2C)), complementary protection allows asylum seekers, who do not meet the definition of a refugee but nonetheless face serious dangers, to claim protection under human rights law.

27. See *DFAT Country Information Report Vietnam*, June 21, 2017, 24, [para. 5.17], https://www.ecoi.net/en/file/local/1419336/4792_1512564532_country-information-report-vietnam.pdf. This assessment is also included in *DFAT Country Information Report Vietnam*, December 13, 2019, 44, [para. 5.35], https://www.ecoi.net/en/file/local/2024449/country-information-report-vietnam.pdf, although the direct reference to the forcible returns of 2016 was omitted. The entire sentence is missing from its 2022 report, DFAT merely concluding that anyone involved in people smuggling, "whether as organizers or travelers," would be held for questioning, with the worst penalty being a fine, the only exception being those "who use their time overseas to publicly oppose the Government" and who are thus punished more harshly (*DFAT Country Information Report Vietnam*, 2022, 33, [paras. 5.30, 5.35]).

28. "Trial Set for Four Vietnamese 'Boat People' Who Were Repatriated by Australia," *RFA*, November 29, 2016, https://www.rfa.org/english/news/vietnam/trial-set-for-four-vietnamese-11292016134257.html/.

29. "Vietnam Jails 'Boat People' Bound for Australia in Breach of Pledge," *RFA*, December 13, 2016, https://www.rfa.org/english/news/vietnam/vietnam-jails-boat-people-12132016135607.html. In Vietnam, all convicted prisoners are required to work full-time without pay, mainly performing agricultural and manufacturing tasks. See, for example, *Report to the United Nations Committee Against Torture*, 22. According to the authorities, "labour during imprisonment was the primary method of education and social rehabilitation" (UNHCR, "Committee Against Torture Considers the Initial Report of Viet Nam," November 15, 2018, https://www.ohchr.org/en/NewsEvents/Pages/DisplayNews.aspx?NewsID=23895&LangID=E).

30. Socialist Republic of Vietnam, Penal Code No. 100/2015/QH13. In the end, the amended law only actually came into effect on January 1, 2018.

31. "Trial Set"; see also "Vũng Tàu Xử Tù Người 'Tổ Chức Vượt Biên'," *BBC*, December 13, 2016, https://www.bbc.com/vietnamese/vietnam-38167677 (translated from Vietnamese).

32. Report of appeal (officially translated from Vietnamese).

33. Interview with Vo An Don, May 25, 2019.
34. "Australia and Vietnam Further Cooperation to Stamp Out People Smuggling," Minister for Immigration and Border Protection Peter Dutton, Media Release, December 12, 2016, https://minister.homeaffairs.gov.au/peterdutton/Pages/Australia-and-Vietnam-further-cooperation-to-stamp-out-people-smuggling.aspx.
35. "UNICEF Statement."
36. See for example "Vietnamese Community Comes to Aid of Syrian Refugees," *SBS*, August 30, 2016, https://www.sbs.com.au/news/vietnamese-community-comes-to-aid-of-syrian-refugees and Lee Brooks, "Australia's Vietnamese Community Pledges $500k to UNHCR to Help Refugees," *ABC News*, August 30, 2016, https://www.abc.net.au/news/2016-08-30/vietnamese-community-gives-thousands-to-refugees/7796796.
37. See www.viettan.org.
38. https://www.bpsos.org/our-history.
39. "Trial Set."
40. In 2019, Australia's official understanding was that fines were much lower than in both Mrs. Loan's and Mrs. Van's experience: "Vietnamese nationals who depart the country unlawfully, including without travel documents, may be subject to a fine upon return. Article 17 of the Decree on Sanctions of Administrative Violations in Social Security, Order and Safety, Prevention and Fighting of Social Evils, Fire, and Domestic Violence mandates a fine of between VND3 million ... [USD130] and VND5 million ... [USD215] for crossing a national border without undergoing official exit procedures; evading, organising or helping others to leave illegally; or departing using another person's travel documents (or permitting another person to use their documents). Fines of between VND5 million ... [USD215] and VND10 million ... [USD430] are mandated for the owners or operators of vehicles that transport people across the border illegally; and for the use of fraudulent travel documents or other identity documents. In practice, the implementation of this legislation varies depending on the person and the circumstances of the illegal departure" (*DFAT Country Information Report Vietnam*, 2019, 43, [para. 5.27]). It should be noted that these details were omitted from DFAT's 2022 report.
41. "Trial Set."

Chapter 3

1. See also "Vietnamese 'Boat People' Attempt to Reach Australia a Second Time," *RFA*, February 8, 2017, https://www.rfa.org/english/news/vietnam/vietnamese-boat-people-attempt-to-reach-australia-a-second-time-02082017131644.html; "Ba Phụ Nữ Bình Thuận 'Lại Vượt Biên Đến

Úc'," *BBC*, February 6, 2017, https://www.bbc.com/vietnamese/vietnam-38878718; "Ba Phụ Nữ Bình Thuận 'Dược Hưởng quy Chế Xin Tỵ Nạn'," April 5, 2017, https://www.bbc.com/vietnamese/vietnam-39362063?ocid=socialflow_facebook (translated from Vietnamese).
2. See https://www.refugeecouncil.org.au, http://www.refugeeaction.org.au, and https://www.hrlc.org.au.
3. This statement, which appears on the home page of our website in English and Vietnamese, is accompanied by a note: "The above is not, and not intended to be, legal advice. Any individual seeking protection in Australia is advised to obtain independent legal advice for their specific circumstances."
4. Anthea Vogl, Email to author, August 12, 2020.
5. Keep and Pham, "Women Flee Vietnam."
6. Keep and Pham, "Women Flee Vietnam."
7. *Tết* is a shortened form of *Tết Nguyên Đán*, which is Sino-Vietnamese for "Feast of the First Morning of the First Day."
8. The Law of the Republic of Indonesia No. 6 of 2011 Concerning Immigration (art. 11) allows for the temporary acceptance of "foreigners" entering in groups, as an exception and based on humanitarian considerations, including those "foreigners anchored or landed somewhere in Indonesia due to engine failure or bad weather, while the conveyance does not intend to dock or land in the Territory of Indonesia." Under the Presidential Regulation (*Peraturan Presiden* or *Perpres* in Indonesian) No. 125 of 2016 on the Handling of Foreign Refugees (art. 1(4), c. II, arts. 5–23), enacted in the wake of the 2015 Andaman Sea crisis when 8,000 Rohingya refugees and Bangladeshi migrants were left stranded at sea, the government reinforced its commitment to rescuing people from emergency situations as a form of temporary humanitarian assistance. See Bilal Dewansyah and Irawati Handayani, "Reconciling Refugee Protection and Sovereignty in ASEAN Member States: Law and Policy Related to Refugee in Indonesia, Malaysia and Thailand," *Central European Journal of International and Security Studies* 12, No. 4 (December 2018): 479-481, https://cejiss.org/reconciling-refugee-protection-and-sovereignty-in-asean-member-states-law-and-policy-related-to-refugee-in-indonesia-malaysia-and-thailand.
9. "Vietnamese Asylum Seekers' Boat Stalls in Indonesia," *RFA*, February 10, 2017, https://www.refworld.org/docid/58f9cace21.html.
10. See Keep and Pham, "Women Flee Vietnam" and P. Sinh, "Làm Rõ Nghi Vấn Dối Tượng Tổ Chức Dưa Người Ra Nước Ngoài Trái Phép," *Bình Thuận Online*, February 9, 2017, https://baobinhthuan.com.vn/lam-ro-nghi-van-doi-tuong-to-chuc-dua-nguoi-ra-nuoc-ngoai-trai-phep-13218.html (translated from Vietnamese).
11. Interview with Vo An Don, May 25, 2019;

see also "Authorities Request to Revoke License Vo An Don," Lawyers for Lawyers, January 20, 2015, https://lawyersforlawyers.org/en/vietnam-request-by-authorities-to-revoke-license-of-lawyer-vo-an-don/ and VCHR, *Shrinking Spaces: Assessment of Human Rights in Vietnam During the 2nd Cycle of its Universal Periodic Review*, Paris, February 2018, 19, http://queme.org/app/uploads/2018/02/Shrinking-spaces-VCHR-2018-EN.pdf.

12. "18 Imigran Gelap Ternyata Kabur dari Penjara di Vietnam," *TitikNOL*, February 11, 2017, https://titiknol.co.id/peristiwa/18-imigran-gelap-ternyata-kabur-dari-penjara-di-vietnam/ (translated from Indonesian).

13. According to HRW, guards are sometimes from the Directorate General of Immigration (DGI) and sometimes from the police (*Barely Surviving: Detention, Abuse, and Neglect of Migrant Children in Indonesia*, June 24, 2013, 27, https://www.refworld.org/docid/51cae2724.html).

14. As we shall see below, the overall attitude towards asylum seekers in Indonesia has since become more positive.

15. "Ba Phụ Nữ Việt Vượt Biên Sang Úc Bị Tạm Giữ ở Indonesia," *SBTN*, February 11, 2017, https://www.sbtn.tv/ba-phu-nu-viet-vuot-bien-sang-uc-bi-tam-giu-o-indonesia/ and Cat Linh, "Các Thuyền Nhân VN Được Cho Tạm Tá Túc ở Jakarta Qua Cuối Tuần," *RFA*, February 10, 2017, https://www.rfa.org/vietnamese/news/vietnamnews/vn-asylum-seekers-temporary-stay-in-jakarta-02102017225935.html (translated from Vietnamese).

16. See https://namati.org/network/organization/indonesian-legal-aid-foundation/ and https://www.forum-asia.org.

17. "Since 2009 JRS Indonesia has supported asylum seekers and refugees in urban areas and immigration detention centres by listening to their stories and providing information, advice and practical support for the most vulnerable" (Lars Stenger, "What the Future Might Hold," *Inside Indonesia* 124, April-June 2016, https://www.insideindonesia.org/what-the-future-might-hold); see also https://jrs.net/en/country/indonesia/.

18. https://suaka.or.id/about-us/. In December 2018, SUAKA, together with UNHCR, JRS, and Sandya Institute, published *Know Your Rights: A Handbook for Refugees and Asylum Seekers*, which would have been a most useful document for us had it existed at the time (https://apr.jrs.net/wp-content/uploads/sites/18/2020/03/2019-Know-your-rights-JRS-Indo.pdf).

19. See below for further discussion of the IOM.

20. While a new Indonesian regulation passed in 2016 required "coordination with UNHCR for those seeking asylum in Indonesia," it also granted "authority to initiate communication with countries of origin." See UNHCR, *Submission by the United Nations High Commissioner for Refugees for the Office of the High Commissioner for Human Rights' Compilation Report Universal Periodic Review: 3rd Cycle, 27th session, Indonesia*, September 2016, 4, https://refworld.org/docid/59158ed24.html and Regulation of Director General of Immigration No. IMI-0352.GR.02.07 on the Handling of Illegal Immigrants Claiming to be Asylum-Seekers or Refugees (2016), art. 2(3)b.

21. UN General Assembly, *Protocol relating to the Status of Refugees*, January 31, 1967, 606 UNTS 267.

22. See the Fourth Amendment to the 1945 Constitution of the Republic of Indonesia (August 11, 2002), art. 28G(2); Law of the Republic of Indonesia No. 37 of 1999 on Foreign Relations, arts. 25-27; Law of the Republic of Indonesia No. 39 of 1999 Concerning Human Rights, art. 28. Not having enacted implementing regulations, however, Indonesia has no apparatus that could possibly deal with such rights.

23. SUAKA, "Perpres: Refugee Protection Must Answer Key Issues Regarding Asylum Seekers and Refugees in Indonesia," Media Release, January 18, 2017, https://suaka.or.id/handling-refugees-from-overseas/. Muhammad Hafiz was also speaking in his capacity as Executive Director Human Rights Working Group Indonesia (HRWG).

According to the *Perpres*, art. 1(1): "Foreign refugee, hereinafter referred to as refugee, shall mean a foreigner who resides within the territory of the Republic of Indonesia due to a well-founded fear of persecution due to race, ethnicity, religion, nationality, membership of a particular social group, and different political opinions, and does not wish to avail him/herself of protection from their country of origin and/or has been granted the status of asylum-seeker or refugee by the United Nations through the United Nations High Commissioner for Refugees."

24. "Indonesia has carried out deportations, but because of their high cost there are usually only twenty to thirty deportations each year" (Antje Missbach, *Troubled Transit: Asylum Seekers Stuck in Indonesia* (Singapore: ISEAS-Yusof Ishak Institute, 2015), 132). The *Perpres*, however, included "a greater emphasis on deportations" (Antje Missbach and Nikolas Feith Tan, "No Durable Solutions," *Inside Indonesia*, March 13, 2017, https://www.insideindonesia.org/no-durable-solutions).

25. "Funding required for the handling of refugees can be taken from:

a. The state budget through the relevant ministry/agency; and/or

b. Other legal and unbinding sources in accordance with the prevailing laws and regulations" (*Perpres*, art. 40).

As we will see, until mid-March 2018, IOM, largely funded by Australia, covered most costs relating to housing and basic care for asylum seekers and refugees in Indonesia.

26. As per the "Agreement Between the

Government of the Republic of Indonesia and the United Nations High Commissioner for Refugees Regarding the Establishment of the Office of the UNHCR Representative for Indonesia" (June 15, 1979), https://treaty.kemlu.go.id/apisearch/pdf?filename=OI-1979-0022.pdf. See also Directive from Director General of Immigration No. F-IL.01.10–1297 on Procedures Regarding Aliens Expressing Their Desire to Seek Asylum or Refugee Status (September 30, 2002) and Regulation of Director General of Immigration No. IMI.1489. UM.08.05 Regarding the Handling of Illegal Immigrants (September 17, 2010), which were subsequently replaced by Regulation of Director General of Immigration No. IMI-0352.GR.02.07 on the Handling of Illegal Immigrants Claiming to be Asylum-Seekers or Refugees (2016).

27. UNHCR, *Information for Asylum Seekers in Indonesia*, https://www.unhcr.org/id/wp-content/uploads/sites/42/2017/05/Information-Leaflet-for-Asylum-Seekers-English-Feb-2017.pdf. According to international customary law, all countries are bound by the principle of non-refoulement, ensuring a refugee is not forcibly returned to any country where they have reason to fear persecution. Nevertheless, Indonesia has been accused of not consistently adhering to this obligation.

28. See https://indonesia.iom.int/iom-indonesia. Indonesia is not a member state of IOM, only holding observer status.

29. Jewel Topsfield, "Trapped in Transit: What Next for Asylum Seekers Stranded in Indonesia?" *SMH*, March 19, 2016, https://www.smh.com.au/world/trapped-in-transit-what-next-for-asylum-seekers-stranded-in-indonesia-20160317-gnlmkf.html.

30. See IOM, "Financial Report for the Year Ended 31 December 2017," May 29, 2018, 63, https://governingbodies.iom.int/system/files/en/council/109/C-109-3%20-%20Financial%20Report%20for%20the%20year%202017.pdf and Commonwealth of Australia, *Budget 2016–17: Budget Measures*, Budget Paper No. 2, 2016–17, 124, https://archive.budget.gov.au/2016-17/bp2/BP2_consolidated.pdf. In 2016–2017, the Australian government provided around USD38 million to continue funding the Regional Cooperation Model (RCM) between IOM, Australia, and Indonesia that had come into effect in 2001. An additional USD1.5 million was provided to maintain IOM's outreach offices across Indonesia. The RCM broadly provided for "the interception and detention of asylum seekers, assessment of protection claims, and arrangements for removal of failed asylum seekers or resettlement of recognized refugees" (Jessica Howard, "To Deter and Deny: Australia and the Interdiction of Asylum Seekers," *Refuge: Canada's Journal on Refugees* 21, No. 4 (2003): 41, https://refuge.journals.yorku.ca/index.php/refuge/article/view/21307/19978; see also United States Committee for Refugees and Immigrants, "Paying the Price: Australia,

Indonesia Try to Stop Asylum Seekers," *Refugee Reports* 22, No. 8 (September 1, 2001), https://www.refworld.org/docid/3c58099a1.html).

For further analysis of Australia's funding of IOM in Indonesia and IOM's role in Australia's regional deterrence strategy see Asher Lazarus Hirsch and Cameron Doig, "Outsourcing Control: The International Organization for Migration in Indonesia," *The International Journal of Human Rights* 22, No. 5 (2018): 681–708, http://doi.org/10.1080/13642987.2017.1417261.

31. See Appendix 3 for the full text of the letter.

32. Shira Sebban, "Exclusive: Fate of Vietnamese asylum seeker children hangs in the balance," *Independent Australia*, March 16, 2017, https://independentaustralia.net/australia/australia-display/exclusive-fate-of-vietnamese-asylum-seeker-children-hangs-in-the-balance,10117.

33. Keep and Pham, "Women Flee Vietnam."

34. Standard procedure in Indonesia under the RCM was for the police and local immigration office to inform IOM, which referred those wishing to make asylum claims to UNHCR. See, for example, Savitri Taylor and Brynna Rafferty-Brown, "Difficult Journeys: Accessing Refugee Protection in Indonesia," *Monash University Law Review* 36 No. 3 (2010), http://classic.austlii.edu.au/au/journals/MonashULawRw/2010/29.html and Department of Immigration and Citizenship, *Submission to the Joint Select Committee on Australia's Immigration Detention Network*, September 2011, 29, 106, https://www.homeaffairs.gov.au/reports-and-pubs/files/diac-jscaidn-submission-sept11.pdf.

35. Grace subsequently made a similar statement to the *BBC*, April 5, 2017.

36. Cochrane, "A Bullet Would Be Better."

37. Xem Binh Luan, "Ba Gia Dình Việt Vượt Biên 'Sắp Được Phỏng Vấn'," *VOA*, February 22, 2017, https://www.voatiengviet.com/a/ba-gia-dinh-viet-vuot-bien-bi-giu-o-indonesia-sap-duoc-lhq-phong-van/3735066.html#comments (translated from Vietnamese). The article was subsequently amended at my request.

38. See *Troubled Transit*, Chap. 3.

39. UNHCR in Indonesia has constantly faced funding and staff shortages. For more detail, see for example, Missbach, *Troubled Transit*, Chap. 5. In 2017 specifically, UNHCR was short around USD2.8 million from its total refugee and stateless program budget of just over USD7.2 million (see UNHCR, "Financials, 2017 South East Asia Requirements and Expenditure—Programmed Activities," http://reporting.unhcr.org/financial).

40. See *BBC*, April 5, 2017.

41. UNHCR, *Procedural Standards for Refugee Status Determination Under UNCHR's Mandate*, September 1, 2005, 3–29, https://www.unhcr.org/en-au/publications/legal/4316f0c02/procedural-standards-refugee-status-determination-under-unhcrs-mandate.html and "Indonesia Fact Sheet," December

2016, https://www.unhcr.org/id/wp-content/
uploads/sites/42/2017/05/Indonesia-Fact-Sheet-
December-2016.pdf. In its online "FAQs for refugees and asylum-seekers," UNHCR noted an
even longer delay: "Because of the large number
of asylum-seekers approaching UNHCR, any further interview will take place at least two years
from the date you register" (https://www.unhcr.
org/id/wp-content/uploads/sites/42/2017/05/
UNHCR-website-FAQs.pdf). The process has
since become much more efficient (see https://
help.unhcr.org/indonesia/registration/).
    42. *Procedural Standards*, 3–23, 4–21.
    43. UNHCR, *Information for Asylum Seekers
in Indonesia*, photocopies supplied to the group
when they were registered as asylum seekers on
March 20–21, 2017. UNHCR Indonesia has since
developed a useful website for refugees and asylum seekers, https://help.unhcr.org/indonesia/.
    44. JRS, *The Search: Protection Space in
Malaysia, Thailand, Indonesia, Cambodia and
the Philippines* (Bangkok: JRS Asia Pacific, 2012),
41 https://www.refworld.org/pdfid/506bfb622.
pdf; see also UNHCR, *Procedural Standards*,
4–10. While UNHCR's original core mandate
covered only refugees, it has since been expanded
to include returnees and stateless persons.
    45. UNHCR, *Note on Burden and Standard of
Proof in Refugee Claims*, December 16, 1998, para.
11, https://www.refworld.org/pdfid/3ae6b3338.
pdf and "Part Two: Procedures for the Determination of Refugee Status" in *Handbook on Procedures
and Criteria for Determining Refugee Status and
Guidelines on International Protection Under the
1951 Convention and the 1967 Protocol Relating
to the Status of Refugees*, HCR/1P/4/ENG/REV.4,
reissued Geneva, February 2019, 43–45, https://
www.refworld.org/docid/5cb474b27.html.
    46. See UNHCR, *Procedural Standards*, 2–3.
    47. For an example of the English-language
version of such a campaign see Oliver Laughland, "Angus Campbell Warns Asylum Seekers
Not to Travel to Australia by Boat," *Guardian*,
April 11, 2014, https://www.theguardian.com/
world/2014/apr/11/angus-campbell-stars-in-
videos-warning-asylum-seekers-not-to-travel-
by-boat. See also discussion of "Zero Chance"
campaigns in Chapter 7 below.
    48. "As a general rule, RSD decisions should
be issued within one month following the RSD
interview." In more complicated cases, the decision should be given not "later than two months
from the RSD interview," while "the decision for
claims heard under the Accelerated RSD Processing procedures should generally be issued
within one week of the RSD interview" (UNHCR,
Procedural Standards, 4–20, 4–23).

Chapter 4

    1. The 2011 Immigration Law determined
that "foreigners" without valid travel documents,

including minors, should be placed in immigration detention centers (arts. 83 and 85). Whereas
the Presidential Regulation (*Perpres*) No. 125 of
2016 on the Handling of Foreign Refugees specified that "foreigners suspected of being refugees"
were to be handed over to immigration detention
if possible or else to the police (arts. 9–12, 18–19),
it was still unclear whether all refugees actually had to be detained. For two opposing views
see UNHCR, *Global Strategy: Beyond Detention 2014–2019: National Action Plan Indonesia*,
1, https://www.refworld.org/pdfid/57dff7912.
pdf and Lisa Button, *Unlocking Childhood: Current Immigration Detention Practices and Alternatives for Child Asylum Seekers and Refugees
in Asia and the Pacific*, Save the Children and
Asia Pacific Refugee Rights Network, May 2017,
45, https://resourcecentre.savethechildren.net/
node/12161/pdf/unlocking_chiildhood.pdf.
    2. Trieu, "Lua and Loan."
    3. The 2011 Immigration Law (arts. 83(2) and
87) allowed those "foreigners" who were sick,
pregnant, or children, as well as victims of trafficking and human smuggling, to be housed
outside detention but still under the control of
immigration officers. The *Perpres* of 2016 went
further, discussing the transfer of refugees to
"shelter" with "basic necessities," and specifically
considering those with "special needs," defined
as children, pregnant women, people with a disability, the sick, and elderly (c. III, arts. 24–28).
This has been interpreted to mean that refugees in Indonesia would no longer be accommodated in immigration detention centers. See also
Immigration Regulation No. IMI-0352.GR.02.07
(2016), arts. 4, 5, 13, and 15 and Wicipto Setiadi
and Mario Johanes Caesar Siagian, "The Implementation of Alternatives to Detention to Handle
the Problems of Refugees in Indonesia," *Padjadjaran Journal of Law* 6, No. 1 (2019): 135–136,
https://doi.org/10.22304/pjih.v6n1.a7.
    4. The Montagnard or "mountain people" are
indigenous ethnic groups from Vietnam's central
highlands. Regarded as among the most margin-
alized in the region, many have fled persecution
to Thailand and Cambodia, where they continue
to live without recognition of basic human rights.
Grace originally moved from the U.S. to Bangkok
in 2014 to assist 160 Montagnard families, comprising about 600 people.
    5. Trieu, "Lua and Loan."
    6. Canadian immigration policy is dis-
cussed further in Chapters 5 and 7. For more
information on former Senator Ngo see https://
senatorngo.ca.
    7. While geographical constraints mean that
only a small percentage of asylum seekers reach
Canada by boat, it should be noted that their
treatment has been similar to that of Australia, although "Canadian options were limited
by its Charter of Rights and Freedoms" (David
Scott FitzGerald, *Refuge Beyond Reach: How Rich
Democracies Repel Asylum Seekers* (New York:

Oxford University Press, 2019), 97–99); see also *Canadian Charter of Rights and Freedoms, Constitution Act 1982*, Part 1. Australia does not have such a charter.

8. IOM did not allow me to quote directly from Mr. Getchell's email, explaining that it was not intended for publication.

9. RCOA, "Refugees and International Law," May 10, 2020, https://www.refugeecouncil.org.au/international-law/6/. IOM was operating under the "Management and Care of Irregular Immigrants Project" (MCIIP), launched in 2007 and funded by Australia. The *Perpres* of 2016 aimed to standardize detention centers and shelters, ensuring they meet these basic needs. See also Immigration Regulation No. IMI-0352.GR.02.07 (2016), art. 15 and endnote 30 below.

10. UNHCR, "Beyond Detention," 2 and *Progress Report 2018: A Global Strategy to Support Governments to End the Detention of Asylum-Seekers and Refugees, 2014–2019*, February 2019, 36, https://www.refworld.org/country,,,,IDN,,5c9354074,0.html; Antje Missbach, "Accommodating Asylum Seekers and Refugees in Indonesia: From Immigration Detention to Containment in 'Alternatives to Detention,'" *Refuge* 33, No. 2 (2017): 34, https://doi.org/10.7202/1043061ar; Global Detention Project, "Indonesia Immigration Detention Profile," updated January 2016, https://www.globaldetentionproject.org/countries/asia-pacific/indonesia.

11. See http://www.vanlangsj.org and http://www.viettoon.com/.

12. "UNHCR's unhindered access to detention facilities allowed regular monitoring visits in all detention centres and interception sites, with the frequency of the visits ranging from weekly visits in detention centres where UNHCR also provides daily services, such as access to counselling and protection interventions, to between 1 to 3 monthly visits in other detention centres where UNHCR has no regular presence. Monitoring is also routinely conducted by other UNHCR staff who visit detention facilities for registration purposes, RSD and resettlement interviews" (UNHCR, *Indonesia: Progress Under the Global Strategy Beyond Detention 2014–2019, mid-2016*, 2, https://www.unhcr.org/protection/detention/57b583457/indonesia-progress-report.html?query=indonesia). See also UNHCR, *Operation: Indonesia: 2017 Year-End Report*, July 25, 2018, https://reporting.unhcr.org/sites/default/files/pdfsummaries/GR2017-Indonesia-eng.pdf and *Progress Report 2018*, 37.

13. "Ba Gia Dình Người Việt Vượt Biên Được LHQ Cấp Qui Chế Tị Nạn," *RFA*, May 23, 2017, https://www.rfa.org/vietnamese/news/vietnamnews/vietnamese-boatpeople-in-indonesia-granted-refugee-status-05232017095746.html (translated from Vietnamese).

14. "18 Thuyền Nhân Việt ở Indonesia Được Cấp Qui Chế Tị Nạn," *VOA*, May 24, 2017, https://www.voatiengviet.com/a/muoi-tam-thuyen-nhan-viet-o-indonesia-duoc-cap-qui-che-ti-nan/3868946.html (translated from Vietnamese).

15. The video can be viewed at https://www.youtube.com/watch?v=H6CN00I1yu4.

16. "Migrants, including children, are typically detained without judicial review or bail, access to lawyers, or any way to challenge their detention" (HRW, *Barely Surviving*, 25). The National Law Development Agency, however, later clarified that "refugees are entitled to access state-funded legal aid programs, enhancing their access to lawyers in challenging their detention, among others." For more information see UNHCR, *Progress Report 2018*, 34. To what extent this was enforced in practice is unknown.

17. Shira Sebban, "Turned Back by Australia, Vietnamese Recognised as Refugees in Indonesia," *SMH*, June 11, 2017, https://www.smh.com.au/world/turned-back-by-australia-vietnamese-recognised-as-refugees-in-indonesia-20170608-gwn475.html.

18. Hoa Ai Tran, "Ba Gia Dình Phụ Nữ Vượt Biên Sẽ Tạm Cư ở Trại Tị Nạn Semareng," *RFA*, June 13, 2017, http://www.rfa.org/vietnamese/in_depth/the-three-families-fled-vn-2-time-moved-semareng-refugee-camp-ha-06132017085531.html (translated from Vietnamese).

19. Nevertheless, in recent years, less than one third of those resettled under Australia's Refugee and Humanitarian Program were referred by UNHCR. Reuniting families also became more difficult, most refugees being selected based on their Australian communal connections. See, for example, RCOA, "Less Than One Third of Refugees in Australia's Humanitarian Program Are Resettled From UNHCR," May 9, 2020, https://www.refugeecouncil.org.au/less-one-third-refugees-australias-humanitarian-program-resettled-unhcr/.

20. Exceptionally, a "foreign national may submit the application without a referral if they reside in a geographic area as determined by the Minister" to be one "in which circumstances justify the submission" (*Immigration and Refugee Protection Regulations*, SOR/2002–227 (Can.) (IRPR), Part 8, Div. 1, ss. 140.3(2) and (3)).

21. Paul Power continued:
You can see the question he [Volker Türk] was asked here: https://youtu.be/seR-4dtDKMU?t=7809 and his response here: https://youtu.be/seR-4dtDKMU?t=9170. I have included a transcript, which we made at the time:
Question: … This week we heard that Vietnamese women returned by Australia to Vietnam in 2015 have been recognized as refugees after escaping again to Indonesia …. What actions could and should the international community take against countries which breach the Refugee Convention so clearly?
Response: (Volker Türk): … I was just made aware of that particular news item. We will

obviously look into this and, if necessary, we will raise this with the government.

22. UNHCR, *Information for Asylum Seekers in Indonesia* and *Code of Conduct for Asylum Seekers and Refugees in Indonesia*. Phrases highlighted as per the original text. "Resettlement to a safe third country is not a right, because there is no international obligation for states to accept refugees who are temporarily in transit elsewhere. Resettlement ... depends, therefore, on the goodwill of the countries receiving refugees" (Missbach, *Troubled Transit*, Chap. 5).

23. UNHCR, *Information for Refugees on Resettlement*, https://www.unhcr.org/id/wp-content/uploads/sites/42/2017/05/Resettlement-Information-Leaflet-English-Feb-2017.pdf and "Indonesia: Year-End Report, 2017," https://reporting.unhcr.org/sites/default/files/pdfsummaries/GR2017-Indonesia-eng.pdf.

24. See Chapter 5 for further discussion of integration.

25. Dr. Bui is also a former president of the Vietnamese community in Australia (1982–1991).

26. Khanh Hoang, "Risks and Rewards in Australia's Plan for Private Sponsorship," UNSW Kaldor Centre for International Refugee Law, May 16, 2017, https://www.kaldorcentre.unsw.edu.au/publication/risks-and-rewards-australias-plan-private-sponsorship. According to the 2017–18 Budget, Australia would increase its permanent Refugee and Humanitarian Program from a total of 13,750 places to 16,250 in 2017–18 and 18,750 in 2018–19 (see Commonwealth of Australia, *Budget 2017-18: Budget Measures*, Budget Paper No. 2, 2017-18, 15, https://archive.budget.gov.au/2017-18/bp2/bp2.pdf).

27. See *Migration Regulations 1994* (Cth.), Sch. 1, Item 1402(1)-Item 1402(4) and Sch. 2, Cl. 202.1- Cl. 202.612 (Migration Regulations); DHA, "Subclass 202 Global Special Humanitarian visa," https://immi.homeaffairs.gov.au/visas/getting-a-visa/visa-listing/global-special-humanitarian-202 and "Community Support Program," https://immi.homeaffairs.gov.au/what-we-do/refugee-and-humanitarian-program/community-support-program. The character requirements are set out under the Migration Act, s. 501. The Department also issues regular updates of Procedural Instructions providing "guidance on the administration of the offshore component of Australia's Humanitarian Program," including the CSP. These are available via subscription on LEGENDcom, an electronic database of migration and citizenship legislation and policy (https://immi.homeaffairs.gov.au/help-support/tools/legendcom).

28. *DFAT Country Information Report Vietnam*, 2022, 33, [para. 5.30].

29. Nearby Galang Island, also part of the Riau Archipelago, was where UNHCR and IOM had commenced operations in Indonesia in 1979 with the processing of Indochinese asylum seekers,

who were granted "de facto temporary asylum ... based on general humanitarian considerations." For more details, see for example, Missbach, *Troubled Transit*, Chaps. 2 and 6.

30. Upgrade and refurbishment of detention facilities, as well as developing standard operating procedures for human rights in detention, were other components of the "Management and Care of Irregular Immigrants Project" (MCIIP), funded by Australia and implemented by IOM and Indonesian immigration. See endnote 9 above; Amy Nethery, Brynna Rafferty-Brown, Savitri Taylor, "Exporting Detention: Australia-Funded Immigration Detention in Indonesia," *Journal of Refugee Studies* 26, No. 1 (March 2013): 88–109, https://doi.org/10.1093/jrs/fes027; Simon Kearney and Stephen Fitzpatrick, "'Life of Brutality' in Crowded Indonesian Lock-Up," *Australian*, October 23, 2009, https://www.theaustralian.com.au/news/world/life-of-brutality-in-crowded-indonesian-lock-up/news-story/8b751e651ccbccd0471d41736555e720.

31. For more on the "entrenchment of a culture of embezzlement, extortion and self-enrichment among detention center staff" see, for example, Missbach, *Troubled Transit*, Chap. 3 and "Detaining Asylum Seekers and Refugees in Indonesia" in *Detaining the Immigrant Other: Global and Transnational Issues*, eds. Rich Furman, Douglas Epps, and Greg Lamphear (Oxford: OUP, 2016), 91-104.

32. Missbach has quoted figures of about 60,000 IDR (just over USD4) per detainee per day allocated for food in detention centers, consisting of 15,000 IDR (about USD1) from immigration and an extra allowance of 45,000 IDR (around USD3) provided by IOM to those registered under UNHCR (see *Troubled Transit*, Chap. 3).

33. In "Detaining Asylum Seekers," Missbach discusses the "discretionary powers of center staff, especially the head of detention," highlighting that protection mechanisms for detainees were often ignored.

34. "Indonesian data still includes refugees in counts of 'illegal immigrants.' It is not clear, however, whether the count refers only to refugees and asylum seekers or whether it also includes ordinary immigration offenders" (Antje Missbach, Yunizar Adiputera, Atin Prabandari, Ganesh Cintika, Frysa Yudha Swastika, and Raditya Darningtyas, "Stalemate: Refugees in Indonesia—Presidential Regulation No. 125 of 2016," Centre for Indonesian Law, Islam and Society, Melbourne Law School, Policy Paper (2018), 13, https://law.unimelb.edu.au/__data/assets/file/0006/2777667/CILIS-Paper-14_Missbach-et-al_final.pdf).

35. *Bahasa Indonesia* is the local Indonesian term for the Indonesian language.

36. https://vietnamvoice.org/en/voice/.

37. This is known as the Government-Assisted

Refugee Program (GAR). There are also Shared Government-Private Sponsorship Programs (SGPSP), including Joint Assistance Sponsorship (JAS) and Blended Visa Office-Referred (BVOR). For more information see *UNHCR Resettlement Handbook*, Country Chapter: Canada, revised February 2018, 11–12, https://www.unhcr.org/3c5e55594.html.

38. PSR was introduced by Canada's *Immigration Act*, SC 1976–77, c. 52, s. 1, which was replaced by the *Immigration and Refugee Protection Act*, SC 2001, c. 27 (Can.) (IRPA), accompanied by updated *Immigration and Refugee Protection Regulations*, SOR/2002–227 (Can.) (IRPR): "A Canadian citizen or permanent resident, or a group of Canadian citizens or permanent residents, a corporation incorporated under a law of Canada or of a province or an unincorporated organization or association under federal or provincial law—or any combination of them—may sponsor a foreign national, subject to the regulations" (IRPA, s. 13(1); see also s. 12(3) and IRPR, s. 138). For more information see Refugee Sponsorship Training Program (RSTP), "The Private Sponsorship of Refugees Program," http://www.rstp.ca/en/refugee-sponsorship/the-private-sponsorship-of-refugees-program/ and Canadian Council for Refugees (CCR), "About Refugees and Canada's Response: Resettlement to Canada," https://ccrweb.ca/en/refugee-facts.

39. Immigration, Refugees and Citizenship Canada (IRCC) is the government department responsible for these areas. Until November 2015, it was known as Citizenship and Immigration Canada (CIC).

40. Jennifer Hyndman, Johanna Reynolds, Biftu Yousuf, Anna Purkey, Dawit Demoz, and Kathy Sherrell, "Sustaining the Private Sponsorship of Resettled Refugees in Canada," *Frontiers in Human Dynamics* 3 (May 11, 2021): 8, https://doi.org/10.3389/fhumd.2021.625358.

41. See IRCC, "Sponsorship Agreement Holders: About the Program," https://www.canada.ca/en/immigration-refugees-citizenship/services/refugees/help-outside-canada/private-sponsorship-program/agreement-holders.html and "Global Cap for Sponsorship Agreement Holders," https://www.canada.ca/en/immigration-refugees-citizenship/corporate/mandate/policies-operational-instructions-agreements/timely-protection-privately-sponsored-refugees.html; RSTP, "Sponsorship Agreement Holders (SAH), http://www.rstp.ca/en/refugee-sponsorship/sponsorship-agreement-holders/.

42. Titled "Vietnamese Refugees Pay It Forward: James Nguyen," the Canadian government video can be viewed at https://www.youtube.com/watch?v=TbYUJOW2-Fs. For more information on this campaign see, for example, Cassandra Szklarski, "Vietnamese-Canadian 'Boat People' Rally to Sponsor Syrian Refugees," *Globe and Mail*, December 9, 2015, https://www.theglobeandmail.com/news/national/vietnamese-boat-people-rally-to-sponsor-syrian-refugees/article27661190/.

43. Groups of Five can either sponsor refugees via an arrangement with an SAH or directly with the Canadian government. Other categories of private sponsors include faith communities, ethnic groups, and benevolent organizations, known as Constituent Groups (CG), which are authorized by SAHs to sponsor refugees; Community Sponsors (CS), and Co-Sponsors, which can also include individuals, such as family members of the sponsored refugee living in Canada (see https://www.canada.ca/en/immigration-refugees-citizenship/services/refugees/help-outside-canada/private-sponsorship-program.html).

44. Each family, as well as unmarried adults, had to complete and sign three forms: "Generic Application Form for Canada," "Schedule A—Background/Declaration," and "Schedule 2—Refugees Outside Canada" (see https://www.canada.ca/en/immigration-refugees-citizenship/services/application/application-forms-guides/guide-6000-convention-refugees-abroad-humanitarian-protected-persons-abroad.html).

Chapter 5

1. See Asher Lazarus Hirsch, *After the Boats Have Stopped: Refugees Stranded in Indonesia and Australia's Containment Policies*, RCOA Brief, November 2018, 3, https://www.refugeecouncil.org.au/wp-content/uploads/2018/12/Indonesia_brief.pdf.

2. See, for example, UNHCR, *Beyond Detention: A Global Strategy to Support Governments to End the Detention of Asylum-Seekers and Refugees—2014–2019*, https://www.refworld.org/docid/536b564d4.html; Setiadi and Siagian, "The Implementation of Alternatives to Detention," 135–136; Thomas Brown and Antje Missbach, "Refugee Detention in Indonesia," *Interpreter*, May 12, 2017, https://www.lowyinstitute.org/the-interpreter/refugee-detention-indonesia.

3. Adam Bemma, "Refugees in Indonesia Told to Assimilate But Not Settle," *Refugees Deeply*, February 9, 2018, https://www.newsdeeply.com/refugees/articles/2018/02/09/refugees-in-indonesia-told-to-assimilate-but-not-settle; see also Antje Missbach, "Substituting Immigration Detention Centres with 'Open Prisons' in Indonesia: Alternatives to Detention as the Continuum of Unfreedom," *Citizenship Studies* 25, No. 2 (2021): 228-229, 10.1080/13621025.2020.1859193.

4. Gemima Harvey, "Surviving While Seeking Asylum," *Inside Indonesia*, October 26, 2018, https://www.insideindonesia.org/surviving-while-seeking-asylum. See Indonesian Directorate General of Immigration (DGI) Circular Note No. IMI-UM.01.01–2827 on Restoring the Original Function of Immigration Detention Centers,

July 30, 2018 (translated from Indonesian). I have been unable to find an English translation of this document. "The Australian government stated the reason for ending such funding under the Regional Cooperation Model (RCM) was that it did not want the care under IOM to be a 'pull factor' for refugees to come to Indonesia" (Hirsch, *After the Boats Have Stopped*, 2).

5. "IOM provides refugees adequate, safe, and secure living environments in the form of community housing, where refugees live alongside the host community" ("IOM Indonesia Programmes," https://indonesia.iom. int/sites/g/files/tmzbdl1491/files/documents/ IOM%20Indonesia%20Fact%20Sheet%20 2021%20EN.pdf). See also IOM Indonesia, *Alternatives to Detention*, Issue 4, September 2014, 1–4, https://www.iom.int/files/live/ sites/iom/files/Country/docs/IOM-Indonesia_ Alternatives-to-detention-September-2014. pdf.

6. Ministry of Education and Culture, Circular Note No. 75253/A.A4/HK/2019 on Education for Children of Refugees (translated from Indonesian). I have been unable to find an English translation of this document. See also, for example, "Public schools in Medan, Jakarta, Makassar and Tangerang Open Doors to Refugee Kids," *Coconuts Jakarta*, July 18, 2018, https://coconuts.co/jakarta/news/public-schools-medan-jakarta-makassar-tangerang-open-doors-refugee-kids/.

7. See Realisa D Masardi, "All Alone," *Inside Indonesia* 124, April-June 2016, https://www. insideindonesia.org/all-alone and SUAKA, *Know Your Rights*, 27–31.

8. See UNHCR, "Indonesia Fact Sheet," December 2016; https://cws-asia.org and https:// cwsglobal.org/our-work/asia/indonesia/.

9. See https://www.crs.org/our-work-over seas/where-we-work/indonesia and https://www. dompetdhuafa.org/tag/indonesia/.

10. See notably Cisarua Learning (https:// cisarualearning.com) and the Roshan Learning Center (https://roshanlearning.org).

11. See http://www.lia.co.id.

12. See Amanda Hodge, "Refugees in Limbo Wait for Softening of Rules," *Australian*, November 4, 2018, https://www.theaustralian.com. au/nation/nation/refugees-in-limbo-wait-for-softening-of-rules/news-story/21faec4c12146 0f102c1ceaa4bd3ecbe and Missbach, "Falling Through the Cracks."

13. http://joycarejkt.com.

14. https://paclearninglab.wordpress.com/ 2019/07/11/why-the-learning-lab/.

15. See https://www.uphcollege.com and https://www.uph.edu/about-us/ for more information.

16. See https://jakarta.hmcc.net.

17. See Chapter 7 for more details.

18. See Missbach, *Troubled Transit*, Chap. 4 and "Substituting Immigration Detention

Centers," 226, 230; IOM, "Indonesia Programmes"; https://indonesia.iom.int/migrant-assistance.

19. For more information see https://www. unhcr.org/id/wp-content/uploads/sites/42/ 2018/04/Leaflet-Puskesmas_English.pdf and SUAKA, *Know Your Rights*, 23–26.

20. See Antje Missbach and Gerhard Hoffstaedter, "When Transit States Pursue Their Own Agenda: Malaysian and Indonesian Responses to Australia's Migration and Border Policies," *Migration and Society: Advances in Research* 3 (2020): 1-16, https://doi.org/10.3167/ arms.2020.111405.

21. UNHCR, *Information for Refugees on Resettlement*. See Immigration Regulation No. IMI-0352.GR.02.07 (2016) and Missbach, "Accommodating," 33: "Legal integration into Indonesia and naturalization are not options because the Law on Indonesian Citizenship (Government of Indonesia, 2006) does not permit refugees to apply for citizenship."

22. https://www.unhcr.org/id/wp-content/ uploads/sites/42/2017/10/Poster-on-Com prehensaive-Solutions-ECHO-Oct-2017.pdf. Phrases highlighted as per the campaign. See also Jewel Topsfield, "Most Refugees in Indonesia Will Never Be Resettled: UN Refugee Agency," *SMH*, October 31, 2017, https://www.smh.com. au/world/most-refugees-in-indonesia-will-never-be-resettled-un-refugee-agency-20171031-gzbzhn.html and Immigration Regulation No. IMI-0352.GR.02.07 (2016), arts. 2(1), 3, and 4(4).

23. See *UNHCR Resettlement Handbook* (Geneva: UNHCR, 2011), 288, https://www. refworld.org/pdfid/4ecb973c2.pdf; Missbach, "Accommodating," 36 and "Benevolent Neglect: How Indonesia Handles Its Asylum Seeker Problem," *Conversation*, August 30, 2012, https:// theconversation.com/benevolent-neglect-how-indonesia-handles-its-asylum-seeker-problem-8920; Nikolas Feith Tan, "The Status of Asylum Seekers and Refugees in Indonesia," *International Journal of Refugee Law* 28, No. 3 (October 1, 2016): 367, https://doi.org/10.1093/ ijrl/eew045; *UNHCR Policy on Refugee Protection and Solutions in Urban Areas*, September 2009, 24, paras. 153 and 154, https://www.unhcr.org/ protection/hcdialogue%20/4ab356ab6/unhcr-policy-refugee-protection-solutions-urban-areas.html. "In theory, there is no limit on the length of temporary stay for long-term stayers in Indonesia ..." (Antje Missbach, "Transiting Asylum Seekers in Indonesia: Between Human Rights Protection and Criminalisation," in *Migration and Integration in Europe, Southeast Asia, and Australia: A Comparative Perspective*, eds. Juliet Pietsch and Marshall Clark (Amsterdam: Amsterdam University Press, 2015), 126).

24. Button, *Unlocking Childhood*, 46.

25. https://immi.homeaffairs.gov.au/visas/ getting-a-visa/visa-listing/global-special-humanitarian-202.

26. See https://immi.homeaffairs.gov.au/help-support/meeting-our-requirements/character.

27. See Migration Act, ss. 314, 486E, and 486F and *Migration (Migration Agents Code of Conduct) Regulations 2021* (Cth.), s. 19.

28. See IRPR, s. 153(1)(b) and IRCC, "2.11 What is a Refugee Status Determination and when is it required?" Guide to the Private Sponsorship of Refugees Program, https://www.canada.ca/en/immigration-refugees-citizenship/corporate/publications-manuals/guide-private-sponsorship-refugees-program/section-2.html#a2.11.

29. This situation has since changed, private sponsorship applicants now able to contact UNHCR directly for a status confirmation letter (see https://help.unhcr.org/indonesia/refugee-status-determination/).

30. See https://www.hr4a.com.au.

31. See DHA, *Life in Australia: Australian Values and Principles*, 2020, 1–10, https://immi.homeaffairs.gov.au/support-subsite/files/life-in-australia/life-in-australia.pdf and https://immi.homeaffairs.gov.au/help-support/meeting-our-requirements/australian-values; see also https://immi.homeaffairs.gov.au/visas/getting-a-visa/visa-listing/global-special-humanitarian-202#Eligibility.

32. The Australian government's "Application for an Offshore Humanitarian visa" Form 842 notably asks main applicants and their partners to provide the "status in country of residence" of all relatives, living, dead, or whereabouts unknown (questions 13 and 14). Applicants are asked to choose between the following categories: citizen, permanent or temporary resident, student, visitor/tourist, refugee, illegal resident, asylum/protection applicant, or other (details to be provided). A further question focuses on whether the applicant or their partner has "any relatives not included in this visa application who have current Australian visa applications under consideration" (question 16), while yet another probes whether candidates have "any other relatives residing in Australia" and enquires as to their "resident status" (question 19) (see https://www.ua-au.net/files/842.pdf). The Canadian government, in contrast, simply asks for relatives' "present address" ("Schedule 2 Refugees Outside Canada" [IMM 0008 Schedule 2], questions 8–11) (see https://www.canada.ca/en/immigration-refugees-citizenship/services/application/application-forms-guides/applying-convention-refugee-humanitarian-protected-person-abroad.html).

33. In 2017–2018, these "resettlement priority countries" were "the Democratic Republic of Congo, Afghanistan, Eritrea, Ethiopia, Myanmar, Bhutan, Syria and Iraq." The government confirmed that while "no nationality is excluded from consideration," it established priorities "based on a range of factors," including communal consultation and "UNHCR global priorities" (Commonwealth of Australia, Senate, Legal and Constitutional Affairs Legislation Committee, *Estimates*, Home Affairs Portfolio, May 22, 2018, 173 (Luke Mansfield, First Assistant Secretary, Refugee, Citizenship and Multicultural Programs), https://parlinfo.aph.gov.au/parlInfo/search/display/display.w3p;db=COMMITTEES;id=committees%2Festimate%2F75507344-48f1-4665-8f23-623c6eb5c20d%2F0002;query=Id%3A%22committees%2Festimate%2F75507344-48f1-4665-8f23-623c6eb5c20d%2F0002%22).

"The phrase 'regional and global priorities' refers to caseloads, identified by nationality, ethnic or religious group, or other characteristic, and country, to which places are allocated, by region, post and subclass, each program year, to the offshore humanitarian program as determined by the government" (Procedural Instruction, "Refugee and Humanitarian—Offshore Humanitarian Program—Visa Application and Related Procedures—Class XB Specific Criteria—Regional and Global Priorities").

34. https://immi.homeaffairs.gov.au/visas/getting-a-visa/visa-listing/global-special-humanitarian-202; https://immi.homeaffairs.gov.au/what-we-do/refugee-and-humanitarian-program/community-support-program/how-to-apply. As further information came to light, we were of course proved wrong regarding the linguistic facility required upon arrival in Australia, "adequate English" being officially defined as "comprehension and expression of spoken and written English sufficient for independent daily living and employment, including workplace safety" (see Procedural Instruction, "Offshore Humanitarian Program Management and Class XB (Refugee and Humanitarian) Visa Processing—3.17 The Community Support Program—English Language").

35. See https://immi.homeaffairs.gov.au/change-in-situation/get-a-refund and https://immi.homeaffairs.gov.au/visas/getting-a-visa/fees-and-charges/explanation-of-visa-application-charges/refunds.

36. For the legal definition of an APO see Migration Regulations, Sch. 2, reg. 202.111. For more information subsequently published about the APOs' role regarding the CSP see DHA, *The Community Support Program: Guidelines for Approved Proposing Organisations*, January 22, 2019, 1–30, https://www.homeaffairs.gov.au/foi/files/2019/fa-190301223-document-released.pdf.

37. See DHA, "Community Support Program (CSP)," https://immi.homeaffairs.gov.au/what-we-do/refugee-and-humanitarian-program/community-support-program/approved-proposing-organisations. See also IOM, "Cost of Sponsoring," https://australia.iom.int/sites/g/files/tmzbdl1001/files/documents/CSP%20-IOM%20Process%20Map1%20%281%29.pdf; Asher Lazarus Hirsch, Khanh Hoang, and Anthea Vogl, "Australia's Private

Refugee Sponsorship Program: Creating Complementary Pathways or Privatizing Humanitarianism?" *Refuge* 35, No. 2 (2019): 110, 115–116, 118, https://doi.org/10.7202/1064823ar; DHA, *Findings of the Review of the Community Support Program*, led by the Commonwealth Coordinator-General for Migrant Services, Ms. Alison Larkins, 4–5, https://www.homeaffairs.gov.au/reports-and-pubs/files/csp-review-findings.pdf.

As a result of that review, from August 19, 2022, it would become much cheaper for Australians to sponsor a refugee under the CSP program, the visa application charge being reduced to 40 percent of the then current rate. See Minister for Immigration, Citizenship, Migrant Services, and Multicultural Affairs Alex Hawke, "Enhanced Support for Refugee Resettlement and Integration," Media Release, December 17, 2021, https://minister.homeaffairs.gov.au/AlexHawke/Pages/enhanced-support-for-refugee-settlement-and-integration.aspx and DHA, "Community Sponsorship Reforms: Review of Australia's Community Support Program," https://immi.homeaffairs.gov.au/settling-in-australia/settlement-policy-and-reform/community-sponsorship-reforms.

38. "The first applications under the CSP were lodged in March 2018, with the first visa granted in June 2018." Overall, in 2017–18, 487 CSP applications were received, and 326 visas were granted (DHA, *Australia's Offshore Humanitarian Program: 2017–18*, 2018, 1, 27; the Department has since removed this report from its website). According to the Department's Procedural Instructions, applications for the 202 Global Special Humanitarian Visa, including the CSP, are listed last in the order of "overall priorities," to be "processed according to the urgency of the applicant's need for resettlement in Australia" ("Offshore Humanitarian Program—Visa Application and Related Procedures—Caseload Management—Prioritising Caseload").

39. See IRCC, "Notice—Supplementary Information 2018-2020 Immigration Levels Plan," November 1, 2017, https://www.canada.ca/en/immigration-refugees-citizenship/news/notices/supplementary-immigration-levels-2018.html and "Notice—Supplementary Information for the 2022-2024 Immigration Levels Plan," February 14, 2022, https://www.canada.ca/en/immigration-refugees-citizenship/news/notices/supplementary-immigration-levels-2022-2024.html. The "Levels Plan," which contains the Canadian government's targets for the number of permanent residents to be admitted for the next calendar year, is published via tabling in parliament as required under IRPA.

40. See UNHCR, *Information on Private Sponsorship Programs*, May 29, 2018, https://www.unhcr.org/id/wp-content/uploads/sites/42/2018/09/Leaflet-Sponsorship-Programs.pdf. In addition, even those who had arrived in Indonesia before that date were allocated fewer places than previously—450 down from 600 annually—resulting in a much longer waiting period. "These changes should reduce the movement of asylum seekers to Indonesia and encourage them to seek resettlement in or from countries of first asylum," then Immigration Minister Scott Morrison had announced retrospectively on November 11, 2014 ("Asylum Seekers Registered With UNHCR in Indonesia After June No Longer Eligible for Resettlement in Australia, Scott Morrison Says," *ABC News*, November 18, 2014, https://www.abc.net.au/news/2014-11-18/resettlement-path-for-asylum-seekers-in-indonesia-cut-off/5900962).

41. See https://www.canada.ca/en/immigration-refugees-citizenship/services/new-immigrants/pr-card/apply-renew-replace/photo.html.

42. Immigration Regulation No. IMI-0352. GR.02.07 (2016) includes an attachment stipulating the wording for a much broader "statement letter" to be signed by refugees. While Missbach ("Accommodating," 36) has also maintained that in addition to "restrictions on mobility and housing," such documents included "prohibitions on visiting airport and seaports, biweekly reporting requirements, requests to comply with Indonesian law and display 'cooperative behaviour in the neighbourhood,'" the actual declaration signed by the families was much more limited.

43. Passport holders of certain countries, including Vietnam, are exempt from needing a visa to enter Indonesia, valid for 30 days.

44. Also known as an "attestation letter" or "asylum seeker certificate" (see UNHCR, *Procedural Standards*, 3–17 and Taylor and Rafferty-Brown, "Difficult Journeys"), Indonesian authorities are obliged to take such a document seriously.

45. See Joe Cochrane, "Refugees in Indonesia Hoped for Brief Stay. Many May Be Stuck for Life," *New York Times*, January 26, 2018, https://www.nytimes.com/2018/01/26/world/asia/indonesia-refugees-united-nations.html.

46. "Conclusion: Sponsorship's Success and Sustainability?" in *Strangers to Neighbours*, 360. See UNHCR, *Global Trends: Forced Displacement in 2018*, 30, 32, https://www.unhcr.org/5d08d7ee7.pdf and IRCC, *2019 Annual Report*.

47. See UNHCR, *Progress report 2018*, 34.

48. Amerasians are children of American Vietnam War veterans and Vietnamese women. See https://www.facebook.com/AmerAsiansWithoutBorders.

49. See IRPR, s. 141(1) and IRCC, "Guide to Reunite Family Members Abroad Under the One-Year Window of Opportunity Provision (IMM 5578)," https://www.canada.ca/en/immigration-refugees-citizenship/services/application/application-forms-guides/guide-5578-request-process-following-family-

members-year-window-opportunity-provisions. html. They may still be eligible for processing in a family reunification category, even after the one-year period elapses.

50. See IRPR, ss. 138, 153 (1)(a) and (b), 154(2). At least three members of each G5, which consists of five or more Canadian citizens or permanent residents, must contribute funds towards the sponsorship. For more information see IRCC, "2. Private Sponsorship of Refugees Program," https://www.canada.ca/en/immigration-refugees-citizenship/corporate/publications-manuals/guide-private-sponsorship-refugees-program/section-2.html.

51. See IRCC, "Guide 2200—Groups of Five to Privately Sponsor Refugees," https://www.canada.ca/en/immigration-refugees-citizenship/services/application/application-forms-guides/guide-sponsor-refugee-groups-five.html#appendix. Both the Canadian and Australian private sponsorship programs also allowed for in-kind support, thereby reducing expenses. For a rough cost comparison between the Canadian and Australian programs in 2017–2018 see RCOA and Settlement Services International (SSI), *Canada's Private Sponsorship of Refugees Program: Potential Lessons for Australia*, Discussion Paper, August 2017, 5, https://www.refugeecouncil.org.au/wp-content/uploads/2018/12/Canadian-PSR-paper-1708.pdf and Stephanie Cousins, *Make Refuge: Safer Pathways for Refugees and Asylum Seekers*, Churchill Fellowship Report, December 2018, 131, https://www.churchilltrust.com.au/fellow/stephanie-cousins-nsw-2017/.

52. "A de facto dependant is a person considered by the refugee family to be an integral member of the family unit, but who does not meet IRCC's definition of a family member. Such individuals should be included in the sponsorship." For more information see IRCC, "2.13 What is a De Facto Dependant?" https://www.canada.ca/en/immigration-refugees-citizenship/corporate/publications-manuals/guide-private-sponsorship-refugees-program/section-2.html#a2.13.

53. See, for example, Missbach, "Falling Through the Cracks" and J. N. Joniad, "How Australia's Deterrence Policies Turned Indonesia into a Prison Without Walls," *Overland*, October 29, 2021, https://overland.org.au/2021/10/how-australias-deterrence-policies-have-turned-indonesia-into-a-prison-without-walls/comment-page-1/#comment-1056832. According to DGI Circular Note No IMI-UM.01.01–2827 (July 30, 2018), IOM interpreted this "termination of assistance" as being directed against, among others, asylum seekers like Mr. Loi, "who come independently and enter legally into Indonesian territory then register themselves / report to UNHCR to obtain status as an asylum seeker" (translated from Indonesian); see also SUAKA, *Know Your Rights*, 51.

54. This was in keeping with the "statement letter" to be signed by refugees, attached to Immigration Regulation No. IMI-0352.GR.02.07 (2016)

(see endnote 42 above); see also Missbach, "Substituting Immigration Detention Centers," 231.

55. Mr. Yen's and the rest of the group's qualms about working illegally are not commonly shared, with many refugees prepared to take the risk of entering the informal labor market in Indonesia, despite the discrimination and risks they confront. See, for example, Wayne Palmer and Antje Missbach, "Enforcing Labour Rights of Irregular Migrants in Indonesia," *Third World Quarterly* 40, No. 5 (2019): 915, https://doi.org/10.1080/01436597.2018.1522586.

56. This statistic has since been removed from the website, https://www.canada.ca/en/immigration-refugees-citizenship/services/refugees/help-outside-canada/private-sponsorship-program/how-we-process-applications.html.

57. "Attorney Vo An Don Was Disbarred From Phu Yen Bar Association," *Dan Lam Bao*, November 27, 2017, https://danlambaovn.blogspot.com/2017/11/attorney-vo-don-was-disbarred-from-phu.html.

58. *Report to the United Nations Committee Against Torture*, 49–50.

59. Interview with Vo An Don, May 25, 2019.

Chapter 6

1. The organization has asked not to be named for fear of being perceived in Vietnam as associated with "anti-government propaganda," although that is certainly not the case. All names in this chapter, apart from the advocates, have been changed to maintain the privacy of those involved.

2. See https://avwa.org.au.

3. While initially I was somewhat taken aback by being addressed as "*bà*," commonly translated as "grandma," Mai Pham subsequently explained that it is meant as a title of respect.

4. For the story of Son's parents, Nguyen Tuan Kiet and Huynh Thi My Van, see Chapter 2.

Chapter 7

1. Angela Johnston, "Majority of Canadians Against Accepting More Refugees, Poll Suggests," *CBC News*, July 3, 2019, https://www.cbc.ca/news/canada/manitoba/refugees-tolerance-1.5192769; see also Marc Montgomery, "Canadians: Attitudes Hardening Against Immigrants, Refugees," *Radio Canada International*, July 3, 2019, https://www.rcinet.ca/en/2019/07/03/canadians-attitudes-hardening-against-immigrants-refugees/. Several other surveys at that time reached a similar conclusion; see, for example, Environics Institute for Survey Research, *Canadian Public Opinion About Immigration and Refugees, Focus Canada*, April 29, 2019, 1–7, https://www.environicsinstitute.org/docs/default-source/project-documents/focus-canada-spring-2019/environics-

institute---focus-canada-spring-2019-survey-on-immigration-and-refugees---final-report.pdf?sfvrsn=8dd2597f_2. Interestingly, by September 2020, Canadian public opinion had become more positive: Environics Institute for Survey Research, *Canadian Public Opinion About Immigration and Refugees Final Report, Focus Canada*, October 7, 2020, 1–8, https://www.environicsinstitute.org/docs/default-source/project-documents/fc-fall-2020---immigration/focus-canada-fall-2020---public-opinion-on-immigration-refugees----final-report.pdf?sfvrsn=bd51588f_2&mc_cid=e467489f57&mc_eid=9fb7b20078.

2. See IRCC, "#WelcomeRefugees: Key Figures," https://www.canada.ca/en/immigration-refugees-citizenship/services/refugees/welcome-syrian-refugees/key-figures.html and Robert Vineberg, "25,000 Syrian Refugees in Four Months: How Did Canada Do It?" *Interpreter*, March 9, 2016, https://www.lowyinstitute.org/the-interpreter/25000-syrian-refugees-four-months-how-did-canada-do-it.

3. Vic Satzewich, "'Canadian Exceptionalism': Border Control Also Matters," *Canadian Diversity* 15, No. 2 (2018): 35 and IRPA, s. 101.

4. IRCC, "Claiming Asylum in Canada—What Happens?" https://www.canada.ca/en/immigration-refugees-citizenship/news/2017/03/claiming_asylum_incanadawhathappens.html and interview with Kyanh Do, September 4, 2019; see also UNHCR, "What to Know About Irregular Border Crossings," https://www.unhcr.ca/wp-content/uploads/2019/02/Facts-About-Irregular-Border-Crossings-Feb2019.pdf and IRCC, *2019 Annual Report*.

5. See, for example, IRCC, "By the Numbers—40 Years of Canada's Private Sponsorship of Refugees Program," https://www.canada.ca/en/immigration-refugees-citizenship/news/2019/04/by-the-numbers--40-years-of-canadas-private-sponsorship-of-refugees-program.html. "Six in ten Canadians support accepting an increased number of refugees into the country and … seven percent of Canadian adults—close to two million people—report being personally involved in helping Syrian refugees come to and settle in our country" (Environics Institute for Survey Research, *Canada's World Survey 2018 Final Report*, April 2018, 6, 34–35, https://www.environicsinstitute.org/docs/default-source/project-documents/canada's-world-2018-survey/canada's-world-survey-2018---final-report.pdf?sfvrsn=17208306_2).

6. See, for example, "About the GRSI," https://refugeesponsorship.org/about-the-global-refugee-sponsorship-initiative/ and Hyndman, Reynolds, Yousuf, Purkey, Demoz, and Sherrell, "Sustaining Private Sponsorship," 3. The GRSI is in keeping with the UN *Global Compact on Refugees* (GCR) and the IOM's *Global Compact for Safe, Orderly and Regular Migration* (GCM), both adopted in 2018. See, for example, Lara Coleman, *Resettling*

Refugees: Canada's Humanitarian Commitments, Publication No. 2020–74-E, Ottawa: Library of Parliament, 2021, https://lop.parl.ca/staticfiles/PublicWebsite/Home/ResearchPublications/BackgroundPapers/PDF/2020-74-e.pdf.

7. IRCC, *2020 Annual Report to Parliament on Immigration*, 3, 14, https://www.canada.ca/content/dam/ircc/migration/ircc/english/pdf/pub/annual-report-2020-en.pdf; see also UNHCR, *Global Trends: Forced Displacement in 2019*, 1-83, https://www.unhcr.org/5ee200e37.pdf.

8. Interview with Kyanh Do, May 20, 2020. For more information see https://vietnamvoice.org/en/2018/11/thong-diep-givingtuesday-cua-voice/ and https://vietnamvoice.org/en/2019/07/cap-nhat-ve-chuong-trinh-ti-nan-cua-voice/.

9. See IRPR, ss. 154 (1)(a) and (b).

10. See IRCC, "A New Way Forward for Some Immigration Application Processing Times," News Release, August 9, 2018, https://www.canada.ca/en/immigration-refugees-citizenship/news/2018/08/a-new-way-forward-for-some-immigration-application-processing-times.html.

11. While the estimated time from Indonesia had been slowly increasing by a month or two each time we checked, it should be noted that in the past, private sponsorship applications had taken considerably longer to process. See, for example, IRCC, *Evaluation of the Resettlement Programs (GAR, PSR, BVOR and RAP)*, July 2016, 23, https://www.canada.ca/content/dam/ircc/migration/ircc/english/pdf/pub/resettlement.pdf. More recently, projected processing times would be dramatically reduced, as discussed later in Chapter 7.

12. For more information see RSTP, *Best Practices for Monitoring Resource Kit*, April 2019, 1–29, http://www.rstp.ca/wp-content/uploads/2019/04/Best-Practices-for-Monitoring-Resource-Kit-Apr-2019.pdf. For sponsorship withdrawals see IRCC, "2.23 Sponsorship Withdrawals," https://www.canada.ca/en/immigration-refugees-citizenship/corporate/publications-manuals/guide-private-sponsorship-refugees-program/section-2.html#a2.5.

13. "Adults are expected to be engaged in activities that will lead to self-sufficiency, e.g., enrolled in programs normally outside of the public school system including language or job training programs or attending a post-secondary institution; seeking employment and/or employed" (https://www.canada.ca/en/immigration-refugees-citizenship/corporate/publications-manuals/operational-bulletins-manuals/service-delivery/resettlement-assistance-program/roles.html). For more details see also IRCC, "2.21 What Are the Refugee's Responsibilities?" https://www.canada.ca/en/immigration-refugees-citizenship/corporate/publications-manuals/guide-private-sponsorship-refugees-program/section-2.

html#a2.6 and "Guide 5413—Sponsorship Agreement Holders to Privately Sponsor Refugees," "Post-Arrival Financial Support," https://www.canada.ca/en/immigration-refugees-citizenship/services/application/application-forms-guides/guide-sponsor-refugee-agreement-holder-constituent-group.html.

14. See "Guide 2201—Community Sponsors to Privately Sponsor Refugees," https://www.canada.ca/en/immigration-refugees-citizenship/services/application/application-forms-guides/guide-sponsor-refugee-community.html#appA, notably the "Sponsorship Cost Table for Privately-Sponsored Refugees." Although the Guide was revised on March 1, 2021, the sponsorship costs remained the same.

15. After their first year in Canada, resettled refugees are eligible for means-tested public income support if needed. See, for example, IRCC, "Syrian Refugee Integration—One Year After Arrival: Income Support," https://www.canada.ca/en/immigration-refugees-citizenship/services/refugees/welcome-syrian-refugees/integration.html.

16. For a list of SPOs see IRCC, "Resettlement Assistance Program Service Provider Organizations," https://www.canada.ca/en/immigration-refugees-citizenship/services/refugees/help-within-canada/government-assisted-refugee-program/providers.html.

17. Jennifer Hyndman, William Payne, and Shauna Jiminez, *The State of Private Refugee Sponsorship in Canada: Trends, Issues and Impacts*, Refugee Research Network/Centre for Refugee Studies Policy Brief submitted to the Government of Canada, December 2, 2016, 12, https://refugeeresearch.net/wp-content/uploads/2017/02/hyndman_feb'17.pdf. For a useful summary of private sponsor and publicly funded services see IRCC, "Responsibilities of Sponsors & Availability of IRCC-Funded Services for PSRs and BVORs," updated October 2019, https://www.rstp.ca/wp-content/uploads/2019/11/Responsibilities-of-Sponsors-and-Availability-of-IRCC-funded-Services-for-PSRs-and-BVORs-Oct-2019.pdf. Resettled refugees can also access websites such as https://settlement.org/ontario/immigration-citizenship/refugees/after-you-arrive/what-assistance-can-refugees-get-in-canada/ and https://newyouth.ca/en, which focus on Ontario.

18. Genevieve Richie, "Civil Society, the State, and Private Sponsorship: The Political Economy of Refugee Resettlement," *International Journal of Lifelong Education* 37, No. 6 (2018): 6, https://doi.org/10.1080/02601370.2018.1513429.

19. RSTP, *Private Sponsorship of Refugees (PSR) Program FAQs Post-Arrival Financial Support for PSRs*, updated August 2019, 16, http://www.rstp.ca/wp-content/uploads/2019/08/EN-FAQs-update-Summer-2019-AUG-19-update_FINAL.docx-3.pdf; see also IRCC, "2.6 What Are the Responsibilities of the Sponsoring Group?"

https://www.canada.ca/en/immigration-refugees-citizenship/corporate/publications-manuals/guide-private-sponsorship-refugees-program/section-2.html#a2.6. Considerable guidance is provided to private sponsors in Canada. Administered by Catholic Cross-cultural Services (CCS), RSTP includes a *Handbook for Sponsoring Groups* (see http://www.rstp.ca/en/resources/handbook-for-sponsoring-groups/) and hosts training workshops. Other groups, such as the Canadian Council for Refugees (CCR), offer support too (see https://ccrweb.ca/en).

20. Vu Pham Yen, "Nhà van Shira Sebban: Ân Nhân Nguòi Viêt Ty Nan Tam Trú ö Nam Duong," *Thoi Bao*, February 22, 2019, https://www.thoibao.com/nha-van-shira-sebban-an-nhan-nguoi-viet-ty-nan-tam-tru-o-nam-duong/. *Thoi Bao* is the largest Vietnamese language newspaper in Canada.

21. See https://www.facebook.com/pages/category/Community-Service/Home-For-Amerasians-1244675755729994/.

22. https://www.ancestry.com/dna/.

23. See, for example, Catherine Baillie Abidi and Shiva Nourpanah, *Refugees and Forced Migration: A Canadian Perspective, An A—Z Guide* (Halifax: Nimbus Publishing, 2019), 57; UNHCR, "Are Refugees Good for Canada?" https://www.unhcr.ca/wp-content/uploads/2019/06/economic-integration-onepager-en-2.pdf; IRCC, "Apply for Canadian Citizenship," https://www.canada.ca/en/immigration-refugees-citizenship/services/canadian-citizenship/become-canadian-citizen.html; *UNHCR Resettlement Handbook*, Country Chapter: Canada, 13.

24. According to IRPA, s. 96, the "Convention Refugees Abroad" class includes individuals meeting the refugee definition in the 1951 Refugee Convention, art. 1. See IRPR, ss. 139, 144, 145 and Introduction, endnote 2 above. For more information on the other "Country of Asylum" class, which is for "humanitarian-protected persons abroad," effectively in refugee-like situations outside their home country, involving "civil war, armed conflict or massive violation of human rights," who can also be privately sponsored, see IRPR, ss. 139, 146, and 147. For the eligibility criteria for each category see IRCC, "Resettle in Canada as a Refugee: Determine Your Eligibility," https://www.canada.ca/en/immigration-refugees-citizenship/services/refugees/help-outside-canada.html#conventionrefugee; "Guide for Convention Refugees and Humanitarian-Protected Persons Abroad (IMM 6000)," https://www.canada.ca/en/immigration-refugees-citizenship/services/application/application-forms-guides/guide-6000-convention-refugees-abroad-humanitarian-protected-persons-abroad.html#step1; "Convention Refugees Abroad Class—Conditions," https://www.canada.ca/en/immigration-refugees-citizenship/

corporate/publications-manuals/operational-bulletins-manuals/refugee-protection/resettlement/admissibility/convention.html; "Country of Asylum Class—Conditions," https://www.canada.ca/en/immigration-refugees-citizenship/corporate/publications-manuals/operational-bulletins-manuals/refugee-protection/resettlement/admissibility/asylum.html. Henceforth, I will refer to all such "policy, procedures and guidance used by IRCC staff ... posted on the Department's website as a courtesy to stakeholders" as "IRCC guidelines."

25. See Howard Adelman, "Accepting Refugees: International Law in a Canadian Context in the Twentieth Century" (Working Paper No. 2017/1, Canadian Association for Refugee and Forced Migration Studies, February 2017), 2, http://carfms.org/wp-content/uploads/2015/10/CARFMS-WPS-No9-Howard-Adelman.pdf. The successful establishment requirement is outlined in IRPR, s. 139(1)(g). The only exception to it is those refugees determined "to be vulnerable or in urgent need of protection" (IRPR, s. 139(2)), "vulnerable" being defined as having "a greater need of protection than other applicants for protection abroad because of the person's particular circumstances that give rise to a heightened risk to their physical safety" (IRPR, s. 138). See also *UNHCR Resettlement Handbook*, Country Chapter: Canada, 4 and IRCC, "The Humanitarian and Compassionate Assessment: Ability to Establish in Canada," https://www.canada.ca/en/immigration-refugees-citizenship/corporate/publications-manuals/operational-bulletins-manuals/permanent-residence/humanitarian-compassionate-consideration/processing/assessment-ability-establish-canada.html.

26. Being responsible for bringing an interpreter is contrary to regular practice according to which "refugees are not normally requested to provide their own interpreter" (see IRCC, "Resettlement From Overseas: Conducting Interviews," https://www.canada.ca/en/immigration-refugees-citizenship/corporate/publications-manuals/operational-bulletins-manuals/refugee-protection/resettlement/admissibility/conduct-interview.html).

27. IRCC, "Resettlement: Assessing Credibility," https://www.canada.ca/en/immigration-refugees-citizenship/corporate/publications-manuals/operational-bulletins-manuals/refugee-protection/resettlement/admissibility/credibility.html.

28. For more information see IRCC, "Phase 3: Admissibility Assessment," https://www.canada.ca/en/immigration-refugees-citizenship/services/application/application-forms-guides/guide-6000-convention-refugees-abroad-humanitarian-protected-persons-abroad.html and "Get Medical Services Before You Leave for Canada," https://www.canada.ca/en/immigration-refugees-citizenship/services/

refugees/help-outside-canada/health-care.html;"IOM Indonesia Programmes"; https://indonesia.iom.int/resettlement-and-assisted-voluntary-return.

29. IRCC, "Resettlement: Assessing Credibility" and "Resettlement: Finalizing the Interview," https://www.canada.ca/en/immigration-refugees-citizenship/corporate/publications-manuals/operational-bulletins-manuals/refugee-protection/resettlement/admissibility/final-interview.html.

30. The video can be viewed at https://www.youtube.com/watch?v=v6y1LOUwW3s&list=PLAGur7-GAVv8xo8v_xjfa4fEaKEssCaiv&index=4.

31. The retrospective ban has been introduced and rejected several times since 2016 within the Migration Legislation Amendment (Regional Processing Cohort) Bill (https://www.aph.gov.au/Parliamentary_Business/Bills_LEGislation/Bills_Search_Results/Result?bId=r6344). Having been passed by the House of Representatives on November 10, 2016, the bill was not debated in the Senate and ended up lapsing when the 45th Parliament ended on July 1, 2019. It was reintroduced into the lower house three days later but lapsed once again when the 46th Parliament was dissolved on April 11, 2022. For a useful chronology and history of the bill see Claire Petrie and Harriet Spinks, "Migration Legislation Amendment (Regional Processing Cohort) Bill 2019," Bills Digest No. 54, 2019–20, November 19, 2019, https://www.aph.gov.au/Parliamentary_Business/Bills_Legislation/bd/bd1920a/20bd054. See also, for example, Gareth Hutchens, "Asylum Seekers Face Lifetime Ban from Entering Australia if They Arrive by Boat," *Guardian*, October 30, 2016, https://www.theguardian.com/australia-news/2016/oct/30/asylum-seekers-face-lifetime-ban-on-entering-australia-if-they-arrive-by-boat and Fergus Hunter and Michael Koziol, "Asylum Seekers Who Come by Boat Banned for Life Under New Laws," *SMH*, October 30, 2016, https://www.smh.com.au/politics/federal/asylum-seekers-who-come-by-boat-banned-for-life-under-new-laws-20161030-gsdvf7.html.

32. UNHCR, "IOM, UNHCR Announce Temporary Suspension of Resettlement Travel for Refugees," March 17, 2020, https://www.unhcr.org/news/press/2020/3/5e7103034/iom-unhcr-announce-temporary-suspension-resettlement-travel-refugees.html?fbclid=IwAR0o7YK3YcGvHdWnHypI0TsipgM3WpnL1gPoqmfnyuhO0yYS2-upMDsBPqk; RCOA, "Refugee Resettlement to Fall Short of National and Global Targets, as COVID-19 Pandemic Halts Travel," April 29, 2020, https://www.refugeecouncil.org.au/resettlement-briefing-on-covid-19; Adèle Garnier, "The Covid-19 Resettlement Suspension: Impact, Exemptions and the Road Ahead," *FluchtforschungsBlog*, June 16, 2020,

https://blog.fluchtforschung.net/the-covid-19-resettlement-suspension/.

33. Correspondence with Kyanh Do, May 19, 2020.

34. Anne Barker, "Indonesia is Preparing to Vaccinate Up to 180 million People Against COVID-19 in 15 Months," *ABC News*, February 5, 2021, https://www.abc.net.au/news/2021-01-13/indonesia-starts-rolling-out-jabs-of-chinas-covid-19-vaccine/13051430.

35. Dian Septiari, "UNHCR Works to Ensure No Refugees Left Behind in COVID-19 Crisis in Indonesia," *Jakarta Post*, April 5, 2020, https://www.thejakartapost.com/news/2020/04/05/unhcr-works-to-ensure-no-refugees-left-behind-in-covid-19-crisis-in-indonesia.html; IOM Indonesia, *COVID-19 Strategic Response and Recovery Plan 2021*, 1–9, https://indonesia.iom.int/sites/g/files/tmzbdl1491/files/documents/IOMIndonesiaCOVID19SRRP2021.pdf and "IOM Indonesia—2021 Year in Review," https://indonesia.iom.int/sites/g/files/tmzbdl1491/files/documents/iom-indonesia-2021-year-in-review_final_1.pdf.

36. http://www.lentera.sch.id.

37. See Ismira Lutfia Tisnadibrata, "Surviving as a Refugee Becomes More Testing During Pandemic," *Arab News*, June 19, 2020, https://www.arabnews.com/node/1692426/world. About 3,570 refugees were enrolled in online university courses or community-based education programs.

38. "Immigration, Refugees and Citizenship Canada Service Standards," https://www.canada.ca/en/immigration-refugees-citizenship/corporate/mandate/service-declaration/service-standards.html.

39. Shauna Labman and Adèle Garnier, "Federal Election 2021: What the Conservatives Don't Understand About Refugee Resettlement," *Conversation*, September 12, 2021, https://theconversation.com/federal-election-2021-what-the-conservatives-dont-understand-about-refugee-resettlement-167033.

40. IRCC, *2020 Annual Report*, 24; *2021 Annual Report to Parliament on Immigration*, 29, https://www.canada.ca/content/dam/ircc/documents/pdf/english/corporate/publications-manuals/annual-report-2021-en.pdf; "IRCC Minister Transition Binder 2021: Permanent Immigration—Immigration Levels Planning," https://www.canada.ca/en/immigration-refugees-citizenship/corporate/transparency/transition-binders/minister-2021/levels.html; "Notice—Supplementary Information for the 2021-2023 Immigration Levels Plan," October 30, 2020, https://www.canada.ca/en/immigration-refugees-citizenship/news/notices/supplementary-immigration-levels-2021-2023.html; "Notice—Supplementary Information for the 2022-2024 Immigration Levels Plan"; Kathleen Harris, "Federal Government Plans to Bring in More Than 1.2M Immigrants in Next 3 Years," *CBC News*, October 30, 2020, https://www.cbc.ca/news/politics/mendicino-immigration-pandemic-refugees-1.5782642 and "Refugee Advocates Say Canada Must Step Up Resettlement Efforts Despite Pandemic," *CBC News*, November 12, 2020, https://www.cbc.ca/news/politics/refugees-canada-pandemic-mendicino-1.5797361?fbclid=IwAR0MA8g_EHGJ1LaZU8exgrtg8l8yVpfUoC3TmQLvwdQJvpk1D0eUXDEid1E; Amelia Cheatham, "What Is Canada's Immigration Policy?" Council on Foreign Relations, August 3, 2020, https://www.cfr.org/backgrounder/what-canadas-immigration-policy; Zaini Majeed, "Canada to Admit 45,000 Refugees in 2021; Expedite Permanent Residency Applications," *Republicworld.com*, June 19, 2021, https://www.republicworld.com/world-news/rest-of-the-world-news/canada-to-admit-45000-refugees-in-2021-expedite-permanent-residency-applications.html.

41. Majeed, "Canada to Admit 45,000 Refugees in 2021"; UNHCR, "Indonesia Fact Sheet," December 2020, https://reporting.unhcr.org/sites/default/files/UNHCR%20Indonesia%20fact%20sheet%20-%20December%202020.pdf; *Global Trends: Forced Displacement in 2021*, 37-38, https://www.unhcr.org/62a9d1494/global-trends-report-2021; "Indonesia Fact Sheet," February 2022, https://www.unhcr.org/id/wp-content/uploads/sites/42/2022/04/Indonesia-Fact-Sheet-February-2022-FINAL.pdf; "Resettlement at a Glance," January-December 2020, https://www.unhcr.org/protection/resettlement/600e95094/resettlement-fact-sheet-2020.html; "Refugee Data Finder," https://www.unhcr.org/refugee-statistics/; "With Refugee Resettlement at a Record Low in 2020, UNHCR Calls on States to Offer Places and Save Lives," January 25, 2021, https://www.unhcr.org/news/press/2021/1/600e79ea4/refugee-resettlement-record-low-2020-unhcr-calls-states-offer-places-save.html; IRCC, *2021 Annual Report*, 38.

42. See Chapter 1.

43. See https://coa.iom.int/training-materials.

44. See IRCC, "Phase 2: Eligibility Assessment," https://www.canada.ca/en/immigration-refugees-citizenship/services/application/application-forms-guides/guide-6000-convention-refugees-abroad-humanitarian-protected-persons-abroad.html#step1.

45. IRCC, "Immigration Category on the Confirmation of Permanent Residence (COPR)," https://www.canada.ca/en/immigration-refugees-citizenship/corporate/publications-manuals/immigration-category-confirmation-permanent-residence-copr.html.

46. Majeed, "Canada to Admit 45,000 Refugees in 2021"; IRCC, "Canada Announces 3 New Initiatives to Welcome and Support More Refugees," News Release, June 18, 2021, https://www.canada.ca/en/immigration-refugees-citizenship/

news/2021/06/canada-announces-3-new-initiatives-to-welcome-and-support-more-refugees.html and "Supporting Afghan Nationals: About the Special Programs," https://www.canada.ca/en/immigration-refugees-citizenship/services/refugees/afghanistan/special-measures.html.

47. While usually required, an interview is deemed unnecessary if a Migration Officer determines enough information is available to decide eligibility and admissibility.

48. UNHCR and partners including IOM reported vaccinating more than 7,000 refugees against COVID-19 (see UNHCR, "Fact Sheet," September 2021). Nevertheless, a "bureaucratic glitch," meaning that some refugees were unable to prove they had been vaccinated, would result in them missing out on public services (see Devianti Faridz, "Thousands of Refugees in Indonesia 'Shut Out' From Public Facilities," VOA, March 11, 2022, https://www.voanews.com/a/-thousands-of-refugees-shut-out-from-public-facilities/6480371.html).

49. See IRCC, "Get Medical Services Before You Leave for Canada."

50. A popular informal mode of transportation, angkots are small mini vans running between fixed points in Indonesian cities.

51. In November 2021, UNHCR reported that about 780 of the roughly 3,500 refugee children registered with the organization were enrolled in accredited national schools, the number increasing to 862 by early 2022. "Around 1,700 school aged children are not yet attending formal schools, but among them some 1,000 children are receiving education through refugee learning centres organised by UNHCR, IOM or centres led by the refugee communities" (UNHCR, "Indonesia Fact Sheet," September 2021, https://www.unhcr.org/id/wp-content/uploads/sites/42/2021/11/September-Fact-Sheet-Indonesia-FINAL.pdf); see also UNHCR, "Indonesia: Monthly Statistical Report," February 2022, https://reliefweb.int/report/indonesia/unhcr-indonesia-monthly-statistical-report-february-2022.

52. For more information, see, for example, "How Do I Repay My Travel Loan If I Am a Refugee or Protected Person?" https://settlement.org/ontario/immigration-citizenship/refugees/after-you-arrive/how-do-i-repay-my-travel-loan-if-i-am-a-refugee-or-protected-person/.

53. The interview can be viewed at https://www.youtube.com/watch?v=LCHqCQ_AZe0; see also Nhan Vu, "Cộng Đồng Người Việt Tại Canada Tiếp Dón Thuyền Nhân Việt Nam Từ Indonesia," SBTN, December 3, 2021, https://www.sbtn.tv/cong-dong-nguoi-viet-tai-canada-tiep-don-thuyen-nhan-viet-nam-tu-indonesia/ (translated from Vietnamese).

54. See https://www.cbsa-asfc.gc.ca/menu-eng.html.

55. See IRPA, ss. 95(1) and (2); https://www.canada.ca/en/immigration-refugees-citizenship/corporate/publications-manuals/immigration-category-confirmation-permanent-residence-copr.html.

56. See, for example, Nam Loc, "Những Thuyền Nhân Tị Nạn Muộn Màng," Viet Bao, January 24, 2022, https://vietbao.com/a310922/nhung-thuyen-nhan-ti-nan-muon-mang and Nguoi Viet, January 25, 2022, https://www.nguoi-viet.com/little-saigon/nhung-thuyen-nhan-ti-nan-muon-mang/; Vu Pham Yen, "Cuối Cùng Cũng Dã Dến Bến Bờ Tự Do," Thoi Bao, January 29, 2022 (all translated from Vietnamese). Unfortunately, Thoi Bao suffered a technical mishap in July 2022, which led to the loss of the newspaper's entire database from 2020 onwards.

57. For the latest processing times see IRCC, "Check Processing Times," https://www.canada.ca/en/immigration-refugees-citizenship/services/application/check-processing-times.html. From March 31, 2022, IRCC improved the accuracy of its processing times tool, updating information weekly.

58. See Chapter 6.

59. See Chapter 2 for this family's story.

60. See Chapter 5.

61. "As an added precaution, refugees undergo a fitness-to-fly check for COVID-19 signs and symptoms with an IOM nurse or doctor. This check is done 24 to 72 hours before their flight" (https://www.canada.ca/en/immigration-refugees-citizenship/services/coronavirus-covid19/refugees.html#quarantine).

62. "This session provides refugees with information on how they can monitor their health and prevent the spread of COVID-19. Refugees are also told about the 14-day quarantine upon arrival in Canada, and given information about the supports they'll receive from Resettlement Assistance Program service provider organizations or their private sponsor" (https://www.canada.ca/en/immigration-refugees-citizenship/services/coronavirus-covid19/refugees.html#quarantine).

63. See IRCC, "Interview Process," https://www.canada.ca/en/immigration-refugees-citizenship/services/new-immigrants/prepare-life-canada/border-entry/interviews.html; "Prepare For Arrival—Refugees Resettling to Canada," https://www.canada.ca/en/immigration-refugees-citizenship/services/refugees/help-outside-canada/after-apply-next-steps/prepare-arrival.html.

64. Vu Pham Yen, "Những Thuyền Nhân Muộn Màng Dến Bến Bờ Tự Do," Thoi Bao, July 14, 2022 (translated from Vietnamese). Unfortunately, the article was part of the database lost by the newspaper (see above).

65. Interview with Kyanh Do, July 7, 2022.

Postscript

1. "UNHCR Projected Global Resettlement Needs 2023, 13, https://www.unhcr.org/62b18e714; USA for UNHCR, "Refugee Statistics," https://www.unrefugees.org/refugee-facts/statistics/.

2. Peter Singer, *The Life You Can Save: How to Do Your Part to End World Poverty*, 10th anniversary edition (Sydney: The Life You Can Save, 2019), https://www.thelifeyoucansave.org.au/our-story/.

3. *DFAT Country Information Report Vietnam*, 2022, 33, [paras. 5.31, 5.34].

4. https://m.facebook.com/story.php?story_fbid=pfbid02sVGoHZizSxBnjDqoqSdEAkpXo4cf3mKTPo95daTqLV8xgR4eU2NFT3uR1nZuxbYUl&id=683110988; see also "Vietnam Rights Lawyer Barred from Leaving Country," *RFA*, September 28, 2022, https://www.rfa.org/english/news/vietnam/barred-09282022145939.html/ampRFA?fbclid=-IwAR0E_hLUVWF5JFfU12g4-Ii8oEHEEsspNm3-K6NJPhGhYLDTJVBDQ7EHviA and Le Phan, "Việt Nam Tự Hạ Thấp Trong Mắt Các Nhà Quan Sát Nhân Quyền," *Saigon Nho*, October 4, 2022, https://saigonnhonews.com/thoi-su/van-de-hom-nay/viet-nam-tu-ha-thap-trong-mat-cac-nha-quan-sat-nhan-quyen/.

5. Trevor Hunnicutt, "Exclusive: Vietnam Activists to Seek U.S. Refuge After Biden Administration Deal—U.S. Officials," *Reuters*, September 19, 2023, https://www.reuters.com/world/vietnam-activists-seek-us-refuge-after-biden-administration-deal-us-officials-2023-09-18/.

6. https://www.rfa.org/vietnamese/news/vietnamnews/vietnam-hr-attorney-to-seek-us-refuge-after-biden-visit-09192023080519.

html (translated from Vietnamese); see also "Profile of Vo An Don," *88 Project*, September 2023, https://the88project.org/profile/344/vo-an-don/.

Appendix 1

1. Part B has been omitted to preserve the privacy of those involved.

Appendix 2

1. http://parlinfo.aph.gov.au/parlInfo/search/display/display.w3p;db=COMMITTEES;id=committees%2Festimate%2F0c5973fa-5b41-457f-af39-57df2971a205%2F0000;query=Id%3A%22committees%2Festimate%2F0c5973fa-5b41-457f-af39-57df2971a205%2F0000%22.

Appendix 3

1. https://www.amnesty.org/en/latest/press-release/2016/07/the-secretive-world-of-vietnam-torturous-prisons/.

2. https://www.hrw.org/report/2014/09/16/public-insecurity/deaths-custody-and-police-brutality-vietnam.

Further Reading by Chapter

Chapter 1

Restriction of Human Rights in Vietnam

According to the Constitution of the Socialist Republic of Vietnam (November 28, 2013), art. 14.2, "Human rights and citizens' rights shall only be restricted when prescribed by law in imperative circumstances for the reasons of national defence, national security, social order and security, social morality, and community well-being", while art. 15.4 states: "The practice of human rights and citizens' rights cannot infringe national interests and legal and legitimate rights and interests of others"; see also arts. 11, 46, and 64.

Far from conforming to international human rights standards, advocates maintain that such provisions, ubiquitous in Vietnamese domestic legislation, only ensure that "Vietnam remains a one-party state with a constitution that allows authorities to restrict basic rights on vague grounds whenever it suits them." (Human Rights Watch (HRW), "Vietnam: Amended Constitution a Missed Opportunity on Rights," December 2, 2013, https://www.hrw.org/news/2013/12/02/vietnam-amended-constitution-missed-opportunity-rights and Brad Adams, HRW Executive Director, Asia Division, "Letter to Chairman Nguyen Sinh Hung re: Amended Vietnam Constitution," October 22, 2013, https://www.hrw.org/news/2013/10/22/letter-chairman-nguyen-sinh-hung-re-amended-vietnam-constitution). See also, for example, Freedom House, *Freedom in the World 2020: Vietnam*, https://freedomhouse.org/country/vietnam/freedom-world/2020; US Department of State, Bureau of Democracy, Human Rights and Labor, *Vietnam 2018 Human Rights Report*, 1–43, https://www.state.gov/wp-content/uploads/2019/03/VIETNAM-2018.pdf; Vietnam Committee on Human Rights (VCHR), *Submission to the United Nations Human Rights Committee on the Third Periodic Report of Vietnam*, CCPR/C/VNM/3, 125th session, March 2019, 1–20, https://www.google.com/url?sa=t&rct=j&q=&esrc=s&source=web&cd=&ved=2ahUKEwjw88HnhduBAxXNSmwGHZboCm8QFnoECA4QAQ&url=https%3A%2F%2Fccprcen tre.org%2Ffiles%2Fdocuments%2FINT_CCPR_CSS_VNM_33776_E.docx&usg=AOvVaw2rq0r-M3ioWoFnC83slwO4&opi=89978449; International Federation for Human Rights (FIDH) and VCHR, *Assessment of Vietnam's Implementation of the UN Human Rights Committee's Recommendations on Key Priority Issues*, 136th session, July 18, 2022, 1–6, https://www.fidh.org/IMG/pdf/20220718_vietnam_ccpr_js_en.pdf; Giao Cong Vu and Kien Tran, "Constitutional Debate and Development on Human Rights in Vietnam," *Asian Journal of Comparative Law* 11, No. 2 (December 2016): 235–262, https://doi.org/10.1017/asjcl.2016.27.

For examples of the official Vietnamese view, see UN Permanent Mission of Viet Nam, *Note Verbale Addressed to the President of the General Assembly*, A/68/312, August 27, 2013, 1–6, https://digitallibrary.un.org/record/756375?ln=en and *Note Verbale Addressed to the President of the General Assembly*, A/77/276, August 4, 2022, 1–6, https://the88project.org/wp-content/uploads/2022/09/Note_verbale_-_Vietnam_2022.pdf.

Land Conflicts in Vietnam

See, for example, Huyen Thanh Do, "Land Conflicts in Emerging Suburban Areas in Viet Nam: Causes and Effects," *Local Administration Journal* 13, No. 4 (October–December 2020): 319–346, https://papi.org.vn/wp-content/uploads/2021/06/244548-Article-Text-870777-1-10-20210104.pdf; Phan Xuan Son and Vu Hong Trang, "Causes of Land Conflicts in Vietnam," *Political Theory*, January 22, 2016, http://lyluanchinhtri.vn/home/en/index.php/practice/item/314-causes-of-land-conflicts-in-vietnam.html; Kaitlin Hansen, "Land Law, Land Rights, and Land Reform in Vietnam: A Deeper Look into 'Land Grabbing' for Public and Private Development," Independent Study Project (ISP) Collection, 2013, 1722, https://digitalcollections.sit.edu/isp_collection/1722.

Treatment of Catholics in Vietnam

See, for example, "Catholic Vietnam: Growing Despite Communist Oppression," *Catholic World Report*, December 5, 2016, https://

www.catholicworldreport.com/2016/12/05/
catholic-vietnam-growing-despite-communist-
oppression/; United States Department of State,
Bureau of Democracy, Human Rights, and Labor,
*2016 Report on International Religious Freedom:
Vietnam*, https://www.state.gov/wp-content/
uploads/2019/01/Vietnam-3.pdf; Timothy Fowler,
"Vietnamese Catholics Fleeing to Australia 'to
Avoid Persecution',", *Ecumenical News*, July 19,
2013, https://www.ecumenicalnews.com/article/
vietnamese-catholics-fleeing-to-australia-to-
avoid-persecution/22345.htm; UN Human Rights
Council, *Report of the Special Rapporteur on Free-
dom of Religion or Belief, Addendum: Mission to
Viet Nam (July 21 to 31, 2014)*, January 30, 2015,
A/HRC/28/66/Add.2, 1–20, https://www.refworld.
org/docid/54f432530.html; Bui Ngoc Son, "Legal
Regulation of Religion in Vietnam," in *Regulating
Religion in Asia*, eds. Jaclyn L. Neo, Arif A. Jamal,
and Daniel P.S. Goh (Cambridge: Cambridge University Press, 2019), 160–161; Peter Hansen, "The
Vietnamese State, the Catholic Church and the
Law," in *Asian Socialism and Legal Change: The
Dynamics of Vietnamese and Chinese Reform*, eds.
John Gillespie and Pip Nicholson (Canberra: ANU
E Press; Asia Pacific Press, 2005), 310–334, https://
press-files.anu.edu.au/downloads/press/p125661/
pdf/book.pdf; John Gillespie, "Human Rights as
a Larger Loyalty: The Evolution of Religious Freedom in Vietnam," *Harvard Human Rights Journal* 27 (2014): 127–129, https://web.archive.org/
web/20180409231343/http://harvardhrj.com/
wp-content/uploads/2014/07/V27_Gillespie.pdf.

Australia's "Enhanced Screening" Process

See Australian Government Department
of Immigration and Citizenship, *Enhanced
Screening Policy Guidelines*, April 2013, 1–37,
https://drive.google.com/file/d/0ByW2V3f-
jYBRMEllNEs0X3haN28/edit; Australian Human
Rights Commission (AHRC), *Tell Me About the
"Enhanced Screening Process,"* June 26, 2013, 1–3,
https://www.humanrights.gov.au/our-work/
asylum-seekers-and-refugees/publications/tell-
me-about-enhanced-screening-process and *LA and
LB v Commonwealth of Australia (DIBP): Report
into the "Enhanced Screening" Process*, (2015)
AusHRC 96, 1–29, https://www.humanrights.gov.
au/sites/default/files/document/publication/2015_
AusHRC_96.pdf; Nick Evershed, Paul Farrell, and
Oliver Laughland, "'In' or 'Out': What We Know
About 'Enhanced Screening' of Asylum Seekers,"
Guardian, July 3, 2014, https://www.theguardian.
com/world/2014/jul/03/asylum-seekers-may-be-
subject-to-speedy-on-water-screenings; Anthea
Vogl, "A Matter of Time: Enacting the Exclusion
of Onshore Refugee Applicants Through the
Reform and Acceleration of Refugee Determina-
tion Processes," Oñati Socio-Legal Series 6, No. 1
(2016): 137–162, http://138.25.65.17/au/journals/
UTSLRS/2016/43.html.

Chapter 2

Abuses in Police Custody in Vietnam

Much has been written on this topic. See, for
example, ACAT, BPSOS, CAT-VN, CSW, LIV,
and VN-CAT, *Report to the United Nations Committee Against Torture for the Examination of
the First State Report of the Socialist Republic
of Vietnam*. UNCAT's 65th session in Geneva,
November 12, 2018–December 7, 2018, 13–14,
https://www.acatfrance.fr/public/joint-report-
for-the-examination-of-vietnam-by-uncat_1.
pdf; HRW, *Public Insecurity: Deaths in Custody
and Police Brutality in Vietnam*, September 15,
2014, https://www.hrw.org/report/2014/09/16/
public-insecurity/deaths-custody-and-police-
brutality-vietnam; Campaign to Abolish Torture in Vietnam, *Vietnam: Torture and Abuse
of Political and Religious Prisoners*, January
2014, 1–137, http://www.stoptorture-vn.org/
uploads/2/5/9/2/25923947/report-torture_
in_vn_1-16-2014-final.pdf and "Police Brutality and Lethal Beatings," 2018, http://www.
stoptorture-vn.org/police-brutality-and-lethal-
beatings.html.

Abuses in Administrative Detention Centers in Vietnam

See, for example, *Torture and Abuse of Political and Religious Prisoners*, 83–84; The 88 Project, *Report: Torture and Inhumane Treatment
of Political Prisoners in Vietnam 2018–2019*,
November 5, 2020, 1–32, https://the88project.
org/wp-content/uploads/2020/11/Torture-
Report_final.pdf; *Report to the United Nations
Committee Against Torture*, 16: "Vietnam's laws
authorize the arbitrary 'administrative detention'
without trial of individuals considered threats to
security, social order, or public safety. Normal
legal safeguards relating to imprisonment do not
apply to administrative detention centers, which
operate outside of the criminal justice system.
Administrative detainees are often picked up by
police and sent to detention centers without notification of family members, heightening the risk
that mistreatment of detainees can be carried out
with impunity."

Formosa Disaster

See, for example, Ho Binh Minh, "Vietnam,
Grappling with Mass Fish Deaths, Clamps Down
on Seafood Sales," *Reuters*, April 28, 2016, https://
www.reuters.com/article/us-vietnam-formosa-
plastics-environment-idUSKCN0XP0QD; Steve
Mollman, "A Taiwanese Steel Plant Caused Vietnam's Mass Fish Deaths, the Government Says,"
Quartz, June 30, 2016, https://qz.com/718576/a-
taiwanese-steel-plant-caused-vietnams-mass-

fish-deaths-the-government-says/; Tra Mi, "Vietnam Bans Unsafe Seafood in Central Provinces," *VOA*, May 5, 2016, https://www.voanews.com/a/vietnam-bans-unsafe-seafood-in-central-provinces/3316289.html; "Vietnam Says Taiwan Firm's Pollution Affected 200,000 people," *AP*, July 29, 2016, https://apnews.com/2755bc884d0a4a37b9ccab02ad05e759; "Anger Burns on Vietnam's Poisoned Coast a Year After Spill," *Reuters*, April 4, 2017, https://www.reuters.com/article/us-formosa-plastics-vietnam-idUSKBN1760FH.

Chapter 3

Human Rights in Indonesia

In addition to its Constitution and 1999 Foreign Relations and Human Rights Laws, Indonesia has also ratified various international human rights treaties, such as the *International Covenant on Civil and Political Rights* (ICCPR), *International Covenant on Economic, Social and Cultural Rights* (ICESCR) and *Convention Against Torture and Other Cruel, Inhuman or Degrading Treatment or Punishment* (UNCAT), which engage the non-refoulement principle too. For more information on Indonesia's humanitarian traditions and refugee policies see Nikolas Feith Tan, "The Status of Asylum Seekers and Refugees in Indonesia," *International Journal of Refugee Law* 28, No. 3 (October 1, 2016): 365–383, https://doi.org/10.1093/ijrl/eew045; Febi Yonesta, "Illegal or Protected? Indonesia's Inconsistent Policy on Refugees," *Indonesia at Melbourne*, June 20, 2019, https://indonesiaatmelbourne.unimelb.edu.au/illegal-or-protected-indonesias-inconsistent-policy-on-refugees/; Susan Kneebone, Antje Missbach, and Balawyn Jones, "The False Promise of Presidential Regulation No. 125 of 2016?" *Asian Journal of Law and Society* 8 (2021): 431–450, 10.1017/als.2021.2.

UNHCR's Refugee Status Determination (RSD) Work in Indonesia

For a summary of the RSD procedure see https://www.unhcr.org/id/en/refugee-status-determination; UNHCR, "Part Two: Procedures for the Determination of Refugee Status" in *Handbook on Procedures and Criteria for Determining Refugee Status and Guidelines on International Protection Under the 1951 Convention and the 1967 Protocol Relating to the Status of Refugees*, HCR/1P/4/ENG/REV.4, reissued Geneva, February 2019, 42–45, https://www.refworld.org/docid/5cb474b27.html; SUAKA, UNHCR, JRS, and Sandya Institute, *Know Your Rights: A Handbook for Refugees and Asylum Seekers* (Jakarta: SUAKA, December 2018), 13–16, https://apr.jrs.net/wp-content/uploads/sites/18/2020/03/2019-Know-your-rights-JRS-Indo.pdf.

Since 2018, "UNHCR Indonesia uses a unique merged RSD-Resettlement process whereby applicants are only put through the RSD process if they meet resettlement criteria, a higher standard" ("Refugee Work Rights Report: Refugee Access to Fair and Lawful Work in Asia," *Asylum Access*, October 2019, 19, https://asylumaccess.org/wp-content/uploads/2019/11/Asia-RWR_FINAL.pdf).

Chapter 4

The Montagnard

See, for example, Rebecca Onion, "The Snake-Eaters and the Yards," *Slate*, November 27, 2013, https://slate.com/news-and-politics/2013/11/the-green-berets-and-the-montagnards-how-an-indigenous-tribe-won-the-admiration-of-green-berets-and-lost-everything.html; Office of former Senator Thanh Hai Ngo, *Human Rights Situation in Vietnam: 2019–2020*, Senate Canada, 52–64, https://senatorngo.ca/wp-content/uploads/2019/10/Final_ENG.pdf; Grace Bui, "The Resettlement of Vietnamese and Montagnard Refugees Residing in Thailand," National Bureau of Asian Research, September 10, 2022, https://www.nbr.org/publication/the-resettlement-of-vietnamese-and-montagnard-refugees-residing-in-thailand/.

Canada's Treatment of Asylum Seekers Who Arrive by Boat Similar to That of Australia

See, for example, Luke Taylor, "Designated Inhospitality: The Treatment of Asylum Seekers Who Arrive by Boat in Canada and Australia," *McGill Law Journal* 60, No. 2 (January 2015): 333–379, https://doi.org/10.7202/1029211ar; Canadian Council for Refugees, *Sun Sea: Five Years Later*, August 2015, 1–17, https://ccrweb.ca/sites/ccrweb.ca/files/sun-sea-five-years-later.pdf; Alexandra Mann, "Refugees Who Arrive by Boat and Canada's Commitment to the Refugee Convention: A Discursive Analysis," *Refuge* 26, No. 2 (2009): 191–206, https://doi.org/10.25071/1920-7336.32088.

Harsh Treatment in Vietnamese Jails

See, for example, *DFAT Country Information Report Vietnam*, 2022, 28, 30–31, [paras. 4.6, 5.12-5.17]; *Report to the United Nations Committee Against Torture*, 18–38; Amnesty International, *Prisons Within Prisons: Torture and Ill-Treatment of Prisoners of Conscience in Vietnam*, July 2016, https://www.amnesty.org/download/Documents/ASA4141872016ENGLISH.PDF.

For examples of the official Vietnamese view,

see UNCAT, *Consideration of Reports Sub-mitted by States Parties Under Article 19 of the Convention Pursuant to the Optional Report-ing Procedure: Initial Reports of States Parties Due in 2016: Viet Nam*, CAT/C/VNM/1, Sep-tember 13, 2017, 1–51, https://tbinternet.ohchr.org/_layouts/15/treatybodyexternal/Download.aspx?symbolno=CAT/C/VNM/1&Lang=en and UNHCR, "Committee Against Torture Considers the Initial Report of Viet Nam," November 15, 2018, https://www.ohchr.org/en/NewsEvents/Pages/DisplayNews.aspx?NewsID=23895&LangID=E.

Applying as Refugees for Resettlement to Australia Compared with Canada

See, for example, Australian Government Department of Home Affairs (DHA), *Discus-sion Paper: Australia's Humanitarian Pro-gram 2019–20*, 4–5, https://www.homeaffairs.gov.au/reports-and-pubs/files/2019-20-discussion-paper.pdf; *UNHCR Resettlement Handbook*, Country Chapter: Australia, revised April 2016 and May 2018, 3, https://www.unhcr.org/3c5e542d4.html; IRPA, s. 99(2) and IRPR, ss. 138–158. For more information see https://immi.homeaffairs.gov.au/what-we-do/refugee-and-humanitarian-program/about-the-program/resettle-in-australia and https://www.canada.ca/en/immigration-refugees-citizenship/services/refugees/canada-role.html.

Resettlement for Refugees Is Not a Right

For further information see, for example, UNHCR, *Frequently Asked Questions About Resettlement*, https://www.refworld.org/pdfid/4ac0d7e52.pdf and *UNCHR Resettlement Handbook and Country Chapters*, April 2018, https://www.unhcr.org/4a2ccf4c6.html; Adèle Garnier, Kristin Bergtora Sandvik, and Liliana Lyra Jubilut, "Introduction: Refugee Resettle-ment as Humanitarian Governance," in *Refugee Resettlement: Power, Politics, and Humanitar-ian Governance*, eds. Adèle Garnier, Liliana Lyra Jubilut, and Kristin Bergtora Sandvik, Studies in Forced Migration Series Vol. 38 (New York: Ber-ghahn Books, 2018), 1–27.

Australia's Community Support Program (CSP)

The CSP replaced the Community Pro-posal Pilot (CPP), a national trial, which ran from 2013–2017. Previously, from 1979–1997, more than 30,000 refugees had been inte-grated in Australia via the Community Refugee

Settlement Scheme (CRSS). For more infor-mation, see Khanh Hoang, "Lessons from History: The Community Refugee Settle-ment Scheme," Community Refugee Sponsor-ship Initiative (CRSI), April 27, 2018, https://refugeesponsorship.org.au/lessons-from-history-the-community-refugee-settlement-scheme/. For a detailed overview and critique of the CSP, see Asher Lazarus Hirsch, Khanh Hoang, and Anthea Vogl, "Australia's Private Refugee Sponsorship Program: Creating Com-plementary Pathways or Privatizing Human-itarianism?" *Refuge* 35, No. 2 (2019): 110–119, https://doi.org/10.7202/1064823ar and "Private Humanitarian Sponsorship: Searching for the Community in Australia's Community Refugee Sponsorship Program," in *Strangers to Neigh-bours: Refugee Sponsorship in Context*, eds. Shauna Labman and Geoffrey Cameron (Mon-treal: McGill-Queen's University Press, 2020), 303–325.

Chapter 5

Growing Crisis of Hitherto Independent Refugees Seeking Entry to Indonesian Detention Centers

See, for example, UNHCR, *Progress Report 2018: A Global Strategy to Support Governments to End the Detention of Asylum-Seekers and Ref-ugees, 2014–2019*, February 2019, 35, https://www.refworld.org/country,,,,IDN,,5c9354074,0.html; Kate Lamb and Ben Doherty, "On the Streets with the Desperate Refugees Who Dream of Being Detained," *Guardian*, April 15, 2018, https://www.theguardian.com/world/2018/apr/15/on-the-streets-with-the-desperate-refugees-who-dream-of-being-detained; Antje Missbach, "Accommodating Asylum Seekers and Refugees in Indonesia: From Immigration Detention to Containment in 'Alternatives to Detention,'" *Refuge* 33, No. 2 (2017): 36, https://doi.org/10.7202/1043061ar; "From Darfur to Cipayung: Refugees Are Left Stranded," *Con-versation*, April 7, 2014, https://theconversation.com/from-darfur-to-cipayung-refugees-are-left-stranded-25034; and "Falling Through the Cracks," August 8, 2018, https://www.policyforum.net/falling-through-the-cracks/.

The crisis would only deepen, with protests spreading across various Indonesian cities, cul-minating in over 1,000 homeless asylum seekers and refugees camping outside Jakarta's UNHCR headquarters in July 2019. They were temporar-ily accommodated by Indonesian authorities at a cost of USD18,720 in an ill-equipped former military building that many refused to vacate, rejecting small cash inducements supplied by UNHCR, which had assumed responsibility on August 19. Food and water quickly ran out, leading to its closure and further unrest. While some eventually left, 245 mainly Hazara people from Afghanistan and a few Iraqis, including 28 families, 40 children, and some single men, would remain in self-isolation there during the COVID-19 pandemic from 2020 onwards. See, for example, Amanda Hodge, "Little Food, No Shelter ... Aid Runs Out," *Australian*, August 31, 2019, https://www.theaustralian. com.au/nation/world/no-more-aid-refugees-turn-on-each-other-to-feed-families/news-story/99f3e60b89edc7423e7baddd7dc838b1; Kate Lamb, "'It's Impossible to Do Anything': Indonesia's Refugees in Limbo as Money Runs Out," *Guardian*, September 14, 2019, https://www.theguardian.com/world/2019/sep/13/its-impossible-to-do-anything-indonesias-refugees-in-limbo-as-money-runs-out; Nicole Curby, "Evicted and Arrested: Refugees in Indonesia Under Pressure," *Overland*, September 16, 2019, https://overland.org.au/2019/09/scenes-from-indonesia-near-the-border-with-australia/; Chrisanthi Giotis, "'Stop Playing Politics': Refugees Stuck in Indonesia Rally Against UNHCR for Chronic Waiting," *Conversation*, October 8, 2019, https://theconversation.com/stop-playing-politics-refugees-stuck-in-indonesia-rally-against-unhcr-for-chronic-waiting-124176; Matthew LoCastro and Diovio Alfath, "Indonesia's Refugees Need Sustainable Solutions," *Asean Post*, January 19, 2020, https://theaseanpost.com/article/indonesias-refugees-need-sustainable-solutions; Ismira Lutfia Tisnadibrata, "Surviving as a Refugee Becomes More Testing During Pandemic," *Arab News*, June 19, 2020, https://www.arabnews.com/node/1692426/world; J.N. Joniad, "How Australia's Deterrence Policies Turned Indonesia into a Prison Without Walls," *Overland*, October 29, 2021, https://overland.org.au/2021/10/how-australias-deterrence-policies-have-turned-indonesia-into-a-prison-without-walls/comment-page-1/#comment-1056832.

Education for Refugee Children in Indonesia

For more information on the barriers to education faced by refugee children in Indonesia see Michelle Tauson, *Forgotten Futures: The Lives of Refugee Children in Urban Areas of Indonesia and Thailand*, Save the Children, June 2018, 26–31, 10.13140/RG.2.2.11882.16324; P. Nugroho Adhi, I. Gst Putu Agung, and Bernadette Gitareja, "Challenge and Opportunity to Implement the Right to Education for Child Refugees in Indonesia," Proceedings of the 1st International Conference on Law and Human Rights 2020, *Advances in Social Science, Education and Humanities Research* 549 (2021): 54–62, https://dx.doi.org/10.2991/assehr.k.210506.009; J.N. Joniad, "A Lost Generation of Refugee Children

in Indonesia," *Overland*, May 6, 2020, https://overland.org.au/2020/05/a-lost-generation-of-refugee-children-in-indonesia/; Debby Kristin and Chloryne Trie Isana Dewi, "The Rights of Children Refugee in Transit Country Under the CRC, A Case of Indonesia: An Intended Negligence?" *Padjadjaran Journal of International Law* 5, No. 1 (January 2021), https://doi.org/10.23920/pjil.v5i1.349.

Increasing Numbers Under Canada's "Multi-Year Immigration Levels Plan"

See https://www.canada.ca/en/immigration-refugees-citizenship/corporate/mandate/policies-operational-instructions-agreements/timely-protection-privately-sponsored-refugees.html; IRCC, "Notice – Supplementary Information 2018–2020 Immigration Levels Plan," November 1, 2017, https://www.canada.ca/en/immigration-refugees-citizenship/news/notices/supplementary-immigration-levels-2018.html; *2017 Annual Report to Parliament on Immigration*, https://www.canada.ca/content/dam/ircc/migration/ircc/english/pdf/pub/annual-report-2017.pdf; "Notice—Supplementary Information 2019–2021 Immigration Levels Plan," October 31, 2018, https://www.canada.ca/en/immigration-refugees-citizenship/news/notices/supplementary-immigration-levels-2019.html; *2018 Annual Report to Parliament on Immigration*, https://www.canada.ca/content/dam/ircc/migration/ircc/english/pdf/pub/annual-report-2018.pdf; *2019 Annual Report to Parliament on Immigration*, https://www.canada.ca/content/dam/ircc/migration/ircc/english/pdf/pub/annual-report-2019.pdf; "IRCC Minister Transition Binder 2019: Immigration Levels Planning," https://www.canada.ca/en/immigration-refugees-citizenship/corporate/transparency/transition-binders/minister-2019/levels.html; "Notice—Supplementary Information 2020-2022 Immigration Levels Plan," March 12, 2020, https://www.canada.ca/en/immigration-refugees-citizenship/news/notices/supplementary-immigration-levels-2020.html; *2020 Annual Report to Parliament on Immigration*, https://www.canada.ca/content/dam/ircc/migration/ircc/english/pdf/pub/annual-report-2020-en.pdf; "Notice—Supplementary Information for the 2021–2023 Immigration Levels Plan," October 30, 2020, https://www.canada.ca/en/immigration-refugees-citizenship/news/notices/supplementary-immigration-levels-2021-2023.html; *2021 Annual Report to Parliament on Immigration*, https://www.canada.ca/content/dam/ircc/documents/pdf/english/corporate/publications-manuals/annual-report-2021-en.pdf; "IRCC Minister Transition Binder 2021: Permanent Immigration—Immigration Levels Planning," https://www.canada.ca/en/immigration-refugees-citizenship/corporate/

transparency/transition-binders/minister-2021/levels.html; "Notice—Supplementary Information for the 2022–2024 Immigration Levels Plan," February 14, 2022, https://www.canada.ca/en/immigration-refugees-citizenship/news/notices/supplementary-immigration-levels-2022-2024.html.

Australia's New Community Refugee Sponsorship Program

In 2018, the Community Refugee Sponsorship Initiative (CRSI) was established by various humanitarian organizations, which actively supported the development of a new community sponsorship program for Australia that "draws on the most successful aspects of the Canadian private sponsorship experience." For more information see CSRI, *A New Model for Community Refugee Sponsorship in Australia*, Position Paper, May 2019, 1–18, http://www.ausrefugeesponsorship.com.au/wp-content/uploads/2019/05/CRSIPositionPaper.pdf.

In mid–2021, this initiative developed into an independent non-profit charity, Community Refugee Sponsorship Australia (CRSA) (https://refugeesponsorship.org.au) which, following an official CSP review (DHA, *Findings of the Review of the Community Support Program*, led by the Commonwealth Coordinator-General for Migrant Services, Ms. Alison Larkins, 1–9, https://www.homeaffairs.gov.au/reports-and-pubs/files/csp-review-findings.pdf), would soon partner with the Australian government in designing the Community Refugee Integration and Settlement Pilot (CRISP), launched in the first half of 2022 at a cost of just over USD6.5 million. Immediate plans envisaged trained Australian "Community Supporter Groups" assisting up to 1,500 refugees and humanitarian entrants over the next four years (2022–2025). Each participant would receive 12 months of support from their date of arrival, having been referred for resettlement by UNHCR and with no family links to Australia. While initially these resettled refugees would be counted within Australia's humanitarian quota, the government subsequently announced that if the pilot was successful, it would be expanded by up to 5,000 additional places per year. See Minister for Immigration, Citizenship, Migrant Services, and Multicultural Affairs Alex Hawke, "Enhanced Support for Refugee Resettlement and Integration," Media Release, December 17, 2021, https://minister.homeaffairs.gov.au/AlexHawke/Pages/enhanced-support-for-refugee-settlement-and-integration.aspx; DHA, "Community Sponsorship Reforms: Review of Australia's Community Support Program," https://immi.homeaffairs.gov.au/settling-in-australia/settlement-policy-and-reform/community-sponsorship-reforms, and "Helping Refugees: Community Refugee Integration and Settlement Pilot," https://immi.homeaffairs.gov.au/settling-in-australia/helping-refugees/get-involved/community-refugee-integration-settlement; CRSA, "Community Refugee Integration and Settlement Pilot (CRISP)," https://refugeesponsorship.org.au/what-we-do/crisp/; Minister for Immigration, Citizenship, and Multicultural Affairs Andrew Giles, "Minister Marks First Refugee Arrivals Under the Community Refugee Integration and Settlement Pilot," Media Release, August 26, 2022, https://minister.homeaffairs.gov.au/AndrewGiles/Pages/first-arrivals-community-refugee-integration-settlement-pilot.aspx; Ruby Cornish, "New Community-Led Resettlement Program Provides Year-Long Support to Arriving Refugees," *ABC News*, August 28, 2022, https://www.abc.net.au/news/2022-08-28/new-crisp-community-led-refugee-resettlement-program/101379450.

The new Australian program would become considerably cheaper even than the Canadian program, the difference being Australian refugee participants' ability to access social security within weeks after their arrival (see *CRISP Application Guidebook*, August 2022, 10, https://refugeesponsorship.org.au/wp-content/uploads/2022/08/CRISP-Application-Guidebook-August-2022.pdf; IRCC, "Sponsorship Cost Tables: PSR and BVOR," https://www.canada.ca/en/immigration-refugees-citizenship/services/application/application-forms-guides/guide-sponsor-refugee-groups-five.html#appa2-psr).

Mother Mushroom

For more information about Mother Mushroom, who was eventually released after serving two years of her ten-year sentence on condition she leave for the U.S., see, for example, Shawn W. Crispin, "Undercover in Vietnam: Bloggers Play Risky Game of Cat-and-Mouse to Report," *CPJ*, September 25, 2014, https://cpj.org/blog/2014/09/undercover-in-vietnam-bloggers-play-risky-game-of-.php; Ten Soksreinith, "Vietnamese Blogger Mother Mushroom Tells Activists 'You Are Not Alone,'" *VOA*, November 15, 2018, https://www.voanews.com/a/vietnamese-blogger-mother-mushroom-tells-activists-you-are-not-alone-/4659768.html; "Profile of Nguyen Ngoc Nhu Quynh – Me Nam ('Mother Mushroom')," *88 Project*, October 20, 2016, https://the88project.org/profile-of-nguyen-ngoc-nhu-quynh-me-nam-mother-mushroom/.

Suppression of Human Rights Lawyers, Including Vo An Don, in Vietnam

See, for example, Quynh-Vi Tran, "Vietnam: Lawyer Disbarred for Speaking Ill of Regime and the Communist Party," *Vietnamese*, April 14, 2019, https://www.thevietnamese.org/2019/04/vietnam-lawyer-disbarred-for-speaking-ill-of-regime-and-the-communist-party/; HRW, "Vietnam: EU Should Press for Release of Political Prisoners," November 28, 2017, https://www.hrw.org/news/2017/11/28/vietnam-eu-should-press-release-political-prisoners; "Attorney Vo An Don Was Disbarred From Phu Yen Bar Association," *Dan Lam Bao*, November 27, 2017, https://danlambaovn.blogspot.com/2017/11/attorney-vo-don-was-disbarred-from-phu.html; "Vietnamese Rights Lawyer Stripped of His License to Practice," *RFA*, May 24, 2018, https://www.rfa.org/english/news/vietnam/license-05242018152904.html.

Chapter 7

In-Canada Asylum Program

The In-Canada Asylum Program provides protection to refugees whose claims made from within Canada are heard by the Immigration and Refugee Board of Canada (IRB). For more information see IRCC, "Claim Refugee Status From Inside Canada: About the Process," https://www.canada.ca/en/immigration-refugees-citizenship/services/refugees/claim-protection-inside-canada.html and "Claiming Asylum in Canada—What Happens?" https://www.canada.ca/en/immigration-refugees-citizenship/news/2017/03/claiming_asylum_incanadawhathappens.html; IRB, "Refugee Claims," https://www.irb-cisr.gc.ca/en/refugee-claims/Pages/index.aspx.

Canada's Treatment of Overland Asylum Claimants

See, for example, Sigal Samuel, "There's a Perception That Canada Is Being Invaded," *Atlantic*, May 26, 2018, https://www.theatlantic.com/international/archive/2018/05/theres-a-perception-that-canada-is-being-invaded/561032/ and "Canada to Reject Refugees with Claims in Other Countries," *BBC*, April 9, 2019, https://www.bbc.com/news/world-us-canada-47874012; see also UNHCR, "Irregular Arrivals at the Border: Background Information Jan–May 2019," June 2019, https://www.unhcr.ca/wp-content/uploads/2019/07/IRREGULAR-ARRIVALS-AT-THE-BORDER-Background-information-Jan-May-2019-1.pdf; IRCC, "Irregular Border Crossings—What is Canada Doing?" https://www.canada.ca/en/immigration-refugees-citizenship/news/2018/07/irregular-border-crossings--what-is-canada-doing.html and "Government of Canada Appeal Granted on Safe Third Country Agreement," April 15, 2021, https://www.canada.ca/en/immigration-refugees-citizenship/news/2021/04/government-of-canada-appeal-granted-on-safe-third-country-agreement.html.

Australia's "Zero Chance" Campaigns in Sri Lanka, Afghanistan, and Indonesia

Launched internationally in May 2019, the "Zero Chance" campaign in Sri Lanka would result in media headlines in late 2021, when flash games, as well as a short film competition offering cameras and a drone as prizes to encourage "budding filmmakers ... to creatively express 'Illegal Migration to Australia,'" were met with moral condemnation. See https://zerochance.lk; https://osb.homeaffairs.gov.au; Eden Gillespie, "Tamil-Australians 'Outraged' over Taxpayer-Funded Anti-Migration Film Competition," *SBS*, December 24, 2021, https://www.sbs.com.au/news/tamil-australians-outraged-over-taxpayer-funded-anti-migration-film-competition/d89d29b4-5736-4212-a316-867158d99c89 and "Ad Agency Behind Government's Film Competition Warning Against 'Illegal Migration' Has Won Ethical Awards," *SBS*, February 18, 2022, https://www.sbs.com.au/news/article/ad-agency-behind-governments-film-competition-warning-against-illegal-migration-has-won-ethical-awards/65yaplhkm; Refugee Advice and Casework Service (RACS), "Open Letter: Calling PM Scott Morrison to Shut Down Zero Chance," January 3, 2022, https://www.racs.org.au/news/open-letter-calling-pm-scott-morrison-to-shut-down-zero-chance; Avani Dias, Som Patidar, and Emily Clark, "Federal Government Asks Sri Lankan Filmmakers to Create Work About 'Illegal Migration to Australia,'" *ABC News*, February 14, 2022, https://www.abc.net.au/news/2022-02-14/australian-government-slammed-over-film-competition-in-sri-lanka/100819104; Mark Saunokonoko, "'It Is Not a Game, It's Our Life, It's Our Kids' Lives,'" *9news*, February 16, 2022, https://www.9news.com.au/national/sri-lankan-refugee-advocates-claim-australia-zero-chance-online-games-campaign-misses-mark/e1f2bc73-0511-4b96-aca9-44232e121203; Australian Government Joint Agency Task Force Operation Sovereign Borders (OSB), "Anti-People Smuggling Campaign," Last reviewed May 17, 2021, https://www.homeaffairs.gov.au/foi/files/2022/fa-210900999-document-released.PDF.

In August 2021, in the immediate aftermath of the Taliban takeover of Afghanistan, then Australian Home Affairs Minister Karen Andrews appeared in a video on social media, warning Afghan asylum-seekers against trying to reach Australia by boat. See Richard Ferguson, "Afghan Boatpeople 'Zero Chance,'" *Weekend Australian*, August 23, 2021, https://www.theaustralian.com.au/nation/afghan-boatpeople-zero-chance/

news-story/287c0825233f9c1bd50e31ea7446 62c0 and Yan Zhuang, "Australia Tells Afghan Refugees: 'Do Not Attempt an Illegal Boat Journey,'" *New York Times*, August 23, 2021, https://www.nytimes.com/2021/08/23/world/asia/australia-tells-afghan-refugees-do-not-attempt-an-illegal-boat-journey.html.

In May 2022, anti-refugee playing cards with the Australian government logo were handed out to refugee children as young as four at the Cisarua Learning Center in West Java, Indonesia. See Amber Schultz and Imogen Champagne, "Refugee Children in Indonesia Given Anti-Refugee Cards with Australian Coat of Arms," *Crikey*, May 25, 2022, https://www.crikey.com.au/2022/05/25/refugee-children-in-indonesia-given-anti-refugee-playing-cards/; Imogen Champagne, "Border Force Backs Zero Chance Campaign After Children Given Anti-Refugee Playing Cards," *Crikey*, May 26, 2022, https://www.crikey.com.au/2022/05/26/border-force-backs-stance-despite-refugee-children-given-anti-refugee-playing-cards/.

After the May 2022 Australian federal election resulted in a Labor government, OSB reported intercepting and returning several "maritime people smuggling ventures" to Sri Lanka, and new Home Affairs Minister Clare O'Neil soon visited Sri Lanka where she reiterated support for the "Zero Chance" campaign and struck a deal

including the provision of aerial drone surveillance and fuel for Sri Lankan navy patrol boats to prevent subsequent arrivals. See Australian Border Force, "Operation Sovereign Borders Monthly Update: June 2022," July 29, 2022, https://www.abf.gov.au/newsroom-subsite/Pages/Operation-Sovereign-Borders-monthly-update-June-2022.aspx and "Operation Sovereign Borders Monthly Update: August 2022," September 30, 2022, https://www.abf.gov.au/newsroom-subsite/Pages/Operation-Sovereign-Borders-monthly-update-August-2022.aspx; Minister for Home Affairs Clare O'Neil, "Joint Media Release with Sri Lankan Foreign Minister," June 20, 2022, https://minister.homeaffairs.gov.au/ClareONeil/Pages/meeting-sri-lankan-minister-foreign-affairs.aspx?utm_source=miragenews&utm_medium=miragenews&utm_campaign=news; Ben Packham and Susitha Fernando, "GPS to Track Sri Lankan Fish Fleet," *Australian*, June 22, 2022, https://www.theaustralian.com.au/nation/gps-to-track-sri-lankan-fish-fleet/news-story/be3f234983da4d712e19a2c4ee1bcd9a; Ben Packham, "Secret Sri Lankan Fuel Deal Keeps Patrol Boats on Water," *Australian*, August 8, 2022, https://www.theaustralian.com.au/nation/secret-sri-lankan-fuel-deal-keeps-patrol-boats-on-water/news-story/e9a1c1a99e6c599425bfd64b6a237bab.

Bibliography

Articles, Books and Reports

ACAT, BPSOS, CAT-VN, CSW, LIV, and VN-CAT. *Report to the United Nations Committee Against Torture for the Examination of the First State Report of the Socialist Republic of Vietnam.* UNCAT's 65th session in Geneva, November 12, 2018–December 7, 2018, 1–55. https://www.acatfrance.fr/public/joint-report-for-the-examination-of-vietnam-by-uncat_1.pdf.

Adams, Brad. "Letter to Chairman Nguyen Sinh Hung Re: Amended Vietnam Constitution." October 22, 2013. https://www.hrw.org/news/2013/10/22/letter-chairman-nguyen-sinh-hung-re-amended-vietnam-constitution.

Adelman, Howard. "Accepting Refugees: International Law in a Canadian Context in the Twentieth Century." Working Paper No. 2017/1, Canadian Association for Refugee and Forced Migration Studies, February 2017, 1–37. http://carfms.org/wp-content/uploads/2015/10/CARFMS-WPS-No9-Howard-Adelman.pdf

Adelman, Howard. "We or All: A Review Essay on Refugees—Xenophobia, Idealism and Pragmatic." Parts I-V, March 11, 2018. https://howardadelman.com/2018/03/page/2/.

Adhi, Nugroho P, I Gst Putu Agung, and Bernadette Gitareja. "Challenge and Opportunity to Implement the Right to Education for Child Refugees in Indonesia." Proceedings of the 1st International Conference on Law and Human Rights 2020. *Advances in Social Science, Education and Humanities Research* 549 (2021): 54–62. https://dx.doi.org/10.2991/assehr.k.210506.009.

Agus, Alamsyah, Intan Slipi Lia, and Muh Akbar. "The Role of Social Work in the Context of Refugees and Asylum Seekers Rights in Indonesia." *ASWJ* 3, No. 5 (December 2018), 39–47. https://doi.org/10.47405/aswj.v3i5.60.

Ali, Muzafar, Linda Briskman, and Lucy Fiske. "Asylum Seekers and Refugees in Indonesia: Problems and Potentials." *Cosmopolitan Civil Societies: An Interdisciplinary Journal* 8, No. 2 (2016): 22–43. https://search.informit.com.au/documentSummary;dn=903977044351509;res=IELHSS.

Amnesty International. *Annual Reports 2015–2022: Vietnam.* https://www.amnesty.org/en/annual-report-archive/.

Amnesty International. *'Let Us Breathe!' Censorship and Criminalization of Online Expression in Viet Nam.* December 2020, 1–79. https://www.amnesty.org/en/wp-content/uploads/2021/05/ASA4132432020ENGLISH.pdf.

Amnesty International. *Prisons Within Prisons: Torture and Ill-Treatment of Prisoners of Conscience in Vietnam.* July 2016, 1–52. https://www.amnesty.org/download/Documents/ASA4141872016ENGLISH.PDF.

Amnesty International. "Public Statement." August 11, 2016. https://www.amnesty.org/download/Documents/ASA4146532016ENGLISH.pdf.

Amnesty International. "Viet Nam: Facebook Must Cease Complicity with Government Censorship." April 22, 2020. https://www.amnesty.org/en/latest/news/2020/04/vietnam-facebook-cease-complicity-government-censorship/.

"Anger Burns on Vietnam's Poisoned Coast a Year After Spill." *Reuters,* April 4, 2017. https://www.reuters.com/article/us-formosa-plastics-vietnam-idUSKBN1760FH.

Anker, Deborah. "Regional Refugee Regimes: North America." In *The Oxford Handbook of International Refugee Law,* 296–314.

Arora, Vishal. "Vietnam's Religion Law 'Created to Repress, Control.'" *World Watch Monitor,* April 27, 2016. https://www.worldwatchmonitor.org/2016/04/vietnams-religion-law-created-to-repress-control/.

Aston, Heath. "Australian Navy to Hand 50 Asylum Seekers Back to Vietnam." *SMH,* April 17, 2015. https://www.smh.com.au/politics/federal/australian-navy-to-hand-50-asylum-seekers-back-to-vietnam-20150417-1mnew5.html.

"Asylum Seekers Registered with UNHCR in Indonesia After June No Longer Eligible for Resettlement in Australia, Scott Morrison Says." *ABC News,* November 18, 2014. https://www.abc.net.au/news/2014-11-18/resettlement-path-for-asylum-seekers-in-indonesia-cut-off/5900962.

"Attorney Vo An Don Was Disbarred From Phu

Yen Bar Association." *Dan Lam Bao,* November 27, 2017. https://danlambaovn.blogspot.com/2017/11/attorney-vo-don-was-disbarred-from-phu.html.

Australian Government Department of Foreign Affairs and Trade. *DFAT Country Information Report Vietnam.* June 21, 2017, 1–26. https://www.ecoi.net/en/file/local/1419336/4792_1512564532_country-information-report-vietnam.pdf.

Australian Government Department of Foreign Affairs and Trade. *DFAT Country Information Report Vietnam.* December 13, 2019, 1–47. https://www.ecoi.net/en/file/local/2024449/country-information-report-vietnam.pdf.

Australian Government Department of Foreign Affairs and Trade. *DFAT Country Information Report Vietnam.* January 11, 2022, 1–35. https://www.dfat.gov.au/sites/default/files/country-information-report-vietnam.pdf.

Australian Government Department of Home Affairs. *The Community Support Program: Guidelines for Approved Proposing Organisations.* January 22, 2019, 1–30. https://www.homeaffairs.gov.au/foi/files/2019/fa-190301223-document-released.pdf.

Australian Government Department of Home Affairs. *Discussion Paper: Australia's Humanitarian Program 2019–20.* 1–10. https://www.homeaffairs.gov.au/reports-and-pubs/files/2019-20-discussion-paper.pdf.

Australian Government Department of Home Affairs. *Findings of the Review of the Community Support Program.* Led by the Commonwealth Coordinator-General for Migrant Services, Ms. Alison Larkins, 1–9. https://www.homeaffairs.gov.au/reports-and-pubs/files/csp-review-findings.pdf.

Australian Government Department of Home Affairs. *Life in Australia: Australian values and principles.* 2020, 1–10. https://immi.homeaffairs.gov.au/support-subsite/files/life-in-australia/life-in-australia.pdf.

Australian Government Department of Immigration and Citizenship. *Enhanced Screening Policy Guidelines.* April 2013, 1–37. https://drive.google.com/file/d/0ByW2V3f-jYBRMEllNEs0X3haN28/edit?resourcekey=0-zlHpf36gcaCGv_x3OAX_8A.

Australian Government Department of Immigration and Citizenship. *Submission to the Joint Select Committee on Australia's Immigration Detention Network.* September 2011, 1–238. https://www.homeaffairs.gov.au/reports-and-pubs/files/diac-jscaidn-submission-sept11.pdf.

Australian Government Joint Agency Task Force Operation Sovereign Borders (OSB). "Anti-People Smuggling Campaign." Last reviewed May 17, 2021. https://www.homeaffairs.gov.au/foi/files/2022/fa-210900999-document-released.PDF.

Australian Human Rights Commission (AHRC). *LA and LB v Commonwealth of Australia (DIBP): Report into the 'Enhanced Screening' Process.* [2015] AusHRC 96, 1–29. https://www.humanrights.gov.au/sites/default/files/document/publication/2015_AusHRC_96.pdf.

Australian Human Rights Commission (AHRC). *Tell Me About the 'Enhanced Screening Process.'* June 26, 2013, 1–3. https://www.humanrights.gov.au/our-work/asylum-seekers-and-refugees/publications/tell-me-about-enhanced-screening-process.

"Authorities Request to Revoke License Vo An Don." Lawyers for Lawyers, January 20, 2015. https://lawyersforlawyers.org/en/vietnam-request-by-authorities-to-revoke-license-of-lawyer-vo-an-don/.

"Ba Gia Đình Người Việt Vượt Biên Được LHQ Cấp Qui Chế Tị Nạn." *RFA,* May 23, 2017. https://www.rfa.org/vietnamese/news/vietnamnews/vietnamese-boatpeople-in-indonesia-granted-refugee-status-05232017095746.html (translated from Vietnamese).

"Ba Phụ Nữ Bình Thuận 'Lại Vượt Biên Đến Úc.'" *BBC,* February 6, 2017. https://www.bbc.com/vietnamese/vietnam-38878718 (translated from Vietnamese).

"Ba Phụ Nữ Bình Thuận 'Được Hưởng Quy Chế Xin Ty Nạn.'" *BBC,* April 5, 2017. https://www.bbc.com/vietnamese/vietnam-39362063?ocid=socialflow_facebook (translated from Vietnamese).

"Ba Phụ Nữ Việt Vượt Biên Sang Úc Bị Tạm Giữ ở Indonesia." *SBTN,* February 11, 2017. https://www.sbtn.tv/ba-phu-nu-viet-vuot-bien-sang-uc-bi-tam-giu-o-indonesia/ (translated from Vietnamese).

Baillie Abidi, Catherine, and Shiva Nourpanah. *Refugees and Forced Migration: A Canadian Perspective, An A–Z Guide.* Halifax: Nimbus Publishing, 2019.

Barker, Anne. "Indonesia is Preparing to Vaccinate Up to 180 million People Against COVID-19 in 15 Months." *ABC News,* February 5, 2021. https://www.abc.net.au/news/2021-01-13/indonesia-starts-rolling-out-jabs-of-chinas-covid-19-vaccine/13051430.

Barker, Anne. "Suspected Asylum Seekers Found in Queensland Spark Warnings of Exodus from Vietnam." *ABC News,* August 30, 2018. https://www.abc.net.au/news/2018-08-29/fears-suspected-asylum-seekers-part-of-flood-from-vietnam/10179322.

Bemma, Adam. "Refugees in Indonesia Told to Assimilate but not Settle." *Refugees Deeply,* February 9, 2018. https://www.newsdeeply.com/refugees/articles/2018/02/09/refugees-in-indonesia-told-to-assimilate-but-not-settle.

Best, Laura. "Why Canada Can Safely Meet Its Refugee Commitments." *TheTyee.ca,* November 18, 2015. https://thetyee.ca/Opinion/2015/11/18/Canada-Can-Meet-Syrian-Refugee-Commitments/.

Bloemraad, Irene. *Understanding 'Canadian Exceptionalism' in Immigration and*

Pluralism Policy. Washington, D.C.: Migration Policy Institute, 2012, 1–18. https://www.migrationpolicy.org/research/TCM-canadian-exceptionalism.

Bohane, Ben. "South China Sea: Vietnam Prepares for Dangerous Days Ahead as the Country's Fisheries Clash with Chinese Authorities." *ABC News,* December 9, 2016. http://www.abc.net.au/news/2016-12-09/south-china-sea-vietnam-prepares-for-dangerous-days-ahead/8101192.

Bond, Jennifer. "The Power of Politics: Exploring the True Potential of Community Sponsorship Programs." In *Research Handbook on the Law and Politics of Migration,* edited by Catherine Dauvergne, 155–170. Cheltenham: Edward Elgar Publishing, 2021, https://doi.org/10.4337/9781789902266.00018.

Bond, Jennifer, and Ania Kwadrans. "Resettling Refugees Through Community Sponsorship: A Revolutionary Operational Approach Built on Traditional Legal Infrastructure." *Refuge: Canada's Journal on Refugees* 35, No. 2 (2019): 86–108. 10.7202/1064822ar.

Boykoff, Pamela. "Vietnam Fishermen on the Front Lines of South China Sea Fray." *CNN,* July 12, 2016. https://edition.cnn.com/2016/05/22/asia/vietnam-fisherman-south-china-sea/index.html.

Bradley, Megan, and Cate Duin. "A Port in the Storm: Resettlement and Private Sponsorship in the Broader Context of the Refugee Regime." In *Strangers to Neighbours,* 94–113.

Brooks, Lee. "Australia's Vietnamese Community Pledges $500k to UNHCR to Help Refugees." *ABC News,* August 30, 2016. https://www.abc.net.au/news/2016-08-30/vietnamese-community-gives-thousands-to-refugees/7796796.

Brown, Thomas, and Antje Missbach. "Refugee Detention in Indonesia." *Interpreter,* May 12, 2017. https://www.lowyinstitute.org/the-interpreter/refugee-detention-indonesia.

Bui, Grace. "The Resettlement of Vietnamese and Montagnard Refugees Residing in Thailand." The National Bureau of Asian Research, September 10, 2022. https://www.nbr.org/publication/the-resettlement-of-vietnamese-and-montagnard-refugees-residing-in-thailand/.

Bui, Ngoc Son. "Legal Regulation of Religion in Vietnam." In *Regulating Religion in Asia: Norms, Modes and Challenges,* edited by Jaclyn L. Neo, Arif A. Jamal, and Daniel P.S. Goh, 146–168. Cambridge: Cambridge University Press, 2019.

Butler, Gavin. "Critics Slam Australia's 'Appalling' Campaign to Deter Asylum Seekers." *VICE,* December 23, 2021. https://www.vice.com/en/article/m7vb4q/australian-campaign-asylum-seekers-online-games.

Button, Lisa. *Unlocking Childhood: Current Immigration Detention Practices and Alternatives for Child Asylum Seekers and*

Refugees in Asia and the Pacific. Save the Children and Asia Pacific Refugee Rights Network, May 2017, 1–71. https://resourcecentre.savethechildren.net/node/12161/pdf/unlocking_chiildhood.pdf.

Campaign to Abolish Torture in Vietnam. "Police Brutality and Lethal Beatings." 2018. http://www.stoptorture-vn.org/police-brutality-and-lethal-beatings.html.

Campaign to Abolish Torture in Vietnam. *Vietnam: Torture and Abuse of Political and Religious Prisoners.* January 2014, 1–137. http://www.stoptorture-vn.org/uploads/2/5/9/2/25923947/report-torture_in_vn_1-16-2014-final.pdf.

"Canada to Reject Refugees with Claims in Other Countries." *BBC,* April 9, 2019. https://www.bbc.com/news/world-us-canada-47874012.

Canadian Council for Refugees (CCR). *Sun Sea: Five Years Later.* August 2015, 1–17. https://ccrweb.ca/sites/ccrweb.ca/files/sun-sea-five-years-later.pdf.

Casasola, Michael. "The Indochinese Refugee Movement and the Subsequent Evolution of UNHCR and Canadian Resettlement Selection Policies and Practices." *Refuge* 32, No. 2 (2016): 41–53. https://doi.org/10.25071/1920-7336.40270.

Cassels, Deborah. "'I Cry All Night': The Child Asylum Seekers Stranded in Indonesia," *Guardian,* July 2, 2014. https://www.theguardian.com/world/2014/jul/02/i-cry-all-night-the-child-asylum-seekers-stranded-in-indonesia.

"Catholic Vietnam: Growing Despite Communist Oppression." *Catholic World Report,* December 5, 2016. https://www.catholicworldreport.com/2016/12/05/catholic-vietnam-growing-despite-communist-oppression/.

Champagne, Imogen. "Border Force Backs Zero Chance Campaign After Children Given Anti-Refugee Playing Cards." *Crikey,* May 26, 2022. https://www.crikey.com.au/2022/05/26/border-force-backs-stance-despite-refugee-children-given-anti-refugee-playing-cards/.

Chan, Gabrielle. "Budget Expected to Expand Sponsorship Program for Refugees—At Cost of $40,000 each." *Guardian,* May 5, 2017. https://papers.ssrn.com/sol3/papers.cfm?abstract_id=2809995.

Chantler, Gareth. "Lessons Learned? Canada's Problematic Syrian Resettlement Process." *Atlantic Council,* September 28, 2018. https://www.atlanticcouncil.org/blogs/syriasource/lessons-learned-canada-s-problematic-syrian-resettlement-process/.

Cheatham, Amelia. "What Is Canada's Immigration Policy?" Council on Foreign Relations, August 3, 2020. https://www.cfr.org/backgrounder/what-canadas-immigration-policy.

Cheng, June. "After the Fall." *World Magazine,* March 15, 2018. https://world.wng.org/2018/03/after_the_fall.

Citizens for Public Justice (CPJ). "A Half Welcome: Delays, Limits, and Inequities in Canadian Refugee Sponsorship." April 2017, 1–20. https://cpj.ca/wp-content/uploads/A-Half-Welcome.pdf.

Citizenship and Immigration Canada (CIC). *OP 5: Overseas Selection and Processing of Convention Refugees Abroad Class and Members of the Humanitarian-protected Persons Abroad Classes.* manual [online] (August 13, 2009): 1–166. https://overseastudent.ca/migratetocanada/IMMGuide/CICManual/op/op05-eng.pdf.

Cochrane, Joe. "Refugees in Indonesia Hoped for Brief Stay. Many May Be Stuck for Life." *New York Times,* January 26, 2018. https://www.nytimes.com/2018/01/26/world/asia/indonesia-refugees-united-nations.html.

Cochrane, Liam. "Vietnamese Asylum Seeker Returned by Australia Says 'A Bullet Would Be Better.'" *ABC News,* February 23, 2017. https://www.abc.net.au/news/2017-02-21/vietnam-asylum-seeker-returned-by-australia-speaks-of-beatings/8288226.

Coleman, Lara. *Resettling Refugees: Canada's Humanitarian Commitments.* Publication No. 2020–74-E, Ottawa: Library of Parliament, 2021. https://lop.parl.ca/staticfiles/PublicWebsite/Home/ResearchPublications/BackgroundPapers/PDF/2020-74-e.pdf.

Commonwealth of Australia. *Budget 2016–17: Budget Measures.* Budget Paper No. 2, 2016–17, 1–172. https://archive.budget.gov.au/2016-17/bp2/BP2_consolidated.pdf.

Commonwealth of Australia. *Budget 2017–18: Budget Measures.* Budget Paper No. 2, 2017–18, 1–190. https://archive.budget.gov.au/2017-18/bp2/bp2.pdf.

Commonwealth of Australia. Senate. Legal and Constitutional Affairs Legislation Committee. *Estimates.* Immigration and Citizenship Portfolio, May 28, 2013, 1–178. https://parlinfo.aph.gov.au/parlInfo/download/committees/estimate/0f70343a-b92d-45d8-b692-58b9623ba9cd/toc_pdf/Legal%20and%20Constitutional%20Affairs%20Legislation%20Committee_2013_05_28_1971_Official.pdf;fileType=application/pdf#search=%22committees/estimate/0f70343a-b92d-45d8-b692-58b9623ba9cd/0000%22.

Commonwealth of Australia. Senate. Legal and Constitutional Affairs Legislation Committee. *Estimates.* Immigration and Border Protection Portfolio, February 23, 2015, 1–188. https://parlinfo.aph.gov.au/parlInfo/download/committees/estimate/726d2567-78be-48ef-a9df-f7302dbb884c/toc_pdf/Legal%20and%20Constitutional%20Affairs%20Legislation%20Committee_2015_02_23_3235_Official.pdf;fileType=application%2Fpdf#search=%22committees/estimate/726d2567-78be-48ef-a9df-f7302dbb884c/0000%22.

Commonwealth of Australia. Senate. Legal and Constitutional Affairs Legislation Committee. *Estimates.* Immigration and Border Protection Portfolio, May 25, 2015, 1–134. https://parlinfo.aph.gov.au/parlInfo/download/committees/estimate/0c5973fa-5b41-457f-af39-57df2971a205/toc_pdf/Legal%20and%20Constitutional%20Affairs%20Legislation%20Committee_2015_05_25_3493_Official.pdf;fileType=application%2Fpdf#search=%22committees/estimate/0c5973fa-5b41-457f-af39-57df2971a205/0000%22.

Commonwealth of Australia. Senate. Legal and Constitutional Affairs Legislation Committee. *Estimates.* Attorney-General's Portfolio, October 17, 2016, 1–203. https://parlinfo.aph.gov.au/parlInfo/download/committees/estimate/516239db-3ab5-4777-8b43-33f6d160c55d/toc_pdf/Legal%20and%20Constitutional%20Affairs%20Legislation%20Committee_2016_10_17_4510_Official.pdf;fileType=application%2Fpdf#search=%22committees/estimate/516239db-3ab5-4777-8b43-33f6d160c55d/0000%22.

Commonwealth of Australia. Senate. Legal and Constitutional Affairs Legislation Committee. *Estimates.* Immigration and Border Protection Portfolio, May 22, 2017, 5–203. https://parlinfo.aph.gov.au/parlInfo/download/committees/estimate/3016728a-1732-413a-bdd9-3647f38d88d4/toc_pdf/Legal%20and%20Constitutional%20Affairs%20Legislation%20Committee_2017_05_22_5100_Official.pdf;fileType=application%2Fpdf#search=%22committees/estimate/3016728a-1732-413a-bdd9-3647f38d88d4/0003%22.

Commonwealth of Australia. Senate. Legal and Constitutional Affairs Legislation Committee. *Estimates.* Home Affairs Portfolio, May 22, 2018, 5–190. https://parlinfo.aph.gov.au/parlInfo/search/display/display.w3p;db=COMMITTEES;id=committees%2Festimate%2F75507344-48f1-4665-8f23-623c6eb5c20d%2F0002;query=Id%3A%22committees%2Festimate%2F75507344-48f1-4665-8f23-623c6eb5c20d%2F0002%22.

Community Refugee Sponsorship Australia (CRSA). *Application Guidebook for Community Supporter Groups in the Community Refugee Integration and Settlement Pilot (CRISP).* August 2022, 1–24. https://refugeesponsorship.org.au/wp-content/uploads/2022/08/CRISP-Application-Guidebook-August-2022.pdf.

Community Refugee Sponsorship Australia (CRSA). *Settlement Guidebook for Community Supporter Groups in the Community Refugee Integration and Settlement Pilot (CRISP).* August 2022, 1–36. https://refugeesponsorship.org.au/wp-content/uploads/2022/09/CRISP-Settlement-Guidebook-Version-date-14-September-2022.pdf.

Community Refugee Sponsorship Initiative (CRSI). *A New Model for Community Refugee*

Sponsorship in Australia. Position Paper. May 2019, 1–18. http://www.ausrefugeesponsorship.com.au/wp-content/uploads/2019/05/CRSIPositionPaper.pdf.

Cornish, Ruby. "New Community-Led Resettlement Program Provides Year-Long Support to Arriving Refugees." *ABC News*, August 28, 2022. https://www.abc.net.au/news/2022-08-28/new-crisp-community-led-refugee-resettlement-program/101379450.

Costello, Cathryn, Michelle Foster, and Jane McAdam. *The Oxford Handbook of International Refugee Law*. Oxford: Oxford University Press, 2021.

Cousins, Stephanie. *Make Refuge: Safer Pathways for Refugees and Asylum Seekers*. Churchill Fellowship Report, December 2018, 1–137. https://www.churchilltrust.com.au/fellow/stephanie-cousins-nsw-2017/.

Crispin, Shawn W. "Undercover in Vietnam: Bloggers Play Risky Game of Cat-and-Mouse to Report." *CPJ*, September 25, 2014. https://cpj.org/blog/2014/09/undercover-in-vietnam-bloggers-play-risky-game-of-.php.

Crock, Mary. "'You Have to Be Stronger Than Razor Wire': Legal Issues Relating to the Detention of Refugees and Asylum Seekers." *Australian Journal of Administrative Law* 10 (2002): 33–63. https://www.researchgate.net/publication/228185845_You_Have_to_Be_Stronger_than_Razor_Wire_Legal_Issues_Relating_to_the_Detention_of_Refugees_and_Asylum_Seekers).

Curby, Nicole. "Evicted and Arrested: Refugees in Indonesia Under Pressure." *Overland*, September 16, 2019. https://overland.org.au/2019/09/scenes-from-indonesia-near-the-border-with-australia/.

Dauvergne, Catherine. "Challenges to Sovereignty: Migration Laws for the 21st Century." New Issues in Refugee Research Working Paper No. 92, UNHCR (July 2003), 1–13. https://www.unhcr.org/3f2f69e74.pdf.

Dauvergne, Catherine. "Evaluating Canada's New *Immigration and Refugee Protection Act* in its Global Context." *Alberta Law Review* 41, No. 3 (2003): 725–744. https://www.albertalawreview.com/index.php/ALR/article/view/1321/1310.

Davidson, Helen. "Australia Reportedly Uses Navy Ship to Return Asylum Seekers to Vietnam." *Guardian*, April 17, 2015. https://www.theguardian.com/australia-news/2015/apr/17/asylum-seekers-to-vietnam.

Dewansyah, Bilal, and Irawati Handayani. "Reconciling Refugee Protection and Sovereignty in ASEAN Member States: Law and Policy Related to Refugee in Indonesia, Malaysia and Thailand." *Central European Journal of International and Security Studies* 12, No. 4 (December 2018): 473–485. https://cejiss.org/reconciling-refugee-protection-and-sovereignty-in-asean-member-states-law-and-policy-related-to-refugee-in-indonesia-malaysia-and-thailand.

Dewansyah, Bilal, and Ratu Durotun Nafisah. "The Constitutional Right to Asylum and Humanitarianism in Indonesian Law: 'Foreign Refugees' and PR 125/2016." *Asian Journal of Law and Society* 8, No. 3 (2021): 536–557. 10.1017/als.2021.8.

Dhital, Dikshya. "The Economic Outcomes of Government Assisted Refugees, Privately Sponsored Refugees and Asylum Seekers in Canada." Major research paper, Graduate School of Public and International Affairs, University of Ottawa, March 25, 2015. https://ruor.uottawa.ca/bitstream/10393/32311/1/DIKSHYA,%20Dikshya%2020151.pdf.

Dias, Avani, Som Patidar, and Emily Clark. "Federal Government Asks Sri Lankan Filmmakers to Create Work About 'Illegal Migration to Australia.'" *ABC News*, February 14, 2022. https://www.abc.net.au/news/2022-02-14/australian-government-slammed-over-film-competition-in-sri-lanka/100819104.

Do, Huyen Thanh. "Land Conflicts in Emerging Suburban Areas in Viet Nam: Causes and Effects." *Local Administration Journal* 13, No. 4 (October-December 2020): 319–346. https://papi.org.vn/wp-content/uploads/2021/06/244548-Article-Text-870777-1-10-20210104.pdf.

Doherty, Ben. *Call Me Illegal: The Semantic Struggle Over Seeking Asylum in Australia*. Oxford: Reuters Institute for the Study of Journalism, 2015. https://reutersinstitute.politics.ox.ac.uk/sites/default/files/2017-10/Call_me_illegal_The_semantic_struggle_over_seeking_asylum_in_Australia_0.pdf.

Doherty, Ben. "Coalition Slashes Costs for Sponsoring Refugees as New Resettlement Scheme Hailed as 'Watershed Moment.'" *Guardian*, December 18, 2021. https://www.theguardian.com/australia-news/2021/dec/18/coalition-slashes-costs-for-sponsoring-refugees-as-new-resettlement-scheme-hailed-as-watershed-moment.

Doherty, Ben. "Community Sponsorship Could Transform Refugee Resettlement—and Australia." *Guardian*, September 22, 2018. https://www.theguardian.com/australia-news/2018/sep/22/community-sponsorship-could-transform-refugee-resettlement-and-australia.

Doherty, Ben. "First Refugee Families Welcomed to Australia Under New Community Sponsorship Program," *Guardian*, August 27, 2022. https://www.theguardian.com/australia-news/2022/aug/27/syrian-refugee-family-welcomed-to-australia-under-new-community-sponsorship-program.

Doherty, Ben. "UN Human Rights Expert Decries Boat Turnbacks as Australia Criticised for Secrecy of 'On-Water Matters.'" *Guardian*,

July 8, 2021. https://www.theguardian.com/australia-news/2021/jul/08/un-human-rights-expert-decries-boat-turnbacks-as-australia-criticised-for-secrecy-of-on-water-matters?mc_cid=7425d737fa&mc_eid=9fb7b20078.

Doherty, Ben. "Vietnamese Asylum Seekers Forcibly Returned by Australia Face Jail." *Guardian,* May 24, 2016. https://www.theguardian.com/australianews/2016/may/24/vietnamese-asylum-seekers-forcibly-returned-by-australia-face-jail.

Doherty, Ben. "Vietnamese Asylum Seekers Turned Back After Being Processed at Sea." *Guardian,* June 22, 2016. https://www.theguardian.com/australia-news/2016/jun/22/vietnamese-asylum-seekers-turned-back-after-being-processed-at-sea.

Doherty, Ben, and Paul Farrell. "Detention of 157 Tamil Asylum Seekers on Board Ship Ruled Lawful." *Guardian,* January 28, 2015. https://www.theguardian.com/australia-news/2015/jan/28/detention-157-tamil-asylum-seekers-on-board-ship-ruled-lawful.

Dutton, Peter. "Australia and Vietnam Further Cooperation to Stamp Out People Smuggling." Media Release, December 12, 2016. https://minister.homeaffairs.gov.au/peterdutton/Pages/Australia-and-Vietnam-further-cooperation-to-stamp-out-people-smuggling.aspx.

Duxson, Sophie. "Filling the Legal Vacuum." *Inside Indonesia* 124 (April-June 2016). https://www.insideindonesia.org/filling-the-legal-vacuum.

Dyck, Stephanie. "Private Refugee Sponsorship in Canada: An Opportunity for Mutual Transformation." *Intersections: Challenges and Opportunities in Refugee Resettlement* 5, No. 4 (2017): 13–14. https://mccintersections.wordpress.com/2017/11/20/private-refugee-sponsorship-canada/.

Edis, Bayan. "Seaborne Asylum Seekers in the 21st Century: An Australian's Perspective." *Refugee Review: Re-conceptualizing Refugees and Forced Migration in the 21st Century,* ESPMI Network 2, No. 1 (June 2015): 195–197. https://refugeereview2.files.wordpress.com/2015/06/final-refugee-review-ii-pdf3.pdf.

"18 Imigran Gelap Ternyata Kabur dari Penjara di Vietnam." *TitikNOL,* February 11, 2017. https://titiknol.co.id/peristiwa/18-imigran-gelap-ternyata-kabur-dari-penjara-di-vietnam/ (translated from Indonesian).

"18 Thuyền Nhân Việt ở Indonesia Được Cấp Qui Chế Tị Nạn." *VOA,* May 24, 2017. https://www.voatiengviet.com/a/muoi-tam-thuyen-nhan-viet-o-indonesia-duoc-cap-qui-che-ti-nan/3868946.html (translated from Vietnamese).

The 88 Project. *Human Rights Reports Vietnam 2020–2021.* https://the88project.org/category/reports/.

The 88 Project. *Report: Torture and Inhumane Treatment of Political Prisoners in Vietnam 2018–2019.* November 5, 2020, 1–32. https://the88project.org/wp-content/uploads/2020/11/Torture-Report_final.pdf.

The 88 Project. *2019 Report on Political Prisoners and Activists at Risk in Vietnam.* June 22, 2020, 1–43. https://the88project.org/wp-content/uploads/2020/06/PDF-2019-annual-report.pdf.

The 88 Project and the Global Human Rights Clinic (GHRC). *Joint Submission to the Universal Periodic Review of the Socialist Republic of Vietnam.* UPR mid-term submission to the UN Human Rights Council, third cycle, November 1, 2021, 1–23. https://the88project.org/wp-content/uploads/2021/10/Final-ENG-version_UPR-Submission-GHRC-88-Project-10-28-21-1.pdf.

El-Chidiac, Sabine. "The Success of the Privately Sponsored Refugee System." *Policy Options,* July 20, 2018. https://policyoptions.irpp.org/magazines/july-2018/success-privately-sponsored-refugee-system/.

Elgersma, Sandra. *Immigration Policy Primer.* Publication No. 2015–42-E. Ottawa: Library of Parliament, 2015. https://lop.parl.ca/staticfiles/PublicWebsite/Home/ResearchPublications/InBriefs/PDF/2015-42-e.pdf.

Elgersma, Sandra. *Resettling Refugees: Canada's Humanitarian Commitments.* Publication No. 2015–11-E. Ottawa: Library of Parliament, 2015. https://lop.parl.ca/sites/PublicWebsite/default/en_CA/ResearchPublications/201511E.

Environics Institute for Survey Research. *Canada's World Survey 2018 Final Report.* April 2018, 1–46. https://www.environicsinstitute.org/docs/default-source/project-documents/canada's-world-2018-survey/canada's-world-survey-2018---final-report.pdf?sfvrsn=17208306_2.

Environics Institute for Survey Research. *Canadian Public Opinion About Immigration and Refugees Final Report. Focus Canada,* Executive Summary, October 7, 2020, 1–8. https://www.environicsinstitute.org/docs/default-source/project-documents/fc-fall-2020---immigration/focus-canada-fall-2020---public-opinion-on-immigration-refugees---final-report.pdf?sfvrsn=bd51588f_2&mc_cid=e467489f57&mc_eid=9fb7b20078.

Environics Institute for Survey Research. *Canadian Public Opinion About Immigration and Refugees. Focus Canada,* Executive Summary, April 29, 2019, 1–7. https://www.environicsinstitute.org/docs/default-source/project-documents/focus-canada-spring-2019/environics-institute---focus-canada-spring-2019-survey-on-immigration-and-refugees---final-report.pdf?sfvrsn=8dd2597f_2.

Environics Institute for Survey Research. *Private Refugee Sponsorship in Canada—2021 Market Study Final Report.* June 2021, 1–24.

https://www.environicsinstitute.org/docs/default-source/project-documents/welcome-the-stranger-private-sponsorship-study-2021/environics-r613-private-refugee-sponsorship-market-study-2021---final-report-eng.pdf?sfvrsn=9e66b9b2_4.

Evershed, Nick, Paul Farrell, and Oliver Laughland. "'In' or 'Out': What We Know About 'Enhanced Screening' of Asylum Seekers." *Guardian,* July 3, 2014. https://www.theguardian.com/world/2014/jul/03/asylum-seekers-may-be-subject-to-speedy-on-water-screenings.

"Factcheck." *ABC News,* January 24, 2014. https://www.abc.net.au/news/2014-01-24/tony-abbott-incorrect-on-asylum-seekers-breaking-australian-law/5214802?nw=0.

Faridz, Devianti. "Thousands of Refugees in Indonesia 'Shut Out' From Public Facilities." *VOA,* March 11, 2022. https://www.voanews.com/a/thousands-of-refugees-shut-out-from-public-facilities/6480371.html.

Faux, Imogen. "Vietnam's Law on Belief and Religion 'Deeply Flawed.'" *World Watch Monitor,* December 6, 2016. https://www.worldwatchmonitor.org/2016/12/vietnams-law-on-belief-and-religion-deeply-flawed/.

Ferguson, Richard. "Afghan Boatpeople 'Zero Chance.'" *Weekend Australian,* August 23, 2021. https://www.theaustralian.com.au/nation/afghan-boatpeople-zero-chance/news-story/287c0825233f9c1bd50e31ea744662c0.

Fitzgerald, David Scott. *Refuge Beyond Reach: How Rich Democracies Repel Asylum Seekers.* New York: Oxford University Press, 2019.

Foster, Michelle, and Anna Hood. "Regional Refugee Regimes: Oceania." In *The Oxford Handbook of International Refugee Law,* 441–460.

Fowler, Timothy. "Vietnamese Catholics Fleeing to Australia 'to Avoid Persecution.'" *Ecumenical News,* July 19, 2013. https://www.ecumenicalnews.com/article/vietnamese-catholics-fleeing-to-australia-to-avoid-persecution/22345.htm.

Freedom House. *Freedom in the World 2016–2020 Complete Books: Vietnam.* https://freedomhouse.org/reports/publication-archives.

Freedom House. "Freedom on the Net 2019: Vietnam." June 1, 2018-May 31, 2019. https://freedomhouse.org/country/vietnam/freedom-net/2019.

Garcea, Joseph. "Canada's Refugee Protection System." In *Structural Context of Refugee Integration in Canada and Germany,* edited by Annette Korntheuer, Paul Pritchard, and Debora B Maehler, 31–36. Cologne: GESIS—Leibniz Institute for the Social Sciences, 2017. https://www.gesis.org/fileadmin/upload/forschung/publikationen/gesis_reihen/gesis_schriftenreihe/GS_15_-_Refugee_Integration_in_Canada_and_Germany.pdf.

Garnier, Adèle. "The COVID-19 Resettlement Suspension: Impact, Exemptions and the Road Ahead." *FluchtforschungsBlog,* June 16, 2020. https://blog.fluchtforschung.net/the-covid-19-resettlement-suspension/.

Garnier, Adèle. "Resettled Refugees and Work in Canada and Quebec: Humanitarianism and the Challenge of Mainstream Socioeconomic Participation." In *Refugee Resettlement: Power, Politics, and Humanitarian Governance,* edited by Adèle Garnier, Liliana Lyra Jubilut, and Kristin Bergtora Sandvik, 118–138. Studies in Forced Migration Series Vol. 38. New York: Berghahn Books, 2018.

Garnier, Adèle, Kristin Bergtora Sandvik, and Amanda Cellini. "The COVID-19 Resettlement Freeze: Towards a Permanent Suspension?" UNSW Kaldor Centre for International Refugee Law, April 14, 2020. https://www.kaldorcentre.unsw.edu.au/publication/covid-19-resettlement-freeze-towards-permanent-suspension.

Garnier, Adèle, Kristin Bergtora Sandvik, and Liliana Lyra Jubilut. "Introduction: Refugee Resettlement as Humanitarian Governance." In *Refugee Resettlement,* 1–27.

Giles, Andrew. "Minister Marks First Refugee Arrivals Under the Community Refugee Integration and Settlement Pilot." Media Release, August 26, 2022. https://minister.homeaffairs.gov.au/AndrewGiles/Pages/first-arrivals-community-refugee-integration-settlement-pilot.aspx.

Gillespie, Eden. "Ad Agency Behind Government's Film Competition Warning Against 'Illegal Migration' Has Won Ethical Awards." *SBS,* February 18, 2022. https://www.sbs.com.au/news/article/ad-agency-behind-governments-film-competition-warning-against-illegal-migration-has-won-ethical-awards/65yaplhkm.

Gillespie, Eden. "Tamil-Australians 'Outraged' over Taxpayer-Funded Anti-Migration Film Competition." *SBS,* December 24, 2021. https://www.sbs.com.au/news/tamil-australians-outraged-over-taxpayer-funded-anti-migration-film-competition/d89d29b4-5736-4212-a316-867158d99c89.

Gillespie, John. "Human Rights as a Larger Loyalty: The Evolution of Religious Freedom in Vietnam." *Harvard Human Rights Journal* 27 (2014): 107–149. https://web.archive.org/web/20180409231343/http://harvardhrj.com/wp-content/uploads/2014/07/V27_Gillespie.pdf.

Giotis, Chrisanthi. "'Stop Playing Politics': Refugees Stuck in Indonesia Rally Against UNHCR for Chronic Waiting." *Conversation,* October 8, 2019. https://theconversation.com/stop-playing-politics-refugees-stuck-in-indonesia-rally-against-unhcr-for-chronic-waiting-124176.

Gleeson, Madeline. "How Should Australia Respond to Asylum Seekers Arriving by Sea During the COVID-19 Pandemic?" *ILA Reporter,* February 11, 2021. http://ilareporter.

org.au/2021/02/how-should-australia-respond-to-asylum-seekers-arriving-by-sea-during-the-covid-19-pandemic-madeline-gleeson/.

Gleeson, Madeline. "What is Occurring in the Seas North and West of Australia? We Have No Way of Knowing." UNSW Kaldor Centre for International Refugee Law, July 7, 2021. https://www.kaldorcentre.unsw.edu.au/news/what-occurring-seas-north-and-west-australia-we-have-no-way-knowing?mc_cid=7425d737fa&mc_eid=9fb7b20078.

Global Detention Project. "Indonesia Immigration Detention Profile." Updated January 2016, https://www.globaldetentionproject.org/countries/asia-pacific/indonesia.

Goodwin-Gill, Guy, and Jane McAdam. *The Refugee in International Law.* 4th edition. Oxford: Oxford University Press, 2021.

Gordyn, Carly. "Assessing Indonesia's New Decree on Refugees." *New Mandala,* February 9, 2017. https://www.newmandala.org/assessing-indonesias-new-decree-refugees/.

Government of Canada. "Regulations Amending the Immigration and Refugee Protection Regulations." *Canada Gazette,* Part 1, 146, No. 23, June 9, 2012. http://www.gazette.gc.ca/rp-pr/p1/2012/2012-06-09/html/reg1-eng.html.

Hansen, Kaitlin. "Land Law, Land Rights, and Land Reform in Vietnam: A Deeper Look into 'Land Grabbing' for Public and Private Development." Independent Study Project (ISP) Collection, 2013, 1722. https://digitalcollections.sit.edu/isp_collection/1722.

Hansen, Peter. "The Vietnamese State, the Catholic Church and the Law." In *Asian Socialism and Legal Change: The Dynamics of Vietnamese and Chinese Reform,* edited by John Gillespie and Pip Nicholson, 310–334. Canberra: ANU E Press; Asia Pacific Press, 2005. https://press-files.anu.edu.au/downloads/press/p125661/pdf/book.pdf.

Hanson-Young, Sarah. "Abbott Government Must Lift Veil of Secrecy on Operation Secret Boats." Media Release, April 18, 2015.

Hanson-Young, Sarah. "Grave Concerns for the Plight of Vietnamese Asylum Seekers." Media Release, July 31, 2015.

Hanson-Young, Sarah. "Minister Needs to Come Clean on Boat Arrival." Media Release, July 20, 2015.

Harris, Kathleen. "Federal Government Plans to Bring in More Than 1.2M Immigrants in Next 3 Years." *CBC News,* October 30, 2020. https://www.cbc.ca/news/politics/mendicino-immigration-pandemic-refugees-1.5782642.

Harris, Kathleen. "Refugee Advocates Say Canada Must Step Up Resettlement Efforts Despite Pandemic." *CBC News,* November 12, 2020. https://www.cbc.ca/news/politics/refugees-canada-pandemic-mendicino-1.5797361?fbclid=IwAR0MA8g_EHGJ1LaZU8exgrtg8l8yVpfUoC3TmQLvwdQJvpk1D0eUXDEid1E.

Harvey, Gemima. "Surviving While Seeking Asylum." *Inside Indonesia,* October 26, 2018. https://www.insideindonesia.org/surviving-while-seeking-asylum.

Hasham, Nicole. "Tony Abbott Tight-Lipped on Suspected Vietnamese Asylum Seeker Boat." *SMH,* July 21, 2015. https://www.smh.com.au/politics/federal/tony-abbott-tightlipped-on-suspected-vietnamese-asylum-seeker-boat-20150721-gih1ij.html.

Hasham, Nicole. "Vietnamese Asylum Seekers Returned by Plane in the Dead of Night: Reports." *SMH,* July 27, 2015. https://www.smh.com.au/politics/federal/vietnamese-asylum-seekers-returned-by-plane-in-the-dead-of-night-reports-20150727-gil671.html.

Hawke, Alex. "Enhanced Support for Refugee Resettlement and Integration." Media Release, December 17, 2021. https://minister.home affairs.gov.au/AlexHawke/Pages/enhanced-support-for-refugee-settlement-and-integration.aspx.

Hawley, Samantha. "Asylum Seekers Returned to Vietnam by Australian Navy Had Claims Assessed at Sea, UNHCR Says." *ABC News,* April 21, 2015. https://www.abc.net.au/news/2015-04-21/vietnam-asylum-seekers-returned-australian-navy-screened-at-sea/6407848.

Higgins, Claire. "Protecting Refugees and Australia's Interests." In *Fresh Perspectives in Security,* Centre of Gravity Series Paper 51, ANU Strategic and Defence Studies Centre, March 2020, 30–35. http://sdsc.bellschool.anu.edu.au/sites/default/files/publications/attachments/2020-03/cog_51_web.pdf.

Hirsch, Asher Lazarus. *After the Boats Have Stopped: Refugees Stranded in Indonesia and Australia's Containment Policies.* Refugee Council of Australia Brief, November 2018, 1–5. https://www.refugeecouncil.org.au/wp-content/uploads/2018/12/Indonesia_brief.pdf.

Hirsch, Asher Lazarus. "The Borders Beyond the Border: Australia's Extraterritorial Migration Controls." *Refugee Survey Quarterly* 36, No. 3 (September 1, 2017): 48–80. https://doi.org/10.1093/rsq/hdx008.

Hirsch, Asher Lazarus, and Cameron Doig. "Outsourcing Control: The International Organization for Migration in Indonesia." *International Journal of Human Rights* 22, No. 5 (2018): 681–708. http://doi.org/10.1080/13642987.2017.1417261.

Hirsch, Asher Lazarus, Khanh Hoang, and Anthea Vogl. "Australia's Private Refugee Sponsorship Program: Creating Complementary

Pathways or Privatizing Humanitarianism?" *Refuge: Canada's Journal on Refugees* 35, No. 2 (2019): 109–122. https://doi.org/10.7202/1064823ar.

Ho Binh Minh. "Vietnam, Grappling with Mass Fish Deaths, Clamps Down on Seafood Sales." *Reuters,* April 28, 2016. https://www.reuters.com/article/us-vietnam-formosa-plastics-environment-idUSKCN0XP0QD.

Hoang, Khanh. "Lessons from History: The Community Refugee Settlement Scheme." Community Refugee Sponsorship Initiative (CRSI), April 27, 2018. https://refugeesponsorship.org.au/lessons-from-history-the-community-refugee-settlement-scheme/.

Hoang, Khanh. "Risks and Rewards in Australia's Plan for Private Sponsorship." UNSW Kaldor Centre for International Refugee Law, May 16, 2017. https://www.kaldorcentre.unsw.edu.au/publication/risks-and-rewards-australias-plan-private-sponsorship.

Hodge, Amanda. "Little Food, No Shelter ... Aid Runs Out." *Australian,* August 31, 2019. https://www.theaustralian.com.au/nation/world/no-more-aid-refugees-turn-on-each-other-to-feed-families/news-story/99f3e60b89edc7423e7baddd7dc838b1.

Hodge, Amanda. "Refugees in Limbo Wait for Softening of Rules." *Australian,* November 4, 2018. https://www.theaustralian.com.au/nation/nation/refugees-in-limbo-wait-for-softening-of-rules/news-story/21faec4c121460f102c1ceaa4bd3ecbe.

Hodge, Amanda. "Turnbacks Best Deterrent, Says IOM Chief." *Australian,* January 31, 2019. https://www.theaustralian.com.au/nation/immigration/turnbacks-best-deterrent-says-iom-chief/news-story/bcd31b7a615a0c35e600de852ca25ddd.

Hodge, Amanda, and Nga LH Nguyen. "Kids 'Orphaned' as Vietnam Jails Parents Over Asylum Bid." *Australian,* July 29, 2016. http://www.theaustralian.com.au/news/nation/kids-orphaned-as-vietnam-jails-parents-over-asylum-bid/news-story/fdb6751c38007ea02371b802315e57a9.

Howard, Jessica. "To Deter and Deny: Australia and the Interdiction of Asylum Seekers." *Refuge* 21, No. 4 (2003): 35–50. https://refuge.journals.yorku.ca/index.php/refuge/article/view/21307/19978.

Hugo, Graeme, George Tan, and Caven Jonathan Napitupulu. "Indonesia as a Transit Country in Irregular Migration to Australia." In *A Long Way to Go: Irregular Migration Patterns, Processes, Drivers and Decision-Making,* edited by Marie McAuliffe and Khalid Koser, 167–196. Canberra: ANU Press, 2017. dx.doi.org/10.22459/LWG.12.2017.07.

Human Rights Watch (HRW). *Barely Surviving: Detention, Abuse, and Neglect of Migrant Children in Indonesia.* June 24, 2013, 1–86. https://www.refworld.org/docid/51cae2724.html.

HRW. *'Locked Inside Our Home': Movement Restrictions on Rights Activists in Vietnam.* February 2022, 1–82. https://www.hrw.org/sites/default/files/media_2022/02/vietnam0222_web.pdf.

HRW. *No Country for Human Rights Activists: Assaults on Bloggers and Democracy Campaigners in Vietnam.* June 18, 2017. https://www.hrw.org/report/2017/06/19/no-country-human-rights-activists/assaults-bloggers-and-democracy-campaigners.

HRW. *Public Insecurity: Deaths in Custody and Police Brutality in Vietnam.* September 15, 2014. https://www.hrw.org/report/2014/09/16/public-insecurity/deaths-custody-and-police-brutality-vietnam.

HRW. "Vietnam: Amended Constitution a Missed Opportunity on Rights." December 2, 2013. https://www.hrw.org/news/2013/12/02/vietnam-amended-constitution-missed-opportunity-rights.

HRW. "Vietnam: Drop Charges Against Boat Returnees." May 24, 2016. https://www.hrw.org/news/2016/05/24/vietnam-drop-charges-against-boat-returnees.

HRW. "Vietnam: EU Should Press for Release of Political Prisoners." November 28, 2017. https://www.hrw.org/news/2017/11/28/vietnam-eu-should-press-release-political-prisoners.

HRW. *Vietnam: Events of 2018,* 1–4. http://www.vietnamhumanrights.net/english/documents/HRW_2019.pdf.

HRW. *Vietnam: Events of 2019.* World Report 2020. https://www.hrw.org/world-report/2020/country-chapters/vietnam.

HRW. *Vietnam: Events of 2020.* World Report 2021. https://www.hrw.org/world-report/2021/country-chapters/vietnam.

HRW. *Vietnam: Events of 2021.* World Report 2022. https://www.hrw.org/world-report/2022/country-chapters/vietnam.

HRW. "Vietnam: Show Rights Commitment at Australia Talks." August 1, 2016. https://www.hrw.org/news/2016/08/01/vietnam-show-rights-commitment-australia-talks.

Hunter, Fergus, and Michael Koziol. "Asylum Seekers Who Come by Boat Banned for Life Under New Laws." *SMH,* October 30, 2016. https://www.smh.com.au/politics/federal/asylum-seekers-who-come-by-boat-banned-for-life-under-new-laws-20161030-gsdvf7.html.

Hutchens, Gareth. "Asylum Seekers Face Lifetime Ban from Entering Australia if They Arrive by Boat." *Guardian,* October 30, 2016. https://www.theguardian.com/australia-news/2016/oct/30/asylum-seekers-face-lifetime-ban-on-entering-australia-if-they-arrive-by-boat.

Hutchinson, Anna. "'Welcome to Canada': Hospitality, Inclusion and Diversity in Private Refugee Sponsorship." MSc diss., UCL, 2017. London: UCL Migration Research Unit Working Papers No. 2018/2, 1–38. https://www.

geog.ucl.ac.uk/research/research-centres/migration-research-unit/publications/working-papers/files/MRU%20WP%20Anna%20Hutchinson%202018%202.pdf.

Hyndman, Jennifer, Johanna Reynolds, Biftu Yousuf, Anna Purkey, Dawit Demoz, and Kathy Sherrell. "Sustaining the Private Sponsorship of Resettled Refugees in Canada." *Frontiers in Human Dynamics* 3 (May 11, 2021): 1–13. https://doi.org/10.3389/fhumd.2021.625358.

Hyndman, Jennifer, William Payne, and Shauna Jiminez. *The State of Private Refugee Sponsorship in Canada: Trends, Issues and Impacts.* Refugee Research Network/Centre for Refugee Studies Policy Brief Submitted to the Government of Canada, December 2, 2016, 1–21. https://refugeeresearch.net/wp-content/uploads/2017/02/hyndman_feb'17.pdf.

Hynie, Michaela, and Jennifer Hyndman. "From Newcomer to Canadian: Making Refugee Integration Work." *Policy Options,* May 17, 2016. http://policyoptions.irpp.org/magazines/may-2016/from-newcomer-to-canadian-making-refugee-integration-work.

Ilham. "'We Never Invited You to Come Here.'" *Inside Indonesia,* May 3, 2021, https://www.insideindonesia.org/we-never-invited-you-to-come-here-2.

Immigration, Refugees and Citizenship Canada (IRCC). "Canada Announces 3 New Initiatives to Welcome and Support More Refugees." News Release, June 18, 2021. https://www.canada.ca/en/immigration-refugees-citizenship/news/2021/06/canada-announces-3-new-initiatives-to-welcome-and-support-more-refugees.html.

Immigration, Refugees and Citizenship Canada (IRCC). *Evaluation of the Resettlement Programs (GAR, PSR, BVOR and RAP).* July 2016, 1–47. https://www.canada.ca/content/dam/ircc/migration/ircc/english/pdf/pub/resettlement.pdf.

Immigration, Refugees and Citizenship Canada (IRCC). "Government of Canada Appeal Granted on Safe Third Country Agreement." April 15, 2021. https://www.canada.ca/en/immigration-refugees-citizenship/news/2021/04/government-of-canada-appeal-granted-on-safe-third-country-agreement.html.

Immigration, Refugees and Citizenship Canada (IRCC). Guide to the Private Sponsorship of Refugees Program. https://www.canada.ca/en/immigration-refugees-citizenship/corporate/publications-manuals/guide-private-sponsorship-refugees-program.html.

Immigration, Refugees and Citizenship Canada (IRCC). "A New Way Forward for Some Immigration Application Processing Times." News Release, August 9, 2018. https://www.canada.ca/en/immigration-refugees-citizenship/news/2018/08/a-new-way-forward-for-some-immigration-application-processing-times.html.

Immigration, Refugees and Citizenship Canada (IRCC). "Notice—Supplementary Information 2018–2020 Immigration Levels Plan." November 1, 2017. https://www.canada.ca/en/immigration-refugees-citizenship/news/notices/supplementary-immigration-levels-2018.html.

Immigration, Refugees and Citizenship Canada (IRCC). "Notice—Supplementary Information 2019–2021 Immigration Levels Plan." October 31, 2018. https://www.canada.ca/en/immigration-refugees-citizenship/news/notices/supplementary-immigration-levels-2019.html.

Immigration, Refugees and Citizenship Canada (IRCC). "Notice—Supplementary Information 2020–2022 Immigration Levels Plan." March 12, 2020. https://www.canada.ca/en/immigration-refugees-citizenship/news/notices/supplementary-immigration-levels-2020.html.

Immigration, Refugees and Citizenship Canada (IRCC). "Notice—Supplementary Information for the 2021–2023 Immigration Levels Plan." October 30, 2020. https://www.canada.ca/en/immigration-refugees-citizenship/news/notices/supplementary-immigration-levels-2021-2023.html.

Immigration, Refugees and Citizenship Canada (IRCC). "Notice—Supplementary Information for the 2022–2024 Immigration Levels Plan." February 14, 2022. https://www.canada.ca/en/immigration-refugees-citizenship/news/notices/supplementary-immigration-levels-2022-2024.html.

Immigration, Refugees and Citizenship Canada (IRCC). "Notice—Supplementary Information for the 2023–2025 Immigration Levels Plan." November 1, 2023. https://www.canada.ca/en/immigration-refugees-citizenship/news/notices/supplementary-immigration-levels-2023-2025.html.

Immigration, Refugees and Citizenship Canada (IRCC). *Privately Sponsored Refugee Program: Refugee Resettlement in Canada: Important Information.* 1–13. https://www.canada.ca/content/dam/ircc/migration/ircc/english/pdf/pub/psr_en.pdf.

Immigration, Refugees and Citizenship Canada (IRCC). "Responsibilities of Sponsors & Availability of IRCC-Funded Services for PSRs and BVORs." Updated October 2019. https://www.rstp.ca/wp-content/uploads/2019/11/Responsibilities-of-Sponsors-and-Availability-of-IRCC-funded-Services-for-PSRs-and-BVORs-Oct-2019.pdf.

Immigration, Refugees and Citizenship Canada (IRCC). *2017 Annual Report to Parliament on Immigration.* 1–39. https://www.canada.ca/content/dam/ircc/migration/ircc/english/pdf/pub/annual-report-2017.pdf.

Immigration, Refugees and Citizenship Canada (IRCC). *2018 Annual Report to Parliament on Immigration.* 1–43. https://www.canada.ca/content/dam/ircc/migration/ircc/english/pdf/pub/annual-report-2018.pdf.

Immigration, Refugees and Citizenship Canada

(IRCC). *2019 Annual Report to Parliament on Immigration*. 1–42. https://www.canada.ca/content/dam/ircc/migration/ircc/english/pdf/pub/annual-report-2019.pdf.

Immigration, Refugees and Citizenship Canada (IRCC). *2020 Annual Report to Parliament on Immigration*. 1–39. https://www.canada.ca/content/dam/ircc/migration/ircc/english/pdf/pub/annual-report-2020-en.pdf.

Immigration, Refugees and Citizenship Canada (IRCC). *2021 Annual Report to Parliament on Immigration*. 1–46. https://www.canada.ca/content/dam/ircc/documents/pdf/english/corporate/publications-manuals/annual-report-2021-en.pdf.

Immigration, Refugees and Citizenship Canada (IRCC). *2022 Annual Report to Parliament on Immigration*. 1–58. https://www.canada.ca/content/dam/ircc/documents/pdf/english/corporate/publications-manuals/annual-report-2022-en.pdf.

Immigration, Refugees and Citizenship Canada (IRCC). "IRCC Minister Transition Binder 2021: Permanent Immigration—Immigration Levels Planning." https://www.canada.ca/en/immigration-refugees-citizenship/corporate/transparency/transition-binders/minister-2021/levels.html.

International Crisis Group. *Vietnam Tacks Between Cooperation and Struggle in the South China Sea*. Asia Report No 318, December 7, 2021, 1–39. https://icg-prod.s3.amazonaws.com/318-between-cooperation-and-struggle_1.pdf.

International Federation for Human Rights (FIDH) and Vietnam Committee on Human Rights (VCHR). *Assessment of Vietnam's Implementation of the UN Human Rights Committee's Recommendations on Key Priority Issues*. 136th session, July 18, 2022, 1–6. https://www.fidh.org/IMG/pdf/20220718_vietnam_ccpr_js_en.pdf.

International Organization for Migration (IOM). "Community Support Program Process Map." https://australia.iom.int/sites/default/files/PDFs/CSP%20-IOM%20Process%20Map.pdf.

IOM. *Financial Report for the Year Ended December 31, 2017*. May 29, 2018, 1–115. https://governingbodies.iom.int/system/files/en/council/109/C-109-3%20-%20Financial%20Report%20for%20the%20year%202017.pdf.

IOM. "Indonesian City Admits Migrant Children to Public Schools." July 17, 2018. https://www.iom.int/news/indonesian-city-admits-migrant-children-public-schools.

IOM. "IOM Indonesia Programmes." https://indonesia.iom.int/sites/g/files/tmzbdl1491/files/documents/IOM%20Indonesia%20Fact%20Sheet%202021%20EN.pdf.

IOM Indonesia. *Alternatives to Detention*. Issue 4, September 2014, 1–4. https://www.iom.int/files/live/sites/iom/files/Country/docs/IOM-Indonesia_Alternatives-to-detention-September-2014.pdf.

IOM Indonesia. *COVID-19 Strategic Response and Recovery Plan 2021*. 1–9. https://indonesia.iom.int/sites/g/files/tmzbdl1491/files/documents/IOMIndonesiaCOVID19SRRP2021.pdf.

Jedwab, Jack. "GARs vs. PSRs: Explaining Differences in Outcomes for Recent Refugees to Canada." *Canadian Diversity* 15, No. 2 (2018): 38–46.

Jelita, Angela. "Suicide, Depression and Poverty: Indonesia's Bleak Future Now There's Almost No Chance of Being Resettled," *South China Morning Post,* March 21, 2018. https://www.scmp.com/lifestyle/article/2137993/suicide-depression-and-poverty-indonesias-refugees-bleak-future-now-theres.

Jesuit Refugee Services (JRS). *The Search: Protection Space in Malaysia, Thailand, Indonesia, Cambodia and the Philippines*. Bangkok: JRS Asia Pacific, 2012. https://www.refworld.org/pdfid/506bfb622.pdf.

Jeyakumar, Rhianne. "Australian Government Has Reduced Sri Lankan Civil War Refugees to Knock-Off Gimmicks—Reflections on the Zero Chance Campaign." *SAARI,* March 17, 2022. https://saaricollective.com.au/community/blog/australian-government-has-reduced-sri-lankan-civil-war-refugees-to-knock-off-gimmicks-reflections-on-the-zero-chance-campaign/.

Johnston, Angela. "Majority of Canadians Against Accepting More Refugees, Poll Suggests." *CBC News,* July 3, 2019. https://www.cbc.ca/news/canada/manitoba/refugees-tolerance-1.5192769.

Joniad, J.N. "How Australia's Deterrence Policies Turned Indonesia into a Prison Without Walls." *Overland,* October 29, 2021. https://overland.org.au/2021/10/how-australias-deterrence-policies-have-turned-indonesia-into-a-prison-without-walls/comment-page-1/#comment-1056832.

Joniad, J.N. "A Lost Generation of Refugee Children in Indonesia." *Overland,* May 6, 2020. https://overland.org.au/2020/05/a-lost-generation-of-refugee-children-in-indonesia/.

Kaduuli, Stephen. "Continuing Welcome: A Progress Report on A Half Welcome." *CPJ,* June 2020. https://cpj.ca/wp-content/uploads/2020/06/Continuing-Welcome-Report.pdf.

Kalda, Lisa, Feng Hou, and Max Stick. "The Long-Term Economic Integration of Resettled Refugees in Canada: A Comparison of Privately Sponsored Refugees and Government-Assisted Refugees." *Journal of Ethnic and Migration Studies* 46 No. 9 (2020): 1687–1708. 10.1080/1369183X.2019.1623017.

Kasli, Zeynep. "Integration Outcomes of Recent Sponsorship and Humanitarian Visa Arrivals." *ReSOMA,* Ask the Expert Policy Brief, May 2019. https://pure.eur.nl/ws/portalfiles/portal/49330805/Ask_the_Expert_Brief_Sponsorship_Humanitarian_Visa.pdf.

Kasynathan, Shankar. "Using Prizes to Deter Asylum Seekers Sinks to Next Level 'Depravity.'" *SMH,* December 31, 2021. https://www.smh.com.au/national/using-prizes-to-deter-asylum-seekers-sinks-to-next-level-depravity-20211230-p59kt3.html.

Kearney, Simon, and Stephen Fitzpatrick. "'Life of Brutality' in Crowded Indonesian Lock-Up." *Australian,* October 23, 2009. https://www.theaustralian.com.au/news/world/life-of-brutality-in-crowded-indonesian-lock-up/news-story/8b751e651ccbccd0471d41736555e720.

Keep, Joel, and Mai Hoa Pham. "Women Flee Vietnam for Second Time Following Turn-Back from Australia." *SBS,* February 15, 2017. http://www.sbs.com.au/news/article/2017/02/14/women-flee-vietnam-second-time-following-turn-back-australia.

Kerkvliet, Ben. "Vietnamese Fishermen Versus China." *New Mandala,* July 6, 2016. http://www.newmandala.org/vietnamese-fishermen-versus-china/.

Keung, Nicholas. "Years After Canada Opened its Doors, Thousands of Syrian Refugees Are Still Waiting to Come Here." *Star,* January 2, 2018. https://www.thestar.com/news/immigration/2018/01/02/years-after-canada-opened-its-doors-thousands-of-syrian-refugees-are-still-waiting-to-come-here.html.

Kneebone, Susan. "Australia as a Powerbroker on Refugee Protection in Southeast Asia: The Relationship with Indonesia." *Refuge* 33, No. 1 (2017): 29–41. https://doi.org/10.25071/1920-7336.40446.

Kneebone, Susan, Antje Missbach, and Balawyn Jones. "The False Promise of Presidential Regulation No. 125 of 2016?" *Asian Journal of Law and Society* 8, No. 3 (2021): 431–450. 10.1017/als.2021.2.

Kneebone, Susan, Asher Hirsch, and Audrey Macklin. "Private Resettlement Models Offer a Way for Australia to Lift Its Refugee Intake." *Conversation,* September 19, 2016. https://theconversation.com/private-resettlement-models-offer-a-way-for-australia-to-lift-its-refugee-intake-65030.

Kristin, Debby, and Chloryne Trie Isana Dewi. "The Rights of Children Refugee in Transit Country Under the CRC, A Case of Indonesia: An Intended Negligence?" *Padjadjaran Journal of International Law* 5, No. 1 (January 2021). https://doi.org/10.23920/pjil.v5i1.349.

Kyriadkides, Christopher, Arthur McLuhan, Karen Anderson, and Lubna Bajjali. "Transactions of Worth in Refugee-Host Relations." In *Strangers to Neighbours,* 231–245.

Labman, Shauna. "Conclusion: Sponsorship's Success and Sustainability?" In *Strangers to Neighbours,* 347–364.

Labman, Shauna. *Crossing Law's Border: Canada's Refugee Resettlement Program.* Vancouver: UBC Press, 2019.

Labman, Shauna. "Looking Back, Moving Forward: The History and Future of Refugee Protection." *Chicago Kent Journal of International and Comparative Law* 10 (2010): 1–22. https://studentorgs.kentlaw.iit.edu/jicl/journal/volume-10/.

Labman, Shauna. "Private Sponsorship:

Complementary or Conflicting Interests?" *Refuge* 32, No. 2 (2016): 67–80. https://doi.org/10.25071/1920-7336.40266.

Labman, Shauna. "Queue the Rhetoric: Refugees, Resettlement and Reform." *University of New Brunswick Law Journal* 62 (2011): 55–63. https://papers.ssrn.com/sol3/papers.cfm?abstract_id=2809995.

Labman, Shauna. "Refugee Protection in Canada: Resettlement's Role." *Canadian Diversity* 17, No. 2 (2020): 7–11. http://hdl.handle.net/10222/79384.

Labman, Shauna, and Adèle Garnier. "Federal Election 2021: What the Conservatives Don't Understand About Refugee Resettlement." *Conversation,* September 12, 2021. https://theconversation.com/federal-election-2021-what-the-conservatives-dont-understand-about-refugee-resettlement-167033.

Labman, Shauna, and Geoffrey Cameron, eds. *Strangers to Neighbours: Refugee Sponsorship in Context.* Montreal & Kingston: McGill-Queen's University Press, 2020.

Labman, Shauna, and Jamie Chai Yun Liew. "Law and Moral Licensing in Canada: The Making of Illegality and Illegitimacy Along the Border." *International Journal of Migration and Border Studies* 5, No. 3 (2019): 188. https://doi.org/10.1504/IJMBS.2019.102446.

Labman, Shauna, and Sarah Zell. "The Shift Towards Increased Citizen-Driven Migration in Canada." In *Research Handbook,* 110–124.

Lamb, Kate. "'It's Impossible to Do Anything': Indonesia's Refugees in Limbo as Money Runs Out." *Guardian,* September 14, 2019. https://www.theguardian.com/world/2019/sep/13/its-impossible-to-do-anything-indonesias-refugees-in-limbo-as-money-runs-out.

Lamb, Kate, and Ben Doherty. "On the Streets with the Desperate Refugees Who Dream of Being Detained." *Guardian,* April 15, 2018. https://www.theguardian.com/world/2018/apr/15/on-the-streets-with-the-desperate-refugees-who-dream-of-being-detained.

Lange, Kelsey. "Mobilization of the Legal Community to Support PSR Applications through the Refugee Sponsorship Support Program." In *Strangers to Neighbours,* 246–262.

Lau, Bryony. *A Transit Country No More: Refugees and Asylum Seekers in Indonesia.* Mixed Migration Centre (MMC) research report, May 2021, 1–49. https://mixedmigration.org/wp-content/uploads/2021/05/170_Indonesia_Transit_Country_No_More_Research_Report.pdf.

Laughland, Oliver. "Angus Campbell Warns Asylum Seekers Not to Travel to Australia by Boat." *Guardian,* April 11, 2014. https://www.theguardian.com/world/2014/apr/11/angus-campbell-stars-in-videos-warning-asylum-seekers-not-to-travel-by-boat.

Law Council of Australia. *Asylum Seeker Policy.* September 6, 2014, 1–11. https://www.lawcouncil.asn.au/publicassets/129a0b1b-bed6-

e611-80d2-005056be66b1/Policy-Statement-Asylum-Seeker-Policy.pdf.

Law Council of Australia. *Australia-Vietnam 2016 Human Rights Dialogue: Civil Society Consultation.* DFAT, June 20, 2016, 1–12. https://www.lawcouncil.asn.au/docs/11b58 e10-02bd-e611-80d2-005056be66b1/3158_-_AU-Vietnam_Dialogue_2016.pdf.

Lawlor, Andrea, and Erin Tolley. "Deciding Who's Legitimate: News Media Framing of Immigrants and Refugees." *International Journal of Communication* 11 (2017): 967–991. https://ijoc.org/index.php/ijoc/article/view/6273.

Lehr, Sabine, and Brian Dyck. "'Naming' Refugees in the Canadian Private Sponsorship of Refugees Program: Diverse Intentions and Consequences." In *Strangers to Neighbours,* 57–76.

Lenard, Patti Tamara. "How *Should* We Think about Private Sponsorship of Refugees?" In *Strangers to Neighbours,* 79–92.

Lester, Eve. *Making Migration Law: The Foreigner, Sovereignty, and the Case of Australia.* Cambridge: Cambridge University Press, 2018.

Levitz, Stephanie. "Canada's Refugee Effort Hailed as Model for World by Head of UN Agency," *Canadian Press,* March 21, 2016. https://www.cbc.ca/news/politics/un-refugee-private-government-sponsor-1.3501400.

Liberal Party of Australia and National Party of Australia. *The Coalition's Operation Sovereign Borders Policy.* July 2013, 1–20. https://perma.cc/DV5E-HUN6.

Linh, Cat. "Các Thuyền Nhân VN Được Cho Tạm Tá Túc ở Jakarta Qua Cuối Tuần." *RFA,* February 10, 2017. https://www.rfa.org/vietnamese/news/vietnamnews/vn-asylum-seekers-temporary-stay-in-jakarta-02102017225935.html (translated from Vietnamese).

Loc, Nam. "Những Thuyền Nhân Tị Nạn Muộn Màng." *Nguoi Viet,* January 25, 2022. https://www.nguoi-viet.com/little-saigon/nhung-thuyen-nhan-ti-nan-muon-mang/ (translated from Vietnamese).

Loc, Nam. "Những Thuyền Nhân Tị Nạn Muộn Màng." *Viet Bao,* January 24, 2022. https://vietbao.com/a310922/nhung-thuyen-nhan-ti-nan-muon-mang (translated from Vietnamese).

LoCastro, Matthew, and Diovio Alfath. "Indonesia's Refugees Need Sustainable Solutions." *Asean Post,* January 19, 2020. https://theaseanpost.com/article/indonesias-refugees-need-sustainable-solutions.

Longbottom, Jessica. "Vietnam Jails Four Asylum Seekers Over Voyage to Australia Despite 'No Retribution' Promise." *ABC News,* May 26, 2016. http://www.abc.net.au/news/2016-05-26/asylum-seekers-jailed-in-vietnam-despite-no-retribution-promise/7449516.

Ma, Wayne. "Facebook and Google Balance Booming Business with Censorship Pressure in Vietnam." *Information,* December 10, 2019. https://www.theinformation.com/articles/facebook-and-google-balance-booming-business-with-censorship-pressure-in-vietnam.

MacCallum, Mungo. "Asylum Seekers and the Language of War." *Drum,* January 14, 2014. https://www.abc.net.au/news/2014-01-13/maccallum-operation-sovereign-borders/5196708.

Macklin, Audrey, Kathryn Barber, Luin Goldring, Jennifer Hyndman, Anna Korteweg, and Jona Zyfi. "Kindred Spirits? Links between Refugee Sponsorship and Family Sponsorship." In *Strangers to Neighbours,* 207–228.

Macklin, Audrey, Kathryn Barber, Luin Goldring, Jennifer Hyndman, Anna Korteweg, Shauna Labman, and Jona Zyfi. "A Preliminary Investigation into Private Refugee Sponsors." *Canadian Ethnic Studies* 50 No. 2 (2018): 35–57. doi:10.1353/ces.2018.0014.

Majeed, Zaini. "Canada to Admit 45,000 Refugees in 2021; Expedite Permanent Residency Applications." *Republicworld.com,* June 19, 2021. https://www.republicworld.com/world-news/rest-of-the-world-news/canada-to-admit-45000-refugees-in-2021-expedite-permanent-residency-applications.html.

Mann, Alexandra. "Refugees Who Arrive by Boat and Canada's Commitment to the Refugee Convention: A Discursive Analysis." *Refuge* 26, No. 2 (2009): 191–206. https://doi.org/10.25071/1920-7336.32088.

Martani, Ervis. "Rebalancing and Improving Refugee Resettlement in Canada." *Policy Options,* November 2, 2020. https://policyoptions.irpp.org/magazines/november-2020/rebalancing-and-improving-refugee-resettlement-in-canada/.

Masardi, Realisa D. "All Alone." *Inside Indonesia,* April-June 2016. https://www.insideindonesia.org/all-alone.

McAdam, Jane, and Fiona Chong. *Refugee Rights and Policy Wrongs: A Frank, Up-to-Date Guide by Experts.* Sydney: UNSW Press, 2019.

McNally, Rachel. "15 Ways to Evaluate the Success of Community Sponsorship Programs." CARFMS / ACERMF, January 22, 2020. https://carfms.org/15-ways-to-evaluate-the-success-of-community-sponsorship-programs-by-rachel-mcnally/.

McNevin, Anne, and Antje Missbach. "Luxury Limbo: Temporal Techniques of Border Control and the Humanitarianization of Waiting." *Int. J. Migration and Border Studies* 4, No. 2 (2018): 12–34. 10.1504/IJMBS.2018.091222.

Meurens, Steven. "It is Time for the Government of Canada to Unleash the Private Sector When It Comes to Refugee Resettlement." *Policy Options,* September 25, 2015. https://policyoptions.irpp.org/2015/09/25/the-private-sponsorship-of-refugees-program-after-alan-kurdi/.

Missbach, Antje. "Accommodating Asylum Seekers and Refugees in Indonesia: From Immigration Detention to Containment in 'Alternatives to Detention.'" *Refuge* 33, No. 2 (2017): 32–44. https://doi.org/10.7202/1043061ar.

Missbach, Antje. "Benevolent Neglect: How Indonesia Handles Its Asylum Seeker Problem." *Conversation*, August 30, 2012. https://the conversation.com/benevolent-neglect-how-indonesia-handles-its-asylum-seeker-problem-8920.

Missbach, Antje. "Big Fears About Small Boats: How Asylum Seekers Keep Upsetting the Indonesia-Australia Relationship." In *Strangers Next Door? Australia and Indonesia in the Asian Century*, edited by Tim Lindsey and Dave McRae, 123–144. Melbourne: Bloomsbury Publishing, 2018.

Missbach, Antje. *The Criminalisation of People Smuggling in Indonesia and Australia: Asylum Out of Reach.* Oxford and New York: Routledge, 2022.

Missbach, Antje. "Detaining Asylum Seekers and Refugees in Indonesia." In *Detaining the Immigrant Other: Global and Transnational Issues*, edited by Rich Furman, Douglas Epps, and Greg Lamphear, 91–104. Oxford: Oxford University Press, 2016.

Missbach, Antje. "Falling Through the Cracks." *Policy Forum*, August 8, 2018. https://www.policyforum.net/falling-through-the-cracks/.

Missbach, Antje. "From Darfur to Cipayung: Refugees Are Left Stranded." *Conversation*, April 7, 2014. https://theconversation.com/from-darfur-to-cipayung-refugees-are-left-stranded-25034.

Missbach, Antje. "Substituting Immigration Detention Centres with 'Open Prisons' in Indonesia: Alternatives to Detention as the Continuum of Unfreedom." *Citizenship Studies* 25, No. 2 (2021): 224–237. 10.1080/13621025.2020.1859193.

Missbach, Antje. "Transiting Asylum Seekers in Indonesia: Between Human Rights Protection and Criminalisation." In *Migration and Integration in Europe, Southeast Asia, and Australia: A Comparative Perspective*, edited by Juliet Pietsch and Marshall Clark, 115–135. Amsterdam: Amsterdam University Press, 2015.

Missbach, Antje. *Troubled Transit: Asylum Seekers Stuck in Indonesia.* Singapore: ISEAS-Yusof Ishak Institute, 2015.

Missbach, Antje, and Anne McNevin. "Out of Sight, Out of Mind." *Inside Story*, April 14, 2015. http://insidestory.org.au/out-of-sight-out-of-mind.

Missbach, Antje, and Frieda Sinanu. "Life and Death in Immigration Detention." *Inside Indonesia* 113, July-September 2013. https://www.insideindonesia.org/life-and-death-in-immigration-detention.

Missbach, Antje, and Gerhard Hoffstaedter. "When Transit States Pursue Their Own Agenda: Malaysian and Indonesian Responses to Australia's Migration and Border Policies." *Migration and Society: Advances in Research* 3 (2020): 1–16. https://doi.org/10.3167/arms.2020.111405.

Missbach, Antje, and Nikolas Feith Tan. "Asylum in Indonesia: Can Temporary Refuge Become Permanent Protection?" *Inside Indonesia* 124, April-June 2016. https://www.insideindonesia.org/asylum-in-indonesia-can-temporary-refuge-become-permanent-protection-2.

Missbach, Antje, and Nikolas Feith Tan. "No Durable Solutions." *Inside Indonesia*, March 13, 2017. https://www.insideindonesia.org/no-durable-solutions.

Missbach, Antje, and Yunizar Adiputera. "The Role of Local Governments in Accommodating Refugees in Indonesia: Investigating Best-Case and Worst-Case Scenarios." *Asian Journal of Law and Society* 8, No. 3 (2021): 490–506. https://doi.org/10.1017/als.2021.5.

Missbach, Antje, Yunizar Adiputera, Atin Prabandari, Ganesh Cintika, Frysa Yudha Swastika, and Raditya Darningtyas. "Stalemate: Refugees in Indonesia—Presidential Regulation No 125 of 2016." Centre for Indonesian Law, Islam and Society, Melbourne Law School, Policy Paper (2018): 1- 27. https://law.unimelb.edu.au/__data/assets/file/0006/2777667/CILIS-Paper-14_Missbach-et-al_final.pdf.

Mollman, Steve. "A Taiwanese Steel Plant Caused Vietnam's Mass Fish Deaths, the Government Says." *Quartz*, June 30, 2016. https://qz.com/718576/a-taiwanese-steel-plant-caused-vietnams-mass-fish-deaths-the-government-says/.

Montgomery, Marc. "Canadians: Attitudes Hardening Against Immigrants, Refugees." *Radio Canada International*, July 3, 2019. https://www.rcinet.ca/en/2019/07/03/canadians-attitudes-hardening-against-immigrants-refugees/.

Moreno-Lax, Violeta. *The Interdiction of Asylum Seekers at Sea: Law and (Mal)practice in Europe and Australia.* Policy Brief 4, UNSW Kaldor Centre for International Refugee Law. May 2017, 1–21. https://www.kaldorcentre.unsw.edu.au/sites/default/files/Policy_Brief4_Interdiction_of_asylum_seekers_at_sea.pdf.

Muntarbhorn, Vitit. "Regional Refugee Regimes: Southeast Asia." In *The Oxford Handbook of International Refugee Law*, 423–440.

Nardi, Dominic J. *Country Update: An Assessment of Vietnam's Law on Belief and Religion.* Washington: United States Commission on International Religious Freedom (USCIRF), November 2019, 1–5. https://www.uscirf.gov/sites/default/files/2019%20Vietnam%20Country%20Update_2.pdf.

Nethery, Amy, Brynna Rafferty-Brown, Savitri Taylor. "Exporting Detention: Australia-Funded Immigration Detention in Indonesia." *Journal of Refugee Studies* 26, No. 1 (March 2013): 88–109. https://doi.org/10.1093/jrs/fes027.

Nguyen Quang Duy. "Challenges and Accomplishments: 45 Years (1975–2020) The Vietnamese Community in Victoria, Australia." Unpublished manuscript, Viet Thuc Foundation.

Nguyen Xuan Quynh, Andreo Calonzo, Philip J. Heijmans, Hannah Dormido, and Adrian Leung. "China is Winning the Silent War to Dominate the South China Sea." *Bloomberg*, July 11, 2019. https://www.bloomberg.com/graphics/2019-south-china-sea-silent-war/?leadSource=uverify%20wall&embedded-checkout=true.

"Người Úc Giúp Thuyền Nhân Việt Bị Hồi Hương." *VOA*, September 3, 2016. http://vietjoy.com/viewtopic.php?f=18&p=86926 (translated from Vietnamese).

Norman, Jane. "Election 2016: Peter Dutton, Malcolm Turnbull Confirm Vietnam Asylum Seeker Boat Turn-Back." *ABC News*, June 22, 2016. https://www.abc.net.au/news/2016-06-22/dutton-turnbull-confirm-vietnam-asylum-seeker-boat-turn-back/7532368.

Office of former Senator Thanh Hai Ngo. *Human Rights Situation in Vietnam Reports: 2012–2021.* Senate Canada, https://honourablengo.ca/summer-internship-program/my-work/.

Okhovat Sahar, Asher Hirsch, Khanh Hoang, and Rebecca Dowd. "Rethinking Resettlement and Family Reunion in Australia." *Alternative Law Journal* 42, No. 4 (2017): 273–278. http://journals.sagepub.com/doi/full/10.1177/1037969X17732705.

O'Neil, Clare. "Joint Media Release with Sri Lankan Foreign Minister." June 20, 2022. https://minister.homeaffairs.gov.au/ClareONeil/Pages/meeting-sri-lankan-minister-foreign-affairs.aspx?utm_source=miragenews&utm_medium=miragenews&utm_campaign=news.

Onion, Rebecca. "The Snake-Eaters and the Yards." *Slate*, November 27, 2013. https://slate.com/news-and-politics/2013/11/the-green-berets-and-the-montagnards-how-an-indigenous-tribe-won-the-admiration-of-green-berets-and-lost-everything.html.

Packham, Ben. "Secret Sri Lankan Fuel Deal Keeps Patrol Boats on Water." *Australian*, August 8, 2022. https://www.theaustralian.com.au/nation/secret-sri-lankan-fuel-deal-keeps-patrol-boats-on-water/news-story/e9a1c1a99e6c599425bfd64b6a237bab.

Packham, Ben, and Susitha Fernando. "GPS to Track Sri Lankan Fish Fleet." *Australian*, June 22, 2022. https://www.theaustralian.com.au/nation/gps-to-track-sri-lankan-fish-fleet/news-story/be3f234983da4d712e19a2c4ee1bcd9a.

Palmer, Wayne, and Antje Missbach. "Enforcing Labor Rights of Irregular Migrants in Indonesia." *Third World Quarterly* 40, No. 5 (2019): 908–925. https://doi.org/10.1080/01436597.2018.1522586.

Pearson, James. "Exclusive: Facebook Agreed to Censor Posts After Vietnam Slowed Traffic—Sources." *Reuters*, April 22, 2020. https://www.reuters.com/article/us-vietnam-facebook-exclusive/exclusive-facebook-agreed-to-censor-posts-after-vietnam-slowed-traffic-sources-idUSKCN2232JX.

Pek, Alfred. "Indifference in Diversity: Ignorance and Apathy Towards Refugees in Indonesia." *New Mandala*, October 8, 2021. https://www.newmandala.org/indifference-in-diversity-ignorance-apathy-towards-refugees-in-indonesia/.

Permanent Mission of the Republic of Indonesia to the UN, WTO, and International Organizations in Geneva. "Response to the Questionnaire of the Special Rapporteur on the Human Rights of Migrants: 'Ending Immigration Detention of Children and Seeking Adequate Reception and Care for Them.'" No. 60/Pol-II/IV/2020, April 21, 2020. https://www.ohchr.org/sites/default/files/Documents/Issues/Migration/CallEndingImmigrationDetentionChildren/Member_States/Republic_of_Indonesia_submission.pdf.

Petrie, Claire, and Harriet Spinks. "Migration Legislation Amendment (Regional Processing Cohort) Bill 2019." Bills Digest No. 54, 2019–20, November 19, 2019. https://www.aph.gov.au/Parliamentary_Business/Bills_Legislation/bd/bd1920a/20bd054.

Phan, Lê. "Việt Nam Tự Hạ Thấp Trong Mắt Các Nhà Quan Sát Nhân Quyền." *Saigon Nho*, October 4, 2022. https://saigonnhonews.com/thoi-su/van-de-hom-nay/viet-nam-tu-ha-thap-trong-mat-cac-nha-quan-sat-nhan-quyen/.

Phan, Thi Lan Huong. "Introduction to Constitutional Law in Vietnam: Constitutional Explanation and Review." In *How Public Law is Taught in Asian Universities*, 19–39. Japan: Programs for Asian Global Legal Professions Series IV, 2020.

Phan, Xuan Son, and Vu Hong Trang. "Causes of Land Conflicts in Vietnam." *Political Theory*, January 22, 2016. http://lyluanchinhtri.vn/home/en/index.php/practice/item/314-causes-of-land-conflicts-in-vietnam.html.

"Phúc Thẩm Vụ Vượt Biên Đến Úc." *BBC*, August 31, 2016. https://www.bbc.com/vietnamese/vietnam/2016/08/160831_australia_asylumn_seeker_vietnam (translated from Vietnamese).

Pressé, Debra, and Jessie Thomson. "The Resettlement Challenge: Integration of Refugees from Protracted Refugee Situations," *Refuge*, 25 No. 1 (2008): 94–99. https://refuge.journals.yorku.ca/index.php/refuge/article/view/21402/20072.

"Profile of Nguyen Ngoc Nhu Quynh—Me Nam ('Mother Mushroom')." *88 Project*, October 20, 2016. https://the88project.org/profile-of-nguyen-ngoc-nhu-quynh-me-nam-mother-mushroom/.

Promoting Settlement-Sponsor Collaboration: Best Practices Report. ARI, April 2019, 1–21.

https://ocasi.org/sites/default/files/promoting-settlement-sponsor-collaboration-best-practices-report.pdf.

"Public Schools in Medan, Jakarta, Makassar and Tangerang Open Doors to Refugee Kids." *Coconuts Jakarta,* July 18, 2018. https://coconuts.co/jakarta/news/public-schools-medan-jakarta-makassar-tangerang-open-doors-refugee-kids/.

Putri, Ganesh Cintika. "The Dilemma of Hospitality: Revisiting Indonesia's Policy on Handling Refugees Under International Law." *Jurnal Ham* 13, No. 1 (April 2022): 113–130. https://ejournal.balitbangham.go.id/index.php/ham/article/view/2435/pdf.

Rahmani, Tanita Dhiyaan. "Making the Best Out of the Worst: Utilizing Indonesia's Existing Laws to Protect Asylum Seekers in Transit." *Jurnal Syariah* 5 (November 2016): 57–70.

Refugee Advice and Casework Service (RACS). "Open Letter: Calling PM Scott Morrison to Shut Down Zero Chance." January 3, 2022. https://www.racs.org.au/news/open-letter-calling-pm-scott-morrison-to-shut-down-zero-chance.

Refugee Council of Australia (RCOA). *Addressing the Pain of Separation for Refugee Families.* November 2016, 1–8. https://www.refugeecouncil.org.au/wp-content/uploads/2018/12/Addressing-the-pain-of-separation-for-refugee-families.pdf.

Refugee Council of Australia (RCOA) "Less Than One Third of Refugees in Australia's Humanitarian Program Are Resettled From UNHCR." May 9, 2020. https://www.refugeecouncil.org.au/less-one-third-refugees-australias-humanitarian-program-resettled-unhcr/.

Refugee Council of Australia (RCOA) "Refugee Resettlement to Fall Short of National and Global Targets, as COVID-19 Pandemic Halts Travel." April 29, 2020. https://www.refugeecouncil.org.au/resettlement-briefing-on-covid-19/.

Refugee Council of Australia (RCOA) "Refugees and International Law." May 10, 2020. https://www.refugeecouncil.org.au/international-law/6/.

Refugee Council of Australia (RCOA) and Settlement Services International (SSI). *Canada's Private Sponsorship of Refugees Program: Potential Lessons for Australia.* Discussion Paper, August 2017, 1–6. https://www.refugeecouncil.org.au/wp-content/uploads/2018/12/Canadian-PSR-paper-1708.pdf.

Refugee Sponsorship Training Program (RSTP). *Best Practices for Monitoring Resource Kit.* April 2019, 1–29. http://www.rstp.ca/wp-content/uploads/2019/04/Best-Practices-for-Monitoring-Resource-Kit-Apr-2019.pdf.

Refugee Sponsorship Training Program (RSTP). *Handbook for Sponsoring Groups.* CCS and RSTP, 2014. http://www.rstp.ca/en/resources/hand-book-for-sponsoring-groups/.

Refugee Sponsorship Training Program (RSTP). *Private Sponsorship of Refugees (PSR) Program FAQs Post-Arrival Financial Support for PSRs.* Updated August 2019, 1–20. http://www.rstp.ca/wp-content/uploads/2019/08/EN-FAQs-update-Summer-2019-AUG-19-update_FINAL.docx-3.pdf.

"Refugee Work Rights Report: Refugee Access to Fair and Lawful Work in Asia." *Asylum Access,* October 2019, 1–42. https://asylumaccess.org/wp-content/uploads/2019/11/Asia-RWR_FINAL.pdf.

"Refugees in Canada—Statistics & Facts." Statista Research Department, March 4, 2022. https://www.statista.com/topics/2897/refugees-in-canada/#topicHeader__wrapper.

"Refugees in Indonesia Tackle Life in Limbo Through School." *Daily Mail Australia,* June 19, 2016. https://www.dailymail.co.uk/wires/afp/article-3648849/Refugees-Indonesia-tackle-life-limbo-school.html.

Reilly, Alex, and Rebecca La Forgia. "Secret 'Enhanced Screening' of Asylum Seekers: A Democratic Analysis Centring on the Humanity of the Commonwealth Officer." *Alternative Law Journal,* 38, No. 3 (2013): 143–146. https://journals.sagepub.com/doi/10.1177/1037969X1303800302.

Reimer, Reg. "Vietnam's Religion Law." *World Watch Monitor,* May 8, 2015. https://www.worldwatchmonitor.org/2015/05/vietnams-religion-law/.

Richie, Genevieve. "Civil Society, the State, and Private Sponsorship: The Political Economy of Refugee Resettlement." *International Journal of Lifelong Education* 37, No. 6 (2018): 663–675. https://doi.org/10.1080/02601370.2018.1513429.

Rizqillah, Muhammad Daffa, and Teresa Retno Arsanti. "Appraising the Education Provision for Refugee Children in Indonesia." *RDI Op-Ed,* No. 10 (2021): 1–6. https://www.rdi.or.id/storage/files/publication/1634621289-rdi-op-ed-no-10-cswh-uref-20211019.pdf.

Rudd, Kevin. "Transcript of Joint Press Conference—Brisbane." July 19, 2013. https://pmtranscripts.pmc.gov.au/release/transcript-22763.

"Rừng Luật Và Luật Rừng." *VietInfo,* September 9, 2014. http://vietinfo.eu/luat-vn/rung-luat-va-luat-rung.html (translated from Vietnamese).

Sadjad, Mahardhika Sjamsoe'oed. "What Are Refugees Represented to Be? A Frame Analysis of the Presidential Regulation No. 125 of 2016 Concerning the Treatment of Refugees 'from Abroad.'" *Asian Journal of Law and Society* 8, No. 3 (2021): 451–466. 10.1017/als.2021.3.

Samuel, Sigal. "There's a Perception That Canada is Being Invaded." *Atlantic,* May 26, 2018. https://www.theatlantic.com/international/archive/2018/05/theres-a-perception-that-canada-is-being-invaded/561032/.

Satzewich, Vic. "'Canadian Exceptionalism': Border Control Also Matters." *Canadian Diversity* 15, No. 2 (2018): 34–37.

Satzewich, Vic. *Points of Entry: How Canada's Immigration Officers Decide Who Gets In.* Vancouver: UBC Press, 2014.

Saunokonoko, Mark. "'It Is Not a Game, It's Our Life, It's Our Kids' Lives.'" *9news,* February 16, 2022. https://www.9news.com.au/national/sri-lankan-refugee-advocates-claim-australia-zero-chance-online-games-campaign-misses-mark/e1f2bc73-0511-4b96-aca9-44232e121203.

Schloenhardt Andreas, and C. Craig. "'Turning back the boats': Australia's Interdiction of Irregular Migrants at Sea." *International Journal of Refugee Law* 27, No. 4 (December 2015): 536–572. https://doi.org/10.1093/ijrl/eev045.

Schultz, Amber, and Imogen Champagne. "Refugee Children in Indonesia Given Anti-Refugee Cards with Australian Coat of Arms." *Crikey,* May 25, 2022. https://www.crikey.com.au/2022/05/25/refugee-children-in-indonesia-given-anti-refugee-playing-cards/.

"Scott Morrison Defends Decision to Call Asylum Seekers 'Illegals.'" *Guardian,* October 21, 2013. https://www.theguardian.com/world/2013/oct/21/news-asylumseekers-immigration-government.

Sebban, Shira. "Exclusive: Fate of Vietnamese Asylum Seeker Children Hangs in the Balance." *Independent Australia,* March 16, 2017. https://independentaustralia.net/australia/australia-display/exclusive-fate-of-vietnamese-asylum-seeker-children-hangs-in-the-balance,10117.

Sebban, Shira. "Saving the World, One Life at a Time." *New Matilda,* October 15, 2016. https://newmatilda.com/2016/10/15/saving-the-world-one-life-at-a-time/.

Sebban, Shira. "Turned Back by Australia, Vietnamese Recognised as Refugees in Indonesia." *SMH,* June 11, 2017. https://www.smh.com.au/world/turned-back-by-australia-vietnamese-recognised-as-refugees-in-indonesia-20170608-gwn475.html.

Sebban, Shira. "We're a Disparate Group of Australians Doing the Work Our Government Won't." *Guardian,* August 24, 2016. https://www.theguardian.com/commentisfree/2016/aug/24/were-a-disparate-group-of-australians-doing-the-work-our-government-wont.

Seck, Yee Chung, and Manh Hung Tran. "Vietnam: New Amendments to Draft Regulations on Internet Services, Online Information and Online Games." Blog by Baker McKenzie, January 14, 2022. https://www.globalcompliancenews.com/2022/01/14/vietnam-new-amendments-to-draft-regulations-on-internet-services-online-information-and-online-games-22122021/.

"Seminar on Draft Decree to Replace Decree 162/2017/ND-CP on Belief and Religion." Vietnam Government Committee for Religious Affairs (GCRA), September 6, 2022. http://religion.vn/committee-news/seminar-on-draft-decree-to-replace-decree-1622017nd-cp-on-belief-and-religion-postEm1Nva4P.html.

Septiari, Dian. "UNHCR Works to Ensure No Refugees Left Behind in COVID-19 Crisis in Indonesia." *Jakarta Post,* April 5, 2020. https://www.thejakartapost.com/news/2020/04/05/unhcr-works-to-ensure-no-refugees-left-behind-in-covid-19-crisis-in-indonesia.html.

Setiadi, Wicipto, and Mario Johanes Caesar Siagian. "The Implementation of Alternatives to Detention to Handle the Problems of Refugees in Indonesia." *Padjadjaran Journal of Law* 6, No. 1 (2019): 128–150. https://doi.org/10.22304/pjih.v6n1.a7.

Shahnaz, Liza, and Zainal Abidin Muhja. "The Rights of Children on the Move in Indonesia: Implementation and Challenges." *JUUM* 30 (2022): 99–110. 10.17576/juum-2022–30–09.

Singer, Peter. *The Life You Can Save: How to Do Your Part to End World Poverty.* 10th anniversary edition. Sydney: The Life You Can Save, 2019. https://www.thelifeyoucansave.org.au/the-book/.

Sinh, P. "Làm Rõ Nghi Vấn Đối Tượng Tổ Chức Dưa Người Ra Nước Ngoài Trái Phép." *Binh Thuan Online,* February 9, 2017. https://baobinhthuan.com.vn/lam-ro-nghi-van-doi-tuong-to-chuc-dua-nguoi-ra-nuoc-ngoai-trai-phep-13218.html (translated from Vietnamese).

Soksreinith, Ten. "Vietnamese Blogger Mother Mushroom Tells Activists 'You are not alone.'" *VOA,* November 15, 2018. https://www.voanews.com/a/vietnamese-blogger-mother-mushroom-tells-activists-you-are-not-alone-/4659768.html.

Stenger, Lars. "What the Future Might Hold." *Inside Indonesia* 124, April-June 2016. https://www.insideindonesia.org/what-the-future-might-hold.

SUAKA, UNHCR, JRS, and Sandya Institute. *Know Your Rights: A Handbook for Refugees and Asylum Seekers.* Jakarta: SUAKA, December 2018. https://apr.jrs.net/wp-content/uploads/sites/18/2020/03/2019-Know-your-rights-JRS-Indo.pdf.

SUAKA. "Perpres: Refugee Protection Must Answer Key Issues Regarding Asylum Seekers and Refugees in Indonesia." Media Release, January 18, 2017. https://suaka.or.id/handling-refugees-from-overseas/.

SUAKA Indonesia, RDI UREF, LBH Jakarta, Dompet Dhuafa, Geutanyoe Foundation, HRWG. *Refugee Rights Situation in Indonesia.* Submission for Universal Periodic Review of the UN Human Rights Council (Fourth Cycle), 41st Session, March 30, 2022. https://suaka.or.id/wp-content/uploads/2022/08/upr-joint-submission-on-refugee-rights-situation-in-indonesia-1.pdf.

Susetyo, Heru. "Lost in Transit: Refugees Stranded in a Legal Vacuum in Indonesia." UNSW Kaldor Centre for International Refugee Law, July 22, 2020. https://www.kaldorcentre.unsw.edu.au/publication/lost-transit-refugees-stranded-legal-vacuum-indonesia.

"Suspected Asylum Seeker Vessel Heading for Dampier off WA's North West Coast." *ABC News*, July 20, 2015. https://www.abc.net.au/news/2015-07-20/suspected-asylum-seeker-vessel-seen-heading-for-dampier-wa-coast/6633146.

Sutiarnoto, Jelly Leviza, and Syaiful Azam. "Legal Protection for Refugees in Indonesia in the Perspective of National and International Law." Proceedings of the International Conference of Science, Technology, Engineering, Environmental and Ramification Researches. *Research in Industry* 4.0 (2020): 1752–1754. https://www.scitepress.org/Papers/2018/100979/100979.pdf.

Suyatna, I. Nyoman, I. Made Budi Arsika, Ni Gusti Ayu Dyah Satyawati, Rohaida Nordin, and Balawyn Jones. "Assessment of the Responsibility of Local Governments in Indonesia for the Management of Refugee Care." *Asian Journal of Law and Society*, 8, No. 3 (2021): 467–489. 10.1017/als.2021.4.

Syahrin, M. Alvi. "The Implementation of Non-Refoulement Principle to the Asylum Seekers and Refugees in Indonesia." *Sriwijaya Law Review* 1, No. 2 (July 2017): 168–178.

Szklarski, Cassandra. "Vietnamese-Canadian 'Boat People' Rally to Sponsor Syrian Refugees." *Globe and Mail*, December 9, 2015. https://www.theglobeandmail.com/news/national/vietnamese-boat-people-rally-to-sponsor-syrian-refugees/article27661190/.

Tan, Nikolas Feith. "The Status of Asylum Seekers and Refugees in Indonesia." *International Journal of Refugee Law* 28, No. 3 (October 1, 2016): 365–383. https://doi.org/10.1093/ijrl/eew045.

Tauson, Michelle. *Forgotten Futures: The Lives of Refugee Children in Urban Areas of Indonesia and Thailand.* Save the Children, June 2018, 1–46. 10.13140/RG.2.2.11882.16324.

Taylor, Jesse. *Behind Australian Doors: Examining the Conditions of Detention of Asylum-Seekers in Indonesia.* Asylum Seekers in Indonesia: Project, Findings & Recommendations, November 3, 2009, 1–48. https://www.safecom.org.au/pdfs/behind-australian-doors-examining-the-conditions.pdf.

Taylor, Luke. "Designated Inhospitality: The Treatment of Asylum Seekers Who Arrive by Boat in Canada and Australia." *McGill Law Journal* 60, No. 2 (January 2015): 333–379. https://doi.org/10.7202/1029211ar.

Taylor, Savitri. "Australian Funded Care and Maintenance of Asylum Seekers in Indonesia and PNG: All Care but No Responsibility?" *University of New South Wales Law Journal* 33, No. 2 (2010): 337–359. https://papers.ssrn.com/sol3/papers.cfm?abstract_id=1725508.

Taylor, Savitri, and Brynna Rafferty-Brown. "Difficult Journeys: Accessing Refugee Protection in Indonesia." *Monash University Law Review* 36, No. 3 (2010): 138–161. http://classic.austlii.edu.au/au/journals/MonashULawRw/2010/29.html.

Taylor, Savitri, and Brynna Rafferty-Brown. "Waiting for Life to Begin: The Plight of Asylum Seekers Caught by Australia's Indonesian Solution." *International Journal of Refugee Law* 22, No. 4 (December 1, 2010): 558–592. doi.org/10.1093/url/eeq034.

Thériault, Pierre-André. "Judicial Review in Canada's Refugee Resettlement Program." In *Strangers to Neighbours*, 263–281.

Timmerman, Antonia. "In Indonesia, Desperation Grows for Refugees Trapped in Limbo for Years." *New Humanitarian*, March 22, 2021. https://www.thenewhumanitarian.org/news-feature/2021/3/22/in-indonesia-desperation-grows-for-refugees-trapped-in-limbo-for-years.

Tisnadibrata, Ismira Lutfia. "Surviving as a Refugee Becomes More Testing During Pandemic." *Arab News*, June 19, 2020. https://www.arabnews.com/node/1692426/world.

Tobing, Dio Herdiawan. "Connecting the Obligation Gap: Indonesia's Non-Refoulement Responsibility Beyond the 1951 Refugee Convention." *Asian Journal of Law and Society* 8, No. 3 (2021): 521–535. 10.1017/als.2021.7.

Topsfield, Jewel. "Most Refugees in Indonesia Will Never Be Resettled: UN Refugee Agency." *SMH*, October 31, 2017. https://www.smh.com.au/world/most-refugees-in-indonesia-will-never-be-resettled-un-refugee-agency-20171031-gzbzhn.html.

Topsfield, Jewel. "Trapped in Transit: What Next for Asylum Seekers Stranded in Indonesia?" *SMH*, March 19, 2016. https://www.smh.com.au/world/trapped-in-transit-what-next-for-asylum-seekers-stranded-in-indonesia-20160317-gnlmkf.html.

Tra Mi. "Vietnam Bans Unsafe Seafood in Central Provinces." *VOA*, May 5, 2016. https://www.voanews.com/a/vietnam-bans-unsafe-seafood-in-central-provinces/3316289.html.

Tran, Hoa Ai. "Ba Gia Dình Phụ Nữ Vượt Biên Sẽ Tạm Cư ở Trại Tị Nạn Semareng." *RFA*, June 13, 2017. http://www.rfa.org/vietnamese/in_depth/the-three-families-fled-vn-2-time-moved-semareng-refugee-camp-ha-06132017085531.html (translated from Vietnamese).

Tran, Hoa Ai. "Mạng Xã Hội Và Niềm Tin Từ Thiện." *RFA*, December 6, 2016. https://www.rfa.org/vietnamese/in_depth/social-media-and-charity-fund-raising-12062016140941.html (translated from Vietnamese).

Tran, Quynh-Vi. "Vietnam: Lawyer Disbarred for Speaking Ill of Regime and the Communist Party." *Vietnamese*, April 14, 2019. https://www.thevietnamese.org/2019/04/vietnam-lawyer-disbarred-for-speaking-ill-of-regime-and-the-communist-party/.

Treviranus, Barbara, and Michael Casasola. "Canada's Private Sponsorship of Refugees Program: A Practitioner's Perspective of its Past and Future." Journal of International

Migration and Integration 4 (2003): 177–202. 10.1007/s12134–003–1032–0.

"Trial Set for Four Vietnamese 'Boat People' Who Were Repatriated by Australia." *RFA*, November 29, 2016. https://www.rfa.org/english/news/vietnam/trial-set-for-four-vietnamese-11292016134257.html/.

Trieu, Kathy. "Lua and Loan, Two Asylum Seekers Rejected by Australia." *Loa Broadcasting Vietnam,* Episode 76, July 19, 2017. Audio, 20:24. https://vietbp.org/2017/09/05/lua-and-loan-two-asylum-seekers-rejected-by-australia.htm.

Trung, Doan. "Statement About Two Groups of 46 Vietnamese Asylum Seekers—The 'Plane Group' and the 'Choules Group.'" Unpublished, January 7, 2016. (See Appendix 1).

Trung, Doan. Unpublished Statement. 28 September 2016. (See Appendix 2).

Turning Back Boats. Research Brief, UNSW Kaldor Centre for International Refugee Law. Last updated August 2018, 1–16. https://www.kaldorcentre.unsw.edu.au/sites/kaldorcentre.unsw.edu.au/files/Research%20Brief_Turning%20back%20boats_final.pdf.

Uhlmann, Chris and Peta Donald. "Australian Navy Returns 46 Asylum Seekers to Vietnam After Intercepting Group en Route to Australia." *ABC News,* April 20, 2015. https://www.abc.net.au/news/2015-04-20/government-criticised-over-boat-secrecy/6404950.

UN Committee Against Torture (UNCAT). *Consideration of Reports Submitted by States Parties Under Article 19 of the Convention Pursuant to the Optional Reporting Procedure, Initial Reports of States Parties Due in 2016: Viet Nam.* CAT/C/VNM/1, September 13, 2017, 1–51. https://tbinternet.ohchr.org/_layouts/15/treatybodyexternal/Download.aspx?symbolno=CAT/C/VNM/1&Lang=en.

United Nations High Commissioner for Refugees (UNHCR). "Are Refugees Good for Canada?" https://www.unhcr.ca/wp-content/uploads/2019/06/economic-integration-onepager-en-2.pdf.

UNHCR. "As Global Displacement Grows to Nearly 80 Million People, Canada Shows Itself to be a World Leader in Refugee Resettlement: UNHCR Report Shows." June 18, 2020. https://www.unhcr.ca/news/global-displacement-grows-80-million-people-canada-world-leader-refugee-resettlement/.

UNHCR. *Beyond Detention: A Global Strategy to Support Governments to End the Detention of Asylum-Seekers and Refugees, 2014–2019.* 2014. https://www.refworld.org/docid/536b564d4.html.

UNHCR. "Committee Against Torture Considers the Initial Report of Viet Nam." November 15, 2018. https://www.ohchr.org/en/NewsEvents/Pages/DisplayNews.aspx?NewsID=23895&LangID=E.

UNHCR. "FAQs for Refugees and Asylum-Seekers." https://www.unhcr.org/id/wp-content/uploads/sites/42/2017/05/UNHCR-website-FAQs.pdf.

UNHCR. "Figures at a Glance." https://www.unhcr.org/en-au/figures-at-a-glance.html.

UNHCR. *Frequently Asked Questions About Resettlement.* 1–16. https://www.refworld.org/pdfid/4ac0d7e52.pdf.

UNHCR. "Global Focus: Financials, 2017 South East Asia Requirements and Expenditure—Programmed Activities." http://reporting.unhcr.org/financial.

UNHCR. *Global Strategy: Beyond Detention 2014–2019: National Action Plan Indonesia.* 1–2. https://www.refworld.org/pdfid/57dff7912.pdf.

UNHCR. *Global Trends Reports. 2018–2021.* https://www.unhcr.org/globaltrends.

UNHCR. "Indonesia Country Fact Sheets." March 2014–June 2022. https://www.unhcr.org/id/en/fact-sheets.

UNHCR. *Indonesia: Progress Under the Global Strategy Beyond Detention 2014–2019, Mid-2016.* https://www.unhcr.org/protection/detention/57b583457/indonesia-progress-report.html?query=indonesia.

UNHCR. *Information for Asylum Seekers in Indonesia.* https://www.unhcr.org/id/wp-content/uploads/sites/42/2017/05/Information-Leaflet-for-Asylum-Seekers-English-Feb-2017.pdf.

UNHCR. *Information for Refugees on Resettlement.* https://www.unhcr.org/id/wp-content/uploads/sites/42/2017/05/Resettlement-Information-Leaflet-English-Feb-2017.pdf.

UNHCR. *Information on Private Sponsorship Programs.* May 29, 2018. https://www.unhcr.org/id/wp-content/uploads/sites/42/2018/09/Leaflet-Sponsorship-Programs.pdf.

UNHCR. "IOM, UNHCR Announce Temporary Suspension of Resettlement Travel for Refugees." March 17, 2020. https://www.unhcr.org/news/press/2020/3/5e7103034/iom-unhcr-announce-temporary-suspension-resettlement-travel-refugees.html?fbclid=IwAR0o7YK3YcGvHdWnHypI0TsipgM3WpnL1gPoqmfnyuhO0yYS2-upMDsBPqk.

UNHCR. "Irregular Arrivals at the Border: Background Information Jan-May 2019." June 2019. https://www.unhcr.ca/wp-content/uploads/2019/07/IRREGULAR-ARRIVALS-AT-THE-BORDER-Background-information-Jan-May-2019-1.pdf.

UNHCR. *Note on Burden and Standard of Proof in Refugee Claims.* December 16, 1998, 1–7. https://www.refworld.org/pdfid/3ae6b3338.pdf.

UNHCR. *Operation: Indonesia: 2017 Year-End Report.* July 25, 2018, 1–4. https://reporting.unhcr.org/sites/default/files/pdfsummaries/GR2017-Indonesia-eng.pdf.

UNHCR. "Part Two: Procedures for the Determination of Refugee Status" In *Handbook on Procedures and Criteria for Determining Refugee Status and Guidelines on International Protection Under the 1951 Convention and the 1967*

Protocol Relating to the Status of Refugees. HCR/1P/4/ENG/REV.4, Reissued Geneva, February 2019, 42–47. https://www.refworld.org/docid/5cb474b27.html.

UNHCR. *Procedural Standards for Refugee Status Determination Under UNCHR's Mandate.* September 1, 2005, 3–29. https://www.unhcr.org/en-au/publications/legal/4316f0c02/procedural-standards-refugee-status-determination-under-unhcrs-mandate.html.

UNHCR. *Progress Report 2018: A Global Strategy to Support Governments to End the Detention of Asylum-Seekers and Refugees, 2014–2019.* February 2019, 1–82. https://www.refworld.org/country,,,,IDN,,5c9354074,0.html.

UNHCR. "Resettlement Data Portal." 2016–2022. https://www.unhcr.org/en-au/resettlement-data.html?query=resettlement%20data%20finder.

UNHCR. *Submission by the United Nations High Commissioner for Refugees for the Office of the High Commissioner for Human Rights' Compilation Report Universal Periodic Review: 3rd Cycle, 27th Session, Indonesia,* September 2016, 1–16. https://www.refworld.org/docid/59158ed24.html.

UNHCR. "UNCHR Legal Position: Despite Court Ruling on Sri Lankans Detained at Sea, Australia Bound by International Obligations." Press Release, February 4, 2015. https://www.unhcr.org/54d1e4ac9.html.

UNHCR. *UNHCR Policy on Refugee Protection and Solutions in Urban Areas.* September 2009, 1–29. https://www.unhcr.org/protection/hcdialogue%20/4ab356ab6/unhcr-policy-refugee-protection-solutions-urban-areas.html.

UNHCR. *UNHCR Projected Global Resettlement Needs 2023.* 1–131. https://www.unhcr.org/62b18e714.

UNHCR. *UNHCR Resettlement Handbook.* Geneva: Division of International Protection, 2011, 1–418. https://www.unhcr.org/46f7c0ee2.html.

UNHCR. *UNCHR Resettlement Handbook and Country Chapters.* April 2018. https://www.unhcr.org/4a2ccf4c6.html.

UNHCR. *UNCHR Resettlement Handbook.* Country Chapter: Australia, revised April 2016 and May 2018, 1–15. https://www.unhcr.org/3c5e542d4.html.

UNHCR. *UNHCR Resettlement Handbook.* Country Chapter: Canada, revised February 2018, 1–22. https://www.unhcr.org/3c5e55594.html.

UNHCR. "UNHCR Resettlement Submission Categories." Presentation. https://www.unhcr.org/558bff849.pdf.

UNHCR. "With Refugee Resettlement at a Record Low in 2020, UNHCR Calls on States to Offer Places and Save Lives." January 25, 2021. https://www.unhcr.org/news/press/2021/1/600e79ea4/refugee-resettlement-record-low-2020-unhcr-calls-states-offer-places-save.html.

UN Human Rights Council. *Report of the Special Rapporteur on Freedom of Religion or Belief, Addendum: Mission to Viet Nam (July 21 to 31, 2014).* January 30, 2015, A/HRC/28/66/Add.2, 1–20. https://www.refworld.org/docid/54f432530.html.

UN Human Rights Council. *Report on Means to Address the Human Rights Impact of Pushbacks of Migrants on Land and at Sea.* A/HRC/47/30, May 12, 2021, 1–20. https://documents-dds-ny.un.org/doc/UNDOC/GEN/G21/106/33/PDF/G2110633.pdf?OpenElement.

UN Permanent Mission of Viet Nam. *Note Verbale Addressed to the President of the General Assembly.* A/68/312, August 27, 2013, 1–6. https://digitallibrary.un.org/record/756375?ln=en.

UN Permanent Mission of Viet Nam. *Note Verbale Addressed to the President of the General Assembly.* A/77/276, August 4, 2022, 1–6. https://the88project.org/wp-content/uploads/2022/09/Note_verbale_-_Vietnam_2022.pdf.

UNICEF. "UNICEF Statement on Australia and Vietnam Signing MOU to Return Vietnamese Asylum Seekers." Sydney, December 13, 2016. https://vietbp.org/2017/08/14/unicef-statement-on-australia-and-vietnam-signing-mou-to-return-vietnamese-asylum-seekers.htm.

United States Committee for Refugees and Immigrants. "Paying the Price: Australia, Indonesia Try to Stop Asylum Seekers." *Refugee Reports* 22, No. 8 (September 1, 2001). https://www.refworld.org/docid/3c58099a1.html.

United States Department of State, Bureau of Democracy, Human Rights, and Labor. *Country Reports on Human Rights Practices 2016–2021: Vietnam.* https://www.state.gov/reports-bureau-of-democracy-human-rights-and-labor/country-reports-on-human-rights-practices/.

United States Department of State, Bureau of Democracy, Human Rights, and Labor. *Reports on International Religious Freedom 2016–2021: Vietnam.* https://www.state.gov/international-religious-freedom-reports/.

Van Haren, Ian. "Canada's Private Sponsorship Model Represents a Complementary Pathway for Refugee Resettlement." Migration Policy Institute, July 9, 2021. https://www.migrationpolicy.org/article/canada-private-sponsorship-model-refugee-resettlement.

"Việt Nam Thẳng Tay Xử Tù Ngýời Výợt Biển Sang Úc: Bản Ân Tàn Bạo Và Vô Nhân Đạo." *VietInfo,* August 18, 2016. http://vietinfo.eu/tin-viet-nam/viet-nam-thang-tay-xu-tu-nguoi-vuot-bien-sang-uc-ban-an-tan-bao-va-vo-nhan-dao.html (translated from Vietnamese).

Vietnam Committee on Human Rights (VCHR). *Shrinking Spaces: Assessment of Human Rights in Vietnam During the 2nd Cycle of its Universal Periodic Review.* Paris, February 2018,

1–35. http://queme.org/app/uploads/2018/02/Shrinking-spaces-VCHR-2018-EN.pdf.

Vietnam Committee on Human Rights (VCHR). *Submission to the United Nations Human Rights Committee on the Third Periodic Report of Vietnam.* CCPR/C/VNM/3, 125th session, March 2019, 1–20. https://www.google.com/url?sa=t&rct=j&q=&esrc=s&source=web&cd=&ved=2ahUKEwjw88HnhduBAxXNSmwGHZboCm8QFnoECA4QAQ&url=https%3A%2F%2Fccprcentre.org%2Ffiles%2Fdocuments%2FINT_CCPR_CSS_VNM_33776_E.docx&usg=AOvVaw2rq0r-M3ioWoFnC83slwO4&opi=89978449..

"Vietnam Fisherman Recounts Attacks by China Coast Guard in South China Sea." *South China Morning Post,* October 14, 2022. https://www.scmp.com/news/asia/southeast-asia/article/3196026/vietnam-fisherman-recounts-attacks-china-coast-guard-south.

"Vietnam Floats Draconian New Religion Decrees." *Morning Star News,* June 14, 2022. https://morningstarnews.org/2022/06/vietnam-floats-draconian-new-religion-decrees/.

"Vietnam Jails 'Boat People' Bound for Australia in Breach of Pledge." *RFA,* December 13, 2016. https://www.rfa.org/english/news/vietnam/vietnam-jails-boat-people-12132016135607.html.

"Vietnam Rights Lawyer Barred from Leaving Country." *RFA,* September 28, 2022. https://www.rfa.org/english/news/vietnam/barred-09282022145939.html/ampRFA?fbclid=IwAR0E_hLUVWF5JFfU12g4-Ii8oEHEEsspNm3-K6NJPhGhYLDTJVBDQ7EHviA.

"Vietnam Says Taiwan Firm's Pollution Affected 200,000 People." *AP,* July 29, 2016. https://apnews.com/2755bc884d0a4a37b9ccab02ad05e759.

"Vietnam Strives to Resolve Issues for the Interest of All Parties." *Vietnam Law & Legal Forum,* August 31, 2022. https://vietnamlawmagazine.vn/vietnam-strives-to-resolve-land-issues-for-the-interest-of-all-parties-48907.html?utm_source=link.gov.vn#source=link.gov.vn.

The Vietnamese. "Religion in Vietnam: Monthly Updates." July 2019–May 2022. https://www.thevietnamese.org/tag/religion/.

The Vietnamese. "Vietnam Briefing." November 8, 2017–September 12, 2022. https://www.thevietnamese.org/tag/human-rights/.

"Vietnamese Asylum Seekers' Boat Stalls in Indonesia." *RFA,* February 10, 2017. https://www.refworld.org/docid/58f9cace21.html.

"Vietnamese 'Boat People' Attempt to Reach Australia a Second Time." *RFA,* February 8, 2017. https://www.rfa.org/english/news/vietnam/vietnamese-boat-people-attempt-to-reach-australia-a-second-time-02082017131644.html.

"Vietnamese Community Comes to Aid of Syrian Refugees." *SBS,* August 30, 2016. https://www.sbs.com.au/news/vietnamese-community-comes-to-aid-of-syrian-refugees.

"Vietnamese Face Punishment for Attempt to Flee the Country." *RFA,* April 1, 2016. https://www.rfa.org/english/news/vietnam/vietnamese-face-punishment-04012016142103.html.

"Vietnamese Rights Lawyer Stripped of His License to Practice." *RFA,* May 24, 2018. https://www.rfa.org/english/news/vietnam/license-05242018152904.html.

Vineberg, Robert. "25,000 Syrian Refugees in Four Months: How Did Canada Do It?" *Interpreter,* March 9, 2016. https://www.lowyinstitute.org/the-interpreter/25000-syrian-refugees-four-months-how-did-canada-do-it.

Vo, Hai. "Prioritize ASEAN-China Cooperation on Equal, Humane Treatment of Fishermen: Vietnam." *VNExpress,* November 3, 2020. https://e.vnexpress.net/news/news/prioritize-asean-china-cooperation-on-equal-humane-treatment-of-fishermen-vietnam-4186530.html.

Voegli, Sarah Emily. "Canadian Sponsorship of Refugees Program Reform: A Limit on Canadians' Generosity." (Major research paper, University of Ottawa, 2014), 1–69. https://ruor.uottawa.ca/bitstream/10393/31570/1/VOEGELI%2C%20Sarah%2020145.pdf.

Vogl, Anthea. "A Matter of Time: Enacting the Exclusion of Onshore Refugee Applicants Through the Reform and Acceleration of Refugee Determination Processes." Oñati Socio-legal Series 6, No. 1 (2016): 137–162. http://138.25.65.17/au/journals/UTSLRS/2016/43.html.

Vogl, Anthea, and Asher Hirsch. "Community Members Should Be Able to Sponsor Refugees for the Right Reasons, Not to Save the Government Money." *Conversation,* March 8, 2018. https://theconversation.com/community-members-should-be-able-to-sponsor-refugees-for-the-right-reasons-not-to-save-the-government-money-112230.

Vogl, Anthea, Khanh Hoang, and Asher Hirsch. "Private Humanitarian Sponsorship: Searching for the Community in Australia's Community Refugee Sponsorship Program." In *Strangers to Neighbours,* 303–325.

Vu, Giao Cong, and Kien Tran. "Constitutional Debate and Development on Human Rights in Vietnam." *Asian Journal of Comparative Law* 11, No. 2 (December 2016): 235–262. https://doi.org/10.1017/asjcl.2016.27.

Vu, Nhan. "Cộng Đồng Người Việt Tại Canada Tiếp Dón Thuyền Nhân Việt Nam Từ Indonesia." *SBTN,* December 3, 2021. https://www.sbtn.tv/cong-dong-nguoi-viet-tai-canada-tiep-don-thuyen-nhan-viet-nam-tu-indonesia/ (translated from Vietnamese).

"Vũng Tàu Xử Tù Người 'Tổ Chức Vượt Biên.'" *BBC,* December 13, 2016. https://www.bbc.com/vietnamese/vietnam-38167677 (translated from Vietnamese).

Waldman, Lorne. *Canadian Immigration & Refugee Law Practice.* Markham: Lexisnexis, 2019.

Wibowo, Mardian, and Jefri Porkonanta Tarigan. "Immigration and Refugee Laws in Indonesia." In *Constitutional Justice in Asia: "Migration and Refugee Law,"* edited by Murat Azakli and Dr.Mucahit Aydin, 96–106. Ankara: AACC, 2018. https://www.anayasa.gov.tr/media/5228/5yaz_okulu_7_eylul.pdf.

Wilkinson, Lori, and Joseph Garcea. *The Economic Integration of Refugees in Canada: A Mixed Record?* Migration Policy Institute, April 2017, 1–26. https://www.migrationpolicy.org/research/economic-integration-refugees-canada-mixed-record.

World Watch Monitor. "Two Steps Back?" March 2, 2013. https://www.worldwatchmonitor.org/2013/03/two-steps-back/.

World Watch Monitor. "Vietnam's Religion Policy and Practice—Contradictions Continue." November 23, 2017. https://www.worldwatchmonitor.org/2017/11/vietnams-religion-policy-practice-contradictions-continue/.

Xem Binh Luan. "Ba Gia Dình Việt Vượt Biên 'Sắp Được Phỏng Vấn.'" *VOA,* February 22, 2017. https://www.voatiengviet.com/a/ba-gia-dinh-viet-vuot-bien-bi-giu-o-indonesia-sap-duoc-lhq-phong-van/3735066.html#comments (translated from Vietnamese).

Yahyaoui Krivenko, Ekaterina. "Hospitality and Sovereignty: What Can We Learn from the Canadian Private Sponsorship of Refugees Program?" *International Journal of Refugee Law* 24, No. 3 (2012): 579–602. http://dx.doi.org/10.1093/ijrl/ees039.

Yen, Vu Pham. "Nhà Van Shira Sebban: Ân Nhân Nguòi Việt Ty Nan Tam Trú ö Nam Duong." *Thoi Bao,* February 22, 2019. https://www.thoibao.com/nha-van-shira-sebban-an-nhan-nguoi-viet-ty-nan-tam-tru-o-nam-duong/ (translated from Vietnamese).

Yonesta, Febi. "Illegal or Protected? Indonesia's Inconsistent Policy on Refugees." *Indonesia at Melbourne,* June 20, 2019. https://indonesiaatmelbourne.unimelb.edu.au/illegal-or-protected-indonesias-inconsistent-policy-on-refugees/.

Zhuang, Yan. "Australia Tells Afghan Refugees: 'Do Not Attempt an Illegal Boat Journey.'" *New York Times,* August 23, 2021. https://www.nytimes.com/2021/08/23/world/asia/australia-tells-afghan-refugees-do-not-attempt-an-illegal-boat-journey.html.

Interviews

Kyanh Do, September 4, 2019, May 20, 2020, and July 7, 2022.

Nguyen Quang Duy, June 18, 2020.

Vo An Ðon, May 25, 2019, and June 24, 2022.

Legislation

Australia

Maritime Powers Act 2013 (Cth.).

Migration Act 1958 (Cth.).

Migration Regulations 1994 (Cth.).

Migration (Migration Agents Code of Conduct) Regulations 2021 (Cth.).

Migration Amendment (Excision from Migration Zone) Act 2001 (Cth.).

Migration Amendment (Excision from Migration Zone) (Consequential Provisions) Act 2001 (Cth.).

Migration Amendment (Unauthorised Maritime Arrivals and Other Measures) Act 2013 (Cth.).

Migration and Maritime Powers Legislation Amendment (Resolving the Asylum Legacy Caseload) Act 2014 (Cth.).

Canada

Canadian Charter of Rights and Freedoms, Constitution Act 1982, Part 1.

Immigration and Refugee Protection Act, SC 2001, c. 27 (Can.) (IRPA).

Immigration and Refugee Protection Regulations, SOR/2002–227 (Can.) (IRPR).

Indonesia

Circular Note of Director General of Immigration No. IMI-UM.01.01–2827 on Restoring the Original Function of Immigration Detention Centers (July 30, 2018).

Directive from Director General of Immigration No. F-IL.01.10–1297 on Procedures Regarding Aliens Expressing Their Desire to Seek Asylum or Refugee Status (September 30, 2002).

Fourth Amendment to the 1945 Constitution of the Republic of Indonesia (August 11, 2002).

Law of the Republic of Indonesia No. 37 of 1999 on Foreign Relations.

Law of the Republic of Indonesia No. 39 of 1999 Concerning Human Rights.

Law of the Republic of Indonesia No. 6 of 2011 Concerning Immigration.

Ministry of Education and Culture, Circular Note No. 75253/A.A4/HK/2019 on Education for Children of Refugees.

Presidential Regulation (*Peraturan Presiden* or *Perpres*) No. 125 of 2016 on the Handling of Foreign Refugees.

Regulation of Director General of Immigration No. IMI.1489.UM.08.05 Regarding the Handling of Illegal Immigrants (September 17, 2010).

Regulation of Director General of Immigration No. IMI-0352.GR.02.07 on the Handling of Illegal

Immigrants Claiming to be Asylum-Seekers or Refugees (2016).

International

UN General Assembly. *Convention Relating to the Status of Refugees*, opened for signature July 28, 1951, 189 United Nations, Treaty Series (UNTS) 137 (entered into force April 22, 1954) (Refugee Convention).

UN General Assembly. *Protocol relating to the Status of Refugees*, opened for signature January 31, 1967, 606 UNTS 267 (entered into force October 4, 1967) (1967 Protocol).

UN General Assembly. *International Covenant on Civil and Political Rights,* opened for signature December 16, 1966, 999 UNTS 171 (entered into force March 23, 1976) (ICCPR).

UN General Assembly. *International Covenant on Economic, Social and Cultural Rights,* opened for signature December 16, 1966, 993 UNTS 3 (entered into force January 3, 1976) (ICESCR).

UN General Assembly. *Convention against Torture and Other Cruel, Inhuman or Degrading Treatment or Punishment,* opened for signature December 10, 1984, 1465 UNTS 85 (entered into force June 26, 1987) (UNCAT).

UN General Assembly. *Convention on the Rights of the Child,* opened for signature November 20, 1989, 1557 UNTS 3 (entered into force September 2, 1990) (CRC).

UN General Assembly. *Protocol against the Smuggling of Migrants by Land, Sea and Air, Supplementing the United Nations Convention against Transnational Organized Crime,* November 15, 2000.

Vietnam

Constitution of the Socialist Republic of Vietnam (November 28, 2013).

Socialist Republic of Vietnam, Decree No. 92/2012/ND-CP Detailing and Providing Measures for the Implementation of the Ordinance on Belief and Religion.

Socialist Republic of Vietnam, Decree No. 162/2017/ND-CP Guidelines for Implementation of the Law on Belief and Religion.

Socialist Republic of Vietnam, Land Law No. 45/2013/QH13.

Socialist Republic of Vietnam, Law on Belief and Religion No. 02/2016/QH14.

Socialist Republic of Vietnam, Ordinance on Belief and Religion No. 21/2004/PL-UBTVQH11.

Socialist Republic of Vietnam, Penal Code No. 15/1999/QH10.

Socialist Republic of Vietnam, Penal Code No. 100/2015/QH13.

Index

Numbers in *bold italics* indicate pages with illustrations